Persian Miniature Painting

Also reproduced in color, following p. 16.

Persian Miniature Painting

INCLUDING A CRITICAL AND DESCRIPTIVE CATALOGUE
OF THE MINIATURES EXHIBITED AT BURLINGTON HOUSE
JANUARY–MARCH, 1931

BY

LAURENCE BINYON

J. V. S. WILKINSON

AND

BASIL GRAY

DOVER PUBLICATIONS, INC., NEW YORK

Published in Canada by General Publishing Company, Ltd.,
30 Lesmill Road, Don Mills, Toronto, Ontario.
Published in the United Kingdom by Constable and Company, Ltd.,
10 Orange Street, London WC 2.

This Dover edition, first published in 1971, is an unabridged republication of
the work originally published by Oxford University Press (Humphrey Milford),
London, in 1933.

Most of the plates illustrating items in the collections of the Bodleian Library
(Oxford), the Gulistan Museum (Tehran), the Chester Beatty Library (Dublin),
the India Office Library (London) and the Musée des Arts Décoratifs (Paris) have
been reproduced from color transparencies or black and white prints furnished by
these institutions expressly for the present edition. The publisher is grateful for
the courtesy shown by the respective librarians and curators. (The India Office
Library pictures are reproduced by courtesy of the Secretary of State for Common-
wealth Affairs.)

Plates LII, LVIII, LXIX, LXXII, LXXV and CVI, originally in color, appear
in black and white in the present edition.

In accordance with requests made by the Bodleian and Beatty Libraries, manuscript and/or folio numbers of items in their collections have been added (and a
few errors corrected) in this edition.

The present edition is published by special arrangement with Oxford University
Press, Inc.

International Standard Book Number: 0-486-22054-0
Library of Congress Catalog Card Number: 68-19989

Manufactured in the United States of America

Dover Publications, Inc.
180 Varick Street
New York, N.Y. 10014

PREFACE

THIS book is, primarily, a catalogue of the miniatures and illustrated manuscripts contained in the Exhibition of Persian Art held at Burlington House, January–March 1931. It was felt that a permanent record, more detailed than the catalogue sold at the Exhibition, and fully illustrated, ought to be undertaken; and it was decided that this should not merely be a record of the Exhibition but should cover the whole field of Persian miniature-painting, though illustrated only by examples shown at Burlington House. It should be noted that manuscripts not containing paintings have been excluded, and bindings also.

Many Persian manuscripts illustrated with fine miniatures found their way into European libraries during the seventeenth, eighteenth, and nineteenth centuries, though the travellers who collected them in the East showed little appreciation of the paintings as art, having the usual Western prejudice against the absence of perspective, &c. Moreover, Persian and Indian paintings were much confused. Such manuscripts have been commonly catalogued by librarians more interested in the text than in the miniatures; and no serious attention was paid to Persian painting, save by a few scholars, such as M. Blochet, till the present century. The *Manuel d'Art musulman* of M. Migeon, 1907, *Les Calligraphes et les Miniaturistes de l'orient musulman* of M. Cl. Huart, 1908, and scattered articles by M. Blochet and others, showed the increasing interest in Persian art, stimulated by exhibitions held by the Musée des Arts Décoratifs in Paris, one in 1903 and another in 1907, and by some smaller exhibitions in other countries. In 1910 took place the remarkable exhibition of Islamic art at Munich, organized by Professor Sarre of Berlin and Dr. Martin of Stockholm. The importance of the miniature in the arts of Persia was, however, more fully recognized by a third exhibition at the Musée des Arts Décoratifs in 1912. This revealed the richness and choice quality of the private collections of Paris; for the disturbances and revolution in Persia had brought, notably in 1908, much new material from that country, and it was in Paris especially that the fine examples were acquired.

In the same year, 1912, appeared Dr. F. R. Martin's *Miniature Painting in Persia, India, and Turkey*. This was a pioneer work; for though M. Blochet had already begun a series of erudite books on the subject and had made known the treasures of the Bibliothèque Nationale, Dr. Martin's two volumes were illustrated from collections all over Europe, and revealed for the first time how much lay hidden and unnoticed in public and private libraries till disclosed by the author's ardent research.

There followed, in commemoration of the exhibition at the Musée des Arts Décoratifs, the sumptuous work by MM. G. Marteau and H. Vever, *Miniatures Persanes*, published in 1913. In 1914 appeared Dr. W. Schulz's comprehensive book on the whole subject, rich in detailed facts, if not too happily arranged.

Since the War, activity in this field of study has multiplied. Persian painting, no longer the concern of specialists only, has been recognized as a most fascinating chapter in the pictorial art of the world. At the same time the documentary sources have been more thoroughly explored, the older collections have been re-examined, evidence has been more minutely scrutinized; accepted ideas, especially about particular artists, have been most rigorously tested.

During these years further valuable contributions to our knowledge have been made by writers in various countries. We need only mention the well-known works of Dr. Kühnel, M. Sakisian, Sir Thomas Arnold, M. Blochet. To these, as to the books above mentioned, our debt is immense, though naturally we have often had differences of opinion on one point or another to register.

The Exhibition at Burlington House, and the Congress which coincided with it, brought to London many eminent scholars, and we would like to record our debt to those with whom we had the privilege of discussing the many problems involved in the study of the miniatures and of the new material shown for the first time at Burlington House.

The Exhibition catalogue, for which Professor V. Minorsky was mainly responsible, is the basis of the present work. A chronological order has been attempted, except for the earliest period, where other considerations have sometimes seemed more important.

Folio numbers of manuscripts are not given. Many of the manuscripts lent to the Exhibition had not been foliated, and in the very short time available for examining the manuscripts, which were returned to their owners immediately after the Exhibition, it was impossible to have this done. Owing to these circumstances, the miniatures are not always described in the order in which they appear in the manuscript. And where the miniatures had been removed from the manuscript and framed, the order here given is the order in which they hung on the wall. These, however, are exceptional cases.

The general conclusions given represent our considered agreement; but the account of the miniatures of the earlier periods is mainly the work of Mr. Gray, of the later periods mainly that of Mr. Wilkinson.

In choosing the paintings to be reproduced (choice of which has been confined to the Exhibition), care has been taken to secure, through consultation with the editors of the *Survey of Persian Art*, that there should be no overlapping between this volume and the section devoted to Miniatures in that work; our illustration of paintings exhibited at Burlington House being complemented in the *Survey* by illustration from the collections on which the Exhibition was unable to draw, as well as by further examples from the Exhibition. The two sets of illustrations taken together will form the most complete series of reproductions of Persian Miniatures available for students.

For assistance of various kinds we would express our thanks to Aziz Bey, Director of the Istanbul Museums; Mr. M. A. Chughtai, of the Islamia College, Lahore; Mr. A. S. Fulton, Sir T. Wolseley Haig, Miss Joan Kingsford, Mr. M. Minovi, Professor R. A. Nicholson, Sir E. Denison Ross, and Sir Aurel Stein; to the Printer to the Oxford University Press and his assistants; and above all to the collectors who allowed their miniatures to be reproduced.

CONTENTS

[vii]

LIST OF ILLUSTRATIONS

[ix]

LIST OF ILLUSTRATIONS

[x]

LIST OF ILLUSTRATIONS

[xi]

LIST OF ILLUSTRATIONS

[xii]

LIST OF ILLUSTRATIONS

[xiv]

INTRODUCTION

NO section of Persian art was so brilliantly and completely represented at Burlington House in 1931 as the section of Miniatures. It was the largest and finest collection ever displayed in Europe, and could claim to be fully representative. It is true that it could have been still more extensive and magnificent if the two great collections preserved in the Bibliothèque Nationale and the British Museum could have been drawn upon. Neither of these was available. But splendid and desirable additions as a selection from these would have been, their absence—and the absence of a few notable manuscripts such as the famous Bestiary of 1295 in the Pierpont Morgan Library, the *Shāh-nāma* illustrated in 1537 for Shāh Tahmāsp, belonging to Baron Edmond de Rothschild, the Nizāmī in the State Library at Leningrad, and the fifteenth-century anthology once belonging to Mr. Yates Thompson and now to Mr. Gulbenkian —even the absence of these did not detract from the claims of the Exhibition to be richly representative of Persian painting in all its phases.

There was, moreover, abundant compensation for the absence of such known treasures in the presence of hitherto unknown or comparatively unknown works, some of them of the highest interest and importance, lent by the Persian Government, the Egyptian Government, and the Turkish Government. These alone would have made the Exhibition memorable; and they were supplemented by a great deal of fresh material from various sources, chiefly English. It is somewhat remarkable that the fine Persian manuscripts and paintings in English libraries should have remained for so long unknown to Europe, and unknown even in England itself, except to a very few scholars like Sir Thomas Arnold. For, even apart from the British Museum, there is in this country a series of works of high importance in the history of Persian painting. The Bodleian Library, the Libraries of Edinburgh University, the Royal Asiatic Society, and the India Office, lent precious manuscripts and single drawings; but the richest contribution came from that of a private owner, Mr. Chester Beatty.

This material was largely new and unpublished; and its juxtaposition with the splendid loans from private collections in Europe and America, especially famous Paris collections like those of M. Vever, the late M. Claude Anet, and M. Cartier, afforded an unparalleled opportunity for comparative study such as was greatly needed.

It may be convenient to indicate here some of the points on which the Exhibition shed new light. Each of these will be fully discussed later, in its place. For the first time the two portions of the History of the World by Rashīd al-Dīn, one in the Edinburgh University Library and the other in the library of the Royal Asiatic Society, were brought together. Also twenty-two paintings from the 'Demotte' *Shāh-nāma*, a manuscript which had never been seen in its entirety in Europe, and of which only a few pages had been reproduced, were lent by six different owners. For the art of the fourteenth century these two manuscripts are of capital importance.

INTRODUCTION

A group of manuscripts produced at Shīrāz at the turn of the fourteenth–fifteenth centuries revealed the fact that the 'Timurid' style was already established before the invasion of Tīmūr, which the earliest of these manuscripts ante-date. New light was shed on the early Timurid period, which was the period most brilliantly represented in the Exhibition. The fame of the libraries of Shāh Rukh and Baysunqur was always great in the East, and at Burlington House we were enabled at last to substitute for tantalizing literary allusions the actual evidence of superb works. Two masterpieces, the great *Shāh-nāma* made for Baysunqur in 1430, a manuscript which Sir Thomas Arnold in his *Painting in Islam* alludes to as still existing but never described, and the *Kalīla and Dimna* Fables with their remarkable landscapes and their ravishing colour, were of outstanding importance. The Fables enlarged our conceptions of landscape art in Persia.

Another splendid fifteenth-century work now for the first time exhibited was the *Shāh-nāma* belonging to the Royal Asiatic Society; a manuscript which was known to very few and till the date of the Exhibition had never been described. Almost equally little known were the somewhat earlier *Shāh-nāma* from the Bodleian, and the *Gulistān* of Sa'dī in the Chester Beatty collection written in 1426 for Baysunqur by Ja'far, the same scribe who wrote the text of the superb *Shāh-nāma* of 1430 lent by the Persian Government.

It was one of the aims of the Exhibition to collect together as much as was available of the works attributed with more or less plausibility to Bihzād. As every one conversant with the subject knows, there has been the most violent controversy and the utmost difference of opinion as to what are the authentic works of this the most famous of Persian painters. The Exhibition afforded a precious opportunity for examining the material and reaching some definite conclusions. Happily the generosity of owners made it possible to group together all the most important works which have been attributed to the master by one authority or another; and if no final agreement was reached, that is not to be wondered at when we remember the fluctuations of critical opinion over works that have been studied for far longer time in Europe; for instance, the works of Giorgione. Especially interesting was the first appearance in Europe of the *Būstān* from Cairo, containing what seem to be the best authenticated paintings by the master.

Other artists whose individuality the Exhibition set in a clearer light than before are Qāsim 'Alī, whose contemporary reputation approached that of Bihzād, and Mahmūd of Bukhara, a painter whose design is of a quite distinctive character.

Hitherto unknown miniatures by 'Abd al-Samad lent by the Persian Government were of great interest in connexion with the origin of the Mughal school, for this master, who changed his style after becoming court painter at Delhi, was seen in the earlier phase of his art, working in a purely Persian manner.

These are perhaps the most noteworthy instances of additions to our knowledge brought about by the Exhibition of new material or the opportunity of comparison; others will be recorded in the narrative portions of this book.

INTRODUCTION

But before coming to the history of Persian painting, we will briefly examine its achievement from the aesthetic point of view.

Persia contributes to the world's art a type of painting which is unique in character and in its own kind supreme. It is easy to disparage it by dwelling on qualities it does not possess and does not attempt. But rate it high or low, its uniqueness is incontestable; it yields a special kind of pleasure which no other art gives us. Let us take it for what it is, and see, if we can, in what its peculiar excellence consists.

First let us say one word on the question of scale.

The general impression of smallness derived from the small scale of the Persian miniature would be corrected if more of the wall-paintings had survived. But even in the case of the miniatures it will be modified when we study them more attentively: we shall find that while the pages painted by the average painter remain, however magnified, merely enlarged miniatures, the designs of the greater masters, when enlarged, as by a lantern on the screen, appear in their true breadth and vigour, rivalling the scale of a fresco.

Yet it is true that monumental and serene design, especially that which concentrates in a single figure or a group of such figures, is almost absent from Persian painting. This absence is mainly due to the fact that art was so largely cut off from the inspiration of religious conceptions; largely, but not entirely, as we shall see.

Geographically, Persia lies between the Mediterranean border-lands and the Farther East.

If we seek for an extreme expression of the Western spirit in art, we shall find it in Michelangelo. In all his work we divine a passionate preoccupation with the human body, as the sufficing symbol of human desires, sorrows, triumph, and tragic frustration. Of interest in the beautiful surface of the earth, foliage, streams, distant mountain-forms, there is almost nothing. The god-like presence of Man obliterates all other objects of vision. He is all that matters.

In absolute contrast are the Chinese landscapes of the classic period. Man is but a traveller, small and insignificant beside the towering crags and cloudy peaks. He is given his due place, he is at home in this world; but the artist's aim is to hint at the whole vision of the living universe, with its endless change and streaming energies, in which the life of man is included.

The Persian conception is between these two. Man and the doings of Man are in the foreground always: Persian art is largely concerned with heroic story. Yet we feel that the outlook on the world is different from the European outlook. The nude human form, as a means of expression, is entirely absent from Persian painting. We may perhaps find a clue in the thought of the Sufi philosophy, which proved so congenial to the Persian spirit. To paraphrase an authority on the subject: the One Being, from whom all proceeds, knows itself as Nature, yet amidst the multiformity of Nature re-asserts its unity in Man.[1] Such a conception may be present only in certain types of

[1] R. A. Nicholson, *Studies in Islamic Mysticism*, p. 125.

Persian painting; but neither is all European art like Michelangelo's, nor all Chinese art like the Sung landscapes.

Persia, in her art, has affinities with the Mediterranean, but more with the other countries of Asia. Hers is one of the great schools of Asiatic art. Like all the other schools of painting in Asia, it ignores shadow, and unlike the European schools, it does not seek expression through ideas of mass.

Yet it is quite distinct from Indian painting. The Mughal school, modelled at the outset on Persian classics, is nearest to it; but almost from the beginning it differentiates itself, partly because the Indian genius asserts its own character, partly because there is a certain infusion of influence from Europe, shown in a more or less tentative suggestion of atmosphere, so that the jewel-like lustre of the Persian pages is soon lost.

Persian painting is still more different from Chinese. The differences are partly due to difference of mental structure and outlook, partly to difference in the painter's material implements and their usage. In both countries fine writing is prized even above fine painting. This is especially true of Persia, where the two arts are distinct. In China the two melt into one another, since the writing-brush is also a paint-brush, and to form well the Chinese characters requires a painter's skill. Using a full broad brush for the most part (though in certain periods a fine hair-line of the utmost delicacy and sensitiveness was used for figure-drawing), the Chinese were naturally led to employ the tones of graduated ink-washes for aerial perspective; and their early love of landscape induced them to create a pictorial art of modulated tones, such as was quite unknown in Persia.

How little the designing in tone rather than line was congenial to the Persian artist is evident in certain of the pages in the manuscript *History of the World* belonging to the Royal Asiatic Society. There are for instance pictures of the Mountains of India and those 'on the way to Tibet' (Plate XXIII), where the Chinese method of representing the mountain-tops dark and the lower parts blotted with mist is imitated. There is no suggestion of mist, and the washes of dark paint are timidly and clumsily put in. It was something that Persian painting was unable and unwilling to assimilate. If it had survived, it would have survived as a kind of pattern merely.

There are no ink-paintings in Persian art: there are ink-drawings incomparable of their kind; but the paintings are all in colour. And while the Chinese colour depends on the relief of low-toned silk or paper, the empty spaces of which are an integral part of the design, the Persian artist covers the entire ground with colour, and that with intense and glowing contrasts marvellously controlled into harmony. Hardly ever do the Chinese paint the blue of the sky, which to the Persians is a fondly dwelt-on glory.

Deeper than these differences is the difference in the conception of space. Chinese painting in its maturity renders the vision of an unlimited, all-enclosing space. But what is presented to the eye in Persian painting is an enclosed space, the theatre of the events portrayed.

Pictorial art, as soon as it grapples with the problem of representing a complete scene, is bound to invent various devices in order to make the picture clear and convincing to the spectator. If there are many figures not all on the same plane, but some nearer and others farther off, there is a confusion which must be resolved in one way or another. Common to all Asiatic art is the convention by which the spectator is imagined to be looking at the scene from a certain elevation, so that figures or groups do not come in front of each other and the whole can be easily grasped. It was of course only by a very slow process that the scheme of conventions was gradually evolved which finally staged the scene. And it is interesting to note how primitive devices remain undisturbed in mature Persian design. Thus even in Bihzād and his successors a cistern or a carpet will be drawn as if on a ground-plan, while the rest of the picture is seen from the point of view usually adopted, or from two points of view at once (cf. Plate LXIX). The discordance does not seem to have perturbed either the painters or their public. But they had no share of the European feeling that a picture should conform as closely as possible to visual appearances; they had none of the zest in exploration which has made European painting a voyage of discovery; they were content to express themselves in an art without atmospheric effect, without light and shade, an art which owed nothing to the study of anatomy or the study of perspective.

Behind this art is an Oriental mind, which regards the problem of picture-making from a quite different point of view from that of the European mind, at least since the beginnings of the Renaissance. It keeps constantly in view the requirements of the spectator for whom the painting is brought into being; and for the spectator's convenience it performs miracles which to the Western mind, with its scrupulous respect for the laws of nature, seem outrageous: we are enabled, for instance, to contemplate scenes of night where there is no darkness, and the stars shine on a fully illuminated scene, and even greater liberties with actuality are taken with perfect nonchalance by the Persian painter. It is all for the convenience of the spectator, and the satisfaction of his interest in the story. We in Europe do not boggle at the assumption by novelists of superhuman powers, when they wish to show us the thoughts and feelings hidden in the hearts of their characters; but when it comes to going behind the visible world in pictorial art we are apt to be disconcerted or to dismiss the devices used as childish, though by our quite modern artists these traditional scruples are being broken down, if from different motives and with different effects.

It must be admitted that Persian painting betrays no intellectual grasp of the structure of things. The Persian outlook is essentially and incurably romantic. It enjoys what is marvellous, it is quite ready to believe the incredible. The painter stages his scene for his own and the spectator's enjoyment, much as it might be arranged in a theatre. He contrives usually a back-cloth of rising ground, which he likes to adorn with tufts of flowering plants, and since these are delightful for their form he brings them near to the eye by a suitable enlargement; it would not occur to him to make them little coloured smudges because they appeared so at a distance in nature. The slopes and ridges of the background, set off by a sky of gold or purest blue, are convenient for half-hiding and

[5]

half-disclosing figures beyond, which will have a dramatic effect. It is all in a way very ingenuous; but the greater masters knew how to combine these simple artifices into a whole which presents a plausible approximation to reality.

Not that realism is ever an aim of the artists. The absence of shadows of itself makes for a certain ideality: the pictured scene is removed a stage from the actual impression on the eye. It is something like the effect of verse in dramatic dialogue.

Just as in Japanese colour-prints we see actors and courtesans, tea-house interiors, pleasure-parties on river or sea-shore, portrayed in detail, yet by the elimination of light and shade and of the imitation of surface-textures all this popular scene is lifted into a serener air, so in Persian painting the absence of shadow and of atmospheric effects has a similar result. The artist, untroubled by the need to give an equivalent of complicated appearances, concentrates all the more on beauty of design. Thus in the illustrations to the *Shāh-nāma* there are battle-scenes in which the painters abate nothing of the bloodiest detail. But being removed a whole stage from actuality by this simple suppression, they are no longer revolting; especially as the artists will make a decorative design out of any elements whatsoever.

Let us contemplate for a moment one or two Persian miniatures of the finest type and period. We cannot do better than take, for one side of Persian art, at least, the paintings in the *Zafar-nāma* belonging to Mr. Robert Garrett, a double-page from which we have the privilege of reproducing. One of these illustrations depicts the building of the Great Mosque at Samarqand under the superintendence of Tīmūr. It is a scene of busy and crowded action, the left-hand page especially. At first sight all appears to be accidental; there is no obvious controlling of the groups into formal relationships: every group, every man in each group, is entirely engrossed in what he is doing, and all is being done at high pressure under the taskmaster's eye. Some are sawing wood or fitting planks together, others chiselling blocks of marble; a cart laden with slabs of stone has just arrived, and now an elephant with larger slabs intrudes on the scene: at a doorway in the background an officer lifts a rod with an energetic gesture. One could not conceive a more busy and animated scene. It is only when we begin to analyse the composition that we perceive how learned a design it is, how admirably the wheels of the cart and the curve of the elephant's trunk set off the complex play of angles and straight lines, and how the map of colour enforces and enhances the richness of the composition: so that, with all its complexity and seeming acceptance of accidental appearances, the whole contents and reposes the eye. The design is extremely original; it is informed by a masculine vigour: enlarged many times, it would show no sign of smallness.

Other pages of the same manuscript reveal a like masterly control of what might seem almost unmanageable elements, together with a wonderful inventiveness, a vibrant energy, and a seizure of unexpected yet natural gesture, which the great European artists have not surpassed. Were the paintings on a large scale, and this small scale is not in the least essential to them, their power and splendour would be at once acknowledged.

[6]

INTRODUCTION

Like most Persian paintings they are illustrations; and though illustration is in fashionable criticism a depreciatory term, we have to remember that the great Italian painters are also illustrators from beginning to end, taking their subjects from the Bible and poetry, as the Persians took theirs from poetry and romance. But in talking of 'illustration' we are using but a nominal term. The born artist will always be intent on his design; the great artist will fuse into his design the utmost expressiveness in telling his story, his form and colour and the relationships he discovers between them communicating his theme more eloquently than his representation of recognizable figures and objects. At its best, Persian painting attains this fusion. For as a race the Persians are born decorators.

The famous poet Nizāmī, in a sort of introduction to his poem *Haft Paykar* or The Seven Portraits, 'on the cause of writing this book' says:[1]

> If seven lines converge, a single point at last falls on the target of the affair;
> The painter who has ten subservient parts holds to the end of every single thread,
> For if one thread should stray from the main cord, all the subservient threads would be faulty.

And such a subordination and control of the parts, that a harmony of the whole may be achieved, are instinctive aims of the Persian artist. In inferior examples the painter subsides into the decorative craftsman, always with a sense of colour-design, not into the illustrator intent on the mere portrayal of lively incident.

There is, however, a side on which Persian art is admittedly lacking. Exquisitely sensuous as it is, there are largely absent from it those spiritual conceptions with which Christianity and Buddhism alike have inspired painters in East and West. It is not true indeed, as was for long the prevalent notion, that Islam has no religious art. Sir Thomas Arnold, whose death during the first preparations for the Exhibition all who have any interest in Persian studies must for ever deplore, has in his *Painting in Islam* shown that there are plenty of miniatures concerned with religious subjects. Yet there is a radical distinction to be drawn. The grand religious conceptions of Christian and Buddhist art were presented by the painters as symbolic events or, concentrated in a single figure, as incarnations of spiritual power, wisdom, and beauty; they were, for the people, objects of adoration. The religious paintings of Persia were never this. Altar-pieces were unknown. The paintings were simply illustrations of sacred story. In one instance alone, the Ascent of the Prophet to the Seventh Heaven and the Presence of God on a night splendid with stars, is there sublimity of conception; and this has inspired some glorious pages. The earth, which for the Persian painter is so congenial a home, with all its varied delight for human senses, is in this vision dwindled to a little globe swimming among the clouds and starry spaces, though even here a certain irrepressible sensuousness overflows into the ethereal atmosphere.

Much has been written on the prohibition of images and figure-painting by the Traditions of the Prophet, which seems so strangely contradicted by the profusion of pictorial art in Persia. All that need here be said is that while painting was not

---

[1] Translation by C. E. Wilson.

[7]

anti-religious, it was at all times condemned by the theologians. Patronage came, never from the Church, but only from princes and rich men; and the artists had to follow their patrons' taste. Writers on art have sometimes deplored that European painters were so long limited in free expression by being dependent on the Church. In Persia may be seen the complementary case of limitation coming from the Church's ban: it was probably the more injurious limitation of the two.

Drained of spirituality as it might seem to be by these narrowing conditions, Persian painting is not so devoid of such content as a superficial impression would infer. Most of the miniatures are inspired by poetry; and in Persian poetry the Sufi mysticism plays a large part.

'Whether quantity or quality be considered,' says Dr. Nicholson in his *Studies in Islamic Mysticism*, 'the best part of medieval Persian poetry is either genuinely mystical or is so saturated with mystical ideas that it will never be more than half understood by those who read it literally.' Sanā'ī, 'Attār, Jalāl al-Dīn Rūmī, Sa'dī, Hāfiz, and Jāmī are the most eminent of these poets. The last three of these are the most often illustrated, more especially Sa'dī and Jāmī.

Let us turn to a painting in which this mystic feeling is made visible. The painting by Qāsim 'Alī reproduced in colour on Plate LXVI will serve as an example. In a garden where a stream flows winding down verdant slopes to form a pool bordered with mallow and iris and narcissus, a group of mystics are seated on mats, books in their hands, and talking together. It is no animated controversy; one imagines rather a few words dropped now and then from the lips of one or other of these bearded men in the stillness of the twilight. For the painter portrays them not as imposing personages against a perfunctory background; rather they are melted and immersed in the unearthly beauty of the scene enclosing them; the pomegranate-trees with their motionless great blossoms, the slim white sapling between them, the clustered flowers springing from the grass, the first stars and the young moon, all seem to breathe the air of a life such as men in moments of profound insight and happiness desire to be included in.

The language of the mystic is universal. With that picture in our minds we find a congenial mood in the language of Thomas Traherne:

'You never enjoy the world aright, till the sea itself floweth in your veins, till you are clothed with the heavens and crowned with the stars . . . till you more feel it than your private estate, and are more present in the hemisphere, considering the glories and the beauties there, than in your own house; till you remember how lately you were made, and how wonderful it was when you came into it; and more rejoice in the palace of your glory, than if it had been made but to-day morning.'

And again:

'Suppose a river, or a drop of water, an apple or a sand, an ear of corn, or an herb: God knoweth infinite excellencies in it more than we: He seeth how it relateth to angels and men; how it proceedeth from the most perfect Lover to the most perfectly Beloved; how it representeth all His attributes; how it conduceth in its place, by the best of means to the best of ends; and for this cause it cannot be beloved too much.'

'Enjoy the world!' It is the phrase associated with the sensualist. What a different depth of meaning it takes here! Could the senses alone ever enjoy with such intensity? The Persian painters have been praised for their refined sensuality; and certainly their senses are exquisitely cultivated. But just as the Sūfī poetry, taking its symbols from the ecstasy of the lover and his beloved and the intoxication of the wine-cup, can easily be misread, so in the paintings who shall say where the intoxication of the eye in light and colour, in sky and blossom, merges into the profounder ecstatic vision of the glory of the world and its creator? At any rate there is in the painters the same dwelling on the glowing distinctness of things (the 'apple', the 'grain of sand', the 'ear of corn'), each in its place with its own 'infinite excellencies', which is habitual to the mystic poet: whereas we in Europe are accustomed to approach the idea of unity in the world through a process of understanding rather than through intuition.

Without dwelling overmuch on this disguised spirituality in Persian art, it is necessary to point out that it exists. We may easily miss it, because there is no overt expression of emotion; and European art uses so readily the features of the face as a means of expression that when this is absent we are disconcerted. Throughout Persian painting such expression of emotion, as Arnold has pointed out in his *Painting in Islam*, is stinted to a remarkable degree.

On the other hand, there is nothing of the rhetorical gesticulation which in many European pictures of imaginary scenes, by its very effort to impress and catch the spectator's attention, provokes him to tedium or disgust. How moving by exception is the strange and massive calm of the personages created by Piero della Francesca!

But in spite of the stinted or suppressed emotion in Persian art, it is often dramatic. Sometimes this sense of drama is in the design itself, in such contrasts as we see in the page from the Oxford *Shāh-nāma* reproduced on the Frontispiece, where the violent action of the man digging in the garden contrasts so strangely with the impassive height of the tower, with the ladies watching above, and the closed door below: we experience a sense of expectation, of events about to happen; or it may be merely a dramatic opposition of colour. But dramatic motives abound in the 'Demotte' *Shāh-nāma*; and we may instance the miniature from the Royal Asiatic Society's *Shāh-nāma* of the 'Paladins in the Snow' (Plate LVIII), where the very quietness of the figures seated and telling stories of their great chief enhances the sense of doom coming upon them in the curdling clouds of snow above. Or look at the scene in the *Shāh-nāma* of 1430 (reproduced in colour in the *Survey of Persian Art*), where the hero Farāmurz mourns over the coffin of Rustam and his brother, while the courtiers wait below; or the dramatic motives to be found in groups and figures of the miniatures in Mr. Garrett's *Zafar-nāma*, all of which have been reproduced in Arnold's *Bihzad and his Paintings in the Zafar-nāmah MS.*

All through Persian painting this gift for expressing dramatic relations, dramatic expectancy, through design rather than through the features, is to be found. And it is always singularly combined with the decorative gift and instinct.

Constable said: 'There is nothing ugly. I never saw an ugly thing in my life—for let the form of the object be what it may, light and shade and perspective will always make it beautiful.' A native of England, where so much squalor in great cities would surely be intolerable to its inhabitants if it were not veiled in tender mists or blotted by smoky exhalations, might well write thus. But this particular thought would not have occurred to a Persian, used to the sharp sunlight and lucid atmosphere of his country. Chardin, the traveller, says: 'Those who have never visited the Eastern countries are strangers to the shining and bright part of Nature.'

Whether influenced by conditions of climate or no, Persian painting derives its peculiar beauty and splendour first from the fact that it admits no shadows to muddy the pure tones of colour, and secondly from its consummate use of the most brilliant colours, which it knows how to unite into a harmony. No other art uses so full and brilliant a palette without being garish.

Thus it is that it communicates in a manner nowhere else surpassed a sense of the glory of the world; the radiance of the sky, the incredible beauty of the spring blossoms, among which, clothed in their beautiful dresses, human beings love and hate, exult and grieve.

But just when we may have decided that the peculiar beauty of Persian painting is its colour, we are arrested by the recollection of drawings in line, which have no colour, in which indeed we feel no need for colour. Here again the quality of the Persian line is distinct and a thing by itself. If we try to differentiate this line-drawing from the Chinese and Japanese 'hair-line' drawings—for of course the vehement, decisive strokes and sudden blots of the brush-strokes of a Mu Ch'i or a Sesshū do not come into competition—we may miss the intellectual subtlety communicated by the masters of the Far East, but, just as Persian colour has a kind of intoxicating potency, so the Persian line gives a physical thrill of pleasure. Nearest to it is the line of the Rajput painters of India, but in that a more lyrical mood is communicated, it is perhaps less directly sensuous. In both cases it is a calligraphic line; that is, we share the artist's pleasure in tracing the sensitive living strokes for their own sake, apart from the forms they enclose; but it is astonishing how, in fine examples, the Persian painter combines this calligraphic beauty with a vital expressiveness of attitude and gesture. In the later periods the calligraphic element becomes over-dominant, significance is impaired or lost.

One of the finest and most famous of Persian line-drawings was lent to the Exhibition by Mr. Philip Hofer: the 'Camel with his driver', dating from the earlier part of the sixteenth century. Calligraphy and expressive draughtsmanship are there in perfect equilibrium. This drawing, a masterpiece in its kind, has not been chosen for reproduction, simply because it has been several times reproduced and is therefore well known. But the qualities of the Persian line can be seen in other drawings reproduced; the legendary subject for instance (Plate XCIII A) in which Solomon sits on a throne supported in the air by winged genii. What extraordinary pleasure there is to the eye in the drawing of the magic carpet held over the floating throne! This and the 'Scene in Paradise', from the same collection, Frau Sarre's, are examples of a rather rare type of intricate and elaborate line-drawing with many figures, made apparently without any intention of adding colour. But in the 'Picnic in the Mountains' (Plate C) we see the kind of exquisite work in line which underlies the finest paintings; for this is a drawing the colouring of which has been begun but left unfinished. Another very beautiful example of unfinished painting is in the British Museum Print Room. In the drawing which has been attributed to Bihzād (Plate LXXIV B) the colouring has been carried a little farther. Another drawing in an earlier stage, a sketch-design with *pentimenti,* has the interest of showing us how the artists began their work (Plate CVIII A). Such sketches and preparatory studies are uncommon, but a number of such are contained in the book of drawings published by F. Sarre and E. Mittwoch (*Zeichnungen von Riza Abbasi,* 1914) and leaves from this book were lent to the Exhibition.

In the period before the fifteenth century the calligraphic element was not marked, even where colour was subordinated, as in the *History of the World* manuscript. Even in the charming ink-drawings, where Chinese influence is so apparent, of the *Diwān* of Sultān Ahmad Jalā'ir (Plate LXXIV A) the actual pen-line yields little of the peculiar pleasure we have noted. But late in the sixteenth century calligraphy begins to be obtrusive. In such examples as the nude study of a girl (Plate CVIII B), a rarity in Persian art, or the figure of a man (Plate CVIII C), the line is still sensitive and fine, though lacking in the thrill that the greater masters communicate so magically. But in such a drawing as that reproduced on Plate XCIX B a different spirit has come in. The artist has acquired a certain manner; the unforced, even quality of the line has gone, and in its place is a sharp accenting of it in the faces especially, and in accessories a sort of routine stroke pleasing enough but without vitality. And when we turn from drawings of this type to such pen-work as is shown on Plate CIX C, we see how far the tendency has gained; the sharp little accents are everywhere, the forms have lost stability.

We may call this the victory of calligraphy over draughtsmanship; but is not this, after all, a misuse of terms? For that special and intimate pleasure communicated by the beauty of a line which expresses the form it encloses and at the same time moves us by its own intrinsic quality, has evaporated. It is that delicate equilibrium, so rare and difficult, like the perfect gesture of a great actor, which thrills. In this the Persian line at its best is unsurpassed.

How was the peculiar character of the Persian miniature formed? It was a long process, and because of meagre evidence obscure. To examine such relics of pictorial art as have survived the obliterating tempests of the Mongol invasions is like examining the shreds and fragments of wreckage after a storm in which whole fleets have foundered. We are in a world of conjecture, and have little assurance that our conjectures hit the truth. Could we have before our eyes the whole range of that once-existing art, many doubtful points would be resolved, questions of relationship and derivation finally established. We must always have in mind, in venturing on generalizations as to this early period, the scantiness of the material available.

Yet, after all, enough has survived to enable us to discern some, perhaps most, of the elements out of which the mature Persian style in painting was developed. The historical aspect of the matter will be more fully examined in the chapters which follow. At the moment we are concerned rather with the various contributions, from whatever source they came, to the formation of that style.

Casting an eye over the general tendency of its development, we see, not a single germ of definite character gradually unfolding and expanding into flower, but diverse elements and a tentative movement, uncertain at first in its direction, and clogged at times by inherited elements which impede its life.

In the illustrations to Harīrī, such as those in the Oxford manuscript, some of which are here reproduced, the impression given is of artists who have taken over the debris of an old tradition but who are, in spite of that, extremely interested in life and character, and in the dramatic relations between the persons they portray. In the British Museum there is a manuscript of Harīrī where the illustrations are in outline, and the drawing is summary, free, and animated. Here we feel the artist's intention is fully expressed. In the Oxford Harīrī, though the decorative effect of gold and vigorous colour is superb in its way, we cannot help thinking of mosaics or wall-paintings; the sumptuous clothing, the monumental exterior, seems to weigh down the simple vivacity of the drawing. In the famous 'Schefer' Harīrī manuscript of the Bibliothèque Nationale a more original artist is at work; one who is intensely interested in human life and character, also in the camels which men depend on for travelling, but in little else. He is scarcely concerned with decorative design. In the Oxford Harīrī there is less seizure of gesture and movement, but the hands talk, the faces are expressive, there is latent drama in the groups and scenes. Look, however, at the dresses. These have elaborate patterns, but the artist seems to have learnt them by rote. There is one pattern in particular, which occurs in most of these manuscripts, with curious crumpled forms not directly suggestive of anything in nature, yet not a geometrical abstraction. It really seems as if the crumpled forms assumed by the folds at the bottom of a heavy dress where it meets the floor had been taken over as the motive for a pattern after long repetition and stylization. Such misunderstandings are common enough in the history of ornamental design. But what we need to note is the absence of any sensitiveness to the hints offered by a thousand things in nature which the born decorator will use to enrich and enliven his designs. Contrast for a moment the patterns on the dresses in a Japanese colour-print. These artists, working in Mesopotamia, seem hardly to have looked at flowers or trees; they are content with rudimentary, lifeless symbols that do not even suggest things that grow. Sun and sky are represented in equally rudimentary fashion.

The real life of this art, that which has sap and vigour in it, is the interest in human beings and human doings and the expressive representation of them. If such an art is to mature, it is on these lines, we should say. And we should expect the development of this art to be of a character more Western than Oriental. But actually no such development occurred. The evidence has largely been lost, but here and there we find traces of other traditions than that to which the Harīrī illustrations belong; we find a keener interest in forms of vegetation, a more observant eye, also a bent towards decorative design which becomes gradually stronger.

A race which has produced an art consummate in its kind must have an instinct and a genius of its own. Its art cannot have been composed merely of borrowings from other races. It must have known both how to assimilate these borrowed elements and how to fuse them into its own special idiom.

We are bound, therefore, to assume an original genius in Īrān, persisting from Sasanian and earlier times, as the finally dominant strain in Persian art. And even though the tangible evidence surviving is so lamentably scanty, we get hints here and there, as from the hunting-scenes carved on the rock-face at Tāq i Būstān, where the conception is rather pictorial than sculptural, and while recalling Assyrian friezes seems to prefigure the paintings of the fifteenth and sixteenth centuries.

Between the last Sasanian king and the first of the Safawī dynasty Persia was under alien rulers; and the imposed taste of patrons, and the fact that the artists were obliged to go for patronage from court to court, following the fortunes of their masters, may account in part for the difficulties we meet in tracing the formation of a national tradition.

Certainly in the manuscripts of Harīrī and other works of the thirteenth century the Iranian genius seems for the time submerged. If the whole range of the art of the time could have survived we should doubtless see our way plainly enough. What is certain is that before the end of the fourteenth century the full Persian style has been formed; and we are able to mark significant stages on the way.

It has already been mentioned that two most important manuscripts of the fourteenth century were shown, for the first time in an exhibition, at Burlington House. No doubt other types existed in this experimental period when the Persian style was in process of formation. But these two, the *History of the World* by Rashīd al-Dīn and the 'Demotte' *Shāh-nāma*, may be taken as typical, and a comparison of them is of great interest. For they represent two different attempts to assimilate Chinese influence, the one successful, the other unsuccessful. The artists of the *History of the World* (for one may assume in both cases that more than one artist was employed) have obviously looked at Chinese paintings and sought in some measure to emulate them. We have already noted the attempt to borrow the Chinese convention in rendering distant hills: the borrowing is not assimilated. So, too, with the Chinese rendering of foaming water. In Persian hands the curling lines have lost their impetus of sinuous movement and are on the way to become an ornamental pattern. But the power of Chinese example is chiefly visible in the abjuring of colour, the natural birthright of Īrān. Not that colour is absent, but it is not used in the Persian way. At the same time the line has little or none of the sweeping force or the subtlety of the Chinese brush.

All this is not to deny the extraordinary interest of the designs and the immense importance of the manuscript, though the paramount value of the drawings may be thought to lie in their excellence as illustration. The point is that, from the point of view of the development of Persian painting, they were sterile.

What a contrast when we turn to the 'Demotte' *Shāh-nāma*, a manuscript which was broken up on its arrival in Europe but twenty-two pages of which the Exhibition was enabled for the moment to reunite. In these paintings there is less trace in outward aspect or in detail of Chinese example. But the artists, having looked at and admired Chinese paintings, have been stimulated to emulate, not their conventions, but their qualities. They have seen that the Chinese excel in the expression of movement, and they have sought to infuse this movement, this rhythm, into the more static design of inherited tradition. Their borrowing has been assimilated; they have known how to use it, and to use it in their own way.

These *Shāh-nāma* pictures make a landmark in Persian painting. There is in them a vigour of action, a vigour of colour, a power of rhythmical design, which is never afterwards surpassed. A certain crudity is present, congenial to the type of drawing and colour: there is nothing of the preciousness, the exquisite refinement of workmanship which at the end of the fifteenth century disguises power. The pigments are comparatively coarse, the palette is limited. It is not yet Persian painting in its perfect manifestation. But it represents an assimilation of various elements, handled with great energy, which must have been of priceless value to the succeeding generation of artists.

What vitality there is in these heroic scenes! What bigness of design! And again we note the dramatic character of the conceptions.

With the fifteenth century comes again a change. We begin to feel that exquisite cultivation of the senses which belongs so intimately to Persian art. The human forms become more supple, the flowers more delicately formed, the pigments have been refined; a gracious air has breathed over the artists' creations.

But there is a moment in the earlier part of this century when something still survives from the more archaic character of design; when a touch of pleasing awkwardness mingles with spontaneous feeling; when the painters have not yet completely mastered their means of expression and are, perhaps, on that account the more expressive. Such moments in the history of any school have always a peculiar charm. In this phase the women especially have a stature and stateliness that succeeding periods forget. The little miniature from the Claude Anet collection (Plate LI B) of Majnūn brought to Layla's tent betrays a sort of shyness and stiffness in the execution which seems to deepen the emotional import of the scene. And in the delicious page of 'Humāy in the Garden' (Plate XLI), with its tapestry effect, and its figures that seem to partake of the springing of the tall flowers about them, the reticent colours seem like the colours of the dawn which will soon bring the splendours of sunrise.

The splendours come with Bihzād and his school, where all the mingled elements of tradition are now fused in perfection. The consummation has been reached. There is abundance of vigour and inventiveness, masterly drawing and dramatic design; but the masculine side of this art is partly disguised by the lustre of enamelled colour and the extraordinary grace of line. Now appears that taste for the precious and luxurious which is probably what gives a stranger to Persian art his first impression. It is subordinated in the school of Herāt, but in the Safawī period this voluptuous tendency strengthens and expands. With the successors of Bihzād it is full meridian; choiceness of exquisite taste alone prevents a feeling of satiety with the pages now produced, glowing with a festal radiance of colour never known before. There is still vitality of drawing, animated design, fresh invention (cf. Plate LXXV), but we cannot help feeling perilously near to the stage of over-ripeness and decay. And that stage soon comes. Like other Eastern schools, the Persian pays the penalty for its lack of the exploring spirit, intent on conquest of new matter; it has no fresh fuel for the fire of inspiration. But the three centuries that include its time of creative power form a chapter in the history of the world's art that in its own sphere, limited though that is, rises to incomparable beauty.

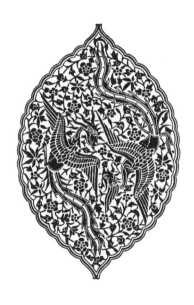

46 (*b*). A garden scene. 1420

(Frontispiece)

PLATE I. 3 (c). Abu Zayd questioned in an Arab encampment. 1337

PLATE X. **29** (*w*). Alexander visiting the city of the Brahmans. *c.* 1340

PLATE XXVIII. **44** (*q*). The King of the Monkeys throws figs to the tortoise. *c.* 1410–20

PLATE XLI. **47.** The meeting of Humāy and Humāyūn in the palace garden
First quarter XV *century*

PLATE L . **49** (*s*). Rustam and Isfandiyār. 1430

PLATE LXVII. **81.** Sultān Husayn Mīrzā in a garden. By Bihzād. *About* 1485

(above and opposite page)

PLATE LXVI. 80 (d). Mystics in a garden. By Qāsim ʿAlī. 1485

I

PERSIAN MINIATURE PAINTING BEFORE THE MONGOL INVASIONS, AND THE MESOPOTAMIAN STYLE

AT BURLINGTON HOUSE the general criterion for the admission of exhibits was production within the political boundaries of Persia. But this left a problem for the medieval period when Persia formed part of the Islamic theocracy. Generally speaking, objects were admitted from the whole area which the Sasanian dynasty had ruled before the Arab invasions of the seventh century A.D. overthrew their empire. But in the field of manuscript art it was not possible to exhibit any example dating back before the Mongol invasions of the thirteenth century which finally divided the Islamic state in Asia. Consequently some later manuscripts representing the style that had then been current were included, though they were produced in areas that were not politically Persian at the time. Some of those manuscripts may even have been produced in Egypt, but this style had developed amid a civilization that was very largely Persian in origin. That they were written in Arabic is of no particular significance; it was long the *lingua franca* of Islam—for all literary purposes down to A.D. 1000, and for philosophical and scientific work for very much longer. Indeed the rapid victory of Arabic over Pahlawī is remarkable, especially since it did not even become the official language of the Government before the eighth century.

It is unnecessary here to go into the question of the legitimacy of representative art under Quranic law, which has been fully discussed by various writers, and recently summed up by Sir Thomas Arnold in *Painting in Islam,* since, by the date of the earliest manuscript shown at Burlington House, the cultured classes had thrown off the restrictions, at least as far as they applied to book illustration. At the same time it is well to remember that manuscript illustration must have been only rarely practised in the Islamic world for two or three centuries after the Hijra (A.D. 622), and that, consequently, when necessary, recourse would have been had to non-Islamic artists, mainly Christians, and to the models of Manichaean[1] and Jacobite[2] manuscripts, which must then have been easily accessible. Small as was the Arab contribution to the arts of Islam, it was probably least of all in painting, in which the Semitic races have never excelled.

A convenient starting-point for the study of Persian miniature painting is the reign of the Turkish Sultān Mahmūd of Ghazna (998–1030), whose empire was comparatively

[1] For the survival of Manichaean artists in Persia till the tenth century, see Sir T. Arnold's contribution to the *Survey of Persian Art*. M. Pelliot, however, holds that any Manichaean elements in later Persian art must have been reintroduced into the country by the Uighurs, and that nothing survived there.

[2] It is improbable that the Nestorians ever illuminated their manuscripts.

short-lived, but extended to include not only what is now Afghanistan, but also most of Persia, and who, in India, established a Muhammadan state which was to have far more lasting influence. A great conqueror and organizer, he was, moreover, anxious to make his court a famous centre of culture and, in this quest, he became the patron of Firdawsī, who completed his great epic the *Shāh-nāma* there in 1010. Firdawsī indeed complained of his treatment at Ghazna, and the Persian epic in fact owed far more to the nationalist dynasty of the Samanids (874–999), who had begun the collection of material for it a generation earlier and had at Merv formed a magnificent library which still existed in 1219 under the Khwārazm Shāh at the time of the visit of the geographer Yāqūt. Whether or no one credits the story told in Baysunqur's preface to his edition of the *Shāh-nāma* (1426), that Sultān Mahmūd decorated the room in which Firdawsī worked with scenes of war from the national story, it seems highly probable that there was then in existence an established iconography for the heroes of Īrān,[1] illustrative of the sources which he used. Probably from the first the manuscripts of the *Shāh-nāma* were provided with illustrations. This would account for the survival in manuscripts of the poem of old Iranian types which seem to be directly descended from Sasanian originals.[2] It is this which makes the early manuscripts of the *Shāh-nāma* particularly interesting and valuable. As in all periods of Persian painting, no doubt most of the costumes and decorative features were borrowed from contemporary fashions, but these painters clearly did not draw from the life, and, for the iconography of their subjects, must have tended to repeat the representations of similar scenes from earlier epics and cycles.

At Mahmūd's court Persian culture was in the ascendant. But this is less remarkable than the fact that by this date it dominated the rest of the Islamic world so far as that was subservient to Baghdad, that is, the whole Near East; and even, to some extent, Egypt. From the first Persian culture had been influential, but it received a great impetus with the establishment of the Abbasid Caliphate and the foundation of Baghdad in A.D. 762. The Abbasids depended on Persian support for their maintenance, and their court was filled with Persians. The 'Persification' of the Caliphate reached its highest point during the rule of the Barmecides, a Persian family all-powerful under Hārūn al-Rashīd from 786 to 803, in the reign of the Shi'ite Caliph Ma'mūn (812–33), and while the Persian dynasty of the Buwayhids were established at Baghdad from 945 to 1055.

During the period of the Caliphate the centre of the Persian nationalist revival was in the extreme east of the country, where intercourse with the peoples of Turkestan must have been fairly close, particularly during the rule of the Samanids in Transoxiana in

[1] e.g. Mas'ūdī (d. 956), writing of A.D. 915 (quoted by Sir Thomas Arnold, *P.I.*, pp. 63 and 82), describes a history of the Persian kings illustrated with their portraits. The author of the *Mujmal al-Tawārīkh* (A.D. 1186) states that there was then in existence an illustrated manuscript showing the portraits of the Sasanian kings from the days of Ardashīr till the extinction of the dynasty. [Blochet, 'Les Origines de la Peinture en Perse', *Gazette des Beaux Arts*, 1905, 3° période, tom. xxxiv, pp. 117, 118.]
[2] At least as early as 1200 incidents from the epic are depicted on Rhages ware.

the tenth century, when an extensive trade was carried on with China,[1] whose products were very fashionable, and Chinese manufacturers were established at Samarqand. At that time the Uighurs who lay across the trade-routes were Manichaeans, to which religion they had been converted by refugees from Persia. On the other hand, large numbers of Christians were scattered about Persia, especially at Rayy[2] (in Azarbayjan), where there was the seat of a metropolitan. They were protected by the Abbasids as they had been by the Sasanian kings. The majority were Nestorians, and so of puritanical persuasion, but there were also many Jacobites and Melkites. So that the court art of Baghdad was likely to be influenced by Christians whether of local origin or imported from Syria and Asia Minor, who filled most of the learned professions such as medicine and had been responsible for the translation of Greek scientific works into Arabic. In the east, where the national legends, crystallized by Firdawsī into the *Shāhnāma*, were in favour, the influence would be mainly from the Manichaean and Buddhist art of Central and Farther Asia. It is notable that this was not one of the most important districts in Sasanian times, as Herzfeld has pointed out, and that most of the rock-carvings are in the south and west.[3] Transoxiana is, however, of particular importance in the cultural history of Persia after the Seljuk invasions, because the Qara Khitā'ī there were more civilized, by contact with the Uighurs, than the Seljuks themselves in Khurāsān.

From the mid-eleventh century till the Mongol conquest in 1220–58, Persia, Mesopotamia, and Asia Minor were all dominated by the Seljuk Turks, first as a united Seljuk empire and then by many separate states under ever-changing Seljuk *atabegs* or generals. The Khwārazm Shah, who had succeeded in swallowing up a number of these states before the Mongol invasions, was himself of similar origin, being descended from a Turkish cupbearer.[4]

The earliest surviving illustrated Mesopotamian manuscript dates from c. 1180,[5] when the Seljuks had been masters of Mesopotamia for considerably over a hundred years—yet this style has frequently been attributed to an Abbasid school. Evidently 'Seljuk' would be a far more correct title; but it would hardly be more significant. Gibb in his classical *History of Ottoman Poetry* (vol. 1, pp. 6–10) has said of the Turkish race, of which the Seljuks were the first wave to roll over Persia and Mesopotamia:

'That great race ... which includes not only the Turks both western and eastern, but all the so-called Tartars and Turkmans as well as the Mongols, has never produced any religion, philosophy or literature which bears the stamp of its individual genius. This is because the true genius of the race lies in action, not in speculation. .... Consequently when brought into close connection with the Persians, although they despised the latter as men, looking upon them as braggarts and cowards, they at once recognised their superiority in learning and culture. .... The Seljuks thus attained a very considerable degree of culture, thanks entirely to Persian tutorage. .... Rapidly the Seljuk Turks pushed their conquests westwards,

[1] Barthold, *Turkestan*, pp. 236–7.
[2] Destroyed in A.D. 1220.
[3] It is doubtful whether the Sasanians ever ruled in Transoxiana; on the other hand, in early Islamic times the tombs of both Afrāsiyāb and Siyāwush were pointed out to travellers at Bukhara (Barthold, *Turkestan*,

p. 107), but of course these would be on the 'Turanian' soil.
[4] From Gharjistān in Khurāsān, east of Herāt.
[5] Bib. Nat. Arabe 3929; cf. Blochet, *Enluminures*, pls. II, III.

ever carrying with them Persian culture,' till 'under Malik Shāh (1072–92) the Seljuk empire extended from the frontiers of China to the confines of Syria.'

At the time of its greatest extent and highest development this wide empire was administered by a Persian minister, the Nizām al-Mulk (1017–92), like Firdawsī by origin a *dihqān* or small landholder of Tūs in Khurāsān. Malik Shāh himself lived principally at Isfahān and only twice during his reign visited Baghdad. Though it is probably true that in art, as well as in philosophy and religion, the Turkish race has not shown original genius, yet in this department they did not simply adopt Persian models. In their Central Asian homes they had not advanced very far in civilization, but during their sojourn in Turkestan they had assimilated something from the ancient Chinese Buddhist civilization established there and also from the Uighur Manichaeans. If, as seems very probable, their art derived from the ancient art of Sasanian Persia,[1] the Seljuks would be returning to the Persians their own idiom, which would naturally be widely accepted in its original land of origin. Something of this had also survived farther west, for Mahmūd had Sasanian books in his library at Ghazna. This survival and recrudescence of Sasanian influence is not mere deduction from this historical sequence, but is visible in the non-Mongol figures in the earliest surviving manuscripts of the *Shāh-nāma*. The costume and facial types in these are close to those in the scanty Manichaean remains[2] found by von Le Coq in Chotscho, which represent for us the classical Persian style. So, too, there is striking similarity between the headgear in the ceiling-painting of the first cave at Ajanta, supposed to represent Khusraw and Shīrīn, and that of many figures in the early *Shāh-nāmas*. The Sasanian character of these roof-paintings is borne out by the association with this group of animals and foliage similar to those in the vaults at Qusayr 'Amra[3] (A.D. 715), though these, of course, go back eventually to Hellenistic models.

The importance of the Uighurs themselves as carriers of the Sasanian tradition has probably been rather exaggerated: their greatest influence was exercised under the early Mongols, when they competed successfully with the Persians, who had monopolized positions in the bureaucracy under the Samanids and Ghaznawids. The Uighurs, though they never produced a civilization of their own, had then long been under civilizing influences: they had been converted to Manichaeism by refugees from Persia in the ninth century, but by the thirteenth they were divided between Buddhism and Nestorian Christianity (though in both communities traces of the older faith remained), the partisans of each religion being remarkably tolerant of their rivals, a tolerance which was shared by the early Mongols.

But it is clear that the influence of Manichaeism and Buddhism might have been brought to bear in Persia and Mesopotamia by the Seljuks long before the Mongol

[1] Judging from the specimens recovered by von Le Coq, however, there was a considerable infusion of Central Asian influence.
[2] The date of these is uncertain. Le Coq placed them in the ninth–tenth century; M. Blochet, however, considers them to be much later, apparently placing them in the fourteenth century. Sir Aurel Stein writes: 'The language and writing of the texts to which they belong speak distinctly against such late dating.'
[3] On the Sasanian affinities of the paintings at Qusayr 'Amra, see Dalton, *Treasure of the Oxus*, p. lxxii.

invasion of 1220. This would account for features reminiscent of Central Asia, not only in the *Shāh-nāmas* and other examples of the Persian style proper, but also in the manuscripts of the Mesopotamian school. Such features will later be discussed in detail. Meanwhile it is important to emphasize that at the earliest date from which we have illuminated manuscripts surviving, there is a mingling of the politically dominant Seljuk Turk and the culturally dominant Iranian Persian. Such a mixture is again found under the Mongols and the Timurids, who were of similar nomad stock; so that throughout its history, till 1502, the Persian miniature style was the product of Persian artists working for great Turkish and Mongol patrons.

For this reason there is a steady development and no break in style corresponding to the terrific devastations of Chingīz Khān, Hūlāgū, and Tīmūr. How it came about that there was a notable change of spirit in the work after the thirteenth-century Mongol invasions will be explained when the manuscripts of the fourteenth century are discussed. But that the earlier style cannot justly be called either Abbasid or Seljuk should now be evident. It is more satisfactory to call it either Mesopotamian or Baghdādī from the central area of Islam and its metropolis, where the bulk of its examples must have been produced, in an atmosphere saturated with Persian culture. Here the Arabs had found a very ancient civilization in existence, which had, moreover, been in constant touch with the Roman Empire in the East. So that the earliest manuscripts of the Mesopotamian school are essentially medieval and present parallel features with the contemporary Christian manuscripts.[1] The formative influence seems, however, to have been from the mosaic rather than the manuscript art of the West.

By the thirteenth century Islamic culture had ceased to progress as it had done in the tenth and eleventh centuries; but it was well maintained, and many copies of the great classics of the earlier period must have been made, though few indeed survived the troubled fourteenth century and the devastations of Tīmūr. The manuscripts of the fourteenth-century Mesopotamian school that survive show the end of a conventionalized naturalistic style that had run its course—a course which in all probability began in Egypt with ink-sketches, like those which have recently been found in the neighbourhood of Fustāt. This would agree with the history of the development of the other arts of the book in Islam, especially binding and illumination, which are probably of Egyptian origin. At Burlington House every class of manuscript in the Mesopotamian style was represented, though none of the manuscripts showed the freedom of drawing and brilliant characterization of the famous 'Schefer' Harīrī of the Bibliothèque Nationale[2] or the other copy at Leningrad from the Ardabīl shrine.[3] The Bodleian *Harīrī* (no. 3) is a fine example of the later, more finished type and is in exceptionally good condition, its gold backgrounds having a smooth burnished quality, unlike the gold painting of later

[1] Compare, for instance, a Jacobite Lectionary of the first quarter of the thirteenth century, in Syriac, at the British Museum (Add. 7170) with such a typical manuscript in the Mesopotamian style as the Bodleian *Harīrī* (no. 3). Each has burnished gold backgrounds, and similar highly formalized conventions for trees and hills.

[2] Blochet, *Enluminures*, pls. x–xiii; *Musulman Painting*, pls. xxiv–xxxi.

[3] Kühnel, *I.M.*, pls. 7–11.

periods in Persia which depends for its effect on the play of light and shade over its minutely broken surface where the gold has entered into the irregularities in the hand-made paper. The blue and manganese make a particularly good contrast against this ground; a colour-scheme which may well be due to Byzantine or Syrian example. There is also considerable use of white. The Bodleian *Kalīla wa Dimna* (no. 4) is also an excellent manuscript, if of somewhat coarser quality. It is properly, as a fable book, more romantic in feeling than the Bestiaries such as the superb though sadly defaced *Naʿt al-Hayawān*[1] of the thirteenth century in the British Museum. These miniatures preserve the old custom of drawing no clear distinction between the miniature and the text; there is no framework, and the calligraphy runs right round the illustration. Indeed, it was probably usual for both to be carried out by the same man, as was the case with the Dioscorides of 1222, from which folios were exhibited, and also with the Schefer Harīrī.

Harīrī's *Maqāmāt* and the *Kalīla wa Dimna* were the most popular Arabic reading for centuries, and the only other illustrated books of the Mesopotamian style that have survived are scientific works where the miniatures fall into rather a different class as essential illustrations to the text. Of the cosmographers the most popular was Qazwīnī. Of his book on the Marvels of Creation three examples were shown, one a complete copy, the other two only fragments. The general iconography of these volumes with its fantastic animals and astrological signs is of great antiquity and is naturally copied with great conservatism. But it is possible to follow an evolutionary progress, particularly in costume, with a general tendency to more calligraphic drawing.

Two other examples of the Mesopotamian style, which were shown at the Exhibition, deserve especial mention. From the Arabic version of Dioscorides copied in A.D. 1222 four miniatures were exhibited (no. 14 and Plate IX A). This manuscript contains what are, in some ways, the finest surviving examples of the Mesopotamian style: the drawing is vigorous and the colours exceptionally fine, particularly in the page belonging to Dr. Sarre which is on loan to the Kaiser-Friedrich Museum. The plants and trees are rather closer to late classical herbals, such as the famous Dioscorides at Vienna which was published by de Vries, than in such a manuscript as no. 6; and this, together with the colouring, probably led Schulz to think it the direct copy of a Syrian manuscript. There is, however, no real reason for seeing in it any more particular derivation from a Syrian source than in many other examples of the Mesopotamian style.

The Edinburgh manuscript of al-Bīrūnī's history (no. 8) is included in this chapter because the style of it is still overwhelmingly Mesopotamian, as is apparent from the highly conventionalized folds of the drapery, most of the facial types, and the colouring. On the other hand, even if it were not dated 1307, it would be easy to assign it, on stylistic grounds, to the early Mongol period. There is Chinese influence in much of the tree-drawing, and the ground is represented in the same way as in the Morgan manuscript discussed in the next chapter (see p. 30). But there is another influence to be seen in it, which is especially noticeable in some illustrations of the life of Christ, such

---

[1] Or. 2784; Martin, pls. 17–20.

as the Annunciation (Plate XV A) and the Baptism (Arnold, *Survivals*, pl. 17). This influence Sir Thomas Arnold considered to be due to the artist having taken as his model a Manichaean original. But of the miniatures which he mentioned in support of this, one, the temptation of Adam and Eve by Ahriman in human form (ib., pl. 15), is admittedly Zoroastrian in origin; and it is practically certain that there were many more Mazdeans than Manichaeans in Persia by this date: while the Baptism looks as near to an Armenian original as to the fragments of Manichaean painting from Turfan. We may, then, admit in this highly eclectic manuscript, so typical of Tabrīz at the time, a number of influences, of which the Manichaean is possibly one; but the predominant strain is still the Mesopotamian.

To sum up. In spite of the fact that in the early days of Islamic book-illustration Persian culture was generally dominant, and that no very definite contribution to the art of the book appears to have been made by any other of the nations under the Caliphate,[1] yet the general characteristic of the illustrations of the Mesopotamian style is a debased Hellenism, in which they are very little distinguished from the Christian examples of the period, which represent a similar descent. It is evident that in Syria, centring round the great cities like Antioch, Hellenistic taste in ornament and decoration persisted well into the Muhammadan period and that the latent artistic genius of the Persians was long in asserting itself against the outworn conventions of Hellenistic Syria and ʿIrāq. Such monuments as Qusayr ʿAmra in the eighth century and Sāmarrā in the ninth still show the last relics of this style, whose characteristic is impressionistic naturalism even when concealed by a short-hand convention which has reduced water, folds, and trees to mere pattern. Such conventions are quite unlike the hieratic conventions of Buddhist art or the decorative conventions which appear in Persian miniatures of the Timurid period and later. They are a sign of weakness of imagination, though the actual execution may be full of vigour; while, for their understanding, it would be necessary to follow back a long sequence of use and change, in a way that is often impossible in face of the lack of evidence for the early medieval period.

[1] Of the few fragments of miniatures found in Egypt which are attributed to the tenth–eleventh centuries the more advanced are strongly oriental in type. Cf. Arnold and Grohmann, pl. 4.

CATALOGUE

1 [531 c] *MANĀFI' AL-AHJĀR* (Properties of stones and talismans), by 'Utārid b. Muhammad al-Hāsib, a mathematician of the third century of the Hijra. In Arabic. Numerous illustrations in the text, human figures with haloes, with touches of ochre in place of gold. Mesopotamia. XII century (?). The date 417/1026 probably belongs to the manuscript from which this copy was made, but the writing is of considerable antiquity. Very similar figures are reproduced by Arnold, *Schweich Lecture*, pl. I.

23·5 × 19 *cm.* ¶ Lent by J. GAZDAR, Bombay.

2 [531 D] IMĀM ABU'L-HASAN NĪSHĀPŪRĪ'S *'ILM AL-USTURLĀB,* 'Treatise on the Astrolabe', part I. Copied in 522/1128 by Ahmad al-Bayhaqī. One hundred and thirty-one diagrams. Dark-brown leather binding.

28 × 20 *cm.* ¶ Lent by A. CHESTER BEATTY, ESQ.

3 [533 B] HARĪRĪ'S *MAQĀMĀT,* in Arabic. The famous 'discourses', in highly ornate and rhetorical diction, tell of the adventures of Abu Zayd, a disreputable old man, who obtains money by craft and spends it on indulgences. Dated 738/1337. Thirty-nine miniatures. Modern leather binding. Formerly in the library of Nāsir al-Dīn Muhammad, son of Husām al-Dīn Tarantay Silahdār.

> 38 × 28 *cm.* Bequeathed to the Bodleian by Archbishop Marsh in 1713. Uri, *Cat.,* no. 353. Arnold, *P.I.,* pl. XII. ¶ Lent by BODLEIAN LIBRARY, Oxford [Marsh 458].
>
> (*a*) An illustration to the 13th Discourse. An old woman, after obtaining money for her recitation of some verses, is followed into a ruined mosque by al-Hāris, the narrator, who recognizes her as Abu Zayd. Abu Zayd is depicted lying down and reciting verses glorifying his own cunning, while al-Hāris peeps through a chink in the door (fol. 29ᵛ). PLATE II B.
>
> (*b*) An illustration to the 14th Discourse. Al-Hāris and his companions, while on a pilgrimage to Mecca, are conversing in a tent, when an old man, who is Abu Zayd, comes with his son and asks for help as his camel has broken down (fol. 30ᵛ). PLATE II A.
>
> (*c*) An illustration to the 32nd Discourse. Abu Zayd, in the character of a jurisconsult, answering questions on points of religious law in an Arab encampment (fol. 59ʳ). COLOUR PLATE I.

4 [534 C] *KALĪLA WA DIMNA,* in Arabic, copied by Muhammad b. Ahmad. Dated 755/1354. Seventy-six miniatures. XVII century Persian binding. These historic fables, mainly originating from India, were translated from Pahlawī into Arabic by 'Abd Allāh b. al-Muqaffa' in the eighth century A.D. From this version the subsequent Persian editions all descend.

> 36·5 × 26·5 *cm.* From the collection of Edward Pococke (1604–91), first Professor of Arabic at Oxford, formed in the Near East in the years 1630–6 and 1637–40. Uri, *Cat.,* no. 356; Arnold, *P.I.,* pl. LXIII *a*; Gray, pl. 2. ¶ Lent by BODLEIAN LIBRARY, Oxford [Pococke 400].
>
> (*a*) The lion-king, falsely induced by the jackals, Kalīla and Dimna, to suspect his friend the bull, attacks and kills him (fol. 63ʳ). PLATE III B.

(*b*) The animals in council (fol. 75ᵛ).   PLATE III A.

(*c*) The crows carry dry sticks to the cave in which their enemies the owls are assembled, and, lighting a fire, cause their destruction (fol. 107ʳ). The hill-convention here used occurs also in a Jacobite Lectionary of the thirteenth century (B.M. Add. 7170).   PLATE IV B.

(*d*) The tortoise, with the intention of betraying his friend the ape, carries him across the water on his back (fol. 114ʳ).   PLATE IV A.

Compare the manuscript of *Kalīla wa Dimna* in the Bibliothèque Nationale (Arabe 3467) for a close parallel. This must surely be later than about 1230, to which date it is assigned by M. Blochet.

5 [534 B] *KALĪLA WA DIMNA*, in Arabic. Many miniatures. Copy dated 791/1388. From the library of Nasr al-Dīn Muhammad.

30 × 22·5 *cm.* ❡ Lent by CORPUS CHRISTI COLLEGE, Cambridge.

6 [535 A] DIOSCORIDES' *KHAWĀSS AL-ASHJĀR*, on the Properties of Plants. An Arabic version of the *Materia medica* of Dioscorides. The notes are in Syriac. The original work, composed in the first century A.D., and consisting of short accounts of the plants and their uses, is the main source of subsequent herbals.[1] 284 fol. Six hundred and seventy-seven figures of plants and two hundred and eighty-four figures of animals. Mesopotamian school, XIII century. Bound in new red leather. Given by Shāh 'Abbās to the Mashhad shrine in 1017/1608.

47 × 30 *cm.* ❡ Lent by PERSIAN GOVERNMENT from the Mashhad shrine.

(*a*) A representation of the quince (safarjal).   PLATE V A.

(*b*) A berry-bearing plant named Milākus (?).   PLATE V B.

7 [535 C] SECOND PART OF *MUFĪD AL-KHĀSS*, an Arabic work by the celebrated physician Abu Bakr Muhammad b. Zakariyyā al-Rāzī (d. at Rayy 311/923). Dedicated to the ruler of Māzandarān. Miniatures. Three pages decorated in gold. New binding in red morocco. XII century (?). Former possessor the Egyptian Sultan, Malik Sālih Ismā'īl ibn Nāsir al-Dīn Abu'l-Ma'ālī Muhammad ibn al-Malik al-Mansūr Qalāwūn (743–6/1342–5). Given by Nādir Shāh to the Mashhad shrine in 1145/1732.

24 × 16 *cm.* Wiet, *Bulletin de l'Institut d'Égypte*, t. XIII, p. 92. ❡ Lent by PERSIAN GOVERNMENT from the Mashhad shrine.

8 [532 B] AL-BĪRŪNĪ'S *AL-ĀSĀR AL-BĀQIYA*, an Arabic work on the chronology and history of ancient nations, copied by Ibn al-Qutbī. Dated 707/1307. 212 fol., twenty-four illustrations. Lacquer binding.

31 × 19 *cm. Catalogue of the Arabic and Persian Manuscripts in Edinburgh University Library*, no. 161. Arnold, *Survivals*, figs. 15–17; Arnold, *P.I.*, pl. XVIII; Arnold and Grohmann, pls. 36–9. ❡ Lent by EDINBURGH UNIVERSITY LIBRARY.

---

[1] *Vide* Charles Singer, *From Magic to Science* (London, Benn, 1928, p. 182): 'As the general character of the Greek mind deteriorated, such science as survived passed into the hands of the various Oriental peoples who went to make up the Byzantine Empire. Of these the Nestorian Christians entered most freely into medical studies and turned into Syriac the more popular of the Greek medical works. . . . First Gondisapur and then Baghdad became the centre of their activities. . . . It was thus that Dioscorides passed into Arabic and later into Persian. The figures of the plants of the Greek Dioscorides tradition, taken mostly from the Mediterranean littoral, were, however, useless to the Oriental reader. New figures were prepared and items were added.'

(*a*) The Angel Gabriel announcing to the Virgin Mary the coming of the Messiah. The mention occurs in al-Bīrūnī's account of the festivals, &c., of the Syrian Church. The draperies of the angel are very peculiar and may be the result of a misunderstanding of a Jacobite or Armenian Christian source from which the miniature was derived. PLATE XV A.

Cf. the extremely close copy in the Bibliothèque Nationale (Arabe 1489) [Blochet, *Enluminures*, pls. XIV, xv], which M. Blochet attributes on the ground of calligraphy and paper to Cairo and the XVIIth century.

9 [535 B] QAZWĪNĪ'S *ʿAJĀʾIB AL-MAKHLŪQĀT*, on the Marvels of Creation. In Arabic. Four hundred and fifty-one pages in *naskh* with miniatures of animals, plants, mythological beings and astronomical figures. Oriental leather binding. Incomplete and undated. XIV century.

33 × 23 *cm. Meisterwerke*, pls. 11 and 12; Kühnel, *I.M.*, pls. 33 and 34; Schulz, pls. B, C, and 13; Arnold, *P.I.*, pl. XVI. Exh. Orientalische Buchkunst, Berlin, 1910, no. 136; Munich, 1910, no. 650. ¶ Lent by FRAU MARIA SARRE-HUMANN, Berlin.

(*a*) The *Sannāja*. An animal found in Tibet, so huge that it needs a house three miles long. Every wild beast that looks on it dies; while if it looks on other beasts itself dies. Other animals, knowing this, come into its presence with closed eyes, so that it may see them and perish. PLATE VI A.

(*b*) The wild deer, which sprouts horns and sheds them every year. It is said to be fond of music and to eat vipers. PLATE VI B.

10 FOUR MINIATURES from QAZWĪNĪ'S *ʿAJĀʾIB AL-MAKHLŪQĀT*. Late XIV century.

(*a*) [465, *a*] Mercury. A figure in a blue dress writing on a scroll. Red background. 10·5 × 12 *cm.*
(*b*) [465, *b*] Mars. A man with a sword and severed head. 15 × 13 *cm.*
(*c*) [453] Emblems of the Four Evangelists. 13·5 × 12·5 *cm.* ¶ (*a*), (*b*), and (*c*) Lent by M. CLAUDE ANET, Paris.
(*d*) [452] An Angel, probably Isrāfīl. 15·5 × 13·5 *cm.* ¶ Lent by M. A. HENRAUX, Paris.
Reproduced: Marteau-Vever, nos. 48–51; C. Anet, *Burl. Mag.*, vol. XXII, p. 15, pl. III G.

11 [536 A] QAZWĪNĪ'S *ʿAJĀʾIB AL-MAKHLŪQĀT*; 465 miniatures. Probably Mesopotamian. Early XV century. The miniatures are somewhat archaistic, but can be dated approximately by the costumes.

37 × 27 *cm.* Lent by MUSÉE ASIATIQUE DE L'ACADÉMIE DES SCIENCES, Leningrad.

(*a*) The planet Jupiter (Mushtarī), with two angels. PLATE VII A.
(*b*) Isrāfīl, the angel who will sound the last trump at the Resurrection. PLATE VII B.

12 [421] MINIATURE from a manuscript on *Automata* by al-Jazarī, dated 755/1354, written in Egypt. Automaton pouring from a bottle into a cup.

24·5 × 12 *cm.* For dating and provenance see F. M. Riefstahl in *Art Bulletin*, vol. XI, no. 2. Reproduced: Martin, II, pl. 3. ¶ Lent by M. H. VEVER, Paris.

13 [534 A] *KITĀB AL-BULHĀN*, &c. An astrological work, in Arabic, containing the nativity days of Abu Maʿshar al-Balkhī, the rules of times and seasons, conjunctions of planets, &c. XIV century. Fols. 1–80 (al-Bulhān) written for Husayn of Irbīl (near Mosul) before 812/1409, in which year he sold it.

> (*a*) The sign of *al-Sunbula*, or the Ear of Corn (=Virgo) (fol. 11ᵛ). Below are small figures representing Mercury, Venus (?), and the Sun.   PLATE VIII A.
> (*b*) The astrological sign of the House of the Idol (fol. 37ᵛ).   PLATE VIII B.
> 25 × 18 *cm.* Nicholls, *Cat.*, no. 283, pp. 270 et seq.; Arnold, *P.I.*, pls. XV and LI. Exh. Oriental Congress, Oxford, 1928. ¶ Lent by BODLEIAN LIBRARY, Oxford [Bodl. Or. 133].

14 FOUR FOLIOS, FROM A DIOSCORIDES, copied and illustrated in 619/1222 by 'Abd Allāh ibn al-Fazl. There are in all some thirty miniatures, divided among many collections.

> (*a*) [25] Three figures (one with eyes bound).
> (*b*) [415] Two figures under a tree.
> (*a*) and (*b*) 32 × 21 *cm.* ¶ Lent by M. H. VEVER, Paris.
> (*c*) [416] Two seated figures with a mixing-bowl between them. Inscribed 'makers of lead'.
> 32 × 24·5 *cm.* Stchoukine, *Louvre Cat.* no. 1. ¶ Lent by M. RAYMOND KOECHLIN, Paris.
>   PLATE IX A.
> (*d*) [417] Birds and flowers. 39·5 × 35 *cm.* ¶ Lent by PAUL J. SACHS, ESQ., through FOGG ART MUSEUM, Harvard University.
> For other reproductions, see *Meisterwerke*, Bd. I, Taf. 4, 5; Martin, II, pls. 5–7; Kühnel, *I.M.*, pls. 4–6; Schulz, pl. 5; Marteau-Vever, nos. 1, 38.

15 [177, 181, 190, 191, 454] FIFTEEN MINIATURES from a fragmentary and undated manuscript of Qazwīnī's *Wonders of Creation*. Early XV century. The miniatures are copied from originals of earlier Mesopotamian style.

> 30 × 23 *cm.* ¶ Lent by A. CHESTER BEATTY, ESQ.

PLATE II-A. 3 (b). Mecca pilgrims in a tent. 1337

Plate I is reproduced in color, following p. 16.

وکگرزنگ بذین بذین علیهصتدو نبتکر
اصعلاد فوناپوغظاواتختربتسعس
واستعینگاعنلدیک ناازختمی

PLATE II-B. 3 (a). Abu Zayd in a mosque, disguised as an old woman. 1337

PLATE III·A·4 (*b*). The Animals in Council. 1354

PLATE III-B. 4 (a). The Lion-king attacks the Bull. 1354

PLATE IV. A. 4 (d). The Tortoise swimming with the Ape on his back. 1354

PLATE IV-B. 4 (c). The Crows burn out the Owls. 1354

PLATE V-A. 6 (*a*). The Quince. XIII *century*

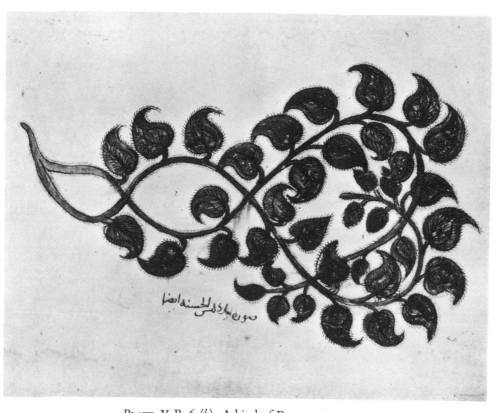

PLATE V-B. 6 (*b*). A kind of Berry. XIII *century*

عوت ذلك فى تلك البلاد فمعترض فنها على الضناعة غامضة اعينها ليقع نظر الصباحة علبها فيموت

فيقى طعمة للحيوانات ذما أناطو بلا ضنت حيوان بقال له ناالفا ربية سوتمار وقوحوان كبن

PLATE VI-A. 9 (*a*). The Sannāja, an animal of Tibet. XIV *century*

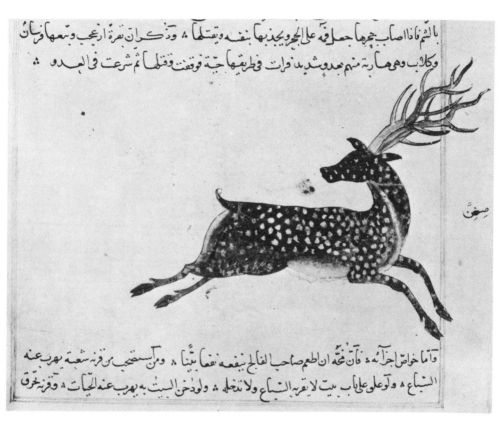

بالسهم فاذا اصاب بجمها جملها على الحجر ويجذبها بنفه ويقتلهآ ۵ وذ كران نمرة ارنحب وبنعها فرنان
وكلاب وهوهارية منهم بعدو يشد يد نرات فى طريقها حتة فوقفت وقتلها ثم شرعت فى الهدو ۵

وأما خاصل اجز آؤه ۵ فأن لمحه ان اطعم صاحب الفالج بنفعه نفعا بينا ۵ ومن اسنجي من قرنه شعبة يهرب عنه
السباع ۵ وآو على عاباب بيت لا يقربه السباع ولا تدخله ۵ ولو دخن البيت به يهرب عنده الحيات ۵ وقرنه بحرق

PLATE VI-B. 9 (b). The Wild Deer. XIV *century*

PLATE VII- A. 11 (*a*). The planet Jupiter. *Early* XV *century*

والمولّدات من المعادن والنبات والحيوان   وهذا الملك اعظم من الأملاك واقوى منها واشرف واعلى من الخلائق
الجمانية وهو الذى يعتمد على تمكين الأملاك كما يقدر على غيركم بتقدير العزيز العليم

ومنهم اسرافيل
صلوات الله عليه
وهو مبلّغ الاوامر ونافخ الارواح فى الاجساد   قال صلى الله عليه وسلم كيف انعم وصاحب القرن قد التقم القرن
واصغى الاذن حتى يؤمر فينفخ فيه   قال مقال القرن الصور واسرافيل واضعه حتى يؤمر فينفخ فيه والقرن

PLATE VII-B. 11 (*b*). The Angel Isrāfil. *Early* xv *century*

PLATE VIII-A. 13 (*a*). The Sign of Virgo. XIV *century*

PLATE VIII-B. 13 (b). The Sign of the House of the Idol. XIV *century*

PLATE IX- A. 14 (c). Leadmakers. 1222

PLATE IX-B. 18 (*a*). Two Asses. *Late* XIII *century*

II

THE EARLY PERSIAN STYLE AND FOURTEENTH-CENTURY CHANGES

CERTAINLY one of the most important results of assembling together the Persian miniatures and manuscripts at Burlington House was to make it possible to form a more definite idea of Islamic painting in the thirteenth and fourteenth centuries and to trace the evolution of a distinctively Persian style from among the various influences then at work. Beside pages from the well-known Dioscorides of 1222 (no. 14) and the *Kalīla wa Dimna* of 1236, and certain later examples of typical Mesopotamian work, were shown such paintings as those from Mr. Chester Beatty's small *Shāh-nāma* (no. 19) and the Royal Asiatic Society *Jāmi' al-Tawārīkh*, at first sight so hard to reconcile. As was to be expected of such a period of transition as the fourteenth century, the style of illustration of the manuscripts in different degrees revealed connexions with the Mesopotamian school of the previous century, as exemplified in the Harīrī of 1180 in the Bibliothèque Nationale, and also traces of the new influences which began to be felt when the Mongol invasions, otherwise so disastrous to Muslim culture, opened up communications across the continent of Asia.

Terrific as were the destructions wrought by the Mongols and especially by Chingīz Khān, and permanent as was the resulting impoverishment of Persia, it is evident that they caused no break in culture, partly because they brought nothing to take its place. Here is a contemporary account of them by Friar John de Plano Carpini, writing in 1246 (Hakluyt's version, Chapter IV):

'The Mongals or Tartars, in outward shape, are unlike to all other people. For they are broader betweene the eyes, and the balles of their cheekes, than men of other nations bee. They have flat and small noses, little eyes, and eye liddes standing streight upright, they are shaven on the crownes like priests. They wear their haire somewhat longer about their eares, than upon their foreheads: but behind they let it growe long like womans haire, whereof they braide two lockes behind binding eche of them behind either eare. They have short feet also. . . . Their habitations bee rounde and cunningly made with wickers and staves in manner of a tent. . . . Some of these Tabernacles may quickly be taken asunder, and set together againe, and are carried upon beastes backes. Other some cannot be taken insunder, but are stowed upon carts. . . . They are very rich in cattel, and in camels, oxen, sheep and goats. And I think they have more horses and mares than all the world besides. . . . Their Emperors, Dukes, and other of their nobles doe abound with silk, gold, silver and precious stones.'

From this account and others we get the picture of a people still nomad, moving with all its possessions from a summer to a winter grazing ground.

But a more important reason for the continuity of civilization in Persia and the wonderful revival, after the destruction by Chingīz Khan in 1219–20 and Hūlāgū in his campaign culminating in the capture of Baghdad in 1258, is to be found in the enlightened patronage, no doubt mainly a matter of policy, of the later Il-khāns, which made the period from 1267 to 1335 one of the most fruitful in the history of Persian literature. In China also the Mongol conquerors welcomed at their court all the artists and literati who had worked under the Sung dynasty which they overthrew. So that it must be an exaggeration to say that Islamic culture was nearly destroyed: its material apparatus, cities, palaces, libraries did indeed suffer severely, but such disasters had been unhappily common in earlier centuries, under Buwayhids, Samanids, and Ghaznawids. As far as possible the Mongol conquerors spared the lives of scholars and craftsmen, and they brought a strong central government, which is the first requisite of civilization. Probably the chaos that succeeded the break-up of the Mongol power in Persia in 1335 was actually more disastrous than the invasions had been. It was only the action of another great conqueror, Tīmūr, that then stopped this process of decay.

As after the Arab invasions of the seventh century and the Seljuk invasions of the eleventh, the central government was mainly carried on by Persians, taken over perforce by conquerors who themselves lacked all skill for such work. In the Il-khānī period the most prominent of those Persians were the members of the Juwaynī family. They are of particular importance to us because they included the great historian of the *Tārīkh i Jahān-Gushā* and were all generous patrons of learning and literature.[1] The barbarous character of the Mongol rulers, even of Arghūn and Ghāzān, is shown by the tragic fate of this family, which was exterminated between 1283 and 1288 as the result of an intrigue. But their power as ministers and governors shows how it was possible for Persian culture to continue and even advance during this period.

It was particularly unfortunate that it proved impossible to show the noble Bestiary, a translation of *Manāfi' al-Hayawān*[2] into Persian, belonging to Mr. Pierpont Morgan, as this is the earliest known manuscript produced for the Mongol conquerors. As stated in the preface, it was presented to Ghāzān Khān (1295–1304), who, though not the first Il-khān to profess Islam, restored it to a prominent position in the State. The advance seen in this book over the best work of the Mesopotamian school in technique is not great; but no great change was to be expected, for it was the work of artists taken over by the Mongol conquerors. But there is a new interest in the drawing: compared with the illustrations in the British Museum thirteenth-century *Na't al-Hayawān* (Or. 2784),[3] it is more naturalistic, though these too are the last product of worn-out Hellenistic naturalism,[4] and an essential difference is made by the attempt to indicate movement and spatial relations. The less masterly copy of the same book represented by several pages (no. 18) at the Exhibition perhaps shows even more clearly the infusion of new elements. In Plate XIX B the old conventions for vegetation are still used; but, compared with no. 16 (Pl. XI), there is a greater freedom and some success in representing perspective. In other pages from this manuscript reproduced by Schulz (Bd. I, Taf. L)

[1] See E. G. Browne, *Literary History of Persia*, vol. III, pp. 20–31.
[2] Martin, pls. 21–6; Claude Anet, *Burl. Mag.*, vol. XXIII, pp. 224–31, 261.
[3] Martin, pls. 17–20.

[4] Compare such animals as are represented in the mosaic pavement of the church of SS. Cosmas and Damian at Jerash (A.D. 533) (Crowfoot, *Churches at Jerash*, 1931, pl. x).

more definite naturalism is visible, which may be taken as evidence of Chinese influence. In these pages, too, the Chinese *tai* cloud convention occurs and in the Morgan manuscript the first traces of Chinese landscape painting are visible. The ibex and goats (*Burl. Mag.*, vol. XXIII, p. 224, pl. b; Martin, pls. 24, 25) live in a world of rocks certainly derived from China, and even more direct copying is seen in the horses (Martin, ib.). Very striking and curious are the conventions for rock drawing in these miniatures, the decapitated cones and the streaky stratification are closely paralleled in the paintings from Tun-Huang. They occur also in the early manuscripts of the *Shāh-nāma*, but are ultimately of Western origin.[1]

Of the manuscripts of the *Shāh-nāma*, from which miniatures were shown, Mr. Chester Beatty's (no. 19) appears to be the oldest. It still preserves certain early features such as the filling of spaces with stiffly built-up vegetation, and the throne and architectural forms common to the Mesopotamian school. For general colouring and style perhaps the closest parallel is with the frontispiece of the well-known Galen manuscript at Vienna (Staatsbibliothek, A.F. 10; Arnold and Grohmann, pl. 13; Martin, pl. 13). So far as can be judged in its present poor condition, the large frontispiece from a manuscript, included in the Album from the Serai Library exhibited at the Munich Exhibition (*Meisterwerke*, Taf. 8), was closely similar. Both these miniatures are painted on red backgrounds. The armour, which M. Blochet says was borrowed by the Mongols from China,[2] is exactly paralleled in M. Kevorkian's *Tabarī*.[3] This has been, probably correctly, assigned to the extreme end of the thirteenth century. Except for the heavy ear-pieces, it also occurs in the Royal Asiatic Society *Jāmiʿ al-Tawārīkh* and the Istanbul and Demotte *Shāh-nāmas*, all of the first half of the fourteenth century.[4] Apart from this feature which seems to connect them with Central Asia, a primitive *horreur de vide* and the simplicity of the compositions give this group, containing the Vienna Galen, the Kevorkian *Tabarī*, and the Beatty *Shāh-nāma*, the appearance of priority to the dated fourteenth-century manuscripts. Consequently one would be inclined to place them about the year 1300. Probably about the same date, or a little earlier, is the Persian novel in the Bodleian Library (no. 17), which preserves a number of very interesting Iranian features and is far less under Chinese influence, which is also the case with the two closely connected rather later copies of the *Shāh-nāma* of the early fourteenth century exhibited for the first time at Burlington House (nos. 22 and 23). Indeed, so striking was their greater Iranianism that at first it appeared as though it would be necessary to place the Chester Beatty *Shāh-nāma* (no. 19) later than the dated Istanbul manuscript of 1330 (no. 23). The small format of his manuscript also seemed to connect it with the closely written and extremely regular manuscripts of the

---

[1] Creswell, *Early Muslim Architecture*, vol. I, p. 249.
[2] *Rupam*, no. 41, Jan. 1930, p. 6. It is, however, to be noted that a sort of chain-armour was used by the Sasanians; cf. the figure of Khusraw II at Tāq i Būstān (Sarre und Herzfeld, *Iranische Felsreliefs*, Taf. XXXVII, S. 203). Dr. Sarre also quotes a passage from Am-

mianus Marcellinus (XXV. 1, 12) in support of its use among the Persians so early as the fourth century A.D.
[3] Schulz, Bd. I, Taf. H–K; Marteau-Vever, pls. XLVII, XLVIII.
[4] Nos. 25, 23, 29.

end of the fourteenth century, such as the Cairo *Shāh-nāma* (no. 32) and the British Museum *Khwājū Kirmānī* of 1396. But a close study of the style of the drawing and colouring, in which there is an unusual amount of blue, makes this later dating even more unacceptable. Possibly some of the divergence between these early *Shāh-nāmas* is more superficial than real. The strongly marked black beards of the Istanbul group contrast with the scanty fringes of the more Mongol figures in Mr. Beatty's book, and suggest that it was rather intended for one of the conquering princes, who would a little later prefer the more thoroughgoing Chinese style of the Demotte book. The Istanbul *Shāh-nāma* (no. 23), on the other hand, is of rougher workmanship, and is more conservative in its treatment of the national epic. The red background, which is found here, probably has a long history reaching back to Sasanian wall-paintings, and associated with it is a rather broad treatment of clouds, drapery and vegetation to be expected of frescoes. The most thoroughgoing use of this style, and also probably its earliest example at Burlington House, was in the long novel mentioned above, called *Kitāb i Samak ʿAyyār*, two volumes of which were lent by the Bodleian Library (no. 17). This may be the original copy of the work, and therefore the artist who illustrated it would be likely to have done so out of his head; but most of the scenes represented in it are so close to those in the *Shāh-nāma* that too much importance should not be attached to it as a faithful mirror of contemporary ideas. In any case, these two manuscripts, the Istanbul *Shāh-nāma* of 1330 and the Bodleian novel, may be considered together.

The coloured background is certainly the most striking feature of these manuscripts; for by that the drawing of the cloud-forms and vegetation is conditioned. On the red background the clouds are in white swirls, which in a battle-scene will fill every vacant space, doing duty for dust as well as rain-clouds. But some of the backgrounds are painted in ochre, which was clearly used as a substitute for gold, and then the clouds may be drawn in red. Manganese, green, and a slate-blue are the only other colours generally used in addition to those mentioned; and with this simple colour-scheme only broad effects are possible, while the hieratic stiffness of the grouping of the figures seems to demand a highly conventionalized style for flowers and trees. The same convention as in the Chester Beatty *Shāh-nāma* is sometimes employed (as in Pl. XII A); but more often more substantial trees are represented, whose peculiar feature is a flower something like a Tudor rose with leaves arranged round it, rather like sepals round a flower. These elements may either be distributed along a sinuous bough or closely collected in a bunch at the top of the tree, broadly following the form of a fruit or a shade tree. The leaves are gold, ochre, or olive, and the flowers red. Very often some gold is sparingly used to lighten a passage mainly carried out with ochre. Sometimes fruit is indicated by round gold berries. The origin of this sort of tree convention is unknown, but it is probably Western, which is certainly the case with that in the Dioscorides of 1222, though there it is finer and more elaborate;[1] and it seems very likely that it

[1] A similar tree-form, based on the palm in shape but with a good deal of colour, is found on a Syrian enamelled glass bottle of the thirteenth century in the British Museum. It must originate in Syria.

derives ultimately from mosaics.[1] Such a convention of a dark ground, with lighter leaves and fruit indicated upon it, is found in Syria both in the Christian and Umayyad periods.

There are rather different flower-forms in the *Kalīla wa Dimna* of 1236 (cf. Pl. XI A), where, in addition to these conventions, there are unmistakable lotus flowers which must have been of Central Asian origin, whether they were introduced into Persia by the Seljuks and Uighurs or only by the Mongols. But, otherwise, this manuscript is certainly to be considered as of the same type. Not only has it also red or ochre backgrounds, but the rare figure scenes in it (cf. Marteau-Vever, I, Pl. III) are closely similar. In all these manuscripts with red backgrounds the Chinese elements introduced by the Mongols are extremely rare and it is interesting to note that, while they share with the Morgan *Manāfiʿ al-Hayawān* the rock conventions, the foliage in that manuscript is totally different and distinctly naturalistic.

Schulz in speaking of the frontispiece to the Vienna Galen had called the general arrangement of the court Seljuk, but had pointed out the occurrence of Mongol hats and of dress-patterns derived from Turkestan. After examining and dating as far as possible some of the more important manuscripts produced during the formative period of the thirteenth and early fourteenth century, it is possible to turn to the several influences which were moulding the new style. It has long been recognized by most writers on the subject that the most important of these influences was from China. M. Blochet has indeed objected that the Mongols when they conquered Persia were possessed of no civilization of their own, that the period when the whole width of Asia was united under their rule was a short one, and that in any case there is no trace, in the manuscripts of the Mongol period, of Chinese influence except in details. He would reduce it to a matter of costume and Mongol facial types. But, leaving aside the literary evidence for the close connexions between the opposite ends of the Mongol Empire, it is only necessary to study the material provided by the manuscripts of the period to see the influence of China in much more than detail.

Sir Thomas Arnold left behind him at his death unpublished material, some of which was communicated to the Oriental Congress in London in January 1931, which emphasized the considerable extent of the knowledge of China in Mesopotamia long before the thirteenth century. The silk trade between Rome and China, of course, passed by this route, and it is well known that the Persians controlled this trade for centuries, so that there was a free interchange of textile designs across Asia between Parthian and Sasanian Persia and China. Though this trade greatly diminished after the introduction of the silkworm into the Byzantine Empire in 552,[2] and the break-up of the T'ang Empire in the tenth century, the reputation of Chinese work, not only silk, but also paintings, was very high, as numerous casual references in the *Shāh-nāma* show.

---

[1] At an earlier period, in 533, Khusraw Anūshīrwān is said to have carried off mosaics from Antioch and re-erected them in Mesopotamia (cf. Blochet, *Peintures*, p. 94), where they apparently survived till the time of Masʿūdī (d. 956).

[2] Cf. G. F. Hudson, *Europe and China*, p. 122 *et passim*.

This reputation must have rested largely on hearsay, but the Mongol conquests made it much easier for the Persians to satisfy their curiosity in such matters. The international connexions of the Mongols are well exemplified by the ease with which Rashīd al-Dīn at Tabrīz could obtain the assistance of Franks, Armenians, and Chinese in the compilation of his Universal History in the first years of the fourteenth century. Marco Polo,[1] who visited Tabrīz about 1295, found it a flourishing and wealthy place with an extremely mixed population, resorting there for trade, especially in silks and precious stones. The consequent opportunities which the painters of Persia had of studying Chinese paintings is increasingly reflected in their work up to 1335, when the Mongol Empire began to break up. This is probably about the date of the big-paged Demotte Shāh-nāma, in which Chinese influence is marked. Twenty-two miniatures from this manuscript, now dispersed, were collected together and shown at Burlington House (no. 29).

After that date, till the time of Tīmūr, manuscripts are scarce owing to the disturbed state of the country, but two fragmentary examples at Constantinople evidently belong to about the mid-fourteenth century. With this evidence it is possible to say that during the fourteenth century Persian painting was strongly influenced by the contemporary school of Chinese painting, that of the Yüan dynasty (1280–1368). Equally in China the Mongols brought no art of their own, but, as Mr. Waley has put it, 'the court painters and poets felt that nothing less than the large allure of the T'ang dynasty was suitable to the triumphant times in which they lived'. Such a style is reflected in the vigorous and spacious treatment of the illustrations to the Demotte Shāh-nāma, which suit its epic character better than the style of any other period of Persian painting. On the other hand, the ink style which was the glory of the Sung period still persisted, and the influence of this too is to be seen in the Royal Asiatic Society and Edinburgh University Jāmiʿ al-Tawārīkh (nos. 25, 26). Its miniatures are very restricted in colouring and show linear work in strong contrast with the style of a hundred years later in Persia. For it attempts the use of line in the Chinese rather than the Persian manner; but it is not very consistent. Its crucial importance as a work produced under the eye of the author in his studio at Rashīdiyya, the suburb of Tabrīz, the capital of the Il-khāns, has been recognized. But it has been difficult to follow this style in its later developments, and, consequently, it has been regarded as an unusual manuscript, perhaps produced under special conditions. It is in fact the most important example of the Tabrīz school in the early fourteenth century, a position which has been obscured by the rival claim of the Bibliothèque Nationale[2] copy of the same work, in Persian, which is admittedly in a different style. This claim will soon be discussed, but it can be pointed out at once that the Royal Asiatic Society and Edinburgh manuscript is paralleled by the Demotte Shāh-nāma (no. 29), with which it is connected by its format; while there is in the Serai Library at Istanbul another copy of the Jāmiʿ al-Tawārīkh of the same size and style of production.[3] In

[1] Ed. Yule, I, pp. 74 et seq.   [2] Sup. pers. 1113.   [3] Nos. 1863, 2475, 2 volumes, 36×26 cm.

it are a few miniatures practically identical with those in the incomplete copy exhibited at Burlington House (nos. 25, 26). At the time of the fall of Rashīd al-Dīn this was all that had been completed, and in this condition the manuscript must have remained for about a hundred years, until Shāh Rukh determined to save this important historical work from oblivion.[1]

As no complete copy was then available and the work was in danger of disappearance, he collected all the manuscripts he could find in order to establish the text. Among them must have been the Serai copy, and probably also the copy exhibited at Philadelphia in 1926, which is said to have been dated 1318, and from which a number of detached miniatures were shown at Burlington House (no. 28). To these manuscripts he must have added more miniatures by his artists, who copied the compositions of the earlier period, but used the Timurid palette of the early fifteenth century. In colouring and other details the famous copy in the Bibliothèque Nationale[2] also shows evidence of a Timurid date, but is less closely modelled on the original compositions. It is undated, comes from the Ardabīl Shrine,[3] and contains the first part of the work, the *History of the Mongols*, with 106 miniatures, many damaged. M. Blochet has attacked this supposition of a Timurid date at length;[4] but he was unaware of the existence of the copy at Istanbul, in which there is clearly work of two different periods (and still a few pages left blank for miniatures). In spite of his assertion to the contrary, the colouring and technique is infinitely nearer to such manuscripts as the Bibliothèque Nationale and Claude Anet *Juwaynī* of 1438, from which three detached pages were shown at the Exhibition (no. 55), than to the early fourteenth-century style. They are of rougher workmanship than the finest miniatures produced for Shāh Rukh or Baysunqur, but in costume, facial types, drawing of horses, and of landscape agree with them very well.[5] The position of the dispersed manuscript of the *Jāmiʿ al-Tawārīkh*, from which a score of pages were shown at the Exhibition (no. 28), many by Messrs. Parish-Watson, is not so clear. When this was first exhibited at the International Exhibition of Persian Art at the Pennsylvania Museum in 1926, it had a colophon giving the date 1318. From the style of the page and the calligraphy this seems to be quite justified, but in their present state the miniatures cannot date from that time. There is evidence of much work on them in the early Timurid period and considerable additions at a much later date.[6] But several, including the page reproduced (Pl. XXIV B), seem to preserve work contemporary with the text. This fine composition with the hound driving off wolves is repeated in the Istanbul copy, but not in the London and Edinburgh manuscript. Even here it is not impossible that the drawing is a Timurid copy of a fourteenth-century original, for the spongy rock-convention does not seem to occur before the end of the century.

[1] Barthold, *Turkestan*, pp. 47–8.
[2] Sup. pers. 1113; Blochet, *Enluminures*, pls. xxiii–xxviii; *Peintures*, pls. xiii–xx; *Musulman Painting*, lix–lxv; Martin, pls. 42–4.
[3] It is perhaps the manuscript dated 1407, formerly in the Public Library of St. Petersburg. Barthold, *Turkestan*, p. 48.

[4] *Peintures*, pp. 263–70.
[5] The inscription in honour of Ghāzān Khān (d. 1304) which occurs on one of the miniatures of this manuscript (*Peintures*, pl. xx) directly illustrates the text and has no bearing on the date of the painting.
[6] Dr. Kühnel is also of opinion that there is later work in these miniatures.

This leaves the position of the copy exhibited from the collections of the Royal Asiatic Society and Edinburgh University unassailable. Its large scale is evidently typical of the workshop established near Tabrīz by its author, the trusted minister of the Il-khāns, at his suburb of Rashīdiyya. When he fell in 1318 and this city was destroyed in 1336 and its library dispersed, his far-seeing plans for preserving his works from destruction by an endowment enabling copies in Persian and Arabic to be sent each year to the principal cities of the country were brought to nothing. But the scribes and illuminators must have returned to the capital and carried on there the tradition of book-production. A regular descent from master to pupil is provided by the notes of Dūst Muhammad, which are translated in Appendix I. From this school must have come the Demotte *Shāh-nāma*, and another copy of the epic, now preserved only in mutilated fragments in the Library of the Serai at Istanbul.[1] At a rather later date this great page persists in the *Kalīla wa Dimna*, from which miniatures are inserted in the *Muraqqaʻ* of Shāh Tahmāsp in the Istanbul University Library.[2] (The complete page of this measures about 28×20 *cm.* within the margins.) But with the turn of the century the fashion completely changed, and the typical royal volume of the Timurid period is comparatively small.[3] The great epic of the *Shāh-nāma* might seem to demand a big page, but this large style does not seem particularly suited to the comparatively short *Fables*.

At the Exhibition the principal examples of this big style were the two copies of the *Jāmiʻ al-Tawārīkh* already mentioned, the Demotte *Shāh-nāma*, and the India Office manuscript of the *Dīwāns* copied by ʻAbd al-Muʼmin al-ʻAlawī al-Kāshī, dated 1313–15 (no. 27). In the *Jāmiʻ al-Tawārīkh*, in spite of the varied iconography to be expected in a book treating of the history of the world, the unity of the execution makes it evident that it was the work of a well-controlled body of artists in Rashīd al-Dīn's workshop. The peculiar features of this school, heavy linear drawing, vigorous rather than sensitive, the extensive use of vermilion and of silver for shading, in a 'hatched' convention deriving from the work of the Tʻang artists of China, persist throughout it and are also found in the India Office manuscript. The use of silver is probably to be attributed to the example of Christian manuscripts. For instance, in an early thirteenth-century Jacobite Lectionary (B.M. no. 7170) much silver is introduced into the miniatures. In this manuscript of the *Jāmiʻ al-Tawārīkh* (nos. 25–6), and naturally above all in the parts dealing with Chinese history, the highest degree of Chinese influence was reached. But it is quite evident that the drawings are not either by a Chinese hand or direct copies of Chinese originals. M. Blochet is perfectly justified in saying that no one conversant with the subject could ever for a moment mistake any Persian miniature for Chinese work. But this does not dispose of Chinese influence or reduce it finally to a question of detail. The fact remains that in the fourteenth century the formative influence is

---

[1] In *Muraqqaʻ* 1720; the full size of the page was 38·5 ×27 *cm.* One miniature from this album is reproduced by Migeon, *Manuel* (1907), II, fig. 35. In the 2nd edition it is for some reason described as *Turkish* (fig. 72)! The rug-pattern occurs also in the Istanbul University *Kalīla wa Dimna*.

[2] Sakisian, pls. III–X (as XII century).

[3] Long historical works such as the *Jāmiʻ al-Tawārīkh* naturally still appear in big volumes.

Chinese, and in these most extreme instances it is difficult to detect in what way the older Persian style persists. However, while the more ambitious experiments with line and composition unmistakably show Chinese influence, the grouping and movement remain Persian. In the court scenes there is a formal balance foreign to Chinese paintings, in the battle-scenes a vigour of action which gives a Persian equivalent for some of the best work of the Yüan school. If colour is more subdued and line more emphasized than at other periods of Persian miniature painting, it is not employed calligraphically, but dramatically with the same happy seizure of character as in the Mesopotamian Harīrīs and fable books. And though the conventions for mountains, clouds, and water are borrowed from China, they are used in a way quite un-Chinese, to fill a gap or break up a scene, or as a means of indicating distance. This is not a landscape art, though there are unmistakable signs of interest in landscape. It is indeed remarkable how fine an effect the artists of this book have obtained while using these borrowed natural forms merely as conventions. The miniatures, running in bands across the big page of the manuscript, and admirably suited to the calligraphy of the writer, are the finest illustrations that ever appeared in Persia, always seizing the dramatic interest of the incident described.

Similar Chinese influence is also present in the Demotte *Shāh-nāma* (no. 29), but here it is far better assimilated, the artist understands what he is doing, and the conventional trees and hills are more freely treated and have become once more alive. At the same time the influences to be traced in it are of more varied origin. The sort of patterns that occur in the architectural details is close to those on the tomb of Uljāytū, built in 1318, which would confirm a dating between 1320 and 1330 for the manuscript. They are of the rather complicated geometrical type that is associated with the Seljuks, but is found among other Islamic peoples. It is noticeable that it also contains the variant on the palmette which Dr. Sarre[1] took to indicate a Hellenic admixture acquired by the Seljuks after their settlement at Qonya. If it is found a hundred years later in Persia, it may well on the contrary have been brought with them from their sojourn near the Oxus frontier, and introduced, as were the tile mosaics at Qonya[1] signed by refugee Persian workmen fleeing from cities like Tūs before the Mongol invaders of the thirteenth century. The Seljuq emperor 'Alā al-Dīn Kay Qubād I (1219–36) welcomed such fugitive craftsmen and was a noted bibliophile.[2]

The most obviously Chinese of the pages from the Demotte book exhibited was that depicting the funeral of Isfandiyār (Pl. XXVI A). Apart from the fine linear drawing, the well-known Chinese design of the three swans in flight betrays its origin immediately. But the mourners with unbound hair crowd the composition, and what space remains is filled with conventional flowers. The brocade covering the bier has a design of deer among running foliage which looks like a Persian adaptation of a Chinese design. Perhaps the most successful are the battle-scenes where the large page is used to the full.

---

[1] Sarre, *Reise in Kleinasien*, pp. 54 and 60.
[2] Gustave Mendel, 'Les Monuments Seldjoukides', *Revue de l'Art*, XXIII, pp. 9–24, 1908.

Even here many of the miniatures show an affinity with the other fourteenth-century manuscripts of the *Shāh-nāma* which are probably later in date of actual production but preserve an older and a more Western style of miniature painting.

The *Shāh-nāma* lent by the Serai Museum (no. 23) and dated 1330 was previously unknown, and its form was only represented by an unillustrated manuscript of about the same date in the British Museum, and a much rougher copy of which Mr. Chester Beatty has a part and of which other separate pages are in different private collections or on the market (no. 24).[1] But, in addition, at the Exhibition was shown another *Shāh-nāma* of the same type (no. 22), which, though smaller and in less good preservation, seems to contain a few older features. It has no colophon and can only be said, from the date of an ex-libris bound up in the middle of the volume, to be earlier than 1353. In these three manuscripts Chinese influence, properly speaking, is non-existent. The apparently Chinese features are simply due to the introduction of Mongol armour and occasional Mongol faces. The main lines of composition, colouring, dress-pattern, and vegetation-forms are quite unlike anything Chinese.

It is natural that the older tradition should persist longer in illustrations of the national epic. With all except the conquerors conservatism would be a merit. Many years ago Noeldeke[2] pointed out the archaic nature of the illustrations to the early manuscripts of the *Shāh-nāma*, and, from the nature of the book, suspected that they represented a very old tradition. Firdawsī's poem rested on a number of earlier sources, most of which no longer survive at all; but, from the occurrence of the heroic names in the days of the Arsacids, it is evident that many of the cycles of legend were already then in existence. Although Arsacid and Sasanian history appear in the poem in a curiously abbreviated and distorted way, Noeldeke was able to trace a clear unbroken tradition from the *Shāh-nāma* back to Sasanian and Parthian days. No doubt it would be possible to multiply the interesting examples of strictly iconographic survival from Sasanian into Muhammadan times in Persia given by Sir Thomas Arnold in his Charlton Lecture;[3] but they are less remarkable than the survivals in technique and convention which seem to be present, particularly, in the *Shāh-nāma* manuscripts. Some of these more general characteristics will here be considered, leaving any detailed iconographic points to be mentioned in the catalogue of the miniatures in which they occur.

The miniatures, in conformity with the poem, reflect the extreme respect for the monarchy which was so marked in Sasanian days. In all the fourteenth-century manuscripts there is a great preference for throne scenes representing the king in the midst of the paladins.[4] There was quite a different atmosphere about the work of the Mesopotamian school, which was more democratic, and, although of earlier date, represented a less ancient tradition. In these royal scenes the emphasis on the central figure and the disposition of the court about him seem to show clearly the influence of a mural school.

---

[1] A colophon of this manuscript is in existence in another portion recently for sale in Paris and gives the date 741/1341.
[2] *Das Iranische Nationalepos*, § 61.

[3] *Survivals of Sasanian and Manichaean Art in Persian Painting*, 1924.
[4] But true 'inverted perspective' is hardly used.

This is particularly noticeable in the Bodleian novel, where also the red background is almost certainly a survival from the surface prepared for frescoes, such as that to be seen in those from Qizyl in the Museum für Völkerkunde in Berlin. The cloud and vegetable conventions in this book also recall the frescoes from Qizyl. Similar conventions without the red background, though sometimes with gold substituted, occur in Mr. Chester Beatty's little *Shāh-nāma* miniatures (no. 19). A similar hieratic court arrangement, but without a coloured background or the old conventions, occurs in the London and Edinburgh *Jāmi' al-Tawārīkh* (nos. 25, 26), especially in Pl. XX b, where the donning of the royal robe is the subject. It would naturally be a great mistake to seek for Sasanian influence only in the illustrations to the *Shāh-nāma*. Even in the work of the Mesopotamian school certain survivals are to be noted: the spotted textile designs are probably Iranian, as they agree with the evidence afforded by the textiles and paintings in the Stein collection. So, too, the rouged cheeks, which were universal in Turkestan, appearing in the fragments of Manichaean paintings (though they may be ultimately a fashion borrowed from China), are found not only in the Bodleian novel, but also in the fourteenth-century *Shāh-nāmas* and the *Kalīla wa Dimna* bequeathed by Marteau to the Bibliothèque Nationale.[1]

There can be no doubt that this small[2] but fine fragment must belong to the same group of manuscripts, both in date and locality. Even if it is rather earlier in date than any of the other manuscripts of this Iranian group and should actually have been executed in the thirteenth century (for which there is no satisfactory evidence), there cannot be claimed for it that essential priority which M. Blochet postulates (*Enluminures*, p. 66) on the ground of the mention, in one of its pages which evidently formed part of the preface, of a certain minister, Fākhir b. 'Abd al-Wāhid, who is otherwise unknown, but whom M. Blochet assumes to have been both the original owner of the book and also a courtier of the Ghaznawid Sultān Bahrām for whom Nasr Allāh made this translation from the Arabic. The date of about A.D. 1150 to which he consequently attributes these pages would certainly make them a very important document for the history of art; but it would also make it even more difficult to follow a consistent development in Persian miniature painting.

In the twelfth century, and probably earlier, the Iranian qualities of Islamic book illustration were partly hidden under the Mesopotamian style, which derives originally from the Hellenistic West and is paralleled by certain Christian Arab work such as the Gospel book in the British Museum (Add. 11856). Even in the finest 'Mesopotamian' manuscripts, such as the St. Petersburg Harīrī and the Vienna Galen, there are obvious Iranian or old Sasanian features such as the winged genii of the Galen frontispiece, or the vegetation built up in cactus fashion or like paper chains made of different coloured links, in just the same way as in the Central Asian frescoes, and this is echoed very closely in the pottery of Rhages. In the 1236 *Kalīla wa Dimna* (no. 16) this feeling is stronger:

[1] Cf. Blochet, *Musulman Painting*, pl. 11; *Enluminures*, pl. XVIII.
[2] The miniatures measure only about 48×35 mm.

the red background is used, recalling, as has been suggested, not only the Central Asian frescoes, but also, probably, similar work in Persia, while the flowers are unmistakably like the lotus of Buddhist iconography and not at all like anything Western. In the small Bibliothèque Nationale *Kalīla wa Dimna* the red background is also used at least once (fol. 15 *v.*; cf. *Notices et Extraits*, t. XLI, p. 324), and the flying draperies look very like a survival from Sasanian times. The halo is, however, still used to give emphasis to the head, and this is probably, though by no means certainly, a custom of Western origin; and the curious markings on the dresses, which had once been intended to represent folds,[1] still occur, though not on all the figures, some of whom have the more decorative Chinese patterns to be found in the fourteenth-century *Shāh-nāmas*. Consequently, it would seem probable that these twenty-five leaves with their twenty miniatures date from about 1300 or a little later, and that there was a very small type of book made for convenience, in contrast to the very large type discussed above. M. Blochet indeed mentions that there is another copy of Nasr Allāh's version of the *Kalīla wa Dimna* fables in the Bibliothèque Nationale which is even smaller and which is actually dated 1318, but it is without miniatures. The connexion between the little Marteau *Kalīla wa Dimna* and Mr. Chester Beatty's *Shāh-nāma* pages is obvious, and it is probably this which has led M. Blochet to assign the latter to the early thirteenth century (cf. *Rupam*, no. 41).

The conclusion, then, seems to be that the distinction immediately apparent between the big style of manuscript produced at Tabrīz, which is alone properly entitled to the epithet 'Mongol', as peculiarly the court art of the Ilkhāns, and the style exemplified in the *Shāh-nāmas* of the fourteenth century should not be pushed too far. They have many elements in common, and it may be said that in the Demotte *Shāh-nāma* and the Istanbul University *Kalīla wa Dimna* they are practically fused together—a cross-breeding of remarkable fertility; for from it was developed, by a pedigree which is still somewhat obscure, the great Timurid style of the fifteenth century.

[1] Cf. Introduction, p. 12.

CATALOGUE

16 SEVEN PAGES FROM NASR ALLĀH'S PERSIAN VERSION OF *KALĪLA WA DIMNA.* XIII century. This manuscript has always been said to have been copied by Yahya b. Muhammad b. Yahya, called Jaddī Rūmī (or Rūdī), in 633/1236; but there may be some confusion, as it is an undoubted fact that the famous 'Schefer' Harīrī of the Bibliothèque Nationale (Arabe 5847) was copied and illustrated by Yahya b. Mahmūd b. Yahya b. Abi'l-Hasan b. Kuwwariha al-Wāsitī in 634/1237, and it is very different in style.

> (*a*) [420] The camel devoured by other animals. Ochre ground. 32 × 20 *cm.* Exh. Memorial Art Gallery, Rochester, 1930; Pennsylvania Univ. Museum, 1930; Detroit Inst. of Arts, 1930, cat. no. 14. ¶ Lent by DEMOTTE, New York.   PLATE XI B.
> (*b*) [427] Miniature illustrating the story of the ascetic, the thief, and the ox. 33 × 21 *cm.* ¶ Lent by MALLON, Paris.
> (*c*) [426] A Sultān seated with his courtiers (all of dark complexion). Red background. 34·5 × 26 *cm.* Exh. Paris, 1925; Repr. Marteau-Vever, no. III; Kühnel, *I.M.,* pl. 19. ¶ Lent by M. CHARLES GILLET, Lyon.
> (*d*) [50] Elephant and lion. 9 × 17·5 *cm.* Marteau-Vever, no. 45.
> (*e*) [430] Couple in bed. 10 × 17·5 *cm.*
> (*f*) [428 *a*] Lion and ox. Red ground. The ox, straying into the domain of the lion-king, becomes his friend, but subsequently, through the machinations of the jackals Kalīla and Dimna, the two quarrel, and the lion slays the ox. 9·5 × 18 *cm.*   PLATE XI A.
> (*g*) [428 *b*] Ox and fox. 9·5 × 18 *cm.*
> ¶ (*d*)-(*g*) Lent by M. CLAUDE ANET, Paris.
> For other reproductions see *Burl. Mag.,* Oct. 1912, pl. I; Marteau-Vever, pl. XLIV.

17 [531 A and B] *KITĀB I SAMAK 'AYYĀR,* a Persian novel by Sadaqa b. 'Abi'l-Qāsim Shīrāzī, collected—or put in writing—by Farāmurz b. Khudādād b. 'Abd Allāh al-Kātib al-Arrajānī, who states that he began to collect it in 585/1189. Two of the three volumes owned by the Bodleian Library were exhibited at Burlington House; vol. 1 with twenty-five miniatures, vol. 3 with twelve miniatures. No other copy appears to be known, and this may possibly be the holograph of Farāmurz and date from about A.D. 1200. It is unfinished and undated. Arrajān, of which the scribe was a native, was, like Shīrāz, in Fārs, and was in the thirteenth century the capital of the westernmost of its five provinces. XIII century: West Persia.

A translation of part of the novel has been included in *The Three Dervishes* by Mr. R. Levy (London, 1923).

Ethé, *Cat.,* no. 442. From the collection of Sir William Ouseley (*Cat.,* no. 445-7). ¶ Lent by BODLEIAN LIBRARY, Oxford [Ouseley 379, 381].

> (*a*) Qabūs has his Wazīr beaten to induce a confession. Sharwān-Dukht, the daughter of Qabūs, is brought before the king by Mardān-Dukht (Ouseley 381, fol. 251ʳ).   PLATE XII A.
> (*b*) Farrukh-Rūz bursts into tears on beholding Gul-Rū (Ouseley 381, fol. 13ᵛ). PLATE XII B.
> (*c*) Men and women, seated under a canopy, mourning for Farrukh-Rūz (Ouseley 379, fol. 217ᵛ).   PLATE XIII B.

The second volume, which is also in the Bodleian Library (Ouseley Add. 380), was originally part of the first and paginates straight on from it, while the present volume III was always separate and starts with a fresh pagination. Volume II contains fifteen miniatures, in exactly the same style as volume I. The last few pages are restored in another hand (fol. 434 onwards).

18 THREE PAGES FROM *MANĀFI' AL-HAYAWĀN*, an Arabic work on natural history by Ibn Bakhtīshū', written in *naskh*, with very large Kufic capitals. XIII century.

    (*a*) [419 *a*] Two asses and conventionalized foliage. 22·5 × 17·5 *cm*.   PLATE IX B.
    (*b*) [419 *b*] Parrots. 27·5 × 17·5 *cm*. Exh. Paris 1925.
    ¶ (*a*) and (*b*) Lent by M. ALPHONSE KANN, Paris.
    (*c*) [41] Ibex. 21·5 × 16 *cm*. ¶ Lent by MCGILL UNIVERSITY, MONTREAL.
Other reproductions in Schulz, I, pls. K, L.

19 [422] EIGHTEEN MINIATURES from a manuscript of Firdawsī's *Shāh-nāma*. Early XIV century. Eighty miniatures from this manuscript belong to Mr. Chester Beatty and others to Mr. Ajit Ghose.

    The Persian Epic of the Kings is the most celebrated poem in the language. It was finished in 400/1009–10.

    16 × 12·5 (*written surface*). Blochet, *Rupam*, Jan. 1930, no. 41. ¶ Lent by A. CHESTER BEATTY, ESQ. (Beatty Lib., Dublin, Ms. 104, fol. 3, 8, and 46, resp.).

    (*a*) Rustam captures his future steed Rakhsh. The young Rustam, having asked for a steed, is taken by Zāl, his father, among the droves, and choosing out a piebald colt he lassoes it, in spite of being warned by the herdsman of the fierceness of its mare, which has prevented it ever being broken. Rustam throws down the mare, which can be seen on her knees, and secures the colt. Rakhsh henceforward is Rustam's companion in his exploits, and, after performing many marvellous feats, he eventually dies with his master.   PLATE XIV A.
    (*b*) Farīdūn causes Zahhāk to be nailed to a rock. Zahhāk, the demon king, having driven the people to desperation by his cruelty, they revolt under Kāwa the smith. Farīdūn, a prince of the Kayānian line, defeats Zahhāk and causes him to be fettered to a rock on Mount Damāwand and abandoned. Farīdūn carries the ox-headed mace, which is probably a survival from Achaemenid times. The bell-shaped hat, worn by the man behind him, is apparently an early type. It occurs as the head-dress of the principal figure in the early frontispiece in the Serai (*Meisterwerke*, Taf. 8) and in a fragment in Vienna from al-Ushmūnayn, said to be of the tenth century (Arnold and Grohmann, pl. 4, B).   PLATE XIV B.
    (*c*) Qaydāfa, Queen of Barda', recognizes Sikandar (Alexander) who has come to her in disguise, and reproaches him. The falcons on either side of the throne were used as royal symbols among the Mongols, but date back very much further. In Islamic times they are so mentioned at the court of the early Fatimids of Egypt.   PLATE XIV C.

20 [144 B] TWO MINIATURES from the same manuscript as the preceding.

    1. A captive led by horsemen. Repr. *Souvenir*, pl. 32.
    2. Minūchihr's fight with his uncle Salm.
    16 × 12·5 *cm*. ¶ Lent by AJIT GHOSE, Calcutta.

For style, compare the Bibliothèque Nationale *Kalīla wa Dimna* (Sup. pers. 1965) [Blochet, *Enluminures*, pl. XVIII], and M. Kevorkian's Tabari [Schulz, Bd. I, Taf. J]. Unfortunately neither of these manuscripts is dated.
    While much of M. Blochet's reasoning, in the article in *Rupam* (no. 41) devoted to these miniatures, is acceptable, it is impossible to follow him in placing them before the Mongol invasions or in denying any

Chinese influence in them. Not only are the facial types entirely Mongol, a fact which might be explained by an attribution to a Seljuk milieu, but the whole feel of the drawing, which is linear in character, betrays Chinese influence. Special details which betray it are the 'tai' clouds, the mountain and tree conventions, and the armour, which M. Blochet himself admits to be of a Mongol type (cf. the description from John de Plano Carpini, quoted below, p. 45). His principal difficulty in accepting a Chinese influence seems to lie in the gold backgrounds which many of the miniatures have; but it is not in fact the case that these are never found in Chinese paintings of the Sung or Yüan periods.

21 [418] BAHRĀM GŪR AND HIS MISTRESS. A page from a copy of the *Hasht Bihisht* of Amīr Khusraw (a poem completed in 701/1301–2), possibly executed in Northern India, as is indicated by the pigments. Early XIV century. Red background.

30 × 22·5 *cm.* Repr. Migeon, I, fig. 22. ❡ Lent by M. H. VEVER, Paris.

Bahrām, annoyed at the rudeness of his mistress, who derides his prowess at shooting deer, throws her from her horse. The story is a variation of the better-known versions of Firdawsī (for which see no. 23, *e*) and Nizāmī, the latter being mainly followed by the poet, whose *Hasht Bihisht* or 'Eight Paradises' is an imitation of Nizāmī's *Haft Paykar*, 'Seven Portraits'.

22 [532] FIRDAWSĪ'S *SHĀH-NĀMA.* 334 fol. Two *sarlawhs*, eight '*unwāns*, one hundred and six miniatures (twelve repainted, many defaced). Early XIV century. Ex-libris dated 753/1352. Leather binding, gold-stamped.

29 × 20 *cm.* ❡ Lent by MRS. STEPHENS.

(*a*) When Rūdāba was pregnant, she suffered such pain that Zāl, her husband, called for assistance to the Sīmurgh, the guardian bird of his family. By the Sīmurgh's advice Rūdāba was drugged with wine, and the future hero, so different from other mortals even in his birth, was delivered by the Caesarian operation. PLATE XIII A.

This manuscript is undated, but there are some reasons for thinking it earlier than the *Shāh-nāma* from Istanbul of 1330 (no. 23). The horses are spotted, as in the Morgan *Natural History*; one of the miniatures is surrounded with an intertwined border of typical Seljuk form; the vegetation is less highly developed; and, generally speaking, the Mongol influence seems to be less in it than in any of the other *Shāh-nāma* manuscripts. The border of the miniature illustrated is of a type that goes back to the earliest Arabic illuminated manuscripts.

23 [532 c] FIRDAWSĪ'S *SHĀH-NĀMA*, copied in 731/1330 by Hasan b. 'Alī b. Husayn al-Bahmanī. 281 fol. Five decorated pages and eighty-nine miniatures. The manuscript bears the seal of the Timurid Shāh Rukh (died A.D. 1447) on the last folio. There is a fine dedication page in gold, with a design of peonies. The royal name on it is illegible, and the patron, who is depicted in the double frontispiece, among his attendants, is unidentified.

33·5 × 28·5 *cm.* ❡ Lent by MUSEUM OF TOP-KAPU, Istanbul.

(*a*) The death of the Paladins in the snow. The five faithful Paladins, who have accompanied the Shāh Kay Khusraw on his last journey, perish in a snowstorm on a mountain after the Shāh's disappearance. It is interesting to compare this miniature with the very different treatment of the same scene in the Royal Asiatic Society MS. (Pl. LVIII). This mountain convention with contours in bright colours is probably of Western origin and was only introduced thence into China. PLATE XVI A.

(*b*) The introduction of the game of chess into Persia. The Rāja of India sends a chess-board and chess-men to the Shāh Nūshīrwān, and offers to pay tribute if Nūshīrwān can find out how the game is played. In the illustration the Indian envoys are showing the board to the Shāh. PLATE XVI B.

(c) Zardusht (Zoroaster), after converting the Shāh Gushtāsp to the Zoroastrian faith, plants a cypress tree, over which the Shāh builds a shrine. The Shāh is of a strongly Iranian type, reminiscent of a playing-card king, the type of which may indeed have reached Europe in the Crusades from a Persian source.　　　　　　　　　　　　　　　　　　PLATE XVII B.

(d) The Persian general Bahrām Chūbīn is insulted by the Shāh Hurmuzd, who sends him a woman's dress and a distaff. Bahrām puts on the red and yellow dress and appears before the chiefs. 'Obedient to the will of his sovereign, he showed himself to the soldiers in this unworthy disguise: they resented his ignominy and their own; a shout of rebellion ran through the ranks, and the general accepted their oath of fidelity and vows of revenge' (Gibbon, *Decline and Fall*, chapter XLVI). The ground of this miniature is uncoloured.　　PLATE XVII A.

(e) Bahrām Gūr punishing the damsel Azāda for mocking him. Bahrām Gūr—so called from his fondness for hunting the wild ass (gūr)—was once accompanied to the chase by his favourite Azāda, a musician. Azāda dared him to show his skill with the bow in such a way as to turn a buck into a doe, and a doe into a buck, and afterwards to transfix the ear and the foot of a deer with a single arrow. So Bahrām with his first arrow carried away the horns of a buck; and with two more he furnished the doe with arrows for horns; with a fourth he grazed the buck's ear, so that it raised its foot to scratch its ear; and immediately he sent another shaft through foot and ear together. But Azāda mocked at Bahrām, saying that Āhriman had aided him; whereupon he flung her from the saddle, and rode the dromedary, on which they had both been riding, over her so that she died. This famous story is found illustrated both in Sasanian silverwork and in twelfth-century pottery, and was for centuries a favourite subject with the miniaturists.　　　　　　　　　　　　　　　　　　　　　　　PLATE XV B.

The miniatures in this manuscript are usually at the bottom of the page and of irregular shape with the top stepped like a pyramid. This device gives greater lightness to a page which might be overburdened with the strong reds and blues, and also accentuates the formal arrangement of the Iranian court. Further lightening is achieved by the introduction of an unusual emerald green. The backgrounds are either red or gold. The trees are indicated by drawing the leaves suitable to the species intended against a solid olive ground. Clouds and dust are both represented as grey swirling masses.

24 [533 A] FRAGMENTS OF FIRDAWSĪ'S *Shāh-nāma*, copied in 741/1341 and dedicated to Wazīr al-Hasan Qawām al-Dawla wa'l-Dīn.

(a) [533 A] Portion containing the original preface in the name of Abu Mansūr al-Ma'marī. 81 fols. Ten miniatures. Brown leather binding with gold geometrical designs. 36·5 × 28·5 cm.
¶ Lent by A. CHESTER BEATTY, ESQ.

(b) [44] Miniature on a red ground: Fight between Rustam and Isfandiyār. 36·5 × 30·5 cm.
¶ Lent by H. NAZARE-AGA, Paris.

(c) [423] Miniature: gold on a red ground. 36·5 × 30 cm. ¶ Lent by D. KELEKIAN, Paris.

(d) [424] Miniature: two parties of horsemen fighting. 34 × 26 cm. Exh. Paris, 1925, no. 255.
¶ Lent by M. CHARLES GILLET, Lyons.

(e) [425] Miniature: Mourning over Alexander's bier. 29 × 24 cm. ¶ Lent by MCGILL UNIVERSITY, MONTREAL.

(f) [429] Miniature: Lahhāk and Farshīdward before King Afrāsiyāb. 28 × 24 cm. ¶ Lent by M. H. VEVER, Paris.

A further portion of this manuscript, which was for sale in Paris in 1931, contained a colophon with the date 741 and the above dedication.

25–26 RASHĪD AL-DĪN'S *JĀMI' AL-TAWĀRĪKH*, 'Universal History', in Arabic. Dated 707–14/1306–14. The two surviving portions of this famous manuscript were reunited here for the first time. Copied for the author at Rashīdiyya, near Tabrīz.

25 [537 A] THE EDINBURGH PORTION, containing a history of the prophets and the early Persian kings, the life of Muhammad, and portions on the Abbasids, Ghaznawids, and Seljuks. 277 fol. Seventy miniatures. Dated 707/1306.

42 × 32 *cm. Catalogue of the Arabic and Persian Manuscripts in Edinburgh University Library*, 1925, no. 20. For other reproductions see Arnold, *P.I.*, pls. xix, xx, liii; Blochet, *Musulman Painting*, pls. liii–lviii; Martin, 1, figs. 12–15; Arnold and Grohmann, pl. 41. ¶ Lent by EDINBURGH UNIVERSITY LIBRARY.

(*a*) The child Moses, abandoned by his mother and cast adrift in a box, is discovered by the women of Pharaoh's household and brought before Pharaoh's wife, who nurtures him.
                                                                                    PLATE XVIII A.

(*b*) Samson destroying the temple of the Philistines. Cf. Judges xvi. 30: And Samson said, Let me die with the Philistines.   PLATE XVIII B.

(*c*) The miracle at the Red Sea. The sea is miraculously divided to allow the Israelites under Moses to pass through in safety; the pursuing Egyptians are drowned in the sight of Moses.
                                                                                    PLATE XIX A.

(*d*) Qārūn and his companions swallowed by the earth. Qārūn, the biblical Korah, is represented in the Qur'ān as a wicked minister of Pharaoh. He was immensely wealthy, and boasted that his wealth was due to his knowledge, whereupon God caused the ground to cleave in sunder and swallow him up with his palace.   PLATE XIX B.

(*e*) David being called to govern Israel. In this miniature note the architectural features, which are of a type inherited by the Mongols from their Seljuk predecessors in Persia.
                                                                                    PLATE XX A.

(*f*) Yamīn al-Dawla, surrounded by his nobles, wearing a robe which he received from the Caliph al-Qādir Billāh. Note that several of the men wear their hair in pigtails.
                                                                                    PLATE XX B.

(*g*) The Seven Sleepers of Ephesus. The well-known Christian story, of which there is a version in the eighteenth Sūra of the Qur'ān ('The Cave'), tells of seven Christian youths of Ephesus who, taking refuge from the Emperor Decius, slept with their dog in a cave for over three hundred years. They are here discovered by Alexander. The story is probably Syrian in origin. For an account of the many versions in Eastern and European authors, cf. P. M. Huber, *Die Wanderlegende von den Siebenschläfern*, 1910.   PLATE XXI A.

(*h*) Joshua, after the taking of Jericho, orders the property seized by the army to be destroyed.
                                                                                    PLATE XXI B.

(*i*) Two miniatures on a single page, of which the upper represents the meeting in battle of Abu'l-Qāsim b. Sīmjūr with Muntasir; while the lower represents Muntasir with 700 men crossing the frozen river Jīhūn (Oxus).   PLATE XXII.

The following description of Mongol arms and armour, taken from *The Voyage of Friar Johannes de Plano Carpini* [1246] (Hakluyt's translation, Chapter 17), is of interest for comparison with the upper miniature: 'They beate out many thinne plates a finger broad, and a handful long, and making in every one of them eight little holes, they put thereunto three strong and straight leather thongs. So they joine the plates one to another, as it were, ascending by degrees. Then they tie the plates with other small and slender thongs, drawn through the holes aforesayd, and in the upper part, on each side thereof, they fasten one small doubled thong unto another, that the plates may firmly be knit together. These they make, as well for their horses caparisons, as for the armour of their men: And they skowre them so bright that a man may behold his face in them.'

26 [537 B] THE ROYAL ASIATIC SOCIETY'S PORTION, containing fragments from the history of the Prophet and his followers, the history of India, with the account of Buddha, and part of the history of the Jews. 59 fol. One hundred miniatures. Dated 714/1314.

43·5 × 30·5 cm. Morley, *Cat.*, no. 1. For other reproductions, see Martin, II, pls. 27–32; Blochet, *Musulman Painting*, pls. 48–52; Kühnel, pls. 23–7; Gray, pl. 3. ❡ Lent by ROYAL ASIATIC SOCIETY.

(*a*) The Indian Mountains. In the foreground a river with fish and ducks.   PLATE XXIII A.

(*b*) The mountains on the way to Tibet.   PLATE XXIII B.

In these pictures no knowledge of India is shown by the artist, who has, as usual, drawn on scenery represented in Chinese paintings for his landscape. The author, Rashīd al-Dīn, used as his principal source for Indian geography al-Bīrūnī: he here states that the road into Tibet from the west is very bad, so that the people have to carry their baggage on their shoulders. The water flowing from the mountains is about a hundred cubits deep. It is related that the gazelles here have four eyes.

27 [537 c] MANUSCRIPT OF SIX *DĪWĀNS*, copied by 'Abd al-Mu'min al-'Alawī al-Kāshī. Dated 713–14/1313–15. Probably executed at Tabrīz. Formerly in the possession of Shāh Ismā'īl Safawī, whose seal it bears. The *dīwāns* are illustrated by *sarlawhs* and miniatures (some of which are repeated) of a type similar to those in the *Jāmi' al-Tawārīkh* (nos. 25–6), and the manuscript may have been copied by the same scribe.

The *Dīwāns* are of (1) Mu'izzī, (2) Asīr al-Dīn Akhsīkatī, (3) Adīb Sābir, (4) Nizām al-Dīn Mahmūd Qamar, (5) Shams al-Dīn Mahmūd al-Tabasī, (6) Nāsir i Khusraw.

45 × 30 cm. E. G. Browne, *Literary History of Persia*, II, frontispiece; Arnold and Grohmann, *The Islamic Book*, pl. 42; Ethé, nos. 903, 911, and 913. ❡ Lent by INDIA OFFICE LIBRARY.

28 FOURTEEN MINIATURES from a manuscript of Rashīd al-Dīn's *Universal History*, now dispersed, but said to have borne the date 1318. Also said (with great likelihood) to have borne the seal of Shāh Rukh, to whose reign some of the miniatures must belong.

(*a*) [219 *a*] Nawdar on his throne. 15 × 22 cm.

(*b*) [219 *b*] Mu'āwiya conversing with the representatives of 'Amr b. al-'Ās. 14 × 22·5 cm.

(*c*) [219 *c*] The Prophets Caleb and Ezekiel conversing. 15 × 25 cm.

(*d*) [219 *d*] King Hūshang on his throne. 12 × 25 cm.

(*e*) [219 *e*] The miraculous river and fishes which nourished the followers of Muhammad in the desert. 14 × 22 cm.

(*f*) [448 *a*] Shāpūr I on his throne. 15 × 22·5 cm.

(*g*) [448 *b*] The Khwārazmshāh Tukush listening to the poet Watwāt. 17·5 × 26 cm.

(*a*)–(*g*) ❡ Lent by PARISH-WATSON, New York.

(*h*) [431 *a*] Portrait, apparently having no connexion with the accompanying text (reign of the Caliph Mustansir Billāh).

(*i*) [431 *b*] Buddha (named *Shākmūnī*) giving news of another prophet.

(*k*) [431 *c*] A young saint with a flame halo.

(*l*) [431 *d*] Moses striking Og's ('Uj) ankle.

(*h*)–(*l*) 33 × 23 cm. ❡ Lent by ÉMILE TABBAGH, Paris.

(*m*) [447 *a*] 'Abd al-Muttalib and his son discovering the well Zamzam. 42·5 × 30 cm. ❡ Lent by D. KELEKIAN, Paris.

(*n*) [447 *b*] The dog Qarā Burāq, 'Black Lightning', driving off wolves from a flock of sheep. This convention for rock drawing is apparently unknown before the early Timurid period. 42·5 × 30 cm. ❡ Lent by D. KELEKIAN, Paris.   PLATE XXIV B.

(*o*) [449] Jonah and the Whale. 40 × 27·8 cm. ❡ Lent by ESTATE OF V. EVERITT MACY, ESQ., New York.

The entire manuscript was exhibited at the International Exhibition of Persian Art, Pennsylvania Museum, Philadelphia, Oct.-Dec. 1926.

29 TWENTY-TWO MINIATURES from a copy of the *Shāh-nāma*, formerly owned by M. Demotte, by whose name it is generally known. The colophon has never appeared. About 1330. Probably made at Tabrīz. It is written in six columns with headings on hatched and more elaborately patterned grounds. The miniatures are usually of the full width of the page, and though not as big as half its height, are distinctly broader than those in the *Jāmiʿ al-Tawārīkh* (nos. 25–6).

(*a*) [445] Ardawān brought before Ardashīr. Firdawsī tells at considerable length how Ardawān, the last of the Parthian rulers, entertained Ardashīr, the descendant of the old Kayānian kings, but subsequently, being displeased with him, sent him to serve in his stables. Ardashīr (Artaxerxes) flees with the maiden Gulnār, and afterwards wars with the Parthians and defeats them. He then founds the Sasanian dynasty. In the illustration Ardashīr is ordering the death of the captured Ardawān. 40 × 29 *cm.* ¶ Lent by M. H. VEVER, Paris.   PLATE XXV A.

(*b*) [446 *a*] Rustam slaying Isfandiyār with a double-pointed arrow. 40·2 × 29·6 *cm.* Repr. Sakisian, *Syria*, 1931, pl. XXXI (2). ¶ Lent by E. WELLS, New York.

(*c*) [446 *b*] Zāl interrogated by Mūbids (Zoroastrian priests). 39·4 × 29·7 *cm.* ¶ Lent by E. WELLS, New York.

(*d*) [440] The Funeral of Isfandiyār. The body of Isfandiyār, who had been slain in fight by his rival Rustam, is sent by Rustam to Gushtāsp, King of Persia, his father. The body of the prince, wrapped in a brocade shroud, lies on a stretcher carried by two mules: his plumed head-gear rests on the body, and his charger, with saddle reversed, is led in front. Mourners accompany the procession, tearing their hair and lacerating their faces. The whole land is filled with lamentations, and the nobles, holding the king responsible for Isfandiyār's death, revile him and leave the palace. 22 × 29 *cm.* ¶ Lent by DEMOTTE, New York.   PLATE XXVI A.

(*e*) [71] Sīndukht, mother of Rūdāba, questioning the go-between employed by her daughter and Zāl and discovering from her their love. 40 × 29 *cm.* Repr. Schulz, Taf. 23. ¶ Lent by M. H. VEVER, Paris.   PLATE XXVII A.

(*f*) [433] Bahrām killing a dragon. The extent to which the Chinese dragon had been adopted in Persia at this date is shown by the introduction of one, closely similar to the one in this miniature, as a decorative element among lettering on the portal of the Veramin mosque executed for Abu Saʿīd in 1322 (cf. Sarre, *Denkmäler Persischer Baukunst*, Bd. I, fig. 70). 44 × 29·2 *cm.* ¶ Lent by MRS. RAINEY ROGERS, New York.   PLATE XXIV A.

(*g*) [436] Bahrām Gūr shooting a gazelle, and the death of Āzāda. 60 × 41 *cm.* Schulz, pl. 27; Sakisian, fig. 35. ¶ Lent by EDWARD W. FORBES, ESQ., Cambridge, Mass.

(*h*) [434] Khusraw Anūshīrwān dictating a letter to the Khāqān of Chīn to the Chief Mūbid. 41 × 29·5 *cm.* ¶ Lent by DEMOTTE, Paris.

(*i*) [438] Alexander building the iron barrier against Gog and Magog. Yājūj and Mājūj (Gog and Magog) represent the uncivilized tribes of the north against whom Sikandar built this protective fortification, traces of which are still shown in the Caucasus. This well-known story, which is mentioned in the Qurʾān, derives from the Christian Alexander legend. The fortifications made of stone and metal were vitrified by fire, the preparation of which is shown in the miniature. 40 × 29 *cm.* Schulz, Taf. 28. ¶ Lent by M. H. VEVER, Paris.   PLATE XXV B.

(*k*) [435] The Shāh Zaw, son of Tahmāsp. 40 × 29 *cm.* ¶ Lent by M. H. VEVER, Paris.

(*l*) [444] Bahrām in a peasant's house. 40·5 × 29·5 *cm.* ¶ Lent by MCGILL UNIVERSITY, Montreal.

(*m*) [442] Farīdūn mourning for his murdered son Iraj. 40 × 29 *cm.* ¶ Lent by M. H. VEVER, Paris.

(*n*) [441] Ardashīr and his wife. 40 × 29 *cm.* ¶ Lent by M. H. VEVER, Paris.

(*o*) [432] The coffin of Iraj brought to Farīdūn. 29 × 28·5 *cm.* ¶ Lent by M. H. VEVER, Paris.

(*p*) [218 *a*] Bahrām Gūr hunting onagers. He is wearing a crown and his head is surrounded with a halo. 21 × 30 *cm.* ¶ Lent by DEMOTTE, New York.

(*q*) [218 *b*] Bahrām Bahrāmiyān, enthroned, with courtiers and attendants. He wears a diadem: the form of the throne is Chinese. 40×29 *cm.* ¶ Lent by DEMOTTE, New York.

PLATE XXVII B.

(*r*) [218 *c*] Zāl, as his father's messenger, kissing the feet of Shāh Minūchihr, who is seated on his throne. 17×20 *cm.* ¶ Lent by DEMOTTE, New York.

(*s*) [218 *d*] Farīdūn watching his sons fight against the dragon. 40×29 *cm.* ¶ Lent by DEMOTTE, New York.

(*t*) [67] Battle exploit of Isfandiyār. 60×41 *cm.* ¶ Lent by EDWARD W. FORBES, ESQ., Cambridge, Mass. (through FOGG ART MUSEUM).

(*u*) [437] The sons of Isfandiyār killed in battle. 57·5×42·5 *cm.* ¶ Lent by EDWARD W. FORBES, ESQ., Cambridge, Mass. (through FOGG ART MUSEUM).

(*w*) [439] Alexander visiting the city of the Brahmans, whom he questions, in company with the philosophers of Rūm, about their mysteries. This episode, like much of Firdawsī's account of Sikandar's adventures, derives ultimately from the Pseudo-Callisthenes. 29×16 *cm.* ¶ Lent by M. H. VEVER, Paris. COLOUR PLATE X.

(*x*) [443] Sikandar defeats the army of Fūr of Hind. The battle of the Hydaspes (the modern Jhelum), in which Alexander the Great defeated the army of Porus, the Indian king, took place in 326 B.C. It was a brilliant feat of arms and one of Alexander's greatest military achievements.

According to the *Shāh-nāma* story, also derived from Pseudo-Callisthenes, Sikandar, in order to cope with the elephants of the Indian army, ordered his artificers—men of Rūm, Egypt, and Persia—to construct horses and horsemen of iron. These were set on wheels and filled with naphtha. The naphtha was lighted, and the figures, belching out flame, were drawn by real horsemen against the enemy, who were routed. Subsequently Sikandar and Porus met in single combat, and Porus was slain. Horses are terrified at elephants; and the iron army was no doubt invented to explain the success of the Macedonian cavalry, whose victory, against heavy odds and in flooded country, was actually gained by their fighting quality and Alexander's tactical skill. Porus was in fact taken prisoner, not slain in battle. He requested Alexander to 'treat him as a king', and he was handsomely entertained by his conqueror. 60×41 *cm.* ¶ Lent by EDWARD W. FORBES, ESQ., Cambridge, Mass. (through FOGG ART MUSEUM). PLATE XXVI B.

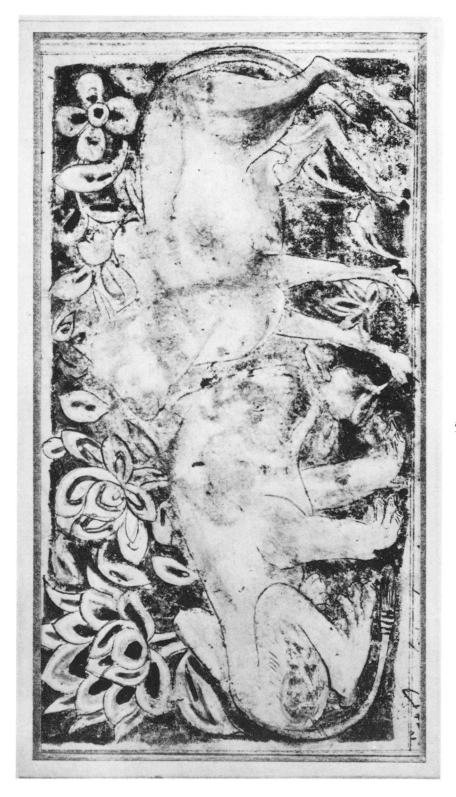

PLATE XI·A. 16 (f). Lion and Ox. XIII *century*

Plate X is reproduced in color, following p. 16.

PLATE XI-B. 16 (*a*). The Camel devoured by the other animals. XIII *century*

PLATE XII-A. 17 (*a*). The King has his Wazir beaten. XIII *century*

PLATE XII-B. 17 (b). Farrukh-Rūz weeps at the sight of Gul-Rū. XIII *century*

PLATE XIII-A. 22. The Birth of Rustam. *Early XIV century*

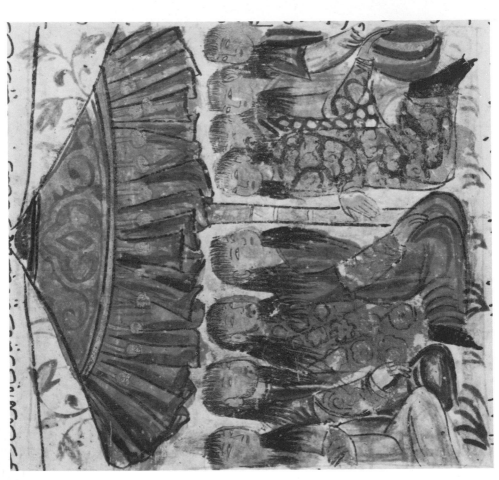

PLATE XIII · B. 17 (c). Mourning for Farrukh-Rūz. XIII *century*

PLATE XIV-A. 19 (*a*). Rustam catches Rakhsh from the herd. *Early* XIV *century*

PLATE XIV-B. 19 (*b*). Zahhāk nailed to Mount Damāwand. *Early* XIV *century*

PLATE XIV-C. 19 (*c*). Sikandar recognized by the Queen of Barda'. *Early* XIV *century*

PLATE XV-A. 8. The Annunciation. 1307

PLATE XV-B. 23 (*e*). Bahrām Gūr punishing Azāda for mocking him. 1330

PLATE XVI-A. 23 (*a*). The Death of the Paladins in the snow. 1330

PLATE XVI-B. 23 (b). The Introduction of the game of Chess. 1330

PLATE XVII-A. 23 (d). Bahrām Chūbīn with women's gear sent by Shāh Hurmuzd. 1330

PLATE XVII. B. 23 (c). Zoroaster plants a cypress tree. 1330

PLATE XVIII-A. 25 (*a*). Moses discovered by Pharaoh's servants. 1306

PLATE XVIII· B. 25 (*b*). Samson destroying the temple of the Philistines. 1306

PLATE XIX-A. 25 (c). The Egyptians drowned in the Red Sea. 1306

PLATE XIX·B. 25 (*d*). Qārūn swallowed by the earth. 1306

PLATE XX-A. 25 (e). David called to govern Israel. 1306

PLATE XX. B. 25 (f). Yamīn al-Dawla displays the robe sent by the Caliph. 1306

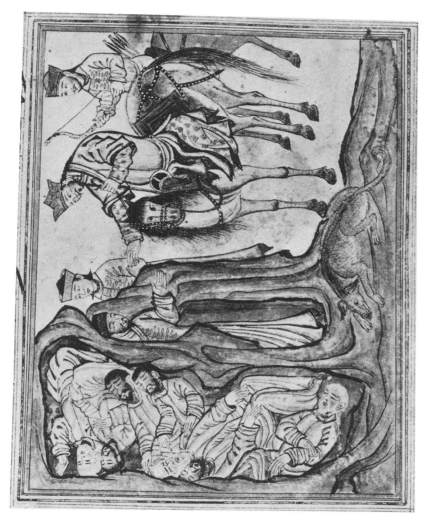

PLATE XXI-A. 25 (g). The Seven Sleepers of Ephesus. 1306

PLATE XXI-B. 25 (h). Joshua orders the destruction of the spoil of Jericho. 1306

PLATE XXII- 25 (i)—*above*, Battle between Abu'l-Qāsim and Muntasir.
below, Muntasir's army on the ice. 1306

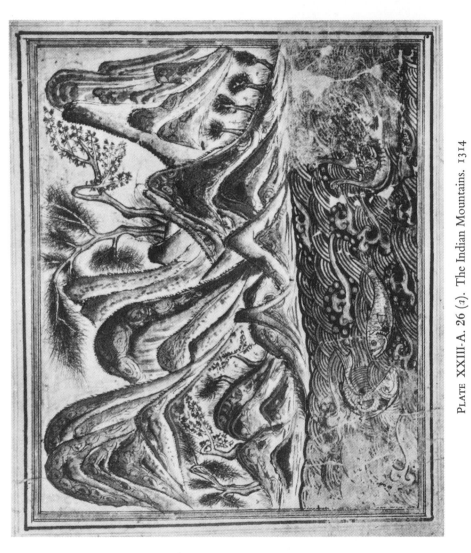

PLATE XXIII-A. 26 (7). The Indian Mountains. 1314

Plate XXIII-B. 26 (b). The Mountains on the way to Tibet. 1314

PLATE XXIV. A. 29 (*f*). Bahrām killing a dragon. c. 1340

بازمنتاینه بوکرکهکنت طباانازبلهش نوداواز تک عظیمجال اولاکنده نبانده انتر باوعن کرکهادانت بود اتنجودن کرکشه وینتازتنایان تک ادانت کرد بند گرنتایاندانا اتاونوا انت کارد انکگوان نازد ایتگکازان دانانی انت بازنامعدرنبا شات بانتدرکند زاره دوازکهان دازواناناتانه کانود نکگعنان دانانازواناقان بالت دادنکگا نتانت انود کاچاشزنت ازتجودن عظجعدرد ندان تنجودن کوعدکاازان زبالت انود کنواناقانگ نان دادنه اندنمعدود نتن کهشونعیعگرد اندنبا شزانه ازجودکاعودن انازوان اقان انوبندود نتک دند نبا بندود درکهاودن دازدربوعم گرنازبورک بابدان ذنتک انگوعان ذبدود

PLATE XXIV · B. 28 (n). 'Black Lightning' drives off wolves from the sheep. 1318?

PLATE XXV-A. 29 (*a*). Ardawān captive before Ardashīr. *c.* 1340

PLATE XXV-B. 29 (*i*). Alexander building the wall against Gog and Magog. *c.* 1340

PLATE XXVI. A. 29 (*d*). The Funeral of Isfandiyār. *c.* 1340

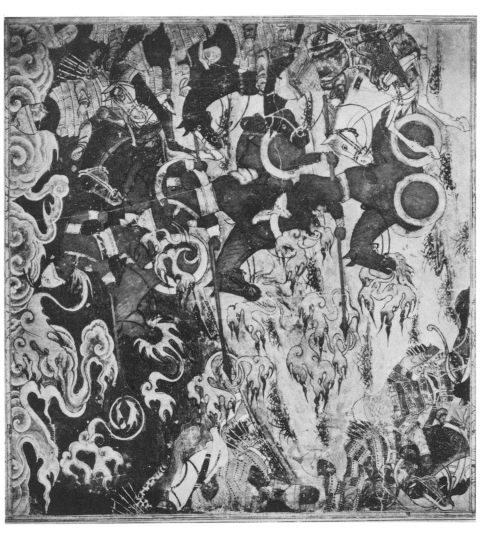

PLATE XXVI-B. 29 (x). Iron Warriors. c. 1340

PLATE XXVII-A. 29 (e). The Mother of Rūdāba discovers her love for Zāl. c.1340

PLATE XXVII-B. 29 (q). Bahrām Bahrāmiyān on his throne. c. 1340

III

THE TIMURID SCHOOL

THOUGH it is true that the style which has long made famous the name of the Timurid school is the natural development of the miniature art of the fourteenth century, and even that it was substantially in existence before the invasions of Tīmūr, yet the noble patronage of his descendants in the second and third generation make it a singularly appropriate title. Tīmūr himself indeed was probably in no way connected with the progress of the school. Not that he was not, in his way, a great patron of artists; he had a passion for fine building, and gathered to the new capital that he established at Samarqand all the finest craftsmen from the conquered cities of Iran, Mesopotamia, and Asia Minor. But his interest in literature seems to have been confined to historical works like the *Zafarnāma*, recording his own stupendous conquests. Several fine manuscripts with miniatures from the period of Tīmūr do in fact exist, of which two were exhibited at Burlington House. But there are special reasons for not associating these manuscripts with Tīmūr himself. Thus the famous British Museum example of the poems of Khwājū of Kirmān[1] was written at Baghdad in 1396, at a time between the first capture by Tīmūr in 1393 and the second in 1401, when it was in the hands of the Jalā'ir Sultān Ahmad: the *Shāh-nāma* from the Bibliothèque Égyptienne, Cairo (no. 32), was copied at Shīrāz in 1393, probably before Tīmūr's entry into the city in that year. So, too, the *Shāh-nāma* lent by Mr. Chester Beatty (no. 33), with its fellow volume in the British Museum (Or. 2780), containing the *Garshāsp-nāma* and other imitations of the *Shāh-nāma* and dated 1397, was produced at a time when Shīrāz, though submissive to Tīmūr, retained its old social structure.[2] Unfortunately it is impossible to say for whom these two books—originally one volume—were copied. Each poem in the British Museum part is preceded by an *'unwān* of marvellous delicacy. The six columns of small script connect this manuscript with the *Shāh-nāma* of 1393 from Cairo (no. 32); but it represents a great improvement on that volume, which, apart from its present damaged state, would make a comparatively poor show with its badly mixed colours and simple though energetic compositions. Its chief charm is its naïve directness, while its date and provenance make it a document of considerable importance.

The 1397 volume, on the other hand, is most sumptuously produced on thin, highly-polished paper with colours, especially the gold, carefully mixed and finely applied. The line is vigorous and the compositions are interesting and varied. In it, and in the British Museum *Khwājū Kirmānī*, effective miniatures are made by extending the design

---

[1] Add. MS. 18113. Martin, pls. 45–50; Sakisian, figs. 37, 38. The artist, Junayd *naqqāsh*, took his title of *Sultānī* from the Jalā'ir Sultān, and not (as Blochet, *Les Peintures*, p. 265) from Tīmūr.

[2] For Tīmūr's policy towards Shīrāz see Gertrude Bell, *Poems from the Divan of Hafiz*, introduction, pp. 32 et seq.

into the margin of the page.[1] Its production at Baghdad may give this latter manuscript something of a Mesopotamian appearance in its colour-scheme, but it is essentially an Iranian manuscript, as is to be expected of one made at the court of the Jalā'ir Sultān, whose dominions originally stretched over all western Persia. Indeed it serves to show clearly the wide diffusion of a Persian style in the west before the appearance of Tīmūr.[2] It has other claims to attention as containing the first artist's signature, if the Mesopotamian calligrapher-illuminator is excluded, and in its clear drawing of carpets and other textiles of a period from which no actual stuffs survive. This artist, Junayd, is mentioned by Dūst Muhammad in his short history of Persian painting prefixed to the Album in the Serai, but unfortunately with no details.[3] Above all, he shows in his carefully detailed drawing an observation of bird and flower life as intimate as that of Botticelli. In this group of manuscripts from the last decade of the fourteenth century first appear the glowing colours and spring landscapes which are afterwards typical of Persian work, and in them too the artist has found a suitable scale for the figures and a convenient relation between the miniature and the text. It seems evident from this that to the Jalā'ir house must belong the credit of having watched over the development of Persian miniature painting during its formative period. According to Dawlatshāh, Ahmad was himself a painter, which is borne out by Dūst Muhammad, who calls Ahmad a pupil of 'Abd al-Hayy.[3]

But with Tīmūr's sons Shāh Rukh and 'Umar Shaykh and his grandsons Baysunqur, Ibrāhīm Sultān, and Iskandar b. 'Umar Shaykh, we reach the great age of the Persian book. There is no longer any question of detecting foreign influences or disentangling various elements; the whole now forms a perfectly fused unity and expresses to the full the Persian genius. To an eye familiar with the modelling of great European draughts-men or to the masterly summary of the Far Eastern calligraphic drawings, there may seem to be in the Persian miniature too meticulous care in the indication of minute detail. But if the Persian artist drew contours instead of modelling, he arranged his composition so that every line in the drawing should be beautiful in its curve, and he thus built up a pattern which was made more articulate by the skilful use of contrasting colours. These effects were achieved by a complicated balance of warm and cool tones, which, inevitably, sometimes fails. But the brilliance of the colouring is in itself a delight; for at this period great pains were always taken in their mixing, so that they have survived with very little deterioration. Such dependence of the composition on a tonal system throws too great a strain on the colouring for reproduction in black and white, however true, to be fully adequate.

Till recently very few manuscripts of this period, illuminated for the libraries of the

---

[1] This device had already been used in the Istanbul University *Kalīla wa Dimna* (cf. Sakisian, pl. VI).

[2] A further proof of this is to be found in a manuscript of Qazwīnī in the Bibliothèque Nationale (Sup. pers. 332), which dates from 1388 and was also made for Sultān Ahmad (see Blochet, *Catalogue*, no. 814). It is

notable that the miniatures in it approach in style those in the Shīrāz *Shāh-nāma* of 1393 (no. 32). The same high horizon, large plants, and curious tree-formations occur in both (cf. Blochet, *Musulman Painting*, pls. LXVIII–LXXI with our pls. XXIX, XXX).

[3] See Appendix I.

princely house, were known to have survived. Of these two of the most famous were made for Iskandar b. 'Umar Shaykh in 1410–11, a Compendium in the British Museum (Add. 27261),[1] and the Yates Thompson Anthology, now in the possession of M. Gulbenkian in Paris.[2] Both of these manuscripts have miniatures in varied styles, and between them they represent practically every variety to be found under the early Timurids. But recently several other manuscripts of this class have become known and several of them were publicly shown for the first time at the Persian Exhibition. Thus Mr. Chester Beatty's *Gulistān* of 1426 (no. 48), written for Baysunqur, has never been published, and the Bodleian *Shāh-nāma* (no. 46) of about 1420, though known, had not been correctly assigned. The prefatory dedication to Ibrāhīm Sultān has been misplaced by careless rebinding, and consequently had not been noticed by Sir Thomas Arnold, who was led into considerably post-dating a miniature from it which he published in *Painting in Islam* (pl. xxxviii). More important still is the very fine manuscript of the *Shāh-nāma* in the possession of the Royal Asiatic Society, which was known only to a few in the Society, which has owned it for many years, until they sanctioned Mr. Wilkinson's publication of it, which coincided with the opening of the Exhibition at Burlington House. He was able to assign it approximately to 1440. A few years ago the Kaiser-Friedrich Museum was able to acquire an anthology dated 1420 and illuminated for Baysunqur at Shīrāz: this manuscript, from which four pages were shown (no. 45), had then only been published in a note, but has since formed the subject of a full article by Dr. Kühnel in the *Jahrbuch der Preuszischen Kunstsammlungen*.[3] But most unhoped for and of the greatest importance were the two completely unknown manuscripts sent over to the Exhibition by the Persian Government. The *Shāh-nāma* of 1430 (no. 49) has already become one of the most famous Persian manuscripts, while the exquisite *Kalīla wa Dimna* (no. 44) should certainly not rank far behind it. These manuscripts add very greatly to the first-rate material from this period.

It is at once striking that several of these early manuscripts were produced at Shīrāz; the Berlin Anthology (no. 45) and the Cairo *Shāh-nāma* (no. 32) are so inscribed, while it is very probable that the *Shāh-nāma* of Ibrāhīm Sultān at Oxford (no. 46) and the two manuscripts made for Iskandar Sultān, which were made while their owners were successively governors of Fārs, would have been produced at Shīrāz, which was the capital of the province and the residence of the governor. If these manuscripts are compared with the almost contemporary volumes produced at Herāt, such as Mr. Chester Beatty's *Gulistān* of 1426 or the Tehran *Shāh-nāma*, there is not a degree of difference to justify a distinction into two schools. But the priority seems to rest with Shīrāz; while it is possible to detect greater academic unity and less individualism in the Herāt work. A speciality of Shīrāz evidently lay in the delicious, fine illumination of whatever space on the page the calligrapher left unfilled, with freely drawn bird and flower

[1] Martin, pl. 53; Sakisian, figs. 47, 80, 82, 83, 86.
[2] *Miniatures . . . from the Period of Tīmūr*, pls. xiv–xvi; Sakisian, figs. 44–6, 48.
[3] Bd. 52, Heft iii, pp. 133–52.

motives, especially where the verses are written transversely. At the end of the British Museum anthology of 1410[1] and the Oxford *Shāh-nāma* (no. 46) are several pages devoted to this kind of work, in which the illuminator seems to have wished to display his whole repertory : in the former the work is still designed in panels of different shapes, but in the latter it is free; and delicate sanguine birds fly amid gold and silver clouds.

Much more formal, regular, and geometrical is the elaborate patterning used at Herāt, particularly in the Chester Beatty *Gulistān* (no. 48) and a manuscript of Amīr Khusraw from Cairo which is dated 1447 (no. 127 c).[2] Under Shāh Rukh's patronage the intricate illumination of dedications, title-page, and heading ('*unwān*) was brought to its highest development, and the variations, mainly in two shades of blue, green, red-brown, and gold, seem infinite in such magnificent volumes as Mr. Chester Beatty's Qur'ān (214 A),[2] the Tehran *Shāh-nāma*, and, above all, in a universal history in the Serai Library which was made for Shāh Rukh himself (Serai no. 282). This was, of course, generally the work of a separate profession and consequently falls outside the scope of this book; but two examples from the Tehran *Shāh-nāma*, illustrated on Plate XLIII, will give some idea of its quality.

Tīmūr's successor, Shāh Rukh, became governor of Khurāsān with his seat at Herāt in 1397, when he was in his twentieth year. There, and in the growing number of provinces assigned to him by his father, he was practically absolute. He soon showed himself an enlightened ruler and patron. Sir John Malcolm[3] has well summed up his character :

'He desired not to extend but to repair the ravages committed by his father. He rebuilt the walls of the cities of Herāt and Merv, and restored almost every town and province in his dominions to prosperity. This prince also encouraged men of science and learning, and his Court was very splendid. He cultivated the friendship of contemporary monarchs, and we read in the pages of his historian a very curious account of some embassies which passed between him and the Emperor of China.'

Shāh Rukh's reign certainly seems to have been one of the most prosperous periods in Persian history—a prosperity which is fittingly reflected in the manuscripts of unexampled magnificence then produced. Herāt became the unrivalled centre of this Timurid miniature art.

In the miniature painting itself there thus took place an extension of the school, which, as has been indicated, had grown up at Shīrāz, to Herāt, whither all the best craftsmen were gradually attracted after the establishment there of the libraries of Shāh Rukh and Baysunqur about 1397 and 1420. The conclusion certainly seems to be that Shīrāz was at least the principal cradle of the Timurid style: the claim of Tabrīz is, however, definite, though its principal legacy may have been the *nasta'līq* script. The Muzaffarid princes must have been good patrons of miniature-painters as well as of poets, of whom by far the most famous is Hāfiz, during their rule at Yezd and Shīrāz from 1313 to 1393; though there may be nothing, except perhaps the Cairo *Shāh-nāma* of 1393, surviving from the period. At any rate, as has been pointed out by M. Sakisian

---

[1] Cf. Martin, II, pl. 239.
[2] These MSS., which are without miniatures, are not included in the present catalogue.
[3] *History of Persia*, 1815, I, p. 487.

and other writers, one of the main results of the Timurid conquest in the realm of art was to carry the Persian style farther to the east, though its centre was never again beyond the Oxus as it had been before the Mongol invasions. In spite of Tīmūr's well-known interest in Samarqand, the prosperity of Transoxiana, resting on its extensive irrigation system, was never fully restored. Throughout the Timurid period and later there is a complete failure of indigenous or original work in these regions.

When Dr. Martin wrote in 1912 he gave the full praise of tradition to Baysunqur as one of the greatest patrons of the art of the book that the world has ever seen, comparing him justly with René of Anjou; and he quoted (from Dawlatshāh) the passage giving the name of Ja'far al-Tabrīzī as the head of the library staff of forty calligraphers that he maintained at Herāt, but he did not mention by name or illustrate any manuscript from this famous atelier. At that time no material was available. There was indeed a fine copy of the history of Hamza Isfahānī, written by Ja'far for him in 1431, at the British Museum (Or. 2773), but this and a few others are unillustrated.[1] Consequently the appearance of the *Shāh-nāma* from the Gulistan Museum (no. 49) at the Persian Exhibition was of great importance, especially as it was supported by two unpublished manuscripts from the collection of Mr. Chester Beatty, also copied by Ja'far. It is therefore for the first time possible for Europe to get an idea of the work of this school, long so famous in the East.

Baysunqur was the fifth son of Shāh Rukh. He was born in 1399, and died in 1433 of the effects of dissipation and drink at the age of thirty-five, apparently as the result of a fall. He was evidently never very vigorous, and remained at Herāt during most of his life as wazīr or lieutenant to his father, from 1414 to 1432. This was probably in agreement with his own personal tastes, which were essentially social and literary. The court at Herāt is celebrated by Dawlatshāh as a great centre of poets, historians, and scientists. Baysunqur's most famous enterprise was his new critical edition of the *Shāh-nāma*, though this is depreciated by modern scholars. But the preface in his name was generally prefixed to copies of the poem after the issue of the new edition in 1426, and several have representations on the frontispiece of Baysunqur receiving the first copy from the hands of the scribe. One such miniature was reproduced by Sir Thomas Arnold (*Painting in Islam*, pl. VI) from a manuscript dated 1494, but it shows nothing more than a conventional bearded Timurid type, though the attitude is extremely languid. In the Tehran *Shāh-nāma*, instead of this scene is represented a hunting-party in which the principal figure is seated on his horse under a state umbrella. There is little doubt that this represents Baysunqur, in which case it would be a genuine contemporary portrait of him. He has no beard, but a small moustache and a rather weak, puffy face, and holds a wine-cup in his hand. Yet whatever may be his reputation as a ruler and a scholar, there is no doubt of his importance as a patron of the makers of the book.

Almost the only appearance of Baysunqur in military history is in 1420, when it is

[1] There is also a manuscript with miniatures executed for Baysunqur in the Evkaf Museum, Istanbul. Cf. Sakisian, p. 43, figs. 52, 56, 57.

recorded that he captured the city of Tabrīz on behalf of his father from Qara Yūsuf. It may be nothing more than a coincidence that the man chosen as the head of his library staff, which was probably formed at about this date, was a native of Tabrīz, Ja'far al-Tabrīzī, and this seems too slender a foundation for arguing that the Herāt school of painters was an offshoot from Tabrīz.[1] Ja'far himself was a calligrapher, the pupil of 'Abd Allāh, son of Mīr 'Alī of Tabrīz the inventor of *nasta'līq* writing, and not a painter; and the other names given by M. Huart[2] show that the body of forty under him was recruited from places well distributed over the north of Persia. A definite reason for not believing in the paternity of Tabrīz is provided by the condition of the city at this time. Between 1387 and 1420 it was constantly changing hands,[3] as the Jalā'irs were unable to protect it from Qara Yūsuf on the one hand, and the Timurids on the other. Although Clavijo found it still a flourishing place in 1405/6, he remarks that it was not so big as it had been, which probably represents a considerable decay for it to be apparent to a stranger. In fact no illustrated manuscript from Tabrīz is certainly known between the middle of the fourteenth century and the coming of the Safawīs, though the unique copy of Sultān Ahmad's *dīwān* (no. 36) may very well come from there. But too great emphasis should not be laid on this distinction between Tabrīz and Shīrāz: such work as may have been done at the former would have been for the Jalā'ir house which ruled there from 1335 but whose capital was Baghdad. It was at the court of the last of these rulers, Ahmad, who died in 1410, that the British Museum *Khwājū Kirmānī* was copied in 1396. The style in which this book is illuminated must have been practised also at Tabrīz. Both the Jalā'irs and the Muzaffarids were employing artists trained in the Mongol school, and there is no reason to suspect any great difference between the styles of Baghdad and Shīrāz at the end of the fourteenth century,[4] but it was apparently actually the Shīrāz atelier that trained the earliest Timurid craftsmen.

To Shīrāz Baysunqur seems to have turned for the earliest known book illuminated for him, the Berlin anthology of 1420, which was copied there.[5] It has the same simple compositions as the Cairo *Shāh-nāma* and the vigour of the 1397 volume of Epics (no. 33), and, though not so highly finished, there is a greater freedom in the drawing of the best pages (which were shown at Burlington House, no. 45). In some of the other miniatures another hand is visible which is distinctly inferior.

The last of this little group of Shīrāz manuscripts is probably the Oxford *Shāh-nāma* (no. 46) dedicated to Ibrāhīm Sultān, which may be assigned to about 1420 or a little later. It is convenient to include it here, thus breaking the sequence of Baysunqur's bibliophilic progress, because it clearly belongs to the same workshop. Ibrāhīm Sultān was indeed a literary correspondent as well as cousin of Baysunqur, as Dawlatshāh records (p. 351 of Browne's edition), and he probably employed the same craftsmen. No other

---

[1] That such was in fact the reasoning of Dūst Muham-mad may be suspected. See Appendix I.
[2] *Les Calligraphes et les Miniaturistes de l'Orient Musul-man*, pp. 209–10.
[3] See Appendix I.

[4] See above, p. 50, note 2.
[5] And not at Herāt as Kühnel in Springer's *Kunstge-schichte*. See his later article in *Jahrbuch der Preuszischen Kunstsammlungen*, Bd. III, pp. 133–52.

book illuminated for him is known to survive beside the present manuscript, except a *Jāmi' al-sahīh* dated 832/1429 in the Fatih Library at Istanbul (Faizullah, no. 489).[1] This has fine headings but no miniatures. Ibrāhīm is said to have studied the art of illumination under Sharaf al-Dīn 'Alī Yazdī. M. Sakisian (p. 40) was able to correct the information of Lane Poole and Zambaur that Shāh Rukh himself acted as governor of Fārs from 1414 to 1435, by quoting the Turkish chronicler 'Ālī to the effect that Ibrāhīm Sultān governed Fārs from 1414 till his death in 1435/6. The Bodleian *Shāh-nāma* may have been produced at any date between these years. Attention has already been called to the pages at the end with their gold and silver drawings of clouds and birds, which seem to have been a peculiarity of the Shīrāz workshop. The miniatures in the text are highly romantic, and the two full-page miniatures, now bound up to face one another in the middle of the book, between the two volumes of the epic, give for the first time the full effect of the brilliant colouring of the fifteenth century. One of these pages is here reproduced in monochrome and the other in colour (Pl. XXXVIII and Frontispiece). The tiled housewall, and the contrast between cypress, plane-tree, and fruit-blossom, are here made full use of. In the miniature showing the battle of Rustam with the crocodiles a more subdued tone is employed, and the surface of the water is ingeniously varied with several different conventions. In some of the miniatures more primitive features survive, such as the rounded high horizon (Pl. XL A) which recalls the Cairo *Shāh-nāma*, in which it is the general rule. Throughout the book there is a rather marked tendency towards a simple scheme of balance, while as far as possible the scenes are confined to only two planes. In the miniature showing King Gayūmars and his courtiers (Pl. XXXIX A) there is a more subtle pattern of curves, in which, by a pathetic fallacy, the vegetation seems to echo the human gestures and sentiment.

By this date Baysunqur had probably established his own library at Herāt. Dawlatshāh's short account of Baysunqur mentions that he drew his forty calligraphers from all parts, but that Ja'far al-Tabrīzī was at their head. He does not state where they were established, but Mr. Chester Beatty's Sa'dī's *Gulistān* (no. 48) is clearly dated from Herāt in 1426 and signed *Ja'far Baysunqurī*. Mr. Beatty also owns a small oblong anthology (no. 51), dated 1432, signed *Ja'far al-Tabrīzī*. It has very beautiful decorative panels, one of which is here reproduced (Pl. XLII A), but only one miniature, and that a somewhat rough and impressionistic piece of work in a style that seems to have become popular about this date. But the earlier volume by Ja'far, the *Gulistān* of 1426, is possibly the most advanced work of the early Timurid school. Its eight miniatures are in an unusually cool tone, perhaps intended to give a more rarefied effect, which the artist may have thought better suited to a mystical interpretation: there seems to be a good deal of white mixed with the pigments—presumably calcium, as they have not oxidized as they would have done had white lead been used. The experiment is a most interesting one and seems highly successful, but it was not copied. To give greater value to the

[1] Copied by Mahmūd al-Husaynī, who also copied no. 45 for Baysunqur and the Gulbenkian *Anthology* for Iskandar (Kühnel, *Jhrb.* p. 142).

landscape, especially in the sea scenes, the figures are very much reduced in scale, while architectural subjects are introduced as 'properties' to give depth to the scene, and to suggest 'action off'. It would be unreasonable to attack as literary a style developed in the illustration of poetry, or as romantic what is clearly intended to beguile one till lost in an ideal world. Such work has never been better done, and the drawing is too fine and clear for the colour to appear over-sweet.

In the same year that Baysunqur received this small volume he also saw his edition of the *Shāh-nāma* finished. Magnificent as was the copy of this new edition exhibited at Burlington House (no.49), it is evidently not the original, as it is three years later in date—having been finished in January 1430. But in every respect it is a royal volume—the sort of work at a consistently high level which could only be produced by a well-disciplined school. It is therefore idle to attempt to identify several hands in it, though slight differences of style are visible. Among the members of the library staff whose names have survived,[1] only Amīr Shāhī of Sabzawār is mentioned as a painter; while from the account of Shāh Rukh's embassy to China we have also the name of Ghiyās al-Dīn as a painter at Baysunqur's court. But both of these must remain nothing more than names, and an attribution to them can add nothing to Ja'far Baysunqurī's signature in the colophon: he may be taken as having signed on behalf of the whole library staff. This volume must be considered the central work of the early Timurid miniature school. It would make almost everything else produced before the time of Bihzād look amateurish if placed beside it. When the study of the evolution of the illustrations to the *Shāh-nāma* is seriously undertaken it will probably be found that these miniatures often represent the first use of a design. So that, in spite of some apparent lack of spontaneity, the artists of this book were probably brilliant innovators as well as superb executants. The tone of each miniature is well kept and the rich colour is never garish. As has been pointed out, the figures in the *Gulistān* of 1426 (no. 48) are not the main object, so that it is here for the first time that the figures are fully realized in space. The artists have gained such freedom that they do not appear cramped even in the most crowded battle-scenes (e.g. Pl. XLVIII A).

Baysunqur died fourteen years before his father Shāh Rukh, and it is difficult to avoid thinking that during his lifetime he was the most important patron of miniature painting in Persia: the impression given by the Exhibition cannot be altogether accidental. It is noteworthy that it was he who attached the painter to Shāh Rukh's embassy to the court of China in 1420–3. This man, Ghiyās al-Dīn, was ordered to write an account of all that he saw on the way, and this was presented on the return of the embassy to Shāh Rukh. It is in the main preserved by Kamāl al-Dīn 'Abd al-Razzāq in his *Matla' al-Sa'davn*.[2] In his writing he shows great interest in the ceremonies and costumes of the Chinese court and has an artist's eye for details—the discerning praise for the craftsmanship of the Chinese in building, which could not be equalled in his own country. He always

---

[1] See also Appendix I.
[2] Cf. the French translation by Quatremère in *Notices et Extraits*, xiv, pt. i, pp. 387–426.

describes structures, whether tombs or temples, and records the colours of the costumes worn: twice over he mentions the wall-paintings 'of the idolaters' in Buddhist temples which he passed on the route.[1] Although there is no record of his having copied or brought back Chinese paintings it seems highly probable that he may have laid the foundation of that collection which now survives in several big albums in the Serai Library at Istanbul.[2] These are made up in the roughest way and much of the work is of course later, as in the two albums which were sent from that Library to Burlington House. But in some of them, and especially in that known as the *Muraqqaʿ* of Yaʿqūb Beg (no. 1720), much more interesting work of Chinese style is preserved. The big album, which takes its name from the son of Ūzūn Hasan of the late fifteenth century, for the most part might have been formed with the express purpose of illustrating the interest of the Persians in Chinese painting, which is so well attested in the literary sources.

In it there are Chinese paintings which may well be of the early fifteenth century, including some copies of earlier compositions; but more interesting are a number of hybrid works, half Persian and half Chinese. There are Persian figures and buildings set awkwardly in Chinese landscapes, and yet apparently by the same hand; there are some paintings which look Persian at first sight except for their unusually large scale— such as that in the album exhibited at the Munich Exhibition[3]—but which on closer examination prove to be Chinese copies of Persian designs; and there are a number of pages which must belong to the borderlands of Central Asia, through which the Embassy passed on the journey to China. An example in this style, belonging to M. Claude Anet, was shown in Gallery X at Burlington House during the first few days of the Exhibition, but was afterwards removed to the room illustrating influences on the ground that it was not Persian. Ghiyās al-Dīn's account is full of the devil-worshippers of these regions.[4] It was not unnatural that the Buddhists should appear to Muslims in this light, when they saw some of the Buddhist paintings, especially those produced under Tibetan influence. Probably such paintings as those of M. Claude Anet (cf. Schulz, Taf. 31) are caricatures of the inhabitants of those regions, confused with recollections of the frescoes to be seen in their country, especially scenes of the last judgement.

Never was connexion with China closer nor more constant than during the reign of Shāh Rukh, when the chronicles are full of the receipt and dispatch of embassies. In view of this close impact of Chinese influence it is remarkable that the Persian miniature style should have been so firmly established before the invasions of Tīmūr that it was able to resist the fashionable Chinese style. Yet fashionable it must have been, or the court artists would not have troubled to make all these copies now to be seen at Istanbul.[5] But by 1392 the force of Chinese influence was spent. During the fourteenth

---

[1] At Turfan and Kamil (Hāmi).
[2] Especially in *muraqqaʿ*'s nos. 1720 and 47985. At Sedinfu' [identified by Yule with Chʿeng Tong-fu] he admired the landscape and animal painting on the walls.
[3] *Meisterwerke*, Bd. I, Taf. 14; Kühnel, *I.M.*, pl. 37.

[4] *Notices et Extraits*, XIV, p. 389.
[5] At a much earlier date there is a similar instance of court patronage of Chinese art, when the Samanid ruler Nasr II b. Ahmad (913–42) had a *Kalīla wa Dimna* illustrated by a Chinese artist (cf. Blochet, *Peintures*, pp. 191–3). This had equally little permanent influence.

century the Persian miniaturist had assimilated from it whatever he found favourable to his aims. At the beginning of that century he had, on the one hand, the Mesopotamian style with its figure-drawing derived ultimately from Hellenistic Syria; its perspective limited to that arrangement of figures in overlapping profile which seems to have been indigenous to Asia Minor, but its animal drawing enlivened with a more eastern element. On the other hand, in the Iranian work which has been classed as a separate school, mainly confined to the *Shāh-nāma* illustrations, he had a monumental style which seems to go back to the wall-paintings and rock-carvings of Sasanian times and to be connected with the rather later examples of wall-painting in Central Asia. It was a style better suited to the hieratic purposes of the Sasanian kings than to illustration of poems and romances. Though the Persian artist for a time seemed inclined to put much of this aside, and having adopted some of the technical achievements of the Chinese to form a new conventionalized and linear art, yet, in the end, he showed himself able to digest these borrowings, and to retain the decorative spirit and dramatic interest of the earlier styles. He fused the whole into a new style which was not less but more Iranian than the old had been. The high horizon may be a sign of his acceptance of eastern rules of perspective, but even this really represents the return to an older native tradition exemplified in the great Sasanian hunting relief at Tāq i Būstān.

The library of Shāh Rukh has the greatest reputation of any formed in Persia, and yet little material remains from a collection that he must have been constantly increasing throughout the fifty years of his active life (from 1397, when he became Governor of Khurāsān, to 1447, when he died aged 72). In spite of its having been scattered far and wide it is impossible not to think and hope that more volumes from it may yet be traced, especially in the libraries of Istanbul. A large historical manuscript bearing his library seal is in the Serai Library (no. 282): it has already been mentioned as the finest example of illuminator's work.[1] There are only about ten miniatures in it, however, and these not of the first class, though evidently contemporary with the book. But these miniatures, though somewhat dull and stiff, especially in contrast with the exquisite *'unwāns*, are of great interest because they are in exactly the same style as the miniatures in the Bibliothèque Nationale *Jāmi' al-Tawārīkh*[2] and some of the miniatures in the Parish-Watson fragment (no. 28) and in the copy at the Serai described above. Shāh Rukh's efforts to preserve the text of Rashīd al-Dīn's great history have already been mentioned. The stylistic agreement of the miniatures in these manuscripts with those admittedly executed in Shāh Rukh's atelier is an additional proof of their having been copies preserved and embellished by him.

This style, it must now be assumed, was the normal product of Shāh Rukh's library staff. It is surprisingly different from the more finished work done for his son Baysunqur; but it may be imagined that Shāh Rukh taxed the resources of his library with the

---

[1] M. Sakisian gives a reference to this manuscript and dates it 1438, but there seems to be some confusion here as he calls it an 'Attār; and there is no date visible in the colophon. See Sakisian, figs. 50, 54, 55, for the binding.
[2] Blochet, *Peintures*, pls. xiv–xx; *Musulman Painting*, pls. lix–lxiv.

quantity of work he expected from it, which would explain these unfinished manuscripts and the rather hasty and poor quality of the work. The compositions are often good, but the execution is clumsy and the colours less pure. Finally, it is a style far nearer to the ordinary products of the day, which will be discussed later. Distinctive features are the large scale of many of the figures, and the dull earthy pigments, which contrast strongly with the burnished metallic surface of the finest Timurid painting.

There can, of course, be no doubt that such miniatures as these do not represent the finest painting done for Shāh Rukh, at whose court at Herāt was working a painter named Khalīl,[1] who was, according to Dawlatshāh, one of the four marvels of the age— a high compliment indeed to be paid to one of his profession—and 'second only to Mānī'. It is at present impossible to make any attribution to him, unless, tentatively, of the Tehran *Kalīla wa Dimna* (no. 44). The grounds for this would be the existence of another copy, closely connected with it, in the Serai Library (no. 1022). This copy is dated 1430 and would, on stylistic grounds, naturally be attributed to the same school as the Gulistan Museum *Shāh-nāma* of the same year; for it is very similar in colouring and has the same hard drawing and the rather unusual style of rendering trees, especially the smooth plane trunks (cf. Pl. XLIX). Although there is no dedication-page it is therefore natural to suppose that this copy at Istanbul was made for Baysunqur like the *Shāh-nāma*.[2] The Tehran manuscript is certainly the original of the Serai manuscript though the miniatures in the latter are not exact copies.

In the absence of any name or date in the colophon of this manuscript of *Kalīla wa Dimna* from Tehran, or of any dedication, it was difficult to date it at first sight as it was of a type previously unknown. Owing to its high finish and rather minute style it was at first assigned to the period of Bihzād and the end of the fifteenth century. But as a result of more thorough examination and of comparison with other material thus available, by the end of the Exhibition most scholars were inclined to attribute it to the very early years of the century. This date agrees with the style of the illumination; with the rather large scale of the flowers in the landscapes, similar to those in the British Museum *Khwājū* discussed above, and with the marked archaism of the figure drawing, especially as compared with the landscape and animals. If the manuscript is placed about 1410 or a little later, the natural attribution for a book of this quality would be to Shāh Rukh's atelier at Herāt, which would besides be the most likely source for a model copied for Baysunqur.

The miniatures in this manuscript show the finest Persian animal-painting that has survived. They are treated in a lively and intimate way that seems to combine the vivid impressionistic drawing of the Mesopotamian school with a new refinement and attention to detail, and to present a complete natural world into which man alone seems to fit

---

[1] Dawlatshāh, ed. E. G. Browne, p. 340. 'There were four talented artists at the court of Shāh Rukh, who in their time had no peer ... [of whom one was] Mawlānā Khalīl the painter, who was second only to Mānī.' It is impossible to say on what grounds Huart identifies him with Ghiyās al-Dīn, Baysunqur's envoy to China.

[2] This is confirmed by the fact that the scribe signs himself Muhammad b. Hasan al-Baysunghurī, while the frontispiece shows a prince certainly intended for Baysunqur.

rather ill. The Sufic emphasis on the unity of all life has taken the place of the narrative character of the illustrations to the fourteenth-century Fable books. In their philosophy, if the visible world was a mirage of the essentially non-existent, its form was a reflection of the divine reality.

The only other miniatures known of a quality to warrant an attribution to Shāh Rukh's painters are those in the well-known *Mi'rājnāma* in the Bibliothèque Nationale (Sup. turc 190), which have often been reproduced,[1] and the still more famous page in the Musée des Arts Décoratifs showing the arrival of Humāy in the Garden of the Emperor of Chīn (Pl. XLI). The *Mi'rājnāma*, which is remarkable for being written in the Uighur character, is dated from Herāt in the year 1436, so that the attribution to Shāh Rukh's atelier is inevitable. It has many fine miniatures, mainly in blue and gold, which produce a dazzling effect and are well suited to its apocalyptic character—it is a history of the Prophet's journey to heaven and hell. The miniatures are unusually square in shape and are always kept quite distinct from the text, which makes for greater formality. This is still further enhanced by the rigid balancing of the figures in many of the pages. It is a fine manuscript, but not characterized by fertility of invention. In one lighter miniature of the *Mi'rājnāma* two *hūrīs* on dromedaries are naïvely exchanging bouquets of flowers beside a heavenly stream. How different is the exquisite scene in the terrestrial paradise of China, where under a night sky resplendent with stars Humāy first saw the princess Humāyūn, by whose face he has been troubled in dreams. Here the artist has made a drawing of great sensibility and in the small space at his disposal has produced a composition that would not look slight on ten times the scale. He must remain anonymous, though it is possible that other miniatures from the manuscript to which this belonged may one day appear.

Apart from the highly finished miniatures in the volumes prepared for the libraries of the Timurid princes, there are many manuscripts surviving from this early fifteenth-century period, all of them showing signs of conscientious craftsmanship, and all, of course, confectioned for wealthy men. Of these there was a representative gathering at Burlington House, the main interest of which was in the idea it gave of the local peculiarities of style existing and surviving alongside of the metropolitan school. At this time, when one house was dominant in all the big cities of Persia owing to Tīmūr's policy of appointing members of his family to the governorship of provinces, there must have been ready and frequent interchange between place and place of the craftsmen engaged in the various arts, including those of the book. In such cases the more highly skilled are naturally the most mobile artists, so that it is not surprising that there very soon ceases to be any difference between a princely volume illustrated at Herāt and another produced at Shīrāz. But the less-esteemed workers would remain in their places of origin and continue to produce work with a stronger local flavour. There is thus in the British Museum a copy of the original version of the *Shāh-nāma* which formerly

[1] See Blochet, *Peintures*, pls. XXI–XXIX; *Enluminures*, pls. XXXIV–XXXVI; *Musulman Painting*, pls. LXXX–LXXXVII. Sakisian, figs. 49, 53. Martin, pl. 56.

belonged to the scholar and translator Jules Mohl (Or. 1403), which is marked by a stiffness in the drawing and by the considerable use of both earth-yellow and indigo. It is dated 841/1438; and to the same place and approximate date may be ascribed a manuscript of Nizāmī's *Khamsa*, also from a famous owner, the seventeenth-century Swedish envoy Fabritius, lent to the Exhibition by the University of Upsala. This volume has similar colouring, and, in addition to its unusual small, square format, is remarkable for the cloud convention, by which the horizon is striped with bars of white in a way that recalls Rajput India rather than Persia (cf. Pl. LIV). Unfortunately it is not at present possible to fix on a locality for this school.

Yet another book which is illustrated in approximately the same style is Juwaynī's *Tārīkh i Jahān-Gushāy*, dated 1438, part of which is in the Bibliothèque Nationale.[1] Some miniatures from this manuscript from the Claude Anet collection were shown at Burlington House (no. 55). The colouring and drawing is closely similar, though it is a finer manuscript with vigorous work. The *Shāh-nāma* from Leningrad (no. 60), whose provincial origin can alone explain its appearance at a date so late as 1445, has a fine double-page opening, full of movement and in unusual colouring. It is probable that the artist had a freer hand in painting these frontispieces, where he would not have to conform strictly to an iconographic model, but would often have been making a pictorial eulogy of his patron. Less than justice is done to the fineness of this drawing in the reproduction (Pl. LVI A) owing to the colouring and bad condition of the original. In some cases the rather freer drawing and less enamelled surface seem to permit the artist to convey a greater sensibility, as in M. Claude Anet's detached miniature of Majnūn in beggar's disguise at Layla's tent (cf. Pl. LI B).

In all the work of this period the painters appear quite unselfconsciously entering with zest into their inheritance of craftsmanship and the illustration of incidents from the traditional stories. One of the most charming, in this way, of the detached pictures of the period is M. Sakisian's 'Garden Scene' (Pl. LII)—showing two young men beneath fruit-trees full of birds. On the ground of costume, as well as of style, this must be placed quite early in the fifteenth century, when the flowers are still large, the sky of the deepest blue, and the trees formal as well as graceful. But all these examples, attractive as we may find them, must be recognized as the work of mere artisans, compared with the fine style shown in the royal volumes. It is this style which leads on through the Royal Asiatic Society *Shāh-nāma* (no. 67) to the later Timurid work at the court of Sultān Husāyn Mīrzā at Herāt, while the broader manner, after being echoed in Mr. Chester Beatty's *Nizāmī* of about 1460 (no. 69), which preserves something of the same colour-scheme, dies out, leaving no direct heirs.

[1] Sup. pers. 206; Blochet, *Catalogue*, no. 444.

CATALOGUE

30 [539 F] SHAYKH 'AṬĪQĪ'S *DĪWĀN*, copied *c.* 1380. Two illuminated title-pages, one *'unwān* with late Kufic script. Headings in gold, small decorated corners. Dark brown binding. The ornamentation of the title-pages, in which the inscriptions are contained in large circular *shamsas*, is of the finest description, black being effectively introduced. All the pages have diagonal floral ornaments in gold.

> *32·5×22 cm.* ¶ Lent by A. CHESTER BEATTY, ESQ.

31 [457] TWO MINIATURES from a manuscript of about 1390–1400. Probably Shīrāz. The high circular horizon, to which the top edge of the miniature forms a tangent, the ground *semé* with conventional flowers and the forward-leaning figures suggest a late fourteenth-century date.

> (*a*) A giraffe, its keeper, and two other figures. The presentation of a giraffe by the Mamlūk Sultān Nāṣir al-Dīn Faraj to Tīmūr in 1403 is recorded by Clavijo, on whom its strange appearance made a great impression. 21 × 17 *cm.* Repr. *Souvenir*, p. 35.
>
> (*b*) Musicians on horseback. 22 × 15 *cm.* ¶ Lent by DEMOTTE, Paris.

32 [536 B] FIRDAWSĪ'S *SHĀH-NĀMA*, copied, at Shīrāz, by Lutf Allāh b. Yahya b. Muhammad in 796/1393. One decorated page and sixty-seven miniatures, many of them defaced. The pigments have worn badly, but were apparently always rather thin and chalky. In the Bibliothèque Nationale is a manuscript of *Kalīla wa Dimna* (Ancien fonds persan 377) which is very close to this in style—landscape, costume, facial types, grouping, &c. (cf. Blochet, *Enluminures*, pl. XXIX). M. Blochet has placed this manuscript at about 1330, which, in view of this dated manuscript, must be some sixty years too early.

> *36×33 cm.* ¶ Lent by BIBLIOTHÈQUE ÉGYPTIENNE, Cairo.
>
> (*a*) Pīrān, the Turanian leader, cousin of Afrāsiyāb, is captured by the Irānian hero Gīw. Note the hills fantastically represented in the forms of wild beasts, a device afterwards popular in Mughal India.   PLATE XXIX A.
>
> (*b*) The Prince Siyāwush is tempted by Sūdāba, his stepmother, in her chamber. In drawing very reminiscent of the British Museum manuscript of Khwājū Kirmānī of 1396.
>   PLATE XXIX B.
>
> (*c*) The Shāh Kay Khusraw, after travelling with some of his paladins into the mountains, and announcing his coming disappearance, bathes in a spring while reciting Avestan texts.
>   PLATE XXX A.
>
> (*d*) Farāmurz, son of Rustam, slays Warāzād, the king of Sipanjāb, in the war of revenge for the murder of Siyāwush.   PLATE XXX B.

33 [539 C] FIRDAWSĪ'S *SHĀH-NĀMA*. 229 fols. Five miniatures. An incomplete manuscript, lacking the early part of the poem. It originally formed part of a collection of Epics, of which a later part containing the *Garshāsp-nāma* and three other poems and twice dated 800/1397 is in the British Museum (Or. 2780: from the collection of the Comte de Gobineau). It is notable for the extraordinary fineness of the blue and gold '*unwāns*, the minuteness of the *naskhī* script, and the thin highly polished paper. The miniatures, which are certainly by the same hand in both parts, show a great advance in technique as compared with earlier work. The colouring is rich and the pigments are very pure: there is a free use of purple and gold, the latter being used for the ground occasionally, and often for the sky. 1397. ? Shīrāz.

26 × 17 *cm.* ¶ Lent by A. CHESTER BEATTY, ESQ. (Beatty Lib., Dublin, Ms. 114).

(*a*) A combat between the Iranian and Turanian armies. The helmets and armour are of gold, as is the sky. The ground is purple (fol. 38).   PLATE XXXI A.

(*b*) Bahrām Gūr wins the crown of Persia, in ordeal, by seizing it from between two lions, whom he slays in turn with his mace. Khusraw, the rival of Bahrām, sits on his horse biting the finger of astonishment. It is noticeable that Khusraw, here represented as a youth, is described as an old man in the poem. The baggy trousers are peculiar to miniatures of about this date (fol. 151b).   PLATE XXXI B.

34 [450, 451] TWO MINIATURES from a *Shāh-nāma. c.* 1395–1400.

(*a*) Rustam fighting a dragon. Rustam, aided by his horse Rakhsh, is cutting off the head of a magnificent black and gold dragon, which has rudimentary golden wings which betray Chinese influence. The dating is pretty certain from a comparison of the landscape, with its very high horizon and few large-sized plants, and that in the *Shāh-nāma* dated 1393, lent by the Cairo Library. 26 × 24·5 *cm.*   PLATE XXXII A.

(*b*) Bīzhan rescued by Rustam from the well in which he has been confined. 30 × 25 *cm.*

¶ Lent by PAUL J. SACHS, ESQ., through FOGG ART MUSEUM, Harvard University.

35 [468] TWO MINIATURES from a *Shāh-nāma. c.* 1395–1400. Apparently from the same manuscript as the preceding.

(*a*) Kay Kāūs attempts to fly to heaven. 15 × 17·5 *cm.*

(*b*) Rustam seizes Afrāsiyāb by the girdle. 17·5 × 17·5 *cm.* Dimand, *Notes on Persian Miniature Painting, Eastern Art*, 1928, 1; Dimand, *Handbook*, p. 28.

¶ Lent by METROPOLITAN MUSEUM OF ART, New York.

36 [456] SULTĀN AHMAD JALĀ'IR'S *DĪWĀN*, copied at the beginning of the fifteenth century in the lifetime of the author, who died in 1410. Dated 508, which must be intended for 805/1402. The last eight pages have the borders filled with line drawings touched with gold and light colour. (These were shown separately at the Exhibition, mounted and framed.) In the margin of the rest of the volume is a copy of the works of Sa'dī written in 1052/1643.

30 × 20 *cm.* From the library of Sultān Bāyazīd II (1481–1512), whose seal it bears. Martin, *Miniatures from the Period of Timur*, 1926. ¶ Lent by JACOB HIRSCH, Geneva.

The text of Sultān Ahmad's *dīwān* is preserved only in this manuscript. Its date is slightly uncertain as the date is in a different hand from the text; but the fine calligraphy and the floral vignettes are in favour of an early fifteenth-century date, when it would naturally have been produced within the Sultān's dominions in west Persia, either at Tabrīz or Baghdad. So that the later endorsement, 'The handwriting of Mīr 'Alī, mercy be upon him',[1] may indeed be correct, as evidently the famous Mīr 'Alī Tabrīzī was intended.

The problem of the border paintings is even more difficult. But the date of the works of Sa'dī gives a final date, though a late one, before which they must have been executed. On one page (op. cit., pl. VII) the spacing of the text round the swimming ducks shows clearly that the calligrapher of the Sa'dī had to

[1] Martin, op. cit., p. 7.

leave room for the decorative works. There is no break in the text of Saʿdī at this point. It must be admitted at once that such border paintings are unique in Persian art. The universal custom was to leave spaces, at this time usually rectangular, for the miniature, which might indeed extend into the margin, but would not be confined to it. At a much later date gold marginal painting such as that in the British Museum *Nizāmī* of 1539 made for Shāh Tahmāsp was introduced; but the character of this is quite different.

In technique the nearest approach to these drawings is found in the Shīrāz decorations of the very early fifteenth century, developed as vignettes, but used in the British Museum Anthology Compendium of 1410 and the Bodleian *Shāh-nāma* dedicated to Ibrāhīm Sultān about 1420 to cover whole pages. But in composition the present examples are much more elaborate and, above all, far closer to Chinese originals. This would seem to connect them with the fourteenth-century school of Tabrīz in which Chinese influence reached its highest point. In the fragmentary *Kalīla wa Dimna* at Istanbul University, so far as can be judged now that practically all the text has been cut out, the page was arranged in a way not unlike the third illustration in Martin's book, though rather less space was occupied by the text. One may conclude, therefore, that these illuminations are contemporary with the text, were probably executed at Tabrīz about 1400, and would have been cut short by the invasions of Tīmūr. They are in a monochrome style of draughtsmanship, which did not appeal to Persian taste, and was rejected in favour of the highly coloured style of the contemporary manuscript of Khwājū's poems made for Sultān Ahmad with which this has so little in common.   PLATE LXXIV A.

37 [474] PAGE, from a manuscript of *Kalīla wa Dimna*. The lion of Aleppo. *c.* 1400.

18·5 × 13 *cm.* ¶ Lent by R. A. DARA.

Cf. the undated manuscript of the fables in the Bibliothèque Nationale (Blochet, *Musulman Painting*, plates LXVI–LXVII), which would appear to date from about 1400.

38 [460] SEVEN FIGURES under a flowering tree, by a stream with ducks. A miniature forming the left-hand part of a divided composition, of which the central part, representing a king seated on his throne, formerly in the Goloubev collection, is in the Fine Arts Museum, Boston (*Cat.* no. 8 and pl. IV). Early fifteenth century.

17 × 11 *cm.* Burl. Mag., Oct. 1912; Marteau-Vever, pl. 6. ¶ Lent by M. CLAUDE ANET, Paris.

A closely similar miniature from M. Sambon's collection was illustrated in Marteau-Vever (no. 61) and said to come from a manuscript dating from the reign of Shāh Rukh—which is in any case very probable.

39 [462] TWO MINIATURES from a manuscript dated 820/1417.

21 × 14 *cm.* Marteau-Vever, nos. 7 and 62. ¶ Lent by M. H. VEVER, Paris.

(*a*) Gulnār sees Ardashīr from the roof and falls in love with him.
(*b*) The call to prayer from a minaret over a flowery landscape. The text has been cut from the upper right-hand corner.

40 [473] LADY RECLINING ON A COUCH, under flowering tree of archaistic appearance, attended by maidens. Early fifteenth century (?).

18·5 × 17·5 *cm.* Souvenir, pl. 40. ¶ Lent by M. H. VEVER, Paris.

41 [464] TĪMŪR FORDING RA'S AL-ʿAYN. Miniature from a *Zafar-nāma* (History of Tīmūr). *c.* 1425. Probably Shīrāz.

25·5 × 18 *cm.* ¶ Lent by MCGILL UNIVERSITY, Montreal.

42 [539 A] NIZĀMĪ'S *KHAMSA*, with many miniatures. The *Khamsa*, or Five Poems, of Nizām al-Dīn Abu Muhammad Ilyās b. Yūsuf, called Nizāmī, who died

598–9/1201–2, are the most celebrated of all romantic *masnawīs*. This copy was probably made about 1410–20, as can be inferred by comparison with the British Museum Anthology of 1411 (Add. 27261). The manuscript bears an inscription in Persian stating that it contained the library seal of Shāh Rukh; but this seems to have disappeared.

26 × 16·5 *cm*. Marteau-Vever, no. 63. ¶ Lent by M. L. CARTIER, Paris.

(*a*) Sikandar and the Sirens. An illustration to the *Sikandar-nāma*. Sikandar (Alexander), after journeying to the Eastern Sea, goes with a sailor to watch the Sirens, 'brides of the water', who sing their songs, which cause men to lose their reason, by night, but 'when they catch the fragrance of the morning, they dive beneath the dark waters'. A close parallel to this miniature is contained in B.M. Add. 27261 mentioned above (folio 286). PLATE XXXII B.

(*b*) Khusraw, in the presence of Shīrīn, slays a lion with his fist. An illustration to the *Khusraw wa Shīrīn*. The work is good, but rather mechanical and not as brilliant as might be expected of Shāh Rukh's atelier. [These plates are two-thirds the size of the originals.] PLATE XXXII C.

(*c*) Shīrīn and Farhād; an illustration from the romance of Khusraw and Shīrīn. Farhād, the young sculptor, who is madly enamoured of Shīrīn, has been promised by Khusraw that if he will cut a road through the mountain Bī-sitūn, he will obtain Shīrīn as a reward. Farhād has carved on the rock figures of Shīrīn and of Khusraw and Shabdīz his charger. Hearing of Farhād's longing for her, Shīrīn goes to visit and comfort him, but he is so overcome at the meeting that she gives him a draught to soothe his emotion.

Farhād's reputed work is still to be seen in the Sasanian sculptured figures in the larger arch at Tāq i Būstān, near Kermānshāh. The figures, which were probably executed in the seventh century A.D., and which long before Nīzāmī's time were held to constitute one of the wonders of the world, bear a rough resemblance to those in the illustration here reproduced. The lower equestrian figure is doubtless the historical Khusraw, the Sasanian king (A.D. 590–628), but there is considerable uncertainty about the other three. Probably, however, they were intended either to represent Khusraw, Shīrīn, and a Zoroastrian priest, or else the investiture of Khusraw, the other two figures being Ormuzd and Anāhita the water-goddess.[1]

PLATE XXXIII B.

(*d*) The visit of Sikandar to Nūshāba, Queen of Barda'. Sikandar, according to Nizāmī's story, which mainly follows that of Firdawsī, disguises himself as a messenger, but is recognized by the Queen, who presents him with a piece of silk, embroidered with portraits of kings. On opening it, he beholds his own portrait. The passage illustrated relates how he was put to shame at being detected, and the colour of his face became like straw through fear. Nūshāba, however, reassures him, and entertains him to a splendid banquet. PLATE XXXIII A.

43 [721 D] PRINCESS SEATED WITH ATTENDANT LADIES. Early fifteenth century (?).

7 × 10 *cm*. ¶ Lent by M. H. VEVER, Paris.

44 [541 B] NASR ALLĀH ABU'L-MA'ĀLĪ'S *Kalīla wa Dimna*; a Persian book of fables. Thirty miniatures. About 1410–20. Bound in red morocco.

29 × 20 *cm*. ¶ Lent by GULISTAN MUSEUM, Tehran.

Title. The library entry at the beginning, entitling the manuscript the *Anwār i Suhaylī*, is

[1] For a discussion on this point see Sarre and Herzfeld, *Iranische Felsreliefs*, p. 220, and A. V. Williams Jackson, *Persia Past and Present*, chapter xv.

incorrect, the *Anwār i Suhaylī* being a late fifteenth-century version of Nasr Allāh's *Kalīla wa Dimna*.

Date. The manuscript is undated, the colophon being lost, and there is no entry of the scribe's name or the place in which the copy was made. On stylistic grounds it is safe to place the manuscript in the first third of the fifteenth century, and, from the quality of the calligraphy and miniature-painting, it must be attributed to a royal library. The frontispiece depicts a young prince, dressed in green and scarlet, aged twenty or rather less, being presented with the manuscript on a garden terrace. The Prince does not appear, from a comparison with other portraits, to represent Baysunqur, and his identity cannot be established with certainty. The probability is that the whole manuscript was prepared at Herāt.

Paper and writing, &c. The paper is of an agreeable brown colour, considerably darker than is usual. The writing is a *nasta'līq* of great beauty. The *'unwāns*, of which there are several, are very fine; green, gold, and a curious smoky blue are the chief colours, and they are enriched with Kufic writing in white and red.

The text differs somewhat from the lithographed text, but it was not examined in detail.

Miniatures. There are thirty miniatures, one, the frontispiece, being a double-page one. The subjects of the miniatures are as follows:

(*a*) Frontispiece. See above. The contrast between the rather stiff figure drawing and the delightful landscape art of the garden is very marked here, as everywhere in this manuscript. Poplars, *arghawāns*, and other trees and flowers make a marvellous pattern against the golden sky.

(*b*) Barzūya the physician brought before Nūshīrwān.

(*c*) The Prophet Muhammad and his Companions (from the introductory portion of the book). The Prophet is shown conversing with the first four Caliphs, Abu Bakr, 'Umar, 'Usmān, and 'Alī. 'Alī is the figure on the left, with his two sons, Hasan and Husayn, seated behind him. The negro slave in the margin is either Bilāl, the first of the muezzins, who call the faithful to prayer, or Qanbar, 'Alī's servant, bearing his master's famous sword.

An immense golden halo embraces all the principal figures, including the angel. The painting is somewhat damaged, and the Prophet's head has been redrawn, the old lines being still visible. PLATE XXXIV B.

(*d*) The thief captured by a ruse and beaten by a rich man whose house he attempted to rob. The sky on the right is blue, but the garden scene has a golden background. The bed covering is scarlet. There is a much inferior version of this picture in a manuscript of the fables in the Top-Kapu Library at Istanbul (no. 1022). PLATE XXXV B.

(*e*) The bull, Shanzaba, after being abandoned by his master in a swamp, frees himself, and wanders at leisure through the country. The sky is golden, the ground grey and light blue, starred with brilliant flowers. PLATE XXXIV A.

(*f*) The heron, the crab, and the fishes. An old heron, unable, owing to its infirmity, to catch fish, tells a crab that a certain pool is about to be netted by fishermen, and arranges to carry the fish to a safe place. Each day it removes some of them, and devours them in secret. The crab, discovering the heron's wickedness, kills it in revenge. PLATE XXXV A.

(*g*) A snake being killed, through the artifice of a crow, whose young the snake had devoured.

(*h*) The tortoise being carried by the two geese, while villagers gaze upon them in surprise. The geese and the tortoise are drawn in the upper margin, the miniature space being filled by the gaily dressed figures of the villagers.

(*i*) The trial of the jackal Dimna.

(*k*) The falconer's eyes pecked out by a hawk.

(*l*) The fowler and the net in which he catches the pigeons. *Gazette des Beaux-Arts*, Avril 1931, fig. 2.

(*m*) The four friends—the crow, the mouse, the tortoise, and the deer. *Gazette des Beaux-Arts*, Avril 1931, fig. 3.

(*n*) The battle of the crows and the owls. *Burl. Mag.*, Jan. 1931, pl. II, *c*.

(*o*) The wise crow telling the king of the crows of his plan to outwit the owls.

(*p*) The crows burning out the owls. The crows, who have a feud with the owls, burn them out in their cave and destroy them. PLATE XXXVI B.

(*q*) The king of the monkeys throwing figs to the tortoise. The aged king of the monkeys, who has been deposed, climbs into a fig-tree and throws down the figs. COLOUR PLATE XXVIII.

(*r*) The monkey carried by the tortoise.

(*s*) The lion killing the ass. A sick lion, unable to pursue his prey, arranges with a fox who entices an ass within the lion's reach. The lion springs too soon and the ass escapes, but later he is again persuaded to approach. This time the lion kills him. The ground is mauve, edged with pale green. The sky is golden. PLATE XXXVI A.

(*t*) The pious man and the faithful weasel whom he kills by mistake.

(*u*) The rat and the cat who is caught in a trap. A very remarkable painting, all in sombre colours, browns, greys, and mauve—except for a deep blue sky with a single scarlet flower. The bare trees are wonderfully drawn.

(*v*) The king and his favourite bird.

(*w*) The faithful jackal falsely accused by the other animals before the lion-king.

(*x*) The lion and the pious jackal conversing.

(*y*) The lion talking with a jackal.

(*z*) The black and the white pigeon conversing.

(*aa*) The gibbeting of the treacherous Brahman counsellors.

(*bb*) The tiger killing the king's daughter.

(*cc*) The husbandman's son gathering wood.

(*dd*) The old man and the two birds.

(*ee*) The duel between Sikandar and Fūrak. (This episode occurs in the introduction of the Arabic version of the fables.)

45 [467] **TITLE-PAGE AND THREE MINIATURES,** from an anthology of Persian poets in *nasta'līq* script, completed in Shīrāz in 823/1420 by Mahmūd al-kātib al-Husaynī, for Prince Baysunqur's library.

> 24×15·7 cm. Kühnel, *Islamische Kunst*, in *Springer's Handbuch*, Bd. VI, Taf. X; *Jahrbuch der Preuszischen Kunstsammlungen*, Bd. 52, pp. 133–52. ¶ Lent by ISLAMISCHE KUNSTABTEILUNG, KAISER-FRIEDRICH MUSEUM, Berlin.

> (*a*) Title-page and on reverse ex-libris of Baysunqur.
>
> (*b*) Khusraw negotiating with Hurmuz.
>
> (*c*) Khusraw finds Shīrīn. PLATE XXXVII A.
>
> (*d*) The battle between the armies of Khusraw Parwīz and Bahrām Chūbīn. PLATE XXXVII B.

46 [538 A] **FIRDAWSĪ'S *SHĀH-NĀMA*,** written in small *nasta'līq* script. Sumptuously ornamented, with many illustrations. Copied at Shīrāz, about 1420, for Ibrāhīm Sultān b. Shāh Rukh (from 1414 to 1435/6 Governor of Fārs, where he received an Embassy from China in 824/1421), at the same place, and about the same date as the two pocket volumes illuminated for his cousin Iskandar b. 'Umar Shaykh and now in the Gulbenkian collection and the British Museum (Add. 27261). This is indicated by the fact that the manuscript contains in addition to the text of the *Shāh-nāma* a poem in honour of this Ibrāhīm Sultān.

> 30×22·5 cm. Ethé, *Cat.*, no. 501; Arnold, *P.I.*, pl. xxxviii. ¶ Lent by BODLEIAN LIBRARY, Oxford. [Ouseley Add. 176.]

(*a*) The Court of Abu'l-Fath Ibrāhīm. This miniature illustrates the laudatory poem mentioned above. It now forms the right-hand page of a double-page miniature, but this is apparently due to faulty binding (fol. 239ᵛ). PLATE XXXVIII.

(*b*) A garden scene with a man digging; five ladies looking down from an upper story. Forming the left-hand page of the same opening (fol. 240ʳ). FRONTISPIECE.

(*c*) Gayūmars, the first of the kings, who instituted a patriarchal monarchy. He dwelt on a mountain and clothed himself and his followers in leopard skins. The Golden Age is indicated by the lion sleeping peacefully below the rocky throne (fol. 20ʳ). PLATE XXXIX A.

(*d*) Rustam in the sea. The demon Akwān, one of the Dīws, finding Rustam asleep, throws him into the sea. Rustam, though set on by crocodiles, fights his way to shore. The Dīw crouches behind the rock on the left (fol. 172ʳ). Compare the rather similar composition from a manuscript dated 1438, reproduced by Martin, II, pl. LIII. PLATE XXXIX B.

(*e*) The wizard king of Māzandarān, in order to elude capture by Rustam, turns himself into stone (fol. 73ʳ). PLATE XL B.

(*f*) Rustam lifts Afrāsiyāb out of the saddle with one hand. The hero of Irān is represented with the tiger-skin coat and the head-dress made out of a leopard's mask (fol. 63ᵛ). He usually has a reddish beard, to indicate the unusual fairness which has always been regarded as a mark of especial beauty in the East, as in Greece, owing to its rarity. PLATE XL A.

47 [471] THE MEETING OF THE PRINCE HUMĀY AND THE CHINESE PRINCESS HUMĀYŪN in the palace gardens, to which he had been led from the West by a dream. From a manuscript of Khwājū i Kirmānī. Herāt, XV century. Kühnel (*I.M.*, pp. 26 and 55) suggests that it may be by Mirzā Ghiyās al-Dīn, who accompanied the embassy of Shāh Rukh to China. Allowing for the subject, however, the details of the miniature are not more influenced by Chinese example than is usual in Timurid miniatures of the period—probably not later than 1425.

29 × 17·5 cm. Martin, pl. 52; *Meisterwerke*, pl. 16; Migeon, I, fig. 26; Kühnel, *I.M.*, pl. 40. Exh. Munich, 1910; The Hague, 1927, no. 10. ❡ Lent by MUSÉE DES ARTS DÉCORATIFS, Paris. COLOUR PLATE XLI.

48 [127 T, 469] SA'DĪ'S *GULISTĀN*, an ethical work in prose and verse by Muslih b. 'Abd Allāh, called Sa'dī, of Shīrāz (d. A.D. 1291). Copied in Herāt in 830/1426 by Ja'far Baysunqurī. *Sarlawh* (blue and gold), *'unwān* headings (blue and gold). Eight miniatures. Numerous blue and gold line fillings. The manuscript bears the mark of Sultān Baysunqur Bahādur Khān's library. Bound in brocade with red leather edging.

25 × 15 cm. ❡ Lent by A. CHESTER BEATTY, ESQ. (Beatty Library, Dublin, Ms. 119).

(*a*) Sa'dī and his teacher Abu'l-Faraj b. al-Jawzī. 17 × 10·5 cm.
(*b*) Scene before a castle. 20·3 × 13·8 cm.
(*c*) A wrestling match. 20·3 × 13·8 cm.
(*d*) The rescue of a drowning man. 20·5 × 13·2 cm.
(*e*) Girl resisting a king's caresses. 17·7 × 10 cm.
(*f*) Mooring a boat to a tower. 20·1 × 13 cm. Repr. *Souvenir*, pl. 35.
(*g*) A poet attacked by dogs. 16·5 × 13·7 cm.
(*h*) Sa'dī, overcome by the heat, is brought a goblet of iced water by a damsel from a neighbouring house. 20·4 × 13·8 cm. (fol. 36b). PLATE XLII B.

49 [538 B]. FIRDAWSĪ'S *SHĀH-NĀMA*, copied by Ja'far Baysunghurī in 833 /1429–30 for the library of Baysunqur b. Shāh Rukh, and containing the preface written for his edition of 829. Three *sarlawhs*, two *khātimas*. Text richly decorated with different designs set inside gold rulings. Double frontispiece and twenty other miniatures. Bound in embossed and gilded leather with double lacquer border; inside, lattice-work.

38 × 26 *cm*. L. Binyon, 'The Persian Exhibition: Paintings', pl. III, *Burl. Mag.*, Jan. 1931. V. Minorsky, 'Two Unknown Persian Manuscripts', *Apollo*, Feb. 1931. ¶ Lent by GULISTAN MUSEUM, Tehran.

This magnificent manuscript is the most important of all those not previously known in Europe which were exhibited at Burlington House. Executed by order of Baysunghur (for that is the contemporary spelling of his name) four years after the completion of that prince's celebrated preface to the national epic, it represents the high-water mark of book-production at the court of the greatest of all Persian bibliophiles. It can hardly, indeed, be the famous original of the revised copy made in 829/1425–6 by Baysunqur's orders, for which editors of the epic have sighed in vain for the last hundred years. But while we may regret that that original, 'masterfully written, elegantly ornamented, and illustrated by beautiful pictures',[1] has disappeared, there is not the slightest reason to suppose that its format surpassed that of this copy.

A fine copy, as a matter of fact, dated 831 A.H., i.e. two years earlier than this one, is, we have been informed, in private possession at Tehran, containing portraits of the writer, gilder, and artist, as well as of Baysunqur, to whom they presented it. But it is not claimed that the earlier copy approaches that of the Gulistan Museum in quality; and it seems probable that numerous copies of the epic of which the Prince was so enthusiastic an admirer would have been produced for his library. That this copy is the most splendid ever made cannot be positively asserted, but that it is the finest surviving manuscript of the period there can be hardly any doubt. It is in an excellent state of preservation almost throughout.

The manuscript is written in six columns, averaging 31 lines to a full page, in an exquisite early *nasta'līq*. The scribe, Mawlānā Ja'far Baysunghurī, was the head of Baysunqur's library[2] and the leading calligrapher of his time.

The ornamentation is particularly sumptuous, a notable feature being the employment of a rich peacock-green, a custom which fell out of use almost entirely later in the fifteenth century. The headings are usually in gold or white on blue and gold, green, or red and blue ground, and are contained in rectangles. The text is, in parts, enclosed in cloud-forms reserved against a gold ground.

The binding, which is much later than the text, is of lacquered leather, with an inset gold-stamped centre panel and marginal panels.

(*a*) On the first folio is a large circular ornamental rosette, painted mainly in green and gold, bearing the following calligraphic inscription:

QAD ZAYYANTU GHURAR HĀDIHI'L-ABYĀT WA-NAWĀDIRHĀ, WA-RATTABTU DURAR HĀDIHI'L-MA'ĀNĪ WA-JAWĀHIRHĀ, BI-RASM KHIZĀNAT AL-SULTĀN AL-A'ZAM, MĀLIK RIQĀB AL-UMAM, HĀMĪ KHAWRAT AL-ISLĀM, A'ZAM SALĀTĪN AL-AYYĀM, GHIYĀTH AL-SALTANA WA'L-DUNYĀ WA'L-DĪN BAISUNGHUR BAHĀDUR KHĀN KHALLAD ALLĀH SALTANAT-HU.

'I adorned the beauties and rarities of these verses, and arranged the pearls and jewels of these sentiments, for the library of the most mighty Sultān, Lord of the necks of the peoples, Defender of the weak places of Islam, the greatest of the Sultāns of the time, Protector of the Sultanate and of things temporal and spiritual, Baysunghur Bahādur Khan; may Allah perpetuate his power.'

The seal above, bearing the name of Ibrāhīm, is modern, as is shown by the date, 1222 A.H.

PLATE XLIII B.

---

[1] See Nöldeke, *Das Iranische Nationalepos*, § 59.   [2] See p. 54.

(*b*) On the reverse of this folio and on the opposite page is a double-page miniature showing, on the right, a prince on horseback. A red umbrella is held over him by one of three mounted attendants. He carries a cup in his right hand, attendants bring him refreshments, and a harpist, mounted, is playing before him. An elaborate battue is in progress, the quarry being wolves, foxes, deer, a hare, a lion, and a bear, against which a company of horsemen are using clubs, arrows, and swords. The curious custom of combining music and hunting appears to be of great antiquity.

The Prince is clearly intended to be Baysunqur, whose intemperate habits were notorious. He died of drink in 1433. He is here represented as a man of about 30 years of age. The miniature is surrounded by a gorgeous border.   PLATE XLIV.

The next two pages are also elaborately ornamented, and contain an inscription, with Baysunqur's name and titles, while the following two pages, on which is written the beginning of Baysunqur's preface to the poem, are also profusely decorated.

(*c*) A few pages later is an illustration of the well-known episode of Firdawsī's meeting with the court poets of Sultān Mahmūd of Ghazna. The story, which is contained in the preface, relates how Firdawsī arrives at a garden in which the poets were making merry. After meeting with a chilly reception he eventually wins their approbation by his skill in a poetical contest, and is subsequently introduced to his patron's favour.   PLATE XLV B.

(*d*) At the end of the Introduction are two dazzling pages containing the names and titles of the kings of Persia from Gayūmars to Yazdigird, written in white letters in gold circles on an ornamental ground enclosed in a decorative frame. The second of these pages is reproduced.
                                                                        PLATE XLIII A.

The colour-scheme here also is mainly made up of a dark peacock-green and gold.

The other illustrations to the manuscript are as follows:

(*e*) Jamshīd and his artisans (a half-page illustration). The early king Jamshīd divided the people into castes, introduced the refinements of civilization, and taught them the trades, crafts, and professions.

(*f*) Zahhāk, the demon-king, being pinned to Mount Damāwand by order of Farīdūn. The serpents growing from Zahhāk's shoulders were the result of a kiss from the fiend Iblīs, with whom Zahhāk had conspired to murder his father.   PLATE XLVI A.

(*g*) The meeting of Zāl and Rūdāba (a full-page illustration). The love-story of the white-haired Zāl and Rūdāba, daughter of the king of Kābul, perhaps the most charming episode in the *Shāh-nāma*, leads up to the birth of their son Rustam, the chief hero of the epic.

(*h*) Kay Kāūs and the minstrel. When the foolish king Kay Kāūs is seated upon his throne, drinking wine, and boasting of his power, a Dīw, in the guise of a minstrel, is introduced into his presence, and sings a song about the beauties of the land of Māzandarān. As a consequence the king invades Māzandarān, where he is taken captive and blinded by the White Dīw.
                                                                        PLATE XLVII A.

(*i*) Rustam slays the White Dīw. Rustam, before rescuing the king, has to perform seven courses, or feats of valour. The final exploit, here illustrated, takes place in a cave. Rustam's famous charger, Rakhsh, stands by a tree, to which is tied his captive Ūlād.   PLATE XLVIII B.

(*k*) The slaying of Siyāwush. Siyāwush, son of Kay Kāūs, is treacherously slain by Gurwī the Turanian. The murder of Siyāwush, who is the hero of a long tragic episode, is one of the main causes of the bitter feud between Īrān and Tūrān.

(*l*) Rustam pulls the Khān of Chīn off his white elephant. The lassoing and capture of the Khān of Chīn is a prominent incident in the war between Īrān and Tūrān.   PLATE XLVIII A.

(*m*) The duel between Rustam and Barzū. This illustrates a story, fairly frequently found in copies of the *Shāh-nāma*, from the *Barzū-nāma*, an eleventh-century addition, not by Firdawsī, to the original epic. Barzū was the son of Rustam's son Suhrāb, and his story is a weaker copy of that of Rustam and Suhrāb, in which the father and son meet in battle without recognizing each other, and the son is killed.

(*n*) The battle of Gūdarz and Pīrān (a full-page illustration). In this, the last of the series of duels known as the Battle of the Twelve Rukhs, between selected heroes of Īrān and Tūrān, Gūdarz finally slays the aged Pīrān.

(*o*) The battle of the hosts of Kay Khusraw and Afrāsiyāb (full-page).

(*p*) Luhrāsp receives the news of the disappearance of Kay Khusraw. Kay Khusraw, having nominated Luhrāsp as his successor, journeys into the mountains, and disappears from among his companions in a snow-storm. In the illustration Luhrāsp is seated on the Kayanian throne in a pavilion, under a night sky. PLATE XLIX B.

(*q*) Isfandiyār slaying the wolves. The hero Isfandiyār, like his rival Rustam, has to perform seven feats of valour. In his first exploit he is confronted by two wolves, with horns like stags and huge tusks, whom he slays with arrows and sword-strokes. *Burl. Mag.*, Jan. 1931, pl. III B. PLATE XLVII B.

(*r*) Isfandiyār slays Arjāsp in the Brazen Hold. Isfandiyār, disguising himself as a merchant, obtains entrance to the Brazen Hold by a stratagem, slays the tyrant Arjāsp, and rescues his sisters from their captivity. *Apollo*, Feb. 1931, fig. 1.

(*s*) Rustam and Isfandiyār seated together before their duel, in which Isfandiyār is slain. Isfandiyār, who has insulted Rustam by seating him on his left, has a trial of strength with him, each gripping the other's hand. COLOUR PLATE L.

(*t*) Farāmurz, son of Rustam, mourning over the coffins of Rustam and Zawāra his brother, who have been slain by treachery. *Burl. Mag.*, Jan. 1931, pl. III, A. *Syria*, 1931, pl. XXXIII.

(*u*) Gulnār (the name signifies Pomegranate Flower), the slave girl of Ardawān the Ashkanian king, looking down from a window of the palace, sees Ardashīr, and falls in love with him. Gulnār subsequently elopes with Ardashīr, who has been degraded by Ardawān to the keepership of the stables, and he eventually becomes Shāh. An inscription on the palace states that 'this building was erected by order of the Great Sultān Baysunghur Bahādur Khān'. *Souvenir*, frontispiece. PLATE XLVI B.

(*w*) Bahrām Gur, son of Yazdigird, as a young man, is consigned to the care of Munzir the Arab, to whom the Shāh presents a robe of honour. The robe is displayed by two women in the foreground. PLATE XLIX A.

(*x*) The bringing of the game of chess to Nūshīrwān from India.

(*y*) The battle between Bahrām Chūbīn and Sāwa the Turk. Bahrām's host, rallied by their leader, attack Sāwa's elephants, Bahrām himself shooting Sāwa dead with an arrow. PLATE XLV A.

The end two pages are again gorgeously illuminated. The colophon records that the manuscript was completed by order of Baysunghur 'by the feeble hand of the weak Ja'far Baysunghurī' on the 5th of Jumādā the first 833 (=31 January 1430).

50 [458] A KING SEATED WITH COURTIERS IN A CAMP. The double-page frontispiece to a manuscript. About 1430.

49 × 29.5 *cm*. Martin, pl. 54. ❡ Lent by M. H. VEVER, Paris.

51 [715 E] ANTHOLOGY OF ARABIC AND PERSIAN MYSTICAL POEMS, copied by Ja'far al-Tabrīzī in 835/1432. Profusely decorated in gold and colours. Some folios on coloured paper. One miniature: Khusraw's portrait examined by Shīrīn and two attendants. Many stencils with birds, &c., against red or gold ground. Dark brown leather, gold ornament.

17 × 8 *cm*. (oblong). ❡ Lent by A. CHESTER BEATTY, ESQ. (Beatty Library, Ms. 122, fol. 45v).

(*a*) Two ducks on a gold ground among formalized flowers, waves, and clouds. Stencil. PLATE XLII A.

Six pages from a similar anthology are in the Museum of Fine Arts, Boston (Goloubev collection; Coomaraswamy, *Cat.*, no. 21; Martin, pl. 240).

52 [539 D] NIZĀMĪ'S *KHAMSA*. Two decorated pages, two *'unwāns*, seven miniatures. Formerly owned by 'Alī b. Lutf Allāh b. al-Sādiq al-Husaynī in 837/1433.
Later lacquer binding.

> 23 × 16 *cm.* ¶ Lent by M. H. VEVER, Paris.
>
> (*a*) Khusraw, in the presence of his beloved Shīrīn, slays a lion with his fist. The pale colour-
> scheme of the miniatures in the manuscript, in which yellow and white predominate, is notable.
> The tall figures are rather archaic.   PLATE LI A.

53 [466] MAJNŪN, the distraught lover, is led by a beggar woman to the tent of his
beloved Laylā. A miniature illustration to Nizāmī's *Laylā wa Majnūn*. About 1430.

> 11·5 × 10·5 *cm.* ¶ Lent by M. CLAUDE ANET, Paris.   PLATE LI B.

54 [470] THREE MINIATURES from an anthology of poetry by Nizāmī, Jalāl
al-Dīn Rūmī, and others, copied by 'Alī Pākir and Zayn al-Isfahānī between the years
838 and 840/1434–6. It formerly belonged to the library of the 'Ādil Shāhs of
Bījāpur, S. India. It has a magnificent gold frontispiece, adorned with figures of angels,
and is beautifully illuminated with many fine *sarlawhs*. It was probably executed in
Shīrāz or western Persia, and the illustrations have certain stylistic affinities with those
in no. 69. The miniatures shown were (*a*) Sikandar watching two birds; (*b*) Sikandar
at the Ka'ba at Mecca; (*c*) Sikandar in a garden.

> 39 × 26 *cm.* ¶ Lent by A. CHESTER BEATTY, ESQ.

55 [455] MINIATURES from a manuscript of Juwaynī's *Tārīkh i Jahān-gushāy*,
copied by Abu Ishāq b. Ahmad al-Sūfī al-Samarqandī in 841/1438, part of which is
in the Bibliothèque Nationale (Sup. pers. 206) [cf. Blochet, *Catalogue*, no. 444; *Musulman Painting*, pl. XCIV; *Enluminures*, pl. XLI]. M. Claude Anet's portion contains
seven miniatures, that in the Bibliothèque Nationale six.

> 27 × 17 *cm.* (the page). Huart, pls. 1–3. ¶ Lent by M. CLAUDE ANET, Paris.
>
> (*a*) Siege of a castle. 15 × 16·5 *cm.*
> (*b*) Battle-scene. 14 × 12 *cm.*
> (*c*) King in garden-pavilion with musicians and attendants. 19 × 11·5 *cm.*
> (*d*) [472] Rosette with pendant, in blue and gold. 13·5 × 10 *cm.*

56 [461] COUPLE STANDING AMONG FLOWERING TREES. Herāt. About
1430–40. An unusually long and narrow miniature.

> 9 × 21 *cm.* Sakisian, fig. 99. ¶ Lent by ARMENAG BEY SAKISIAN, Paris.   PLATE LII.

57 [539 B] THE *KHAMSA*, or Five Poems, of Khwājū of Kirmān. Dated
841/1438. Kamāl al-Dīn Abu'l-'Atā Mahmūd b. 'Alī, who took the name of Khwājū
(679/1281 to 753/1353), wrote five romantic *masnawīs* and a *dīwān* of shorter
poems. The five poems, which are very celebrated, were modelled on the *Khamsa*

of Nizāmī. The present copy is especially notable for its title-pages and '*unwāns*. Judging from the decorative vignettes, this manuscript might be assigned to Shīrāz. Two decorated title-pages, two '*unwāns*, and ten miniatures. Lacquer binding.

22 × 14 *cm.* ❡ Lent by M. H. VEVER, Paris.

(*a*) One of the two decorated title-pages, with figures of angels, bearing arms and offerings, with flowing draperies. In the centre is a panel with reserved disks in which is written the table of contents. The background is covered with a flowing design of conventionalized foliage.

PLATE LIII B.

(*b*) An illustration of a sea-fight, an incident in the tale of Mihr and Mihrbān, which is a story interpolated in the romance of Nawrūz u Gul, the adventures of Prince New Year's Day and Princess Rose.

PLATE LIII A.

58 [539 E] NIZĀMĪ'S *KHAMSA*, dated 843/1439, with fifty-two miniatures of a provincial school. Formerly in the possession of L. Fabritius, Swedish envoy to Persia from Charles XI in 1684–5.

16 × 12·5 *cm.* Tornberg, *Cat.*, no. 151. Exh. Gothenburg, 1928; Copenhagen, 1929, cat. no. 11. ❡ Lent by ROYAL UNIVERSITY LIBRARY, Upsala.

(*a*) Khusraw Parwīz accused before his father, Shāh Hurmuz, of injuring the crops of a peasant and annoying the people by his revels. From the romance of *Khusraw ū Shīrīn*.

PLATE LIV A.

(*b*) The owner of a garden peeps from a window at ladies bathing. An illustration to a story from the *Haft Paykar*, or 'Seven Images'. PLATE LIV C.

(*c*) The garden of the fairies. A dreamer is carried by a great bird to a garden, whither come, in the night, attendant damsels bearing candles, waiting upon their queen, who takes her seat on a throne. Another incident from the *Haft Paykar*. PLATE LIV D.

(*d*) A statue, wearing a veil, is constructed by order of Sikandar so that the women, from seeing it, may learn to cover their faces. A story from the *Sikandar-nāma*. PLATE LIV B.

The miniatures are unusual in colouring as well as in shape. There is a coarse blue and indigo, and the clouds are drawn in white bars rather like a convention used in India at a much later date. The nearest parallel is with a *Shāh-nāma* in the British Museum which is dated 1438, but which also cannot be assigned to any particular locality. But its provincial origin is supported to some extent by the fact that it still retains the old preface seven years after Baysunqur had brought out his new edition.

59 [539 G] FIRDAWSĪ'S *SHĀH-NĀMA*, written by Muhammad b. Muhammad 'Alī Hanafī al-Shushnaqī in Safar 847/1443. Fourteen miniatures, many in bad condition.

26 × 18 *cm.* ❡ Lent by GULISTAN MUSEUM, Tehran.

(*a*) Prince Siyāwush displays his prowess on the polo-ground before the Turanian king Afrā-siyāb. The colours are rather poor and the gold a thin wash, but the horses are well drawn and the characterization is vigorous. PLATE LV A.

60 [539 H] FIRDAWSĪ'S *SHĀH-NĀMA*, copied in 849/1445, twenty-nine miniatures. Fine highly polished paper. A provincial copy, containing the original preface to the poem.

24 × 16·5 *cm.* ❡ Lent by MUSÉE ASIATIQUE DE L'ACADÉMIE DES SCIENCES, Leningrad.

(*a*) Servants setting a feast. The right-hand page of the opening frontispiece representing a king in *dīwān* in a garden. These pages alone are in bad condition, but this reproduction has been included owing to the unusual character of the composition. Judging from the drawing of the tree-trunks, this miniature was originally intended to be mainly landscape. The figure-drawing is vigorous and the faces of great refinement. The thin paper is so worn that reproduction is difficult. PLATE LVI A.

(*b*) Rakhsh, Rustam's charger, slays a lion. The hero Rustam, in his seven days' journey to rescue Kay Kāūs, encounters seven perils. On the evening of the first day, wearied with his journey, he lies down to sleep in a meadow by a lion's lair. The lion appears and is slain by Rakhsh before Rustam wakes. Very high horizon and pale yellow-green foliage. PLATE LVI B.

61 [580] CALLIGRAPHIC DRAWING (in Chinese taste). Animals (bears, monkeys, lions, deer, &c.) in a landscape. Inscribed: 'Work of the painter Master Muhammad'. xv century. Nothing is known of this artist, but the drawing is similar to those in albums 1719 and 1720 in the Serai Library, Istanbul (cf. Kühnel, pls. 28–32).

24×17 *cm. Souvenir*, pl. 40; *Syria*, 1931, pl. XXXII. ¶ Lent by ARMENAG BEY SAKISIAN, Paris.

62 [721 c] TWO MINIATURES (mounted together).

(*a*) Falcon. Herāt school, second half xv century. 5×13·2 *cm.*
(*b*) Ladies in a garden. Mid xv century, as is indicated by the attenuated figures and style of vegetation. 9×10·5 *cm.* Sakisian, figs. 41 and 102. ¶ Lent by ARMENAG BEY SAKISIAN, Paris.

63 [463] MINIATURE, double page. Garden scene with musicians and dancers. Mid xv century.

16·5×10 *cm. Souvenir*, pl. 37. ¶ Lent by M. H. VEVER, Paris. PLATE LVII.

64 [721] *DĪWĀN* OF KAMĀL KHUJANDĪ, copied by Nūr al-Dīn Muhammad al-Harawī in 980/1572. Kamāl of Khujand, a poet renowned for his piety, died at Tabrīz early in the fifteenth century A.D. Lacquer binding with birds and flowers signed by Muhammad Hasan of Shīrāz. Inserted is a double-page frontispiece with musicians playing in a garden. This probably dates from 1450–60. It has the same exotic vegetation as no. 69 and is also very close in style to no. 63. The right-hand part only is reproduced.

24×15 *cm.* ¶ Lent by R. S. GREENSHIELDS, ESQ. PLATE LV B.

65 [538 c] FIRDAWSĪ'S *SHĀH-NĀMA*, copied in 852/1448 in a beautiful *nastaʿlīq* script by ʿAbd Allāh b. Shaʿbān b. Haydar al-Ashtarjānī, with the earlier preface. Spaces left for miniatures, only one of which is finished, in an inferior style, by no means worthy of the exquisite illuminations. Two pages decorated, text profusely ornamented. Contemporary binding, blind-stamped with animal scenes; flap: inside, lattice-work on gold ground. School of Shāh Rukh, though finished shortly after his death, which occurred in 1447.

35×26·5 *cm.* Ethé, *Cat.*, no. 1977. ¶ Lent by BODLEIAN LIBRARY, Oxford.

66 [459] NINE PAGES from an Anthology (Nizāmī, &c.), written in 853/1449. Profusely decorated with stencils of gazelles and ducks in roundels. Three miniatures, of very rich colouring: rather impressionistic in drawing.

21·5×7·5 *cm.* (oblong). Cf. no. 51. ¶ Lent by A. CHESTER BEATTY, ESQ.

(*a*) Majnūn in the desert.
(*b*) Shīrīn and Farhād.
(*c*) Rustam carried by the Dīw Akwān.

PLATE XXIX-A. 32 (*a*). Pīrān is captured by Gīw. 1393

Plate XXVIII is reproduced in color, following p. 16.

PLATE XXIX-B. 32 (b). Siyāwush tempted by Sūdāba. 1393

PLATE XXX-A. 32 (c). The ritual bath of Kay Khusraw. 1393

PLATE XXX-B. 32 (d). Farāmurz slays Warāzād. 1393

PLATE XXXI-A. 33 (a). Combat between Iranian and Turanian armies. 1397

PLATE XXXI-B. 33 (b). Bahrām Gūr wins the crown of Persia by ordeal. 1397

PLATE XXXII·A. 34 (*a*). Rustam slaying a dragon. *c.* 1395–1400

PLATE XXXII-C. 42 (*b*). Khusraw slays a lion with his fist. 1410–20

PLATE XXXII-B. 42 (*a*). Sikandar and the sirens. 1410–20

PLATE XXXIII-A. 42 (d). Sikandar recognized by Nūshāba. 1410–20

PLATE XXXIII· B. 42 (c). Shīrīn and Farhād. 1410–20

PLATE XXXIV-A. 44 (e). The Bull who has escaped from a swamp. c. 1410–20

PLATE XXXIV-B. 44 (c). The Prophet Muhammad and his Companions. c. 1410–20

PLATE XXXV-A. 44 (*f*). The heron, the crab and the fishes. *c.* 1410–20

PLATE XXXV-B. 44 (*d*). A thief captured. *c.* 1410–20

PLATE XXXVI·A. 44 (s). The sick lion is enabled by a fox to kill an ass. c. 1410–20.

PLATE XXXVI-B. 44 (*p*). The crows burning out the owls. *c.* 1410–20

PLATE XXXVII-A. 45 (c). Khusraw discovers Shīrīn. 1420

PLATE XXXVII-B. 45 (*d*). The armies of Khusraw Parwīz and Bahrām Chūbīn fighting. 1420

PLATE **XXXVIII**- 46 (*a*). The Court of Abu'l-Fath Ibrāhīm. *c.* 1420

PLATE XXXIX-A. 46 (c). King Gayūmars, the first of the Kings. c. 1420

PLATE XXXIX-B. 46 (*d*). Rustam fighting a crocodile. *c.* 1420

Plate XL-A. 46 (f). Rustam lifts Afrāsiyāb from the saddle. c. 1420

جوبرق درخشنده ازتیره میغ چو یافت ش ازجوخت ازگزریخ یک سقف دو شک جنگجوی ریفان بروی اندرآوردوی

هشتم جهاندار کاوش شاه سمی آتش برگرفت آن کیانی کلا ببخش جمان اوروستمای بیامد سبوک رکبان پای

ازان پس جهاندار برخاک ازی سمی کفت کای اودرراپت کوی برین نزه دیوان سبه ترس پاک نزوف آ ببند هاداریاپ

پیام توپیروزی درخت می بمن تازه کن نخت شاسلنشی پوشید از انس پس مظفر سرش بیامد برناسو لشکرست

تش ببنلک اندرآمدبخت زریسن انقلب دیلران پشت دست ما زندران زمانی زنز ازان سوگ نمی خون بجوی اندرآمدجوب

بنیشیر درکه کبه پای خویش جو دروی دو دیو پلان برخاش جوی بروی اندرآورد دوبندروی

جهانجوی گرد ازجهان زریاد شان کشت نزآرانز برسم بلاد برکتخت آپس ودرآمدجوش سواکشت ناواآواد جخسه جوش

وزان پس تهتن کنی نیزه خوات پسوی شاه مازندران بروی یکی نیزه نزد وبرکه بنداوی ذبه ستراندرآمدبپوندارر

شدازجاوز ووبی انش یک لخت گشت ازایران نظاره بروبرکرده

PLATE XLII-A. 51 (a). Decorative design with ducks. 1432

Plate XLI is reproduced in color, following p. 16.

PLATE XLII-B. 48 (*h*). Sa'dī is brought iced water by a maiden. 1426

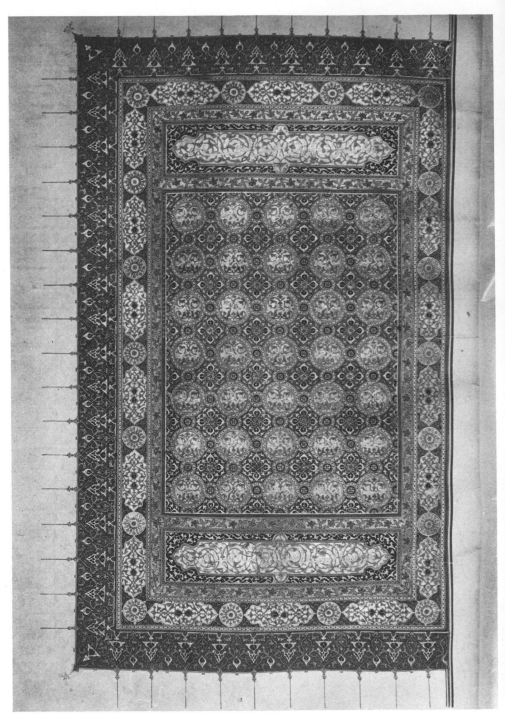

PLATE XLIII-A. 49 (*d*). Table of the Kings of Persia. 1430

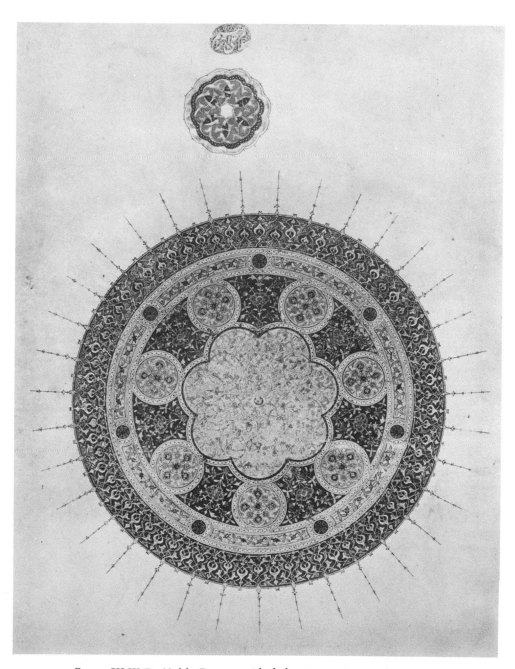

PLATE XLIII-B. 49 (a). Rosette with dedication to Baysunghur. 1430

PLATE XLIV. **49** (*b*). *Frontispiece*. Baysunqur witnesses a battue. 1430

PLATE **XLV-A. 49** (γ). The Battle between Bahrām Chūbīn and Sāwa the Turk. 1430

PLATE XLV-B. 49 (*c*). Firdawsī with the court poets of Ghazna. 1430

PLATE XLVI-A. 49 (*f*). Zahhāk nailed to Mount Damāwand. 1430

PLATE XLVI-B. 49 (u). Gulnār sees Ardashīr from the window. 1430

PLATE XLVII- A. 49 (*h*). The foolish King Kay Kāūs and the minstrel. 1430

PLATE XLVII-B. 49 (*q*). Isfandiyār slaying the wolves. 1430

PLATE XLVIII-A. 49 (l). Rustam pulls the Khān of Chīn off his white elephant. 1430

PLATE XLVIII-B. 49 (*i*). Rustam slaying the White Dīw. 1430

PLATE XLIX-A. 49 (*w*). Presentation of a robe of honour. 1430

PLATE **XLIX-B. 49** (*p*). Luhrāsp hears of the disappearance of Kay Khusraw. 1430

PLATE LI-A. 52 (*a*). Khusraw slays a lion with his fist. 1433

Plate L is reproduced in color, following p. 16.

PLATE LI-B. 53. Majnūn visits Laylā disguised as a beggar. *c.* 1430

PLATE LII. **56**. Couple among flowering trees. *c.* 1430–40

PLATE LIII- A. 57 (*b*). A Sea-fight. 1438

PLATE LIII-B. 57 (*a*). Decorative title-page. 1438

PLATE LIV-A. 58 (a). Khusraw Parwīz accused
before his father. 1439

PLATE LIV-B. 58 (*d*). The veiled statue made by Sikandar
as an example. 1439

PLATE LIV- C. 58 (*b*). Ladies bathing. 1439

PLATE LIV-D. 58 (c). The Garden of the Fairies. 1439

PLATE LV-A. 59 (a). Prince Siyāwush playing polo. 1443

PLATE LV-B. 64. Right-hand page of a frontispiece. *c.* 1450

PLATE LVI- A. 60 (*a*). Stewards setting a feast. 1445

PLATE LVI- B. 60 (b). Rakhsh slays a lion. 1445

PLATE LVIII. 67 (*a*). The Paladins in the snow-storm. *c.* 1440

Plate LVII follows on the next page.

PLATE LVII. 63. Garden scene with dancers. *Mid* XV *century*

IV

THE LATER FIFTEENTH CENTURY: BIHZĀD AND HIS CONTEMPORARIES

ON the death of Shāh Rukh, in 850/1447, disruption followed in the empire which he had tried, with considerable success, to consolidate; the numerous descendants of Tīmūr fighting incessantly against each other, and by their dissensions making it possible for other powers to assert themselves. These powers were, in the first place, the 'Black Sheep' and 'White Sheep' Turkmāns (so called from their battle emblems); the latter of whom ruled, from their capital of Tabrīz, over nearly all Persia except Khurāsān and the Caspian Provinces; and, secondly, the barbarous Uzbeks, whose gradual rise in Transoxiana was to culminate in their invasion and conquest of the dominions of the last two notable Timurid princes, Bābur, first of the Grand Mughals of India, and Husayn Mīrzā of Herāt.

Three cities, above all others in Persia, are associated with the arts of the fifteenth century; Tabrīz in the west, Herāt in the east, and Shīrāz—almost equidistant between the other two—in the south-west.

Tabrīz, throughout most of the century, was the Turkmān capital. Jahān Shāh (1437–67)—builder of the Blue Mosque—of the Black Sheep, and Ūzūn Hasan (1466–78) and his successors (among whom Ya'qūb and Rustam are the most prominent) of the White Sheep, maintained their authority till the coming of Ismā'īl and the foundation of the Safawī power at the beginning of the sixteenth century. Fārs, with its capital Shīrāz—central point of the essential Persian spirit—was lost to the Timurids in 1452, and became part of the Turkmān territory, to which, with a short interlude, it remained attached till their downfall.

Herāt, meanwhile, continued to be the chief capital of the Timurids. It was the scene, at first, of repeated disturbances and of more than one invasion, being contended for both by the members of Tīmūr's family and by the Turkmāns, but from 1457 it was fortunate in being ruled, for nearly fifty years, by two enlightened Timurid princes in succession, first by Abu Sa'īd (1458–68), the grandfather of Bābur, and secondly by Abu'l-Ghāzī Sultān Husayn ibn Mansūr ibn Bayqarā (1468–1506). It was at Herāt, under Sultān Husayn, that painting, and the book arts in general, reached their highest pitch of excellence, in a period which saw the perfect flowering of the Persian artistic genius.

Fine painting can never have been a Herāt monopoly, though, actually, not very many illustrated books of any kind bear clear documentary proof of any but an eastern Persian origin at this epoch. There is a small anthology at the British Museum, written in 1468 (Add. 16561) in far-off Shīrwān, west of the Caspian, with some exquisite

[77]

ornamental headings and a few illustrations notable for the purity of their colouring; but such manuscripts, indubitably produced away from the artistic head-quarters, are extremely rare, throughout the middle and later years of the century. It is a curious fact that details of provenance are almost always missing in cases where a 'western' production is suspected. It is difficult to account for this, considering the known artistic tastes of the White Turkmān rulers. Ūzūn Hasan, who married Despina, daughter of the Christian emperor of Trebizond, kept up a splendid court at Tabrīz, of which a series of Venetian envoys have left admiring accounts. Magnificent buildings were erected, learned men of all kinds were lavishly patronized, and there is evidence that Ūzūn and his successors had caught the prevailing fashion for fine books, calligraphy, and painting. At the Serai Library at Istanbul are two albums,[1] containing many original Chinese paintings, and copies by Persian artists, which once belonged to the Turkmān sovereign Ya'qūb Beg (1479–90). These, however, may have been, as M. Sakisian believes,[2] taken from the Timurid prince Abu Sa'īd, who met his end at Ūzūn Hasan's hands.

An interesting fifteenth-century 'western' manuscript, shown at the Exhibition, is a *Khamsa* of Nizāmī,[3] two miniatures of which are reproduced in Plate LX. This apparently at one time bore the date 868/1463, but the date is now missing, with the colophon. The scale of drawing is fairly large, and the bright colours are of great beauty, but rather lightly painted. (The frontispiece miniatures, since removed from the manuscript (Schulz, pls. 36 and 37), probably date from the fourteenth century.) Especially remarkable is the treatment of foliage, well exemplified in Pl. LX. The unusual facial types recall those of much earlier western Persian art; and at the same time, in some of the miniatures, they prefigure the style associated with Sultān Muhammad.[4] Probably the illustrations are the work of more than one hand.

No. 74, another *Khamsa* of Nizāmī, copied in 886/1481, has several points of resemblance with the manuscript just noticed, both being close akin in drawing and colour. This last-mentioned manuscript too, probably emanates from western Persia, or perhaps Shīrāz.

Even brighter, if less pleasing colour is to be found in other examples, notably a *Nizāmī* in the Cochran collection[5] in the Metropolitan Museum of New York.

No. 70 is again a *Khamsa* of Nizāmī, belonging probably to the third quarter of the fifteenth century, which can also be assigned with some likelihood to western Persia. The colours are strong, and the faces, especially the eyes, are very carefully and expressively drawn in a manner totally foreign to the usual Persian style. There is something European about the facial types.[6] Of great power are the two stray leaves which were found originally inside no. 69, and which probably also belong to western Persia, perhaps to the reign of Ūzūn Hasan, if they are not even earlier. In one of

---

[1] Old no. 37084: new no. 1720.
[2] Op. cit., p. 52.
[3] Cat. no. 69.
[4] As in the Cartier *Hāfiz* (no. 127).

[5] Jackson and Yohannan, *Catalogue of the Collection of Persian Manuscripts* (Cochran collection), 1914, pp. 49 et seq.
[6] Plate LIX b.

these,[1] often reproduced, in which Rustam is depicted sleeping in a marvellous landscape, while his steed Rakhsh battles with a lion, there is an astonishing wealth of fantasy in the richly foliaged landscape, while in another,[2] now at Leipzig and almost equally famous, of a battle exploit of Rustam's, what is perhaps an early representation of the typical Safawī head-dress appears, the Persian warriors having red vertical projections in their helmets, which may be the prototypes of the Shī'a turbans worn under Ismā'īl and his son Tahmāsp.

But the main centre of painting was still in the East, at Herāt.

Of the Herāt miniatures of the middle years of the century something has already been said. If no great masterpiece of sumptuous bookcraft, comparable to the Tehran *Shāh-nāma*, was produced at this time, a good many less pretentious manuscripts, adorned and illustrated with impeccable taste, survive to testify to the further perfecting of a sincerely based tradition of book art. A growing suavity, too, is discernible, in keeping with the themes that were now predominantly pictured, those mysteriously sweet romances of Nizāmī, above all, that were unweariingly illustrated by the miniaturists—as they were endlessly copied by the poets. Such pages as those of no. 66, dated two years after the death of Shāh Rukh, would be difficult to parallel in any age in their delicate richness, and in the harmony of script, ornament, and illustration. Generally speaking, a certain conservatism in drawing combined with an eager delight in colour were the constant marks of the period. Yet the mid-century painters again and again surprise us with new and delightful variations on the familiar models. Garden scenes, especially (nos. 63, 68), have a unique charm of their own which was never quite touched in later times.

Probably the most revealing Herāt manuscript of the 'transition' period is the *Shāhnāma* belonging to the Royal Asiatic Society, dating apparently from about A.D. 1440,[3] and executed for Muhammad Jūkī, one of Shāh Rukh's sons, almost certainly in Herāt.

The miniatures in this manuscript impress at first by their colours, especially the greens and blues; but they reveal, in addition, rare powers both of imagination and of draughtsmanship. Romantic fantasy is given full play, effects of towering heights, of tragic remoteness, of weird unearthly things, are triumphantly achieved. But the most notable advance is in the expression of movement and drama, as in the scenes of Farūd striking down Zarāsp on a hillside with an arrow, of the Paladins in the snow, and of the battle between Gaw and Talhand, where the dying Talhand looks forth from his seat on his elephant, and 'the wind blew cold on his face, and weariness came upon him, for he saw no rest from fighting, and no hope of victory'. This manuscript forms a clear link between the earlier Timurid art and that of the later Herāt school, which is inseparably associated with the name of Bihzād. It has affinities, in some of the miniatures

[1] Kühnel, *I.M.*, pl. 42; Glück and Diez, pl. 507.
[2] Reproduced in colour in Schulz, op. cit., pl. 47; Kühnel, pl. 43.
[3] No. 67. See the separate publication on this manu-script, *The Shāh-nāmah of Firdausī*, described by J. V. S. Wilkinson, with an introduction by Laurence Binyon, Oxford University Press, 1931.

—almost certainly by a second hand—with the work of Baysunqur's painters and even earlier prototypes, but it also exemplifies, still with a certain rude vigour and directness, a new inventiveness which foreshadows a fresh phase of art.

Another fine manuscript, linking the two Herāt styles, is the Persian version of Tabarī's History, dated 1469, belonging to Mr. Chester Beatty, three miniatures from which were shown at Burlington House (no. 71). The treatment is large and spacious, the figure-drawing and colouring strikingly recall the *Kalīla wa Dimna* from Tehrān (no. 44); but at the same time several later features are clearly prefigured, the types of old men, for instance, being very like those of Bihzād's pupil Qāsim 'Alī.

Herāt, under Sultān Husayn Mīrzā, was well fitted to witness the Golden Age of painting. Shāh Rukh, Baysunqur, and Abu Sa'īd had all added to its beauties and amenities; but under Sultān Husayn it attained even greater brilliance, and became the undisputed centre, for the whole world of Islām, of all imaginable refinement. Of several contemporary works containing descriptions of the city, its splendid buildings and gardens, its great men and the life they led, far the most intimate and picturesque is that of Bābur in his delightful *Memoirs*. Bābur stayed there for some weeks shortly before its capture by the Uzbek Muhammad Shaybānī Khān in 1507, and his experiences made a profound impression on him. 'The whole world', he writes, 'has no such town as Herāt had become under Sultān Husayn Mīrzā, by whose directions and efforts its splendour and beauty had increased ten, nay twenty-fold.' 'His was a wonderful age, Khurāsān, and especially Herāt, were filled with men of incomparable talent. Whoever undertook any task, his aim and ambition was to perform it to perfection.' When the princes pressed Bābur with their hospitality he reflected that there could be no place more suitable for him to drink in than Herāt, 'where all the apparatus of luxury and comfort are combined for our enjoyment'. The greatest architectural glory of Herāt was its colossal *Musallā*, with the numerous buildings that surrounded it. To its exquisitely proportioned gateway, and the mellow colours, copper-green, golden-brown, and rich turquoise, of its tiled decorations, every writer alludes with rapture—and now-adays with regret, for nothing but four slender minarets remain of what was once the noblest building in Asia.[1]

Husayn Mīrzā ruled over the extensive territory of Khurāsān from 1468 to his death in 1506. His early career had been adventurous, and he retained his soldierly character and habits. No man of Tīmūr's race was his match, says Bābur, in wielding the sword. Though he was over-fond of the wine-cup, he 'used to abstain till after the midday prayers'. He was lively and pleasant, though hot-tempered, fond of flying pigeons and of ram- and cock-fighting. But he was not all soldier. 'He had a taste for poetry, and composed a *dīwān* in Turkī, many couplets of which are not bad.'

The leading cultural influence in Herāt, however, was the illustrious Mīr 'Alī Shīr

---

[1] 'Words cannot describe their magnificence,' says Dr. Diez, who was quite overawed by their 'fabulous splendour'. (See Niedermayer and Diez, *Afganistan*, 1914.)

Nawā'ī, equally distinguished as a statesman and as the centre of the literary and artistic circle. Musician, poet, and painter himself,[1] 'no such patron and protector of men of parts and accomplishments has ever been heard of'.[2] His vogue was extraordinary, and in compliment people used to call novelties after him, but the poet Banā'ī, who was his rival, when he left Herāt ordered a new pad for his ass, and called it the ''Alī Shīr pad'. The circle presided over by 'Alī Shīr (at least after his withdrawal, about the year 1477, from public affairs) and the illustrious poet and scholar, Jāmī, determined the characteristics of the Herāt school of literature, profuse, rhetorical, and elaborate; though the work of Jāmī himself is, as a matter of fact, mainly free from excesses. This coterie must have been to some extent separated off from that of the lively, rather debauched courtiers whom Bābur describes so vividly. Its tendency was to seek refuge from reality in mystical speculation and romantic art, idealizing and refining upon life, and throwing a mantle of enchantment over the visible world.

It is to this eminent group that Kamāl al-Dīn Bihzād, the most celebrated of all the painters of Islām, must have belonged during his formative years;[3] and the new style of painting, associated with his name, which begins to appear towards the end of the century, is undoubtedly influenced by the standards of that section of Herāt society.

Bihzād's portrait[4] in the Evkaf Library at Istanbul is possibly genuine enough, and in any case it must represent a traditional likeness. It suggests a shy and unassuming, but observant and thoughtful character. That he must have been a capable organizer seems a fair deduction from the fact that in 1522 he was appointed[5] director of Shāh Ismā'īl's extensive atelier of artists, calligraphers, and other craftsmen, and that he was of a friendly and agreeable nature is proved by the terms in which his friend Khwāndamīr alludes to him in the preface to an album.[5] Apart, too, from the 'Alī Shīr connexion, he enjoyed, at Herāt and, later, at Tabrīz, the intimate patronage of four successive rulers, the two last of whom, the Safawid Shāhs Ismā'īl and Tahmāsp, seem to have held him in especial regard. His unique prestige, due in the first place, to his embodying in his work, to perfection, the ideals of his time, was doubtless enhanced, not only by his personal character, but by his association, for many years, with both the intellectual leaders and the great rulers of his age.

It has even been suggested that Bihzād was not as great as his fame, that he was 'written up' by his friend, the historian Khwāndamīr, and that the 'Alī Shīr-Jāmī connexion swelled his reputation unjustifiably. His high position in his contemporaries' esteem is, however, fairly well supported by the testimony both of Bābur and of Bābur's cousin Haydar Mīrzā, who were probably unprejudiced. Yet it is certainly difficult to see in his work

[1] The director of Amīr 'Alī Shīr's library, Hājī Muhammad, was also a painter, in addition to other accomplishments. See the passage from Khwāndamīr translated in Arnold, *P.I.*, p. 139.
[2] Most of the quotations are taken from Bābur's *Memoirs*.
[3] Bihzād died in 1535 or 1536, and cannot have been

very old, therefore, in 1477.
[4] Reproduced in Sakisian, op. cit., fig. 130.
[5] Mirza Mohammed Qazwini et L. Bouvat, 'Deux documents inédits relatifs à Behzâd' (*Revue du Monde Musulman*, vol. XXVI, pp. 146–60, Paris, 1914). The album contained examples of calligraphy and painting, compiled and partly executed by Bihzād.

quite the degree of originality in conceiving new forms or the conspicuous supremacy over all his fellow painters that we should expect from the reputation of a master whose name stands, throughout the Islamic world, for perfection in his art.

Bābur's mention is maddeningly brief, as well as rather puerile. What would we not give for a page or two of further details than the following, from the pen of the most independent and trenchant writer of the day, about Persia's greatest painter while at the height of his powers? All he says is,[1] 'Of the painters, one was Bihzād. His work was very dainty, but he did not draw beardless faces well: he used greatly to lengthen the double chin. Bearded faces he drew admirably.' The only other painter mentioned is Shāh Muzaffar, who died young.

Bābur's cousin, Haydar Mīrzā,[2] is a little more enlightening. Agreeing with what Bābur seems to mean—that no contemporary artist quite equalled Shāh Muzaffar and Bihzād—he praises Bihzād especially for his drawing and composition (*tarh* and *ustukhwān*), and the firmness of his line; 'he is a master painter, though in delicacy of touch he does not come up to Shāh Muzaffar'. It is rather surprising, incidentally, to note that 'delicacy' (*nāzukī*) is not here mentioned as Bihzād's supreme characteristic. Khwāndamīr's allusions to Bihzād are wrapped up in verbiage; but in the documents mentioned above,[3] and in another passage,[4] the qualities of his painting specially noted by this writer are its subtlety and refinement, its enchanting effect, its minute perfection and its 'life-giving' power, qualities which certainly are to be found in what seems most likely to be Bihzād's work.

Apart from the meagre references by Bihzād's contemporaries, a little can be gleaned from the court writings of Mughal times. The early Mughal emperors of India, especially Akbar (1556–1605) and Jahāngīr (1605–27), were both, in their different ways, lovers of painting, and had unrivalled opportunities of studying, in their immense library, the different characteristics of the Persian artists. Their own artists derived much from the Herāt school, and Bihzād's prestige was by this time enormous. Yet Mughal court chronicles and memoirs contain hardly any details about him and his work, many authentic specimens of which must have been easily accessible.

The most curious of these passages occurs in the Memoirs of Jahāngīr.[5] Khān 'Ālam had returned to India from his embassy (1613–18) to Shāh 'Abbās of Persia, bringing various 'beautiful and costly things'. 'Among them was the picture of the fight of Sāhib Qirān (Tīmūr) with Tuqtamish Khān, and the likenesses of him and his glorious children and the great Amīrs who had the good fortune to be with him in that fight, and near each figure was written whose portrait it was. In this picture there were 240 figures. The painter had written his name as "Khalīl Mīrzā Shah Rukhī".[6] The work was very complete and grand, and resembled greatly the paint-brush of Ustād Bihzād. If the name of the painter had not been written, the work would have been

---

[1] Bābur's *Memoirs*, translated by Beveridge, p. 291.
[2] See Appendix II.
[3] p. 81 (footnote).
[4] Quoted in Arnold, *Painting in Islām*, p. 140.
[5] Rogers and Beveridge's translation, vol. II, p. 116.
[6] In the manuscript followed by the translation the last word is 'Savaj'.

believed to be his. As it was executed before Bihzād's date it is probable that the latter was one of Khalīl Mīrzā's pupils and had adopted his style.'

We do not know exactly how much earlier than Bihzād Khalīl was beyond the fact that he worked for Shāh Rukh.[1] Jahāngīr does not seem to have been a very good judge of such matters, in spite of his pride in his critical powers, and it is always unwise to rely on his dicta about Persian miniatures; but the story certainly suggests, first, that Bihzād's style was not essentially different from those of an earlier master, and secondly that he was known at the Mughal court as a painter of battle pictures. The last point receives corroboration from a remark of Evliya Chelebi, the seventeenth-century Turkish traveller. Referring to a certain Turkish painter, he remarks[2] that 'In pictures of battles he may be called a second Bihzād', which may possibly indicate that Bihzād's name was associated with battle themes. The painting of battles and heroes was justified, in Evliya Chelebi's day, in Constantinople, as encouraging beholders to wage the wars of Islam; something of the same notion undoubtedly accounts for the enormous popularity, at all times, of *Shāh-nāma* battle pictures; and no book-miniaturist could neglect such subjects altogether—certainly not the leading court painter of four warrior princes.

The scanty hints provided by contemporary and later writers are not, as may be judged from the quotations just given, of very great assistance in solving problems of detail connected with the later Herāt painting. It is more profitable to consider the paintings themselves in their general character, before approaching the baffling questions of attribution. Though only a fraction of the total number of miniatures which were produced in Persia at this period has survived, we have still many hundreds on which to form impressions and opinions.

Generally speaking, in comparing the best paintings of the age of Shāh Rukh with those of the end of the century, one is struck by an intensification of the distinctively Persian qualities—a pervasive romanticism, a predominantly decorative purpose, love of elegance and finish. Early Timurid painting retains many fourteenth-century characteristics, from which the later work is largely free, though archaistic productions, now as at all periods, appear here and there. In the new painting the handling is more accomplished and there is an advance in the range and disposition of colours, complementary colours being scientifically employed, though the quality of the rich pigments of the middle years of the century was hardly capable of improvement. There is some diminution in the use of reds, and an infinite variety of subtle Watteauesque shades of brown, blue-greys, mauves, greens, and delicate pinks are introduced, with an effective employment of black and pure white. The blues especially sometimes dominate the whole colour-scheme. Compositions are often very elaborate and ambitious, the scale of the figures being reduced, and overcrowding avoided with extreme skill; for the spacing is almost always admirable. And the note of elaboration is continued in the endless ornamental patterns in carpets, canopies, and architectural details. The design tends to be definitely architectural, the feeling for balance, always strong among Persian artists,

---

[1] See p. 59.   [2] *The Travels of Evliya Effendi*, 1834, vol. i, p. 219.

being expressed through new and ingenious relations between the text and the illustrations. Experiments are made in the introduction of varying planes, and diagonal unifying lines are most tellingly used. Signs of perspective, in the European sense, appear occasionally, but there is no obvious Western influence.

In the figure-drawing there is greater diversity of types and attitudes, and a wider command of expressive gesture. The close realism observed in the drawing of animals, trees, and, at times, flowers, is occasionally attempted in the expressions of the human face, but usually the actual faces are expressionless, tradition still holding mainly to the old hieratic rule. Naturalism never extends to a sacrifice of the prevailing decorative intention. Hands and feet are not, as a rule, very carefully drawn.

The broadness of the grand style is seldom attempted, and there is unquestionably some loss of amplitude, but the minuter, suaver manner is better adapted to book-illustration, being perfectly fitted for the themes of mystical romances, lyric love, and the portrayal of the luxury of court life which contemporary taste demanded. The artists seem conscious and proud, as never before, of their world of fastidious connoisseurs.

But, nevertheless, the painting of Herāt in its latest phase does not represent any abrupt break with the past. Many of its formulas are clearly developments from those of the older art; many of its apparent innovations can be found in occasional illustrations dating back to the early fifteenth century or even earlier.[1] Colour and drawing may have greater finesse, but this later Timurid painting grows quite naturally out of what preceded it, just as it leads on to the even richer and more sumptuous style of the Safawīs.

It is always difficult, with the constant interchange of artists from capital to capital, to detect the precise local origin of Persian styles. It is worth noticing, however, that Bihzād, the supposed originator of the new style, is stated by 'Ālī, the Turkish art-historian, to have been a pupil of Pīr Sayyid Ahmad *of Tabrīz*, though Haydar Mīrzā says that Mīrak Naqqāsh[2] (a native of Khurāsān) was his master (*ustād*). Certainly Tabrīz, as the old capital of Persia, must have been the training-ground of great craftsmen from long before Timurid times, and it is probable that through most of the fifteenth century the great capitals continued, in spite of wars and jealousies among their rulers, to influence each other mutually to some extent.

Bihzād must have painted many miniatures during his Herāt period, with which alone we are here concerned, but very few are nowadays accepted by expert opinion as indisputably his. In fact experts differ widely, and often acrimoniously, on this, the central, and probably the most difficult question of Persian painting. The reasons why it is so difficult are several. In the first place stylistic evidence is not enough to go upon. Contemporary writers are not, as has been shown, sufficiently explicit on the differences

---

[1] For instance, the *Khwājū Kirmānī* manuscript in the British Museum, dated 1396 (Add. 18113); or the well-known manuscript of 1410, emanating from Shīrāz, now in the possession of Mr. Gulbenkian, mentioned in the previous chapter.

[2] See below, p. 92, and Appendix II, for this painter —also known as Rūh-Allāh Mīrak.

between Bihzād's work and that of some of his contemporaries to be of much help. It has been already indicated that evidence points to Bihzād being less superior to some at least of his fellows than has been sometimes supposed; especially the evidence of Haydar Mīrzā.[1] Moreover, there is a passing reference by one of Bihzād's contemporaries which is suggestive on this point. It occurs in a supplement to a Persian translation of an account of contemporary poets, originally written in Turki by Mīr 'Alī Shīr,[2] and the author, who was a panegyrist of Shāh Tahmāsp, mentions that one Darwīsh Muhammad, a Turk of Khurāsān, became a pupil of Bihzād, who took the trouble to instruct him in painting after he had entered his service as a maker of oil-colours, and that 'now Master Bihzād entrusts his own work to him'. Bihzād, then, probably made good use of other pupils in the same way, and perhaps signed work which was not properly his. It has to be remembered, besides, that the evidence, in general, of signatures and inscriptions, must be accepted with the greatest caution. Any one who has had to do with Persian manuscripts knows how frequently they present difficult problems, especially, but not exclusively, when they have been in Indian libraries. They are often wrongly dated; miniatures may be much later than the manuscripts which contain them, and vice versa; library officials and owners are not always scrupulous in attaching artists' names to miniatures, while signatures are often forged. Few manuscripts of any value, in short, have altogether escaped the attentions, at some time or other, of the forger, the would-be emender, or the deliberate mutilator. Where Bihzād is concerned, the difficulties of research are particularly great. There is reason to believe that he was not strictly wedded to one style of painting—being able, it would seem, to change his style at will; nor was he, apparently, consistent in the way he signed his name. Probably he did not sign all the miniatures which he painted. He seems to have been the first painter, however, to sign as at all a regular practice, and, perhaps for some reason connected with this, he hides his signatures away in the most unexpected places. They may be written on a book or some other object in the miniature, or between the columns of the text, or in a calligraphic inscription on an architectural façade; or they may be inserted, not by the artist himself, but by the writer of the text—the artist, one imagines, protecting himself from the charge of obtrusiveness under the shield of the calligrapher's greater prestige.

The basis for the study of the Bihzād problem rests, at present, principally on four signed miniatures in the Cairo *Būstān* of 893/1488.[3] The evidence for their genuineness must now be regarded as stronger than that for any other paintings. It may be summarized as follows:

The manuscript, as is obvious from the splendid binding, the exceptionally rich ornamentation, and the quality of the miniatures, is clearly intended as a model of book production, specially designed for Sultān Husayn, whose portrait is contained in the

[1] See also below, pp. 90–1, and Appendix II.
[2] The *Latā'if-nāma* was apparently written in 927 /1520–1. The reference is on fol. 98 of the British

Museum MS. Add. 7669. See also Arnold, *Bihzād and his paintings in the Zafar-Nāmah MS.*, pp. 15–16.
[3] No. 83, pls. LXVIII–LXXI.

[85]

frontispiece, with his name and titles. The text is written by Sultān 'Alī, the greatest calligraphist of the age,[1] and it is natural to suppose that the painting of the miniatures would be entrusted to the greatest artist.

Four[2] of the miniatures actually bear the name of Bihzād, with the modest prefix *al 'abd*, 'the slave'. These signatures, which are introduced with ingenious unobtrusiveness, are quite convincing. Some are incorporated in the contemporary calligraphy on the architecture in the pictures.

The paintings are not only of extraordinary delicacy and distinction, but they correspond closely with the character of Bihzād's work given by his contemporaries.

The inevitable conclusion is that these paintings are by Bihzād. Style, date, signature, occasion, all indicate it. This is his work at the zenith of his Herāt period; and no other known work is so certainly by his hand.

Three miniatures in a little manuscript of the *Khamsa* of Nizāmī at the British Museum (Add. 25900) contain the inscription 'painted by the slave (*al 'abd*) Bihzād' written between the columns of the text. All are perfect examples of the minute style. They are illustrated in Sakisian (op. cit., pl. XLVI). Two of them, of battles, on camels and horseback, in their astonishing rhythm, in their command of dramatic expression and movement, and their intimate feeling for animal life, have never been surpassed in Persian painting, while several others in the same manuscript are probably by the same hand, notably two of Majnūn, in the desert and at the *Ka'ba* at Mecca, the latter[3] a marvellously subtle design in black, white, green, and gold. The manuscript is dated 1442, but this early date is immaterial, for the miniatures which it contains are of various periods, some belonging obviously to the sixteenth century. As M. Sakisian[4] demonstrates, some of these miniatures by Bihzād are clearly modelled on known examples of the early fifteenth century.

The *Būstān* belonging to Mr. Chester Beatty (no. 77), copied in 833/1479, contains eleven unsigned paintings of a very different type from those just noticed. The evidence for their being by Bihzād rests on an entry at the end of the colophon, made by the scribe, 'illustrated by the slave, the sinner (*al 'abd al-muznib*), Bihzād', with a prayer for divine grace on the artist. The miniatures are triumphs of colour, the blues being especially prominent, and the effect is enhanced by the warm-tinted paper, which has perhaps influenced the painter in his choice of contrasting cool colours; but the drawing, though often dramatic and original, lacks the extreme accomplishment of Bihzād's developed style. Hands and feet are indifferently drawn. If these paintings are by him they would seem to be early work. Possibly he was quite a young man at the time. If so, the miniatures in the British Museum *Khamsa* must be rather later. They are much maturer art, but they have some affinity in colouring with these *Būstān* illustrations.

[1] i.e. Sultān 'Alī Mashhadī, or possibly his namesake, instructor of Sultān Husayn's children.
[2] Apparently only two of the miniatures were known to be signed before the manuscript was brought to Burlington House.
[3] Migeon, *Manuel d'art Musulman*, t. I, fig. 34.
[4] pp. 69, 70.

BIHZĀD AND HIS CONTEMPORARIES

The *Zafar-nāma* belonging to Mr. Robert Garrett (no. 84, Pl. LXXII) has been the subject of much controversy, and the late Sir Thomas Arnold has published a special illustrated monograph about it. The manuscript bears the date 872/1467 and was apparently executed for Sultān Husayn Mīrzā, the front page containing an elaborate panel bearing his name. The miniatures, however, are all larger than the written surface, and appear to be subsequent to 1467, having certain characteristics of the work of twenty years or so later. While they are certainly of the school of Bihzād, the only positive evidence of his authorship is the assertion at the beginning of the book by the Emperor Jahāngīr; not, unfortunately, an unimpeachable witness. Alike in the first picture, showing a garden reception by Tīmūr, and in the other miniatures, the construction of the Samarqand mosque, sieges of fortresses and battle-scenes, the painting of these large double-page illustrations is that of a master of remarkable force and varied inventive power: in compositions of great complexity of vigorous movement he diversifies the figures in an endless variety of attitudes without any abandonment of architectural purpose. The miniatures have been partially overpainted, probably in India, and it is a little difficult to judge of the original colouring, especially of the backgrounds. In finish of detail these paintings are inferior to those of the Cairo *Būstān*, but for energy and spirit they are unequalled.

Some of the miniatures in a copy of the *Khamsa* of Nizāmī, at the British Museum (Or. 6810), bear the name of Bihzād. This manuscript, remarkable for the purity and perfection of its colour, is one of the finest Herāt manuscripts known. It was illustrated in 1495 for Mīrzā 'Alī Fārsī-Barlās, one of Sultān Husayn Mīrzā's favourite generals —he is mentioned in Mīrzā Haydar's history. Seven of the most beautiful of the miniatures are signed by Bihzād's pupil, Qāsim 'Alī; all are of Bihzād's school, and the fact that Bihzād's signature is absent does not preclude the possibility of his having a hand in the production of some or all of them. One is tempted to ascribe to him, as sole painter, at least the paintings on folios 27 v. and 135 v., illustrating a scene in a bath and the mourning for the death of Laylā's husband. The disposition of planes, the figure-drawing, the expressive gestures, the wonderful arrangement of blues and blacks, all point to this verdict. The fact that the single word 'Bihzād' is written under many of the miniatures proves, as has been remarked, very little, but Dr. Martin, who has written a monograph[1] on this manuscript, is of the opinion that most of the paintings are from Bihzād's hand, others being possibly finished, from his sketches, by Qāsim 'Alī and other pupils. Other critics do not consider that the manuscript contains any original work by Bihzād. The Mughal Emperor Jahāngīr, in a note, dated 1014 A.H., at the beginning of the manuscript (which formerly belonged to the Mughal Imperial Library), has recorded that out of the 22 miniatures, the work of Bihzād and others, 16 are by Bihzād, 5 by Mīrak, and 1 by 'Abd al-Razzāq. He has made no mention of Qāsim 'Alī. He values the manuscript (he often makes notes of money values) at 5,000 rupees.

[1] *The Nizami MS. . . . .*, by F. R. Martin and Sir Thomas Arnold, Vienna, 1926.

M. Blochet believes that the minute paintings of birds on three folios of *ghazals* by Amīr Shāhī in the Bibliothèque Nationale Supplement persan 1955, copied, as he estimates, between 1480 and 1490,[1] are from Bihzād's hand; also a hunting scene, which he reproduces as well (Arabe 6704). The signatures, of the name Bihzād alone, are written in very minute writing, resembling the writing in the later painting (no. 131), which will be noticed in the next chapter. This most charming manner of painting birds, usually in pairs, to illustrate the lyric poems of Hāfiz, in manuscripts of the period was not apparently uncommon, and it is quite probable that it was invented by Bihzād. A wonderful example of this style was exhibited (no. 97), and there exists a somewhat similar manuscript of Hāfiz, part of which belongs to the British Museum, and part to Mr. Chester Beatty, with Mughal miniatures.

Bihzād's immediate influence, if not his actual hand, may be traced in another splendid manuscript, a *Khamsa* of Amīr Khusraw, dated 1485 (no. 78, Pl. LXII B). None of the miniatures are signed, and though it is natural to attribute to the leading painter of the time co-operation in a manuscript illuminated and illustrated with such careful elaboration, the case for Bihzād is not proved. For one thing it would be surprising, considering the date, if he had not given some indication of his authorship, as in the Chester Beatty *Būstān* of 1478–9 and the Cairo *Būstān* of 1488–9. Enchanting in colour and striking in some cases in their originality as these paintings are, there is perhaps a certain lack of force in the drawing as compared with those—only four years later in date—of the Cairo *Būstān*. The fact that one of them (no. 78 *d*) closely resembles no. 131, which is discussed later, cannot be taken as proof that both are by the same hand. The treatment of the motive is, however, certainly uncommon.

It would serve no useful purpose to detail here the other Herāt manuscripts of the period in which Bihzād's authorship has been seen by various critics, such as the beautiful *Khamsa* at Leningrad (illustrated in Martin, op. cit., pl. 79) which bears no signatures, or the *Haft Paykar* in the Metropolitan Museum in New York, the five illustrations of which, though bearing minute signatures of Bihzād, are now believed, by one who has had an opportunity of studying them closely, to be later copies.[2]

Something, however, must be said of the contemporary detached miniatures which Bihzād is supposed to have painted. M. Sakisian has considered some of these in *La Miniature Persane*, and several of the most interesting were collected at the Exhibition. Among those previously known to us, the portraits of Bihzād's two patrons, Sultān Husayn Mīrzā (no. 89) and the Uzbek conqueror of Herāt, Muhammad Shaybānī (or Shaybak) Khān (no. 88), were placed on opposite walls. In the former, which has been illustrated in both Dr. Martin's and M. Sakisian's publications, the Sultān, looking curiously like Henry VIII of England, is kneeling, wearing a plumed turban, with a dagger at his waist. The portrait is a remarkable one, but the calligraphic inscription, 'the work

---

[1] See *Les Enluminures*, pp. 89 et seq. and pl. XLII; also *Musulman Painting*, pl. xcv. See also *Notices sur les Manuscrits Persans et Arabes de la Collection Marteau* (1923), p. 82.

[2] See Dimand, 'Dated specimens of Muhammadan Art', in *Metropolitan Museum Studies*, vol. I, p. 228.

of the eminent Master Bihzād', is evidently added later,[1] and the same may apply perhaps to the coloured portrait of Shaybānī Khān (Pl. LXXIII B), though here Bihzād is called, as in the Cairo *Būstān*, 'the slave', a word commonly employed in artists' signatures. While, however, it must be admitted that it is difficult to see here the hand of the book-miniature painter of the Cairo *Būstān* and the little British Museum *Khamsa*, to say nothing of the bird-studies noted above, it is possible that Bihzād adopted at this date—for the portrait of Shaybak Khān cannot well be earlier than 1507, when he conquered Herāt—an entirely new style, or abandoned, for the time being, to suit the taste of a ruler whom he disliked and despised, the sensitive drawing and subtle colouring of his more accomplished manner.

Of the fowling scene (no. 99), in which the influence of Far Eastern examples is clearly evident in the lifelike movements of the birds, and the unfinished miniature illustrated in Plate LXXIV B, one cannot feel conviction. Far more probably genuine is the entrancing double-page miniature of Sultān Husayn with his ladies in a garden (no. 81, Pl. LXVII). Here at any rate, in spite of the fact that the colours have suffered, perhaps from the application of some preservative, is one of the masterpieces of Herāt painting, exquisite in technique and feeling. It is difficult to believe that it is a pupil's work.

It is perhaps worth noticing that Sultān Husayn Mīrzā seems always to have been painted in a green dress, as here, in the frontispiece to the Cairo *Būstān* (where also he holds a flower), and in several miniatures in the British Museum *Nizāmī* of 1495, where his portrait has been introduced, after a not unusual custom, in illustrations of the romances.

A well-known painting, sometimes conjecturally attributed to Bihzād, and dating probably from the end of the fifteenth century, is the so-called 'Turkmān prisoner', formerly belonging to the Doucet collection. It was not shown at Burlington House, but has been often illustrated.[2] It appears to be the original of several variations on a popular theme, among which M. Koechlin's fine drawing[3] (no. 160) is the most notable. Underneath the Doucet painting, which is on silk, is written the name of the subject, Māhū Khān.[4] His identity is not known. The meaning of the painting has been much debated, some critics holding that the wooden apparatus in which one of the arms is held is a sling, for support; others that the picture represents a prisoner of high rank, who has been allowed the privilege of retaining his weapons.

Martin considers that the painting is of the captured Murād, the White Turkmān king, perhaps basing his opinion on a version in the Bibliothèque Nationale,[5] which contains the inscription *Kawsaj Murād*, 'Murad the thin-bearded'. This Turkmān ruler was not, as a matter of fact, taken prisoner by the Persians. But the *pālahang* for prisoners, as used by the Mongols, and described by several European travellers, seems

[1] Bihzād especially, who affected the word slave', can hardly have acquiesced in so high-sounding a title as '*Hazrat Ustād*' *Bihzād*.
[2] e.g. in Martin, op. cit., pl. 82; Kühnel, fig. 54; and

Sakisian, fig. 96.
[3] Reproduced in Martin, pl. 83; Sakisian, fig. 97.
[4] The name is not shown in Martin's plate.
[5] Reproduced in Blochet, *Musulman Painting*, pl. 119.

to be the instrument depicted; though it is possible that an Uzbek, rather than a Turk-mān, is the subject of the Doucet painting.

Several well-known drawings of dervishes probably belong to about this period. None of them, however, can be ascribed with certainty to Bihzād.

Before noticing other Herāt artists, mention must be made of an original solution of the whole Bihzād problem which has been put forward by M. Blochet.[1] His suggestion is that Bihzād was a fresco painter, who only occasionally deigned to illustrate books; that he left to his disciples the inferior work of recopying his compositions into the royal manuscripts, and regarded mural painting as the only fitting medium for his talents. The suggestion, which certainly, if accepted, might provide an explanation for the small number of Bihzād's authentic works which are known to exist, nevertheless fails to convince. Why, if the theory is correct, is Bihzād never mentioned specifically as a fresco painter? Painters *are* occasionally so mentioned; for instance, Muzaffar ʿAlī, Bihzād's pupil, is said by Iskandar Munshī to have designed and partly painted the pictures in the royal palace and assembly hall of the Chihil Sutūn.[2] Other painters are similarly referred to. But surely some one fresco by the greatest artist of them all would have been mentioned somewhere in Persian literature if fresco work had been his main occupation. Again, the library of which Bihzād was appointed superintendent was the *kitāb-khāna*, the 'book-house', and when the album of his paintings referred to by Khwāndamīr, and the sample of his work, clearly no mural painting, mentioned by Jahāngīr,[3] are remembered, the evidence, scanty as it is, seems all to conflict with the fresco suggestion. Bihzād may have painted mural paintings, but that he was primarily a mural painter is most unlikely. The best explanation of the scarcity of Bihzād's known work is that only a small fragment of the production of his age has survived.

Mīrzā Haydar Dughlāt, after enumerating some of the chief Herāt artists, remarks 'there are a great many other painters, and so many of them are masters, and proficient in their art, that it is impossible to give an account of them all'. Actually of the twelve contemporary artists mentioned by him, only two or three can be traced in existing paintings. A doubtful example of Shāh Muzaffar's drawing is reproduced in Plate XCV. But fortunately several paintings by a close rival of Bihzād, Qāsim ʿAlī, have come down to us. Seven of these are in the British Museum *Nizāmī* (Or. 6810) mentioned above (p. 87), the signatures being written in the spaces between the columns of the text in the formula 'painted by Qāsim ʿAlī'. Some of these have been partially erased, all, though obviously contemporary, appear to have escaped the notice of the Mughal emperors and their librarians, and their presence does not seem to have been noted before the purchase of the manuscript by the Museum. M. Sakisian has discussed the miniatures in *La Miniature Persane*,[4] and he believes that most of the twenty-two paintings in this manuscript are in fact Qāsim ʿAlī's. The supposition that the signa-

---

[1] See *Bulletin de la Société Française de Reproductions de Manuscrits à Peintures*, 1926, pp. 6 et seq.
[2] The passage is quoted in *Painting in Islām*, p. 141.
[3] p. 82 *ante*.
[4] pp. 74 et seq., and in *La Revue de l'Art*, Feb. 1931 (t. LIX, pp. 87–96).

tures are genuine receives support from the discovery of Qāsim ʿAlī's name in another exquisite miniature of earlier date from the Bodleian (Pl. LXVI, in colour). The signature here is in red, and the formula, *al-ʿabd Qāsim ʿAlī*, 'The slave Qāsim ʿAlī', is different from that in the *Nizāmī*, being the same as that used by Bihzād, but the position between the columns of the text is the same. Ten years separate the two manuscripts, and the artist may have altered his method of signing. The *masnawīs* of Mīr ʿAlī Shīr Nawāʾī, in which this miniature is included, are contained in four manuscripts in the Bodleian, illustrated by eleven paintings, not all of which need necessarily be by the same hand; though they probably are. All four form parts of one series, being similar in size and format, and they were produced for the library of Sultān Husayn's son and joint successor, Mīrzā Badīʿ al-Zamān. The miniatures, of which seven are here reproduced, are brilliantly coloured, and yield little, if anything, in this respect, to those in the Cairo *Būstān*, next to which they were displayed in the Exhibition. They exhibit this artist as one of the greatest and most sensitive colourists in the whole range of Persian painting, astonishingly near akin to his master. In figure-drawing, too, and in the types chosen, especially of old men, there is very little difference between Bihzād and Qāsim ʿAlī.[1] The juxtaposition at Burlington House in fact strikingly bore out the remark of Mīrzā Haydar,[2] that Qāsim ʿAlī was nearly Bihzād's equal (*qarīb i Bihzād ast*). We know too from this author, as we should suspect in any case, that he was actually Bihzād's pupil.[3] Perhaps, if one looks for differences, one can detect them. Bihzād shows greater diversity and elaboration, attempts a greater variety of unusual, lifelike movements. Some of the Bodleian illustrations are rather stiff; they tend to be static and conventional.

Khwāndamīr's references to Qāsim ʿAlī are translated at length in Sir Thomas Arnold's *Painting in Islam*, chapter x. Writing in 1498, Khwāndamīr refers to him as Qāsim ʿAlī, 'portrait painter (*chihra-gushāy*[4]), the cream of the artists of the age and the leader of the painters of lovely pictures'; and he tells us that he learnt his art in the library of Mīr ʿAlī Shīr (not Sultān Husayn, as Arnold translates).

Why Sir Thomas Arnold should regard it as 'rash to identify him' with the artist of the British Museum miniatures is not clear. The signatures of those miniatures, and the very fact that they have been mistaken, both by the Mughal emperor and by later critics, for Bihzād's, leave no doubt of their genuineness.

Qāsim ʿAlī was a pious and learned man, who performed the pilgrimage to Mecca, according to Khwāndamīr; and he subsequently went to live in Sīstān, where he was still alive more than forty years after he had illustrated Mīr ʿAlī Shīr's poems.

Yet another reputed example of this artist's work, from the Gulistan Museum, Tehrān, was exhibited at Burlington House (no. 129, Pl. LXXXVI). It can hardly be genuine; the effective design at any rate has little or nothing in common with his known

---

[1] Compare, for instance, pl. LXVI and pl. LXX A.
[2] See Appendix II.
[3] Compare the identical figures in no. 81 and in the miniature on fol. 190 of the British Museum *Nizāmī*

(Or. 6810). The latter is reproduced in Sakisian, fig. 89.
[4] The same word is used in the inscription on the miniature attributed to this artist in no. 129.

miniatures, though there are certain traces of the Herāt fifteenth-century style in what appears to be, in the main, a later painting.

Haydar Mīrzā[1] and Khwāndamīr[2] both give high praise to Mīrak the painter (*naqqāsh*), whom the former dignifies with the appellation of Mawlānā—which indeed is often applied to the Herāt painters by both writers, a fact which testifies to anything but the degraded status sometimes assumed for all painters in Persia. Whether Mīrak was, in fact, as the Mīrzā says, Bihzād's master seems uncertain, but in any case he must be distinguished carefully from his later, more famous namesake, Āqā Mīrak the Safawī painter. He belonged, it would appear, to a rather older generation than Bihzād, and he died in 1507.[3] The paintings in the British Museum MS. (Or. 6810) to which his name has been added are mostly in a stiffer and more antique style than the rest. The double-page illustration at the beginning is a marvel of impressive richness, and, as Dr. Martin says of it, 'there are few leaves of such beauty in the whole of Persian art'. It is much to be regretted that no absolutely certain work of this painter-athlete (for so Haydar Mīrzā describes him) seems to have survived.

No attempt has been made, in this chapter, to describe every type of the later Herāt painting, but something must be said about the line-drawings. The fifteenth century as a whole, for Persian painting, is pre-eminently the age of colour; at no period perhaps in any country has colour been so profusely used, or with more consummate judgement. Yet line-drawing was, it is clear, extensively practised, if not so extensively now as later; and often, as in such charming examples as the frequently reproduced nos. 145 and 158, the artists reached a wonderfully high pitch of linear beauty and expressive power, precisely perhaps because they were not relying on colour. Whether these were all drawn in Khurāsān or not it is difficult to say. The latest opinion about M. Koech-lin's sensitive drawing of a 'seated youth' (no. 145) is that it represents an Uzbek prince of the fifteenth century; the artist, originally a native of Khurāsān, having worked in succession for two of the White Sheep rulers during the last quarter of the century.[4] Already the custom had started of adding touches of colour and gold to these drawings, with a particularly happy effect. Whether, as has been guessed, Bihzād initiated this type of drawing cannot be determined. There is no particular reason to suppose that he did. Far Eastern practice, with which Timurid Persia became early familiarized, may have suggested the experiment of staking less on colour; and in any case, as has been seen, accomplished masters abounded at Herāt, and Bihzād had no monopoly, presumably, of invention. We do not know positively that he invented anything; he was the greatest, by a little, among many great miniaturists who, in circumstances especially favourable to painters, brought the formulae of their predecessors to a higher perfection of rhythmic grace and refinement, and his fame should be shared by others, from whom his work is hardly to be distinguished.

[1] See Appendix II.
[2] *Painting in Islām*, p. 139.
[3] See also Appendix I.

[4] Sakisian, op. cit., pp. 89–90. We should be inclined, ourselves, to place it in the first quarter of the sixteenth century.

CATALOGUE

67 [475] NINE MINIATURES from a manuscript of the *Shāh-nāma*, copied *c.* 1440 and bearing the seals of the Mughal Emperors from Bābur to Awrangzeb, with an autograph note by Shāh Jahān. The name of Muhammad Jūkī occurs on a banner.

> 23 × 13·5 *cm.* J. V. S. Wilkinson, *The Shāh-nāmah . . . with 24 illustrations from a fifteenth-century Persian Manuscript. With an introduction by Laurence Binyon*, 1931. ¶ Lent by ROYAL ASIATIC SOCIETY.

> (*a*) The Paladins in the snow-storm.   PLATE LVIII.
> (*b*) Isfandiyār kills Arjāsp in the Iron Fortress.
> (*c*) Siyāwush passing the fire test.
> (*d*) Battle between Gaw and Talhand.
> (*e*) Rescue of Bīzhan by Rustam.
> (*f*) Gushtāsp slays a dragon.
> (*g*) Farūd slays Zarāsp in Mount Sapad.
> (*h*) Siege of Kang-bihisht.
> (*i*) Meeting of Rustam and Tahmīna.

68 [540 D] HĀFIZ' *DĪWĀN*, copied *c.* 1435–50. Muhammad Hāfiz of Shīrāz (d. 1389) is universally acknowledged to be the greatest of the Persian lyric poets. Two *'unwāns*, four miniatures. Black leather binding, gold-stamped; inside, lattice-work, brown, blue, and gold.

> 20 × 10 *cm.* ¶ Lent by A. CHESTER BEATTY, ESQ. (Beatty Lib., Dublin, Ms. 146).

> (*a*) Ladies in a Garden. The verses may be translated: 'My soul was consumed in longing to achieve the heart's purpose|And I burned in this vain desire.' An unusually simple and monumental design (fol. 82b).   PLATE LIX A.

69 [540 C] NIZĀMĪ'S *KHAMSA*, copied about 1460; twenty-three miniatures. Isfahān (?). Formerly in the Schulz and Goloubev collections.

> 32 × 21·5 *cm.* Schulz, pls. 38–46. ¶ Lent by A. CHESTER BEATTY, ESQ. (Beatty Lib., Ms. 137).

> (*a*) Khusraw Parwīz is accused before his father, the Shāh Hurmuz, of unruly behaviour. The elders intercede on his behalf (fol. 31a).   PLATE LX A.
> (*b*) Majnūn watches the battle between the hosts of his friend Nawfal and the family of Laylā his beloved (fol. 106v).   PLATE LX B.

> This was previously dated, according to Blochet, 866/1461, and written at Isfahān (cf. Blochet, *Peintures*, p. 165 and note). According to Schulz, who once owned it, the manuscript was copied by Darwīsh 'Abd Allāh of Isfahān in 868/1463. The book has since been re-bound and now lacks the beginning, including the frontispiece reproduced by Schulz (Taf. 36 and 37), and the end, containing the colophon, which may have belonged to the *Amīr Khusraw* with which the *Nizāmī* was bound up. The whole then contained thirty-six miniatures.

70 [540 B] NIZĀMĪ'S *KHAMSA*, the whole of the text on gold background. Six decorated pages, small titles in gold. Fourteen miniatures. Probably 3rd quarter of XV century. Western Persia. Modern Bukhārā brown leather binding, which is signed by Mullā Sharīf Kashgharī, and dated 1276/1859.

> 21·5 × 14 *cm.* ¶ Lent by A. CHESTER BEATTY, ESQ. (Beatty Lib., Dublin, Ms. 141).

(*a*) Majnūn watching the fight between the partisans of his friend Nawfal and the tribesmen of Laylā (fol. 136v). PLATE LIX B.

The curiously careful and expressive drawing of the eyes to be seen in this miniature is characteristic of the manuscript as a whole.

71 [476] THREE MINIATURES from Tabarī's *Annals*. Persian translation copied by Badī' al-Zamān in 874/1469. An important manuscript of the Herāt school middle period, the miniatures being remarkable for the spaciousness of their designs and fine colouring.

35·5 × 24·5 *cm.* ¶ Lent by A. CHESTER BEATTY, ESQ.

(*a*) Jamshīd directing armour-making, weaving, &c. *Souvenir*, pl. 39.
(*b*) Contest between Moses and the sorcerers before Pharaoh.
(*c*) Bahrām Gūr killing a lion and a wild ass.

72 [414 D] SIX MINIATURES from an Anthology written by Sultān 'Alī of Mashhad in 880/1475. Doubtless Herāt. These little miniatures, exquisite in quality, are rather simple in design, and might from their appearance be much earlier than the manuscript. Some of the types and motives bear some resemblance to those in no. 69. The mellow colouring is of extreme beauty, gold and green predominating.

16 × 10·5 *cm.* ¶ Lent by A. CHESTER BEATTY, ESQ.

73 [477] MINIATURES from a *Shāh-nāma*, copied by Muhammad Baqqāl in 855/1480. A typical example of the survival of the archaic style, as in the British Museum *Shāh-nāma* of 891/1486 (Add. 18188). Possibly of Shīrāz.

23·3 × 15·8 *cm.* ¶ Lent by A. CHESTER BEATTY, ESQ.

(*a*) Jamshīd and the first craftsmen.
(*b*) Polo scene.

74 [498 and 541 E] NIZĀMĪ'S *KHAMSA*, copied by Murshid in 886/1481. One *sarlawh*, five *'unwāns*, twenty-five miniatures, of which those representing the pavilions in which Bahrām Gūr was entertained by the princesses were exhibited separately.

21 × 15 *cm.* ¶ Lent by A. CHESTER BEATTY, ESQ.

(*a*) The Yellow Pavilion of the Moorish Princess.
(*b*) The Green Pavilion of the Tartar Princess.
(*c*) The Red Pavilion of the Slav Princess.
(*d*) The Blue Pavilion of the Persian Princess.
(*e*) The Sandal-wood Pavilion of the Chinese Princess.
(*f*) The White Pavilion of the Byzantine Princess.

75 [559] HORSEMEN SHOOTING LION. A brightly coloured drawing in red and blue on a plain ground. The style is similar to that of some drawings in the *muraqqa'* 1720 in the Serai Library which are signed 'Ya'qūbī'. It may therefore be attributed to the Turkmān school of the second half of the fifteenth century.

20 × 13 *cm.* Sakisian, fig. 98. ¶ Lent by ARMENAG BEY SAKISIAN, Paris.

76 [503] DISCOVERY OF THE FOUNTAIN OF LIFE. Page from Nizāmī's *Sikandar-nāma*. Herāt school, second half xv century.

13·5×16 *cm.* Sakisian, frontispiece. ¶ Lent by ARMENAG BEY SAKISIAN, Paris.   PLATE LXI A.

The story is said by Nizāmī to be that related by the 'elders of Rūm'. According to this, Elias and Khizr came together to the Water of Life and prepared a meal by its side. A salted fish fell into the water, which restored it to life. In Nizāmī's story Sikandar (Alexander the Great) goes with the Prophet Khizr to seek the Water of Life: Khizr finds it, but Sikandar is unsuccessful.

77 [480] MINIATURES from a manuscript of Sa'dī's *Būstān*, an ethical poem. Copied by Mīr Shaykh Muhammad b. Shaykh Ahmad in 883/1478–9. Eleven miniatures attributed to Bihzād in the colophon in these words: 'Painted by the slave, the criminal, Bihzād—may God better his condition.'

27·5×18 *cm.* ¶ Lent by A. CHESTER BEATTY, ESQ. (Beatty Library, Dublin, Ms. 156).

(*a*) A saint riding on a tiger and holding a snake.
(*b*) A prince on his throne giving judgement.
(*c*) A man sawing off the branch on which he is seated. The owner of the garden observes: 'If he does harm, he does it to himself and not to me' (fol. 28).   PLATE LXII A.
(*d*) Abraham and an old fire-worshipper. Arnold, *P.I.*, pl. xxx.
(*e*) Majnūn in conversation with a friend.
(*f*) Men in a boat and a holy man standing on the water.
(*g*) Jesus speaking with the devout man and the sinner. Arnold, *P.I.*, pl. xxvi.
(*h*) Prince on his throne with attendants.
(*i*) Story of the archer and the prisoner.
(*k*) A *Sūfī* carried by his accuser on his back.
(*l*) A drunkard in a mosque.

78 [120 B] AMĪR KHUSRAW'S *KHAMSA* (five poems), copied by Muhammad b. Azhar in 890/1485. Sumptuous sixteenth-century gilt leather binding, with animal and arabesque ornament: inside, lattice-work. Dedication-page with inscription illegible. Two fine '*unwāns, sarlawhs*, and rosettes.

25×16·5 *cm.* Martin, II, pls. 75–8; Martin, *Les Miniatures de Bihzad dans un MS. persan, daté de 1485,* Munich, 1912 (22 plates). ¶ Lent by A. CHESTER BEATTY, ESQ. (Beatty Lib., Ms. 163).

[478] Thirteen miniatures attributed to Bihzād:
(*a*) Dervishes dancing in the presence of Nizām al-Dīn Awliyā.
(*b*) A prince and a hermit.
(*c*) Execution of a fratricide.
(*d*) A dervish and a youth in a spring landscape.
(*e*) Shīrīn receiving Khusraw in her palace (fol. 54).   PLATE LXII B.
(*f*) Farhād's death.
(*g*) Khusraw and Shīrīn enjoying music.
(*h*) Majnūn's birth celebrated by his father and mother.
(*i*) The Arab King Nawfal attacks Laylā's tribe.
(*k*) Laylā visiting Majnūn.
(*l*) Bahrām Gūr with the Indian princess.
(*m*) The parrot's evidence in a love-affair.
(*n*) The Queen abducted by her lover in the King's presence.

79 [542 D] MĪR ʿALĪ SHĪR NAWĀʾĪ'S *HAYRAT AL-ABRĀR* (in Chaghatay Turkish), copied in 890/1485, with dedication-page to Badīʿ al-Zāmān (d. 1520), son of Sultān Husayn Mīrzā, joint ruler of Herāt with his brother on his father's death, but shortly afterwards, in 1506, a refugee from the Uzbeks with Shāh Ismāʿīl. In 1514 he returned with Sultān Selim to Constantinople in company with a number of artists and craftsmen and died there in 1520. Two *ʿunwāns*, four miniatures.

27·5×20 *cm*. Ethé, *Cat.*, no. 2116; Arnold, *P.I.*, pl. 22. ¶ Lent by BODLEIAN LIBRARY, Oxford [Elliott 287].

In the Bodleian Library are four of the five *masnawīs* of Mīr ʿAlī Shīr Nawāʾī (Elliot, nos. 287, 339, 317, 408), all from the library of Sir Gore Ouseley, Bt. (1770–1844), who negotiated the treaty of 1812 with Fath ʿAlī Shāh. The volume containing the *Laylā and Majnūn* is missing. Only this first *masnawī* bears a rosace with dedication and a fine illuminated double title-page. The other three have simply *ʿunwāns*, so that it is clear that they are all part of the same set, and may have originally formed one volume. The gold-dusted borders of variegated paper are later. The copyist has not signed any of them, but the calligrapher of each is certainly the same, and each *masnawī* is dated 890, the same year that the last *masnawī*, the *Sadd i Iskandar*, was composed.

It is very probable that the miniatures, of which there are eleven in all, are all by the same hand, which must be that of Qāsim ʿAlī. It is notable that his signature is appended to the last miniature of the last volume.

(*a*) Khwāja ʿAbd Allāh Ansārī, the mystic and theologian, with four disciples (fol. 24ʳ). Probably by Qāsim ʿAlī. A miniature in pale tones, the wall of the house in the background being salmon-coloured. As throughout the work, the geometrical patterning on architecture and textiles is particularly rich and finely executed. Qāsim ʿAlī is noted by Khwāndamīr as being skilled in illumination. The ibex on the sky-line is to be noted, as it is an idea often repeated later.

PLATE LXIII A.

(*b*) The Prophet Muhammad with the Companions (fol. 7ʳ). Probably by Qāsim ʿAlī. The brilliant colouring of this miniature is well reproduced in Sir Thomas Arnold's *Painting in Islam*, pl. XXII.

It is doubtful whether Sir Thomas Arnold is correct in his interpretation of the details of this composition. Probably the four other seated figures, apart from the Prophet, are intended for the first four Caliphs, ʿAlī—in a green robe—being on the right, with his dark-complexioned servant, holding his master's two-pointed sword Zulfiqār, standing behind him. The Abyssinian Bilāl, the first to be appointed to give the call to prayer, stands on the left. The object in the centre is probably not a brazier, but an open Qurʾān, the sacred volume resting on a cloth on a book-chest (*kursī*) of wood inlaid with ivory of a type still common in the East, and being provided, like the Prophet, with a flame halo.

The *mihrāb* or prayer-niche—the portion of a mosque which indicates the direction of Mecca— is surrounded with a suitable Arabic inscription, and on the right is the stepped *mimbar*, or pulpit.

The four figures in the foreground are perhaps mosque students.

On the summit of the green dome over the *mihrāb* is a weathercock in the form of the word الله ʿAllāh'.

PLATE LXIII B.

(*c*) A scene of parting (fol. 34ʳ). Probably by Qāsim ʿAlī. An incident in the life of Shaykh ʿIrāqī, the thirteenth-century poet and mystic (d. 1289). For his life and specimens of his work see E. G. Browne, *Lit. Hist. of Persia*, III, pp. 124–39. He travelled extensively, spending long periods in India, Egypt, Syria, and Qonya. A particularly interesting composition with figures massed on the right and gold ground.

PLATE LXIV B.

(*d*) The Sasanian king, Nūshīrwān, and a lady in a pavilion (fol. 28ʳ). The grass by the stream on the right of this miniature is deep emerald and as it were 'stippled', as is the grass in the miniature by Sultān Muhammad in M. Cartier's manuscript of Hāfiz (pl. LXXXIII A). PLATE LXIV A.

80 [542 A] MĪR ʿALĪ SHĪR NAWĀʾĪ'S *SADD I ISKANDAR* in Chaghatay Turkish, copied in 890/1485 for Badīʿ al-Zāmān, with four miniatures, all probably by Qāsim 'Alī of Herāt, by whom the last is signed. Eighteenth-century lacquer binding. The last *masnawī* by the author, finished in this year, 890. See under no. 79.

> 29 × 19·5 *cm.* Ethé, *Cat.*, no. 2120; Arnold, *P.I.*, pl. 43. ¶ Lent by BODLEIAN LIBRARY, Oxford [Elliott 339].
>
> (*a*) Majnūn coming to the house of Laylā (fol. 39ʳ). An incident from the youth of Laylā and Majnūn.   PLATE LXV B.
>
> (*b*) Iskandar enthroned (fol. 17ʳ). The inscription on the archway contains the name of Sultān Badī' al-Zamān, for whom the manuscript was made (*v. supra*). He was closely intimate with the author, his father's minister, several of whose works, including the present poem, contain verses in his praise.   PLATE LXV A.
>
> (*c*) Iskandar building the rampart (fol. 77ᵛ). A fine miniature, but badly damaged by damp, which has caused a smudge across the middle, so that it is not worth reproducing.
>
> (*d*) Mystics discoursing in a garden (fol. 95ᵛ). Signed by Qāsim 'Alī. The signature *al-'abd Qāsim 'Alī* is written in red between the columns of the text.   COLOUR PLATE LXVI.

> In the Bodleian Library there is also another manuscript of the *Sadd i Iskandar* (Elliot 340), written at Bukhārā in 1553, which contains a miniature of Alexander building the rampart, which is certainly a copy of the third (damaged) miniature of the present volume. This is an interesting direct proof of the influence and reputation of the Timurid school of Herāt in the Uzbek kingdom, whither the pupils of Bihzād and Qāsim 'Alī had fled.

81 [483] DOUBLE PAGE. Sultān Husayn Mīrzā in a garden with attendants, maidens, and musicians. *c.* 1485. By Bihzād. Inscribed, on the book held by two ladies seated in the lower right-hand corner, 'Portrait of Sultān Husayn Mīrzā. The work of Bihzād.' The robe of the lady in white, who is proffering a flower, bears at the foot the words 'Gawhar Shād Begam'.

The first of these inscriptions may well be contemporary with the miniature, even if not written by Bihzād himself, who would probably have prefixed some expression of humility, such as *al-'abd*, 'the slave'.

The authenticity of the likeness of the Sultān is borne out by other portraits (cf. no. 83 (a)). He would have been 45 or 46 years old in 1485.

The other inscription is purely fanciful; Gawhar Shād, the celebrated wife of Shāh Rukh, having been killed in 1457.

> 24 × 14 *cm.* (each). ¶ Lent by GULISTAN MUSEUM, Tehran.   COLOUR PLATE LXVII.

> The two portions of this composition were bound up in different places in the album lent by the Gulistan Museum, which had evidently been put together at the court of Jahāngīr.[1] They clearly originally formed a double-page opening. The discovery of this painting is of great interest, especially as an unfinished version of the left-hand portion was already known and had been secured for the Exhibition (cf. no. 82). A comparison between the two versions was thus possible, but it is not easy to decide on the relation between them. Is the unfinished version a preliminary sketch or a copy of the other? One small fact points to the unfinished version being a copy: in it the tree at the top is continued on to the decorative border, while in the other version the miniature itself is continued upwards beyond the original margination which is visible. This miniature has evidently been cut out and remounted, while the other version clearly retains its original mount and border. A greater precision in the painting of the flowers may be taken to connect it with Bukhārā, but this is very uncertain.
>
> The scene represents the Sultān seated at ease in the enclosure formed by an elaborately embroidered screen, at the entrance of which stands a door-keeper: inside is a eunuch with a staff. Without are musicians playing and men cooking. Within, the ladies are picking flowers and scenting the Mīrzā's cloak. His cushioned seat is set out behind on the left.

[1] See Appendix III.

82 [482] UNFINISHED MINIATURE. Picnic with musicians in a garden. Attributed to Bihzād. From the collection of Charles Ricketts, Esq., R.A. Identical except for small details with the left-hand portion of the preceding, q.v.

24·3 × 14·2 *cm.* Martin, 11, pl. 68. ¶ Lent by PHILIP HOFER, ESQ., New York.　PLATE LXXI A.

83 [543 B] SA'DĪ'S *BŪSTĀN*, copied by Sultān 'Alī al-Kātib in 893/1488 for Sultān Husayn Mīrzā; one page at the end, added later, written in Tabrīz by Shams al-Din Muhammad Kātib in 919/1514. Two *sarlawhs*, two *'unwāns*, five miniatures, of which four are signed by Bihzād. At the end of the manuscript is the seal of *Yarbūdāq, Ghulām Shāh 'Abbās* with the date 1053 (A.D. 1643), i.e. slave of Shāh 'Abbās (presumably a library clerk of Shāh 'Abbās II).

30·5 × 21·5 *cm.* J. V. S. Wilkinson, 'Fresh Light on the Herāt Painters', *Burl. Mag.* Feb. 1931; Martin, 11, pls. 70, 71; Sakisian, *Syria*, t. XII, fasc. 2. ¶ Lent by BIBLIOTHÈQUE ÉGYPTIENNE, Cairo.

This manuscript is of great importance for the study of Persian painting. It has been discussed by Martin and Schulz in their comprehensive works[1] and noticed by Sakisian in an article in *Syria*, published in 1931. All the miniatures were published together for the first time after the reading of the signatures in the *Burlington Magazine* for February 1931, where it was stated that the miniatures 'must, for the present at least, form the main basis of investigation of this, the central problem of Persian painting. . . . The all-round evidence for their genuineness [as works of Bihzād], or at least for that of four of them, is overwhelmingly strong, stronger than any we have for other book-miniatures attributed to Bihzād', with the possible exception of that in the 1524 manuscript (no. 131).

The four signed miniatures each contain the same humble phrase inconspicuously written on them, *'amal al-'abd Bihzād* [the work of the slave Bihzād].

(*a*) *Double-page frontispiece.* A Court party. Sultān Husayn is seated on a carpet in the left-hand page. He is dressed in green and holding a flower, as in the garden scene (pl. LXVII), and is easily recognizable by comparison with his other portraits. Beside him is a youth overcome by intoxication. Above their heads are two canopies, the upper one decorated with hares and birds: in the central cartouche are the Sultān's titles. The right-hand leaf is occupied by stewards decanting wine and bringing in provisions; in the foreground a door-keeper beating a man. Round the gate is a long inscription: the last panel on the left formerly contained the name of the artist, but all is now obliterated except *'amal* ('the work of'), and the last letter which appears to be ﺱ (s or sh), which M. Sakisian has suggested may be the end of the word *naqqāsh*, painter. He says this is an expression not used by Bihzād; but in view of the similarity of the style and the evident appropriateness of the title-page to the volume, it is difficult to attribute it to any one else. M. Sakisian suggests that elusive artist Mīrak, said by Haydar Dughlāt to have been the master of Bihzād (*ustād i Bihzād*). It is difficult to see why the artist's name should have been erased, except out of jealousy or because it was too prominently placed. At this date the former seems the more likely.　PLATE LXVIII.

(*b*) King Dārā and the herdsman. The king, separated from his companions while out hunting, comes upon the herdsman who is in charge of the royal horses. Dārā fails to recognize him, and, taking him for an enemy, fits an arrow to his bow. For this he is reproached by the herdsman, who improves the occasion by lecturing the king on his carelessness of his subjects' interests which he has thus revealed.

The signature of Bihzād can just be distinguished on the black quiver which the king is carrying.

A version of this miniature made at Bukhārā, in a manuscript dated 1535, is reproduced by Martin (vol. I, fig. 28): it bears a false attribution to Shaykh-zāda.　PLATE LXIX.

[1] Martin, I, p. 44; Schulz, Bd. I, p. 112.

(c) An old man refused admittance to a mosque. The old man is seen with a begging-bowl, bare-headed in the foreground. The mosque is represented in considerable detail: in the foreground is the outer wall with water for the essential ablutions. A negro slave holds ready a towel to dry the feet of a worshipper about to enter the mosque. Beyond the wall is the interior of the mosque courtyard, clearly visible in bird's-eye perspective. In the *mihrāb* under the dome is a doctor expounding; on the left, a man in one of the attitudes of prayer. In this miniature, and throughout the manuscript, the illuminator's work in geometrical patterns and calligraphy is exceptionally rich and fine. Note also the disposition of the text.

Bihzād's signature is on the white paper held by the man on the extreme left, behind.
PLATE LXX B.

(d) Theologians disputing in a mosque. A magnificent and elaborate *mihrāb* arch beneath which are seated three doctors with books. In the foreground five others are standing. The signature occurs at the end of the long inscription round the arch: with it is the date 894 in Arabic words: this corresponds to the year A.D. 1489, which is a year later than the completion of the manuscript by the scribe, which would be a normal interval in Persia where the calligrapher always did his work first, leaving spaces for the miniature artist to fill in later. PLATE LXX A.

(e) Yūsuf flees from the temptations of Zulaykhā. The scene represented is Zulaykhā's final attempt to break down the resistance of Yūsuf. She had a pavilion constructed with seven-fold doors and the innermost room decorated with paintings of herself in the arms of Yūsuf. She induced him to enter it hoping that seeing these paintings on every hand he would not be able to turn away his head but would be drawn to look at her and so succumb to her charms. However, Yūsuf, as soon as he perceived the trap, prayed and all the seven doors flew open so that he was able to escape from Zulaykhā. In the painting Yūsuf, as a prophet, has his face covered and his head surmounted by a flame halo. The artist has shown great ingenuity in displaying the seven-fold doors, and the architecture is of considerable interest.

The signature of Bihzād is contained in a small panel between the two windows immediately to the left of Yūsuf, and on a level with his head. In the calligraphic inscription round the arch below occurs the date as in the last miniature. PLATE LXXI B.

The colour-scheme of all these miniatures is rather cold, blues and greens predominating and red being introduced only sparingly. The warmer colours are browns and ochres.

84 [546 B] *ZAFAR-NĀMA*, a History of Tīmūr, by Sharaf al-Dīn 'Alī Yazdī, copied in 872/1467 for Sultān Husayn Mīrzā by Shīr 'Alī. Six double-page miniatures, attributed to Bihzād, added later, c. 1490. On the fly-leaf an inscription, containing an example of the Emperor Akbar's handwriting, certified by the Emperor Jahāngīr, who also states that the miniatures are early work by Bihzād. Also an inscription by the Emperor Shāh Jahān.

21 × 12 cm. Reproduced in Arnold, *Bihzād and his Paintings in the Zafar-nāmah MS.*, 1930; Martin, pl. 69; Schulz, pls. 52–5; Kühnel, *I.M.*, 48–51. ¶ Lent by R. GARRETT, ESQ., Baltimore.

(a) The assault on the fortress of Smyrna. The capture of the 'infidel fortress' of the Knights of St. John took place at the end of 1402. Tīmūr is depicted on horseback on the right. His troops are crossing the moat by a temporary bridge, the drawbridge having been pulled up by the defenders. On the right the attackers are digging a mine. PLATE LXXII.

85 [493] ABDUCTION OF A PRINCESS BY SEA. A page from Amīr Khusraw Dihlawī's works. Herāt school, late xv century.

27 × 19·5 cm. Sakisian, fig. 108. ¶ Lent by ARMENAG BEY SAKISIAN, Paris.

86 [504] FIVE MINIATURES, apparently painted about 1550, from Hātifī's *Timur-nāma* (Poetical History of Tamerlane), copied by Shāh Qāsim in 902/1497 for Husayn Khān Shāmlū (appointed by Ismāʿīl Safawī his counsellor in 906/1501).

24 × 15·5 *cm*. *Architectural Review*, Feb. 1931, pl. 1, fig. 2. ¶ Lent by A. CHESTER BEATTY, ESQ.

87 [491] DOCTOR AND HIS PUPILS IN A GARDEN. Typical work of the late fifteenth-century Herāt style. Possibly by Qāsim ʿAlī. A minute drawing in bright colours.

14 × 10 *cm*. ¶ Lent by GULISTAN MUSEUM, Tehran. 　　　　　　PLATE LXXIII A.

88 [484] A PORTRAIT OF MUHAMMAD SHAYBĀNĪ KHĀN, the Uzbek. Inscribed, in calligraphy, 'Portrait of Shaybak Khān', 'The slave Bihzād'.

12 × 14 *cm*. Sakisian, pl. 11 (in colours). ¶ Lent by ARMENAG BEY SAKISIAN, Paris.
　　　　　　　　　　　　　　　　　　　　　　　　　　PLATE LXXIII B.

The portrait is probably contemporary, and may be by Bihzād, though it is difficult to believe that it is by the same hand that executed the minute and expressive figure-drawing that we know to be by him. The figure is dressed in a blue robe over a green sleeved under-garment, with a white turban showing a flat crimson *kulah*. He leans on a black cushion, and is seated on a crimson carpet. The background is green. M. Sakisian suggests that Bihzād wished to flatter his patron by surrounding him with the implements of a calligrapher or miniaturist, denoting the warrior merely by the archer's ring which he wears.

Muhammad Shaybānī Khān, or Shaybak Khān, was one of the chief military figures of the age, and, like Bābur, a descendant of Chingīz Khān. He conquered Herāt in 1507, and was killed in battle with Shāh Ismāʿīl in 1510. His corpse was barbarously treated, the skull being mounted in gold and made into a drinking-cup by the conqueror. Muhammad Shaybānī Khān was a fanatical Sunnī, and a masterful character who could not tolerate rivals.

Bābur, whose account of him is prejudiced, as the Uzbek leader was the deadly enemy of the Timurids, and the chief cause of their downfall in Central Asia, represents him as an uncouth barbarian, who attempted to instruct the theologians in the exposition of the Qurʾān, and to correct the drawings of Bihzād and the handwriting of the famous calligrapher Sultān ʿAlī, but actually Muhammad Shaybānī, though no doubt falling short of Persian standards of good breeding, was a man of considerable literary culture, besides being a leader of genius.

89 [492] PORTRAIT OF SULTĀN HUSAYN MĪRZĀ. Inscribed in calligraphy in two panels in the top corners 'Sūrat i Sultān Husayn Mīrzā / ʿamal i Hazrat Ustād Bihzād', that is, 'Portrait of Sultān Husayn Mīrzā / the work of the eminent master Bihzād'. Ink with touches of colour.

22 × 12·5 *cm*. Sakisian, fig. 59; Martin, 11, pl. 81. ¶ Lent by M. L. CARTIER, Paris.

While there is no doubt that this is in fact a portrait of Sultān Husayn, there is a flatness about the face and a mechanical appearance which might indicate a copy. This would be in accordance with the evidence of the inscription, which could not have been put on by Bihzād. The illumination of the panels is in a style which was practised at Bukhārā towards the middle of the sixteenth century. That Bihzād's reputation, here, among his pupils, was immense, is shown by the occurrence of such faithful copies of his work as the illustration to the *Būstān* in M. Cartier's copy dated 1535 and written for the Sultān ʿAbd al-ʿAzīz (cf. Martin, 1, fig. 28), which is directly taken from the Cairo *Būstān* of Bihzād (pl. LXIX).

90 [567] A DROMEDARY, FETTERED, WITH ITS KEEPER. Late XV century. The animal, facing right, with head raised, makes a striking pattern, strongly outlined against a pale ground. It wears a gay-flowered covering in crimson, gold, and black. The keeper is dressed in a blue robe.

There are two inscriptions, written in calligraphy, in ornamental cartouches: (1) 'Painted by Bihzād'; (2) 'The sublime work of Master Bihzād'. It is impossible to pronounce definitely whether this work is by Bihzād. The inscriptions are not conclusive evidence; but the work can be placed, on stylistic grounds, at the end of the fifteenth century when Bihzād was in his prime. There is, however, no well-attested drawing by Bihzād which shows a similar bold simplicity of treatment.

14·5 × 11·5 cm. Sakisian, fig. 84. ¶ Lent by ARMENAG BEY SAKISIAN, Paris.

91 [490] A POET ATTACKED BY THE DOGS OF A ROBBER CHIEF. Ascribed to Bihzād. An unfinished miniature, sketched in with touches of colour.

27·5 × 16 cm. Lent by GULISTAN MUSEUM, Tehran.   PLATE LXXIV B.

An illustration to a story in the *Gulistān* of Sa'dī, telling how a robber chief set his dogs on a poet and looked down, laughing, at the scene, from an upper window. The poet is seen, dressed in a cloak, picking up stones to throw at the dogs to keep them back.

The spaces above and below were left for the text of the poem: in the lower one a librarian has written 'Painting by Bihzād'. While it is impossible to be very confident of the justice of this attribution, the miniature is certainly typical of the Bihzād style. Slight additional corroboration of the attribution is obtained from a copy of this drawing made by Āqā Rizā which is reproduced by Martin (I, fig. 39). It is inscribed, at the bottom in a place corresponding to the attribution to Bihzād, 'a composition by the late Ustād Bihzād, copied by Rizā Musawwir in 1028' (A.D. 1619); above is a second inscription which styles it a 'composition by the late Aqā Rizā, coloured by Shafi' 'Abbāsī in 1064' (A.D. 1654). This indicates that the attribution to Bihzād is at least as old as 1619. A comparison between the two versions is of interest in showing the change in Persian style in the intervening century, as the copyist has treated the detail freely.

92 [508] MINIATURE. Fight inside a fortress. School of Bihzād. Beginning XVI century.

23 × 15 cm. ¶ Lent by M. CLAUDE ANET, Paris.

93 [487] PORTRAIT OF A YOUNG MAN PAINTING. He is seated, facing right, in profile, dressed in purple brocade coat decorated with gold arabesque design over a green under-robe. He has a voluminous waistband and a large turban folded in the Turkish fashion. Inscribed at the bottom, 'Painted by the slave Bihzād'. The miniature is copied after a coloured drawing by Gentile Bellini in the Gardner Museum, Boston, which is inscribed 'the work of the son of Mu'azzin who is one of the famous Frankish masters'. Gentile was at Constantinople from September 1479 to December 1480, and Sarre suggests that the subject was a Christian page in the Serai. The copy would appear to be contemporary and must be by a Turkish or Persian artist working at Constantinople—which Bihzād never visited.

19 × 13 cm. *Meisterwerke*, pl. 27; Marteau-Vever, no. 9; Sarre, 'Eine Miniatur Gentile Bellinis', Berlin, 1906, in *Jahrbuch der K. Preuszischen Kunstsammlungen*, Bd. 27, S. 302. ¶ Lent by ÉMILE TABBAGH, Paris.

94 [486] PORTRAIT OF A DERVISH. Inscribed, above, in calligraphy, 'Portrait of a dervish of Baghdad. Work of Hazrat Ustād Bihzād'. He wears a blue robe and a camel-hair cloak. The modelling of the face and turban show European influence. The hands are clumsily drawn, and appear to be later work. Perhaps Turkish, XVI century.

22 × 14 cm. Martin, II, pl. 85; Migeon, fig. 73. ¶ Lent by A. CHESTER BEATTY, ESQ.

95 [495] HUNTING SCENE. A fine well-spaced composition, evidently a page from a manuscript, apparently a *Shāh-nāma*, which may have been executed at Herāt at the end of the fifteenth century, but perhaps a copy of such a composition made at Bukhārā some fifty years later. Probably from the same source as no. 96: they have both suffered severely from repainting at the time that they were mounted in this album for Jahāngīr. Both have been considerably enlarged and the original size of the miniatures appears to have been about 23·2 × 16 *cm.*

It is of particular interest that the reworking of the hills so conspicuous in this miniature bears the inscription *In kūh i tilā az 'amal i faqīr al-haqīr Dawlat*, 'this golden hill is by the poor wretch Dawlat'. Dawlat, who added all the darker-coloured rocks and the present sky, was a well-known artist who flourished in the reigns of Akbar and Jahāngīr: his signature occurs on some of the border paintings in this album (see Appendix III).

29 × 16·5 cm. ¶ Lent by GULISTAN MUSEUM, Tehran.   PLATE CIII B.

96 [496] A KING ON HORSEBACK, with attendants on foot, one holding a state umbrella, arriving at a tent with a *sāyabān* (a movable canopy to keep off the sun), elaborately decorated with arabesques. In the background is a building covered with faience with fine Kufic writing. Apparently from the same manuscript as the preceding (no. 95). Like that miniature it has suffered from enlargement and repainting in India. Late XV century.

27·5 × 16·5 cm. ¶ Lent by GULISTAN MUSEUM, Tehran.

97 [542 c] THE DĪWĀN OF HĀFIZ, copied by Sultān Muhammad Nūr, about 1500. Text inside blue border, headings in gold with pairs of birds, margins with floral and animal designs in gold. One *sarlawh*, two *'unwāns*. Red leather binding, gold-stamped and stencilled inside.

28·5 × 18 cm. ¶ Lent by A. CHESTER BEATTY, ESQ.

It is not impossible that these bird-paintings are by Bihzād. The calligrapher, Sultān Muhammad Nūr, was one of the scribes trained by Mīr 'Alī Shīr Nawā'ī, and some similar drawings of birds in the Bibliothèque Nationale bear Bihzād's minute signature (see also p. 88).

98 [555] MINIATURE. Princess, in blue dress and red robe, kneeling on one knee. About 1500. Many versions of this miniature exist. Cf. Marteau-Vever, 142. Others are in the Serai Library.

28·5 × 20 cm. Sakisian, fig. 60; Kühnel, *I.M.*, pl. 57 (as 'Āqā Mīrak'). ¶ Lent by M. L. CARTIER, Paris.

99 [719 E] PEN-DRAWING, TINTED. Horseman setting a falcon at wild duck. Inscribed 'The work of the master Bihzād'. About 1500.

> 11×20·5 cm. Exh. Memorial Art Gallery, Rochester, 1930; Pennsylvania Univ. Museum, 1930; Detroit Inst. of Arts, 1930, cat. no. 41. Rep. in Demotte, *Cat.*, p. 37. ¶ Lent by DEMOTTE, New York.

100 [721 A] DRAWING, with touches of colour. Two monsters, fettered. One is making music, while the other holds a bottle and hands him a cup. XV century.

> 21×14 cm. ¶ Lent by ARMENAG BEY SAKISIAN, Paris.

101 [544 A] NIZĀMĪ'S *KHAMSA*, 'Five Poems', copied by Naʿīm al-Dīn Kātib Shīrāzī in 907/1501. Forty-four miniatures. Modern binding. Probably West Persian.

> 28×17·5 cm. Ethé, *Cat.*, no. 587; Arnold, *P.I.*, pl. XXVIII; Gray, pl. 8. ¶ Lent by BODLEIAN LIBRARY, Oxford [Elliott, 192].

> (*a*) Majnūn at Mecca. An illustration to the *masnawī* of *Laylā wa Majnūn*. Majnūn, as a last resort, is taken by his relations to Mecca to be cured of his love-frenzy; but even this pilgrimage to the Kaʿba is unavailing for the mad lover, whose longing is undiminished (fol. 115ᵛ).
> Majnūn is represented as about to enter the shrine, in which the Kaʿba is kept, alone. Over it two angels are hovering.
> A provincial style with rather strong coarse colouring.　　　　　PLATE XCVIII A.

102 [545 A] MAWLĀNĀ HAYDAR TILBA'S *Makhzan al-asrār* (a religious poem in Chaghatay Turkish), copied by ʿAlī in 908/1503. Decorated margins. Two *ʿunwāns*, nine miniatures.

> 33×20 cm. ¶ Lent by M. H. VEVER, Paris.

103 [546 A] THE TIMURID SULTĀN HUSAYN'S *MAJĀLIS AL-ʿUSHSHĀQ*, 'Assemblies of Lovers', copied in 908/1503 on coloured paper. Sixteen miniatures. Original leather binding. Presumably Herāt at the very end of the Timurid period.

> 27×17 cm. ¶ Lent by A. GARABED.

> (*a*) The Shaykh of Sanʿā and the Christian maiden. The Shaykh fell in love with a Christian maiden, to gratify whom he even became a swineherd.　　　　　PLATE LXI B.

PLATE LIX-A. 68 (*a*). Ladies in a garden. *c.* 1435–50

PLATE LIX-B. 70 (*a*). Majnūn watches the battle of the clans. 1450–75

PLATE LX-A. 69 (*a*). Khusraw Parwīz accused before his father. *c.* 1460

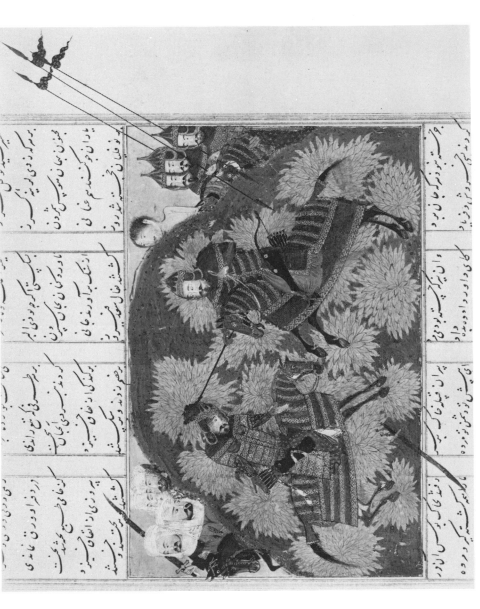

PLATE LX-B. 69 (b). Majnūn watches the battle of the clans. c. 1460

PLATE LXI-A. 76. Elias and Khizr by the Water of Life. *Second half* xv *century*

PLATE LXI-B. **103** (*a*). The Shaykh of San'ā and the Christian maiden. 1503

PLATE LXII-A. 77 (c). A man sawing off the branch on which he is
seated. 1478

۱۰٦

PLATE LXIII-A. 79 (*a*). A Mystic and Four Disciples
By Qāsim ʿAlī. 1485

PLATE LXIII-B. 79 (b). The Prophet Muhammad with the Companions
By Qāsim ʿAlī. 1485

PLATE LXIV- A. 79 (*d*). Nūshīrwān with a lady

By Qāsim ʿAlī. 1485

PLATE LXIV-B. 79 (c). Shaykh 'Irāqī overcome at parting from a friend
By Qāsim 'Alī. 1485

PLATE LXIX. 83 (*b*). King Dārā and the herdsman. By Bihzād. 1488

Plate LXV follows on the next page.

PLATE LXV- A. 80 (*b*). Sikandar enthroned
By Qāsim 'Alī. 1485

PLATE LXV-B. 80 (*a*). Majnūn coming to the house of Laylā
By Qāsim ʿAlī. 1485

Plates LXVI and LXVII are reproduced in color, following p. 16.

PLATE LXVIII. 83 (*a*). Sultān Husayn Mīrzā at a feast. By Bihzād. 1488

PLATE LXX- A. 83 (*d*). Theologians in a mosque. 1489
By Bihzād

Plate LXIX follows Plate LXIV.

PLATE LXX-B. 83 (*c*). An old man refused admittance to a mosque. 1488
By Bihzād

PLATE LXXI- A. 82. Garden scene (unfinished)
Compare pl. LXVII

PLATE LXXI- B. 83 (*e*). Yūsuf flees from Zulaykhā. By Bihzād. 1489

PLATE LXXII. 84 (a). The assault on the fortress of Smyrna. *Attributed to* Bihzād. *c.* 1490

PLATE LXXIII-A. 87. Doctor and pupils in a garden
Late XV *century*

PLATE **LXXIII**-B. **88.** Muhammad Shaybānī Khān, the Uzbek (*d.* 1510)

PLATE LXXIV-A. 36. Border painting in Chinese taste. 1402(?)

PLATE LXXIV-B. 91. A poet attacked by dogs
Attributed to Bihzād

PLATE LXXV. 127 (e). A scene of drunkenness. By Sultān Muhammad. *Between 1517 and 1540*

V

THE EARLY SAFAWĪ PERIOD

HERĀT fell in 1507 before the Uzbek armies of Shaybānī Khān, who, however, was defeated and slain at the battle of Merv, three years later, by the young Shāh Ismā'īl, then twenty-three years of age. Ismā'īl had already, in the first year of the century, annihilated the White Sheep Turkmans, and this further victory secured him in his empire. After eight and a half centuries of Arab, Mongol, and Tartar domination, Persia was again united; a new era had been inaugurated, and the Safawī dynasty, which Ismā'īl founded, was to endure for more than two hundred years, when it, in turn, was to fall before the Afghans.

The tale of the great wave of Shī'a enthusiasm and nationalistic ardour that lifted the Safawīs to power; the details of Ismā'īl's alleged descent, through the hermit of Ardabīl, from 'Alī and the Prophet himself, as well as from the race of the kings of Old Persia; the effect of the half-religious glamour which surrounded the new power,—these make an interesting chapter in history. Ismā'īl's character was a strange mixture of nobility and depravity, generosity and ferocious cruelty; and the secret of his compelling influence over the people who worshipped him as a god, and the soldiers who trusted so blindly in his power that they disdained armour in his battles, is not altogether clear. But Zeno and Angiolello, the two Venetian ambassadors, give a vivid picture of his radiant youth. 'He is as amiable as a girl, left-handed by nature, is as lively as a fawn, and stronger than any of his lords. In the archery trials at the apple he is so expert that of every ten he hits six.' When thirteen years old he was already a great conqueror, and Zeno speaks of him as being then 'of noble presence and a truly royal bearing, as in his eyes there was a something, I know not what, so great and commanding, which plainly showed that he would some day become a great ruler'. It is certain that he had the qualities to appeal to an impressionable race, and could win their devotion as the ideal leader in a supreme moment of national self-assertion.

The capital of the new dynasty was at first Tabrīz, and afterwards Qazwīn, somewhat farther to the south-east. This shifting of interest from the east to the west of Persia had important consequences on the development of Persian painting.

In the first place the Timurid prince Badī' al-Zamān, who had succeeded his father in 1506 as joint ruler of Herāt with his brother, fled to his brother-in-law, Ismā'īl, at Tabrīz on the Uzbek invasion in the following year. Some of the artists of the court probably accompanied him, but Bihzād, the greatest of them, with others, remained on at Herāt under Shaybānī Khān. On the latter's defeat and death in 1510 there appears to have been a greater migration of artists to Tabrīz. Bihzād, at any rate, transferred there either then or shortly afterwards, for though no details are known of this event in his life, he is heard of in Tabrīz in 1514, when (so 'Alī, the Turkish historian, relates)

Shāh Ismāʿīl caused him, together with his favourite calligrapher Shāh Maḥmūd, to be concealed in a cavern before the battle of Chāldirān.[1] Sulṭān Selim the Grim, on his victory, occupied Tabrīz, but withdrew after a week, taking with him to Constantinople Badīʿ al-Zamān and some of the artisans. Some of the Persian manuscripts in the Istanbul collections must have originally reached the Turkish capital in this way.

But other Herāt artists remained on for a time, as appears from the considerable number of illustrated manuscripts produced in that city, still an important provincial capital under the Tabrīz government. Others, again, emigrated to Bukhārā, some quite early in the century (being influenced, possibly, by their dread of Shīʿa fanaticism against remaining on after Herāt came under direct Safawī rule), and there appears to have been a further emigration in 1535, when Herāt suffered one of its periodical Uzbek invasions. From now onwards, till well after the middle of the century, a succession of finely illustrated books, written and painted by calligraphers and artists trained in the formulas of Khurāsān, continued to be produced beyond the Oxus.

Before, therefore, considering the painting of the Safawī school proper, it will be convenient to say something of the miniatures of the early and middle sixteenth century which were executed in Bukhārā.

The best, and apparently the leading, miniaturist of the so-called[2] Bukhārā school was Maḥmūd Muzahhib, 'Maḥmūd the illuminator', as he signs himself. He is stated by the Turkish writer ʿAlī to have been a pupil of the calligrapher Mīr ʿAlī of Herāt, who died in 957/1550, and to have been a better illuminator than calligrapher. M. Sakisian, who has some interesting paragraphs on this artist,[3] thinks that he was probably exiled from Herāt to Bukhārā after Herāt had been sacked by the Uzbeks (1535). He certainly worked at Bukhārā, and must be held primarily responsible for the survival, for about another thirty years, in Transoxiana, of a style of painting closely resembling Herāt work of the fifteenth century.

Bukhārā painting, though mainly traditional, not being stimulated by fresh influences, yet has an individual character and charm, depending partly on a general simplification of earlier formulas and the lavish use of pure colours. Usually, as in the illustration of the stock themes, the types depicted are rather short and sturdy.[4] The influence of Bihzād's school is clearly apparent in design, in colour, attitudes, and gestures.

There is, however, a group of separate figure studies, with one or more figures, of which Maḥmūd may have been the originator, some of which display real inventiveness in new and expressive rhythms and audacious colour combinations.

One of the features of the Exhibition was the number of Bukhārā works, a considerable proportion of which were previously unknown, which were for the first time assembled together. Of especial interest were signed works by Maḥmūd and his pupil

[1] Sakisian, op. cit., p. 105.
[2] It is necessary to emphasize the fact that there was never, at any period, a distinctive Bukhārā school, in any real sense, because some far-reaching theories have been constructed on the hypothesis that there was an old indigenous art tradition emanating from that city.
[3] Op. cit., pp. 97–8.
[4] The short round or conical *kulahs* are distinctive.

'Abd Allāh. In an album from the Mashhad shrine were four signed drawings[1] by Mahmūd, of figure subjects in the characteristic colouring of the Bukhārā school. Previously only one signed drawing by him in this style was known—a small page at Berlin (reproduced by Kühnel, pl. 70). These were larger and much more important, but unfortunately three of the four had been seriously defaced, one so badly that it is not worth reproducing. It is of an angel or hūrī of a well-known type which seems to have found special favour at Constantinople with Shāh Qulī, and his follower Walī Jān. Another is inscribed 'darlings from China' and is a graceful composition, not otherwise known. The Chinese costumes are even more fanciful than those in the famous garden scene of the Musée des Arts Décoratifs.[2] Still finer is a third with a man offering a lady an apple: even in its present state this is a drawing of remarkable beauty and a very sensitive line. It is far finer than the version in the Boston Museum, which must be a copy, probably contemporary. Yet another version signed by 'Abd Allāh was at Burlington House:[3] it well illustrates the relation between these two artists. 'Abd Allāh[4] is said by 'Alī to have been a pupil of Shaykh-zāda, but he was working as late as 1575, as is shown by a signed miniature in a manuscript of Jāmī[5] copied by Mīr Husayn al-Husaynī in that year. In this drawing he shows that he was not afraid to attempt to improve on Mahmūd's designs, but the result is heavy and clumsy compared with the original. Only the dress-pattern remains attractive. That 'Abd Allāh still had access to originals by the artists of the Safawīs as late as 1564 is proved by the existence of a signed miniature[6] of that date which is closely modelled on a page in a Safawī manuscript at Leningrad (cf. Martin, pl. 114).

The fourth example of Mahmūd's work at Burlington House had a very special interest as it was a portrait of Mīr 'Alī Shīr, the faithful and wise minister of Sultān Husayn. He died several years before his master in 1501; this painting has all the appearance of having been done from the life[7] and would therefore date from about 1500, when Mahmūd was in any case still at Herāt where the portrait must have been painted. The old minister is very plainly dressed with a simple turban, in keeping with that side of his character which led him to withdraw from public life and enter an Order of Dervishes, though a strain of arrogance is revealed in his written references to his contemporaries.

Apart from the examples shown at Burlington House, Mahmūd's miniatures are to be found in the Bibliothèque Nationale *Makhzan al-Asrār*[8] (Sup. pers. 985) copied by Mīr 'Alī in 1537, but the miniature dated 1546; and in the *Tuhfat al-Ahrār*[9] (Sup. pers. 1416), copied by Sultān 'Alī Mashhadī in 905/1500 at Herāt, to which, Sakisian

1 No. 104, pls. LXXVI–LXXVII.
2 No. 47, pl. XLI.
3 No. 114, pl. LXXVII A.
4 Sakisian, p. 99.
5 Sakisian, p. 94, fig. 132; Marteau-Vever, pl. CI.
6 In a manuscript of Jāmī's *Subhat al-Abrār* copied by Sultān Muhammad Khandān (see *Burlington Magazine*, vol. XXV, pp. 190–1).
7 There is a copy in an album in the Serai Library.

8 Blochet, *Catalogue*, no. 1264; *Peintures*, pls. XLI, XLII; *Enluminures*, pls. LII, LIII (a).
9 Blochet, *Catalogue*, no. 1683; *Musulman Painting*, pls. CVII, CVIII. Sakisian, fig. 128. Another manuscript of the *Tuhfat al-Ahrār* was sold at the Octave Homberg sale in June 1921 with five pages of illustrations. The fine double-page frontispiece, signed by Mahmūd, was reproduced in plate 39 of the Sale Catalogue. The Bihzadian influence is very clear.

considers,[1] the four miniatures, one signed by Mahmūd, were probably added later. The same writer attributes to Mahmūd the illustrations in a Herāt manuscript, dated 1524, in the Metropolitan Museum of New York,[2] on the basis of an inscription in one of the paintings, in which, however, the word *mahmūd*, 'praised', can hardly have any personal reference.[3] The argument, accordingly, on which M. Sakisian bases his judgement that two of the miniatures in a manuscript of Mīr 'Alī Shīr, in the Bibliothèque Nationale (Sup. turc. 316; Sakisian: figs. 111, 112), dated 1526–7, are also by this painter, on account of the resemblance of one of them to the New York one bearing the inscription, falls to the ground.

The rejection of the attribution of the Metropolitan Museum *Nizāmī* of 1524 removes the argument for Mahmūd's having remained at Herāt so late as this. But whether M. Sakisian is right or not in supposing that Mahmūd moved to Bukhārā after the Uzbek invasion of 1535, it is clear that there was a Bukhārā school in existence before this date. At the Exhibition were two manuscripts written by 'Alī al-Husaynī, and one by Ibrāhīm Khalīl at Bukhārā, dating from the years 1522 to 1524,[4] and all containing miniatures, closely akin and in the Bukhārā style. Transoxiana has always had access to the best sources for minerals for making pigments, which would account for the excellent colours in the works of the school, as in these manuscripts. Bukhārā had fallen to the Shaybānid house in 1500, though it was not till 1540 that 'Abd al-Latīf made it the capital of a separate state. But in 1512 'Ubayd Allāh b. Mahmūd (then a prisoner: he reigned as Khān 1533–9) made Bukhārā his residence, so that these manuscripts must have been written for him. The Shaybānid house had Timurid blood as the progenitor of the family, Abu'l-Khayr, married a granddaughter of Shāh Rukh. Though the Shaybanids did not develop a new art, some credit must be given them for receiving the fugitive artists from Herāt and extending to them their patronage. In this sense the founder of the Bukhārā school would seem to be the 'Ubayd Allāh mentioned above. After him must be mentioned 'Abd al-'Azīz Bahādur Khān (1540–9), into whose library so many of the finest manuscripts passed, and for whom Mahmūd executed the dated miniature[5] in the Bibliothèque Nationale *Makhzan al-Asrār*, which is perhaps the finest of all Bukharan miniatures.

---

[1] Sakisian, p. 88.
[2] Described in Jackson and Yohannan, *Catalogue of Persian Manuscripts—Cochran Collection*, pp. 61 and 66. Illustrated in Martin, *Miniature Painters*, pls. 97–9; *The Nizami MS. from the Library of the Shah of Persia* (1927): (14 plates); Sakisian, pp. 97 and 98: fig. 127.
[3] The inscription, which was misread by Jackson and Yohannan, runs as follows:

شنیدم ام که بر این طارم زر اندود است

خطی که عاقبت کار جمله محمود است

The meaning is, 'I have heard that upon this gilt dome is a writing [in these words] "The end of the work is entirely praiseworthy".' (i.e. In the end, all is for the best.)

The lines are, in fact, parallel to those in the first story of Sa'dī's *Gulistān*: 'These elegant verses were inscribed on the dome of Farīdūn's palace: "The world, my brother, abideth with no one; set thy affections on the world's Creator; that is enough", &c.'

Dr. R. A. Nicholson, who has kindly sent his opinion on the lines, agrees that there is probably no personal allusion. If a pun on Mahmūd's name is intended, the words at the end must form a chronogram, he thinks, based on the numerical value of the letters. But no such chronogram would fit in with the date.
[4] Nos. 105, 106, 107.
[5] Reproduced Blochet, *Musulman Painting*, pls. cxiv–cxv.

But, as has been shown by Blochet and Sakisian, the Bukhārā school in the sixteenth century was little more than a prolongation of the Timurid school of the fifteenth. Its archaism is apparent to any one comparing the products of the two schools. One of the most striking parallels is afforded by the Bibliothèque Nationale *Būstān* of Saʿdī (Sup. pers. 1187),[1] copied at Bukhārā in 1555–6 for Nawrūz Ahmad Khān (1551–5) by Mīr Husayn al-Husaynī, which is illustrated with miniatures closely modelled on those by Bihzād in the Cairo *Būstān* of 1488 and that of Mr. Chester Beatty of 1485.

A series of small-paged volumes, represented at the Exhibition by the little Anthology—ascribed to Mīr ʿAlī's hand—belonging to Mr. Dawud,[2] and by other examples at Boston (*Goloubew Catalogue*, no. 56; Schulz, pl. 138) and Berlin (Kühnel, pl. 70), in the same style seems to represent a departure from anything practised at Herāt under Sultān Husayn, and in some ways a return to the style of the earlier Timurid period.

Shāh Ismāʿīl's short life was too much occupied with fighting and the inauguration of the new régime to give him much time for the arts of the book. His tastes, too, inclined him rather to hunting and field sports. Yet he wrote Turkish and Persian poetry, and seems to have tried his hand at calligraphy; an album at Istanbul contains a specimen of his handiwork.[3] The story, referred to above, of Ismāʿīl's solicitude for Bihzād's welfare in 1514, testifies at least to a tradition that he was appreciative of the great painter's merits, and we find Bihzād, moreover, appointed in 1522 director of the Royal library.[4] The warrant is signed by the Shāh, and the writer of the document was Bihzād's friend, Khwāndamīr. It is of great interest for several reasons. For one thing, it throws some light on the organization of the Shāh's *kitāb-khāna*. By this word nothing like a modern library is implied. The establishment consists rather of many distinct craftsmen, calligraphers, painters, illuminators, margin-drawers, gold-beaters, lapis-lazuli workers, and others. All of these are to recognize Bihzād as director and to submit to his administrative control. In the second place, allowing for the facts that Khwāndamīr was an old personal friend of Bihzād, and that he had a taste for flamboyant language, the warrant contains clear proof that Ismāʿīl was greatly pleased with Bihzād, and had shown him previous favours, and that Bihzād, as both painter and illuminator, enjoyed the confidence, as well as the approbation, of his sovereign—as formerly in Herāt.

And the royal patronage of great artists was continued in the next reign, with the happiest results; for after the ten-year-old Tahmāsp had succeeded his father as Shāh in 1524 it is recorded that he was taught painting by the celebrated Sultān Muhammad, that he himself attained great proficiency in illuminating *sarlawhs*, and that he was so passionately attached to painting in his youth that he gave up all his leisure to it; while

---

[1] Cf. Blochet, *Enluminures*, pls. LVII, LVIII.
[2] No. 109.
[3] Sakisian, fig. 150.
[4] See p. 81. The Persian text of his warrant of appointment—now in the Bibliothèque Nationale, with a French translation, was published in the *Revue du Monde Musulman*, Tome XXVI, 1914 (Mirza Mohammed Qazwini et L. Bouvat, 'Deux documents inédits relatifs à Behzâd'). English translation in Arnold, *P.I.*, pp. 150–1.

such great painters as Bihzād, Sultān Muhammad, and Āqā Mīrak, were admitted to the young king's intimacy.[1] Tahmāsp likewise practised calligraphy and designed carpets.

Conditions were, accordingly, extraordinarily favourable for the development of painting during the first half of the sixteenth century. The patronage of a splendid court, the closer communication, made possible by a unified Persia, between the schools of east and west, and the growth and spread of the technique so carefully elaborated in Herāt and in other fifteenth-century capitals, brought about, at this time, what many critics regard as the culmination of the Persian style—embodying to perfection the prevalent ideals of sumptuous elegance and decorative splendour.

The typical Safawī painting—and a good many examples have survived—is the last word in controlled luxury, reflecting the taste of a court richer and more refined than its predecessors. The pigments are of the finest, designs incline to elaboration, and the favourite subjects are scenes of court life, crowded with richly-dressed figures in sur-roundings of magnificent arched palace chambers or kingly gardens. Compositions tend to be static, with tall graceful youths and maidens, drawn with a new seductiveness and sinuosity of attitude, reclining, feasting, or making music; but the same note of sweetness and costly splendour is struck in the scenes of movement, the hunting and battle pictures, in which the central figure is not infrequently an obvious portrait of the reigning sovereign.

The tendency of the Herāt artists to eschew the warm colours is no longer apparent, every colour combination being attempted impartially, while in the search for sump-tuousness technical processes were further elaborated. In addition to the sprinkling of the paper with gold, or alternating pages of heavy glazed paper of different colours (the last device has not always a happy effect), the margins were sometimes covered with figures of animals, painted in gold, or of trees and foliage, often of great decorative beauty. The miniaturist's art was extended to the covers of books, now frequently lacquered. Many of the motives of the painters, incidentally, appear in contemporary carpets and textiles, which the court miniaturists doubtless often designed.

Side by side with the work of the great painters of the imperial studios many much less pretentious miniatures were painted, to the orders of less wealthy patrons. Some of these are real works of art; very few fail to charm; but a certain amount of perfunctory illustration—in rather greater proportion than in earlier epochs—was undoubtedly done during Tahmāsp's reign, as the breadth of the demand widened.

The earlier Safawī painting can generally be recognized quickly by the details of the costume, among which the characteristic turban is the most conspicuous. This curious head-dress is distinguished by the slender elongated *kulah*, or turban cap, which is pro-longed into a rod, projecting, often for many inches, above the turban which is wound round it.

Evliya Chelebi, the mid-seventeenth-century Turkish traveller, has a ridiculous account of the origin of this Safawī turban. Ibrāhīm, he says, the founder of the dynasty, once

[1] Iskandar Munshī, quoted in Blochet, *Notices sur les Manuscrits . . . de la Collection Marteau*, pp. 227, 228.

dreamed that he bore a child to an ass; and it had seventy fingers. This dream having been interpreted as foreshadowing the Empire, he swore that if it should be fulfilled he would commemorate the circumstance by wearing an ass's phallus in his turban, and by imitating the cries of the animal in music. 'That is the reason why the Persian crown and head-dress have their present shape, and why their music resembles the braying of an ass.' Actually, the red *kulah*, which gave the Safawī Shī'as their name of *Qizil-bāsh* or 'Red-heads', was probably made high so as to support the conical turban, with its twelve folds, representing the Twelve Shī'a *imāms*, 'Alī and his descendants; but it was often exaggeratedly tall, some of the Mullas' being as much as two yards in length. It was not invariably red.

There is in the sixteenth century no absolute distinction to be drawn between the styles of different parts of the Empire. The court artists of the capitals of Tabrīz and Qazwīn set the fashion, and though examples exist of provincial styles, there is little difference, as a rule, between the work of east and west Persia. Herāt painting, in particular, seems to become largely assimilated, fairly early in the century, to the prevailing manner, though in some manuscript miniatures the Khurāsān style still lingers.

Herāt, owing to its great geographical and political importance, retained its prestige for the first third of the century. Tahmāsp and his brother Sām Mīrzā were successively appointed its Governors, and this practice of appointing royal princes as Governors in the eastern province was continued long afterwards, in spite of Uzbek invasions, looting, and persecutions.

Typical of the transition period between the Herāt style of the fifteenth century and that of the Safawīs are the illustrations of a manuscript written at Balkh—then a city of Khurāsān—in 1504 (no. 120). These illustrations[1] are very close to fifteenth-century work, and the Safawī turbans (unless, as seems improbable, these were added later) seem to be an isolated phenomenon at this date, outside Shāh Ismā'īl's territory.

One of the most splendid of the manuscripts of this period is the magnificent copy of the works of Mīr 'Alī Shīr Nawā'ī at the Bibliothèque Nationale, completed in Herāt in A.D. 1527, the miniatures of which have been reproduced in most of the standard works.[2] They are unsigned, but are probably the work of Bihzād's Tabrīz pupils, at least in part. It is at any rate not impossible that the artists accompanied the Shāh on one of his not infrequent visits to Herāt, or the manuscript may have been copied in Herāt and the illustrations subsequently added in Tabrīz. In one of them, a hunting scene, Bahrām Gūr is represented in the likeness of Shāh Ismā'īl, though the Shāh had died three years earlier. In another, representing the death of Farhād, there are strong fifteenth-century traces; but in most of the others the Safawī style is already established. In the scene of the love of the Shaykh of San'ān[3] for the Christian damsel M. Blochet suspects the hand of Bihzād himself, mainly, it would appear, on account of

[1] Marteau and Vever, figs. 84, 85, and 88; Sakisian, fig. 110. Stchoukine (*Louvre Cat.*, p. 17) would date the miniatures 1520–30.
[2] e.g. Blochet, *Les Enluminures*, pls. xlviii–li; Sakisian, figs. 111, 112, 114–16; *Musulman Painting*, pls. cxxi–cxxv.
[3] Blochet, *Les Enluminures*, pl. xlviii.

the resemblance of the figure of the Shaykh to a similar figure in the little miniature in a manuscript of 1524 (no. 131). Bihzād, however, must have been an old man at the time, and the Bibliothèque Nationale miniature shows no trace of failing powers, while no. 131, exquisite as it is, does not quite equal it in sureness of drawing.

A fair number of other miniatures, of this period or earlier, which appear to have been produced in eastern Persia, exist, some of the finest being those in the *Khamsa* of Nizāmī at the Metropolitan Museum of New York,[1] dated 1524, the scribe being Sultān Muhammad Nūr of Herāt,[2] a protégé of Mīr 'Alī Shīr. In the illustrations of both of these manuscripts, and in a few others of somewhat earlier dates, something of the quality of the previous century can be traced; the figures are still a little stiff; the full ripeness of maturity is not yet apparent. The drawing has not reached the limit of facility that was soon to be attained; but the miniatures have a notable grace and beauty, they are the work of gifted artists, who cannot be accused of surrendering overmuch to grandiose ends and the cult of preciosity.

Of even greater individuality are the miniatures in M. Cartier's *Dīwān* of Hāfiz, which was shown at Burlington House.[3] This manuscript, which is discussed elsewhere, is partly illustrated by the celebrated Sultān Muhammad and Shaykh-zāda. Its exact date is problematical, but it cannot well be earlier than the birth of Sām Mīrzā, Shāh Tahmāsp's brother, whose name appears in an inscription in one of the miniatures, unless this inscription was added later, which there is no reason to believe. This prince was born in 1517, and one would naturally therefore be disposed to date the miniatures at least fifteen or twenty years later, when he would have been of an age to appreciate them. They may, however, be earlier, and they certainly possess qualities of liveliness and sincerity which tend to disappear in the great aristocratic painting of the beginning of the second third of the century, with marked Khurasanian traces, in the figure-drawing and grouping, which do not occur a little later on.

A notable manuscript of the early years of Shāh Tahmāsp's reign is the profusely illustrated *Zafar-nāma*, or history of Tīmūr, copied in 1529 by Sultān Muhammad Nūr, which was lent to the Exhibition by the Persian Government (no. 137, Pl. LXXXIX). The difficulty in accepting the statement in the colophon that the miniatures are by Bihzād consists in the fact that it is hard to detect in them any trace of Bihzād's style, as we know it. The designs are varied and interesting, and often show great skill in spacing and general arrangement, but there is a certain lack of mastery in the working out of the details, and the colouring is not of uniform beauty. Some of these miniatures, however, are very arresting, and the standard maintained throughout is one of high if not supreme accomplishment.

The same remarks partly apply to the even more sumptuous *Shāh-nāma* belonging

---

[1] Jackson and Yohannan, *Catalogue of Persian Manuscripts—Cochran Collection*, pp. 58–67, pls. 3–6. Martin, *The Nizami MS. from the Library of the Shah of Persia*, 1927. See also p. 108, above.
[2] A very fine *Dīwān* of Hāfiz, copied by Sultān

Muhammad Nūr in 930/1524, with seven miniatures closely resembling in style those noted, formerly belonged to M. Claude Anet. It was auctioned at Sotheby's on June 4, 1920 (lot 67, pl. v).
[3] No. 127, pls. LXXXIII–LXXXIV, colour plate LXXV.

to Baron Edmond de Rothschild, dated a few years later, in 1537. This manuscript, unique in the number of its illustrations, of which there are 256, apparently by the chief court artists of the day, is a wonderful monument of industry and skill. A good selection of the miniatures is reproduced in Martin, pls. 122–9. There is something unsatisfying and a trifle mechanical about these paintings. Technically excellent, they somehow just fail to 'come off', and give the impression of a set task conscientiously performed, without particular enthusiasm, by talented and carefully trained painters.

But unquestionably the finest known manuscript of the first half, and indeed of the whole, of the sixteenth century is the great *Khamsa* of Nizāmī belonging to the British Museum (Or. 2265), which was copied by a great scribe, Shāh Maḥmūd of Nīshā-pūr, for Shāh Tahmāsp between the years 1539 and 1543, at Tabrīz, and is lavishly ornamented and illustrated with fourteen large miniatures of dazzling beauty and refine-ment by Mīrak, Sultān Muhammad, Mīr Sayyid 'Alī, Mirzā 'Alī, and Muzaffar 'Alī, with, possibly, other collaborators. The miniatures have been frequently reproduced, and can be seen in colour in the *Studio* publication on this manuscript.[1] They represent the climax of the grand style, and the richest and ripest achievement of Persian technique.[2]

Many hundreds of examples of the work of the sixteenth-century painters have been preserved. For the most part these are still unsigned, and only a small proportion con-tain any clue to the identity of the artists; moreover, when a painting contains a name, it is frequently difficult to judge between a genuine signature and an ascription written by an owner or a library clerk. Such ascriptions, moreover, may be contemporary, in which case they have some likelihood of being genuine; or they may be much later than the paintings, when they are obviously of little value, even when they are not dishonest forgeries. It is often impossible to judge the date when a name was written, even approxi-mately, as expert scribes can imitate earlier writing with marvellous skill. Obscure names are, of course, less likely to be forged than celebrated ones; and due weight has to be given, in trying to identify artists' work, to a picture's history. A 'find' in the bazaar, for instance, is more likely to have been forged than a miniature that has been preserved for many years in a great library, public or private.

Though, however, most miniatures are unsigned, and though many signatures and ascriptions are certainly forged or erroneous, there are still far more genuinely signed examples belonging to the sixteenth than to the fifteenth century, while the number of known artists shows a considerable increase. A certain amount of material has been collected, in the present century, on the history of the painters, by such writers as M. Blochet, Sir Thomas Arnold, and M. Sakisian, from Persian and Turkish sources, but the results of their painstaking researches are meagre, fragmentary, and sometimes

---

[1] *The Poems of Nizami*, described by Laurence Binyon, London, 1928.
[2] It is not absolutely certain that the ascriptions to the artists are genuine, and it is not absolutely impossible that they are all by one hand; but the manuscript must always have been famous, it is obviously illustrated by

the greatest master, or masters, of the day, and it is difficult to see why any but correct names should have been given. M. Blochet considers that two of the pictures are signed by the calligrapher on behalf of Mīrak and Sayyid 'Alī, and that all may possibly be by these artists.

conflicting, and we are still very much in the dark on such matters as the stylistic character of different schools and the individual works of the painters.

No attempt will be made, in what follows, to do more than summarize some of the known facts about a few of the chief artists of the early Safawī period, with some remarks on their apparent characteristics and probable works.

Little remains to be said about Bihzād. He lived for about thirteen years after his appointment as head of the royal atelier in 1522, and his death occurred, according to the chronogram noted elsewhere,[1] in 1535 or 1536, though another account places it some two years earlier.[2]

Practically nothing that can be attributed with confidence to Bihzād in his Safawī period has survived. One miniature, however, which was exhibited at Burlington House, and which bears the date 930 A.H. (= 1524), seems to be undoubtedly his. The evidence for its genuineness is discussed farther on.[3] This little circular painting, of a sage and a youth conversing, is a brilliant example of minute work, most charming to the eye, but the drawing is a trifle less certain than in the Herāt period. It is not impossible that the lack of known examples of Bihzād's work towards the end of his life may be accounted for by a consciousness that his powers were beginning to fail. The drawing of the two fighting camels from Tehran (no. 132, Plate LXXXVII A) does, perhaps, contain a suggestion of decline.

There is a drawing[4] in the Louvre, slightly coloured, of the young Shāh Tahmāsp looking down from a platform fixed in a *chenar* tree, with courtiers and attendants on foot. On the left of the ladder by which the Shāh has climbed up is the inscription, in very minute writing, *Pīr i ghulām Bihzād* ('The old slave Bihzād'); and on the skirt of the figure of an old attendant, at the right of the picture, are the words *Pīr i qāpujī* ('The old door-keeper'). The drawing also bears the name of the Shāh, who appears to be about sixteen years old; and this would date it somewhere near the year 1530. The sketch is full of happy characterization, and may be genuine.

The chronicler Iskandar Munshī, writing early in the succeeding century,[5] couples with Bihzād the painter Sultān Muhammad. Both, he tells us, had attained the greatest eminence and world-wide fame for the delicacy of their brush; and Tahmāsp, who in his early youth had the greatest enthusiasm for painting, was Sultān Muhammad's pupil in the art. There is a tendency nowadays to ascribe any fine painting of the early years of Shāh Tahmāsp's reign to this painter or to Mīrak, but actually the data for forming a judgement of his style are very meagre. He is credited with two of the finest of the miniatures in the great *Nizāmī* in the British Museum (Or. 2265), mentioned above, and he may have painted others in the same manuscript. Both have his name attached to them. These two paintings, of Khusraw discovering Shīrīn bathing, and of Bahrām hunting lions, reveal a superb colourist, a master of the sumptuous style. 'He was

---

[1] See Appendix I.
[2] See Sakisian, p. 105.
[3] Catalogue no. 131.

[4] Sakisian, fig. 133; Migeon, fig. 38.
[5] A.D. 1616. Arnold, *P.I.*, p. 141.

a close observer of natural action in men and animals; his figures are graceful, his horses of marvellous elegance; and he excels in movement.'¹ Sultān Muhammad shows himself a powerful caricaturist in the unique scene of revelry in M. Cartier's *Hāfiz* (Pl. LXXV), while the picture of the prince surrounded by his youthful court in the same manuscript (Pl. LXXXIV A) exemplifies his power to fuse traditional elements into a fresh design of rare poetry and grace.

Shāh Tahmāsp's brother, Sām Mīrzā, and Iskandar Munshī both speak of Āqā Mīrak, the former in terms of the highest praise, as being, in the year 957/1550 when he wrote, the unrivalled leader of the court painters. He was a man of high status, a Sayyid of Isfahān, and also wrote poetry.² Possibly the fact that he was descended from the Prophet may have influenced the Shāh, who was, at any rate later in life, fanatically scrupulous in matters of religion, in his choice of Mīrak as his special intimate. Mīrak is said by ʿAlī, the Turkish historian, to have been the pupil of Bihzād and the master of Sultān Muhammad. Five of the paintings in the British Museum *Nizāmī* are attributed to this artist. Three are of magnificent court scenes, and the subjects of the other two are Nūshīrwān listening to the owls conversing among the ruins (clearly signed), and Majnūn among the wild animals—each, in its way, a masterpiece, showing how Mīrak, like Sultān Muhammad, was not hampered by conventional themes and motives. No other known works can be attributed to this great painter with anything like certainty.

One of the most sumptuous miniatures of the British Museum *Nizāmī* (Or. 2265) depicts the famous incident of Bahrām Gūr transfixing the foot and ear of a wild ass with a single arrow. The picture is inscribed 'the work of the Master Muzaffar ʿAlī'. This artist, who also painted two miniatures in the public library at Leningrad,³ is highly praised by Iskandar Munshī, who tells us that he was a pupil of Bihzād, that he was especially distinguished as a portrait-painter, that he designed, and for the most part executed, the pictures in the royal palace and the hall of the Chihil Sutūn at Isfahān, and that he did not long survive the death of Shāh Tahmāsp (1576). He was apparently the acknowledged master in his art in the period succeeding that of Mīrak and Sultān Muhammad. Iskandar speaks of his 'golden' painting, and to judge by the specimen which we have of his work, a blaze of gold with a good deal of red in the details, the epithet may be meant in a literal sense. Of Mirzā ʿAlī of Tabrīz, another collaborator in this manuscript, little is known except that he was greatly renowned in his time, and that he had a pupil named Kamāl, several of whose works have survived.⁴ Of Mīr Sayyid ʿAlī, the fifth named painter of this monumental *Nizāmī*, something will be said later.

The Sayyid Mīr Naqqāsh, mentioned in Appendix I, is presumably the same painter as the follower of Bihzād of whom ʿAlī tells. He was director of Tahmāsp's Tabrīz

---

¹ Binyon, *The Poems of Nizami*, p. 5.
² See Blochet, 'Les Manuscrits Orientaux de la Collection Marteau' (*Notices et Extraits*, t. xli), pp. 226 and 227; Arnold, *Painting in Islam*, p. 141. See also
Appendix I.
³ Martin, i, p. 118.
⁴ Sakisian, pp. 124, 125, with references.

atelier and his painter-in-chief (Sakisian, pp. 108, 111). His place of origin was Isfahān or Sultānia. Sayyid 'Alī was probably his son (see footnote on p. 119)—a point of considerable interest in tracing the influence of the 'Bihzadian' teaching.

In M. Cartier's *Dīwān* of Hāfiz (no. 127) there is a miniature of a scene in a mosque, signed by Shaykh-zāda, illustrating some satirical lines on the hypocrisy of preachers (Pl. LXXXIV B). The painting is the work of a great draughtsman; and a keen sense of character is shown in the expressions and attitudes of the audience, who are differently affected by the sermon.

Shaykh-zāda is mentioned by 'Ālī as a native of Khurāsān, and a pupil of Bihzād. Whether he subsequently came to Tabrīz, or whether Sultān Muhammad, his collaborator in the Cartier *Hāfiz*, worked with him in Khurāsān, cannot be determined.

One of the most delicious line-drawings in all Persian art is that, often reproduced, of a seated boy, holding a book and a flower, lent to the Exhibition by M. Koechlin (no. 145), and signed by Shaykh Muhammad. This drawing, of which several versions exist, probably belongs to the first half of the sixteenth century; but it is difficult to believe that the same artist painted the brilliantly coloured 'Camel with its keeper', inscribed with his name, and dated 1556 (no. 146). Possibly there were several artists and calligraphers of this name. Iskandar Munshī refers to a Shaykh Muhammad of Shīrāz as an expert painter and calligrapher, who imitated European models and created a vogue for them. He joined the royal library staff in the reign of Ismā'īl Mīrzā (1576–8), and later, under Shāh 'Abbās, took part in the building of the new palace of Qazwīn.

A few years later than the British Museum *Nizāmī* of 1539–43 an unknown painter illustrated the Persian version of Qazwīnī's *'Ajā'ib al-Makhlūqāt* with over six hundred illustrations of a very different character. This manuscript (no. 176, Pls. XCVI and XCVII) would be hard to parallel for variety, sustained fertility of invention, and the delightful ease and humour of the animal-drawing. All the miniatures are probably by the same artist, who may possibly have been, like the copyist, a native of Shīrāz. There is something of the perennial Shīrāz spirit, at any rate, in the gaiety, wit, and poetry of the drawing and colour. But this is far removed from typical court art.

Iskandar Munshī remarks that, in the latter part of his reign, Shāh Tahmāsp paid less attention to the work of his artists,[1] owing to the multitude of his occupations which left him no leisure. Tahmāsp certainly had plenty to occupy his time. His armies were almost continuously at war with the Ottoman forces of Sulaymān the Magnificent, the Uzbeks, and the Georgians, not to speak of smaller operations; while two of his own brothers, Sām Mīrzā and Alqās Mīrzā, rebelled against his authority. But the waning of the Shāh's interest in painting was more probably due to his increasing religious fanaticism, fostered, no doubt, by a naturally superstitious nature and the extraordinary semi-religious devotion of his people. The accounts of Queen Elizabeth's stouthearted

---

[1] He kept up his library, however, and Iskandar tells of a fine writer of *Suls* being appointed librarian towards the end of the reign.

envoy, Anthony Jenkinson, in 1562, and of the Venetian ambassador nine years later give the impression of a most unattractive character, gloomy, bigoted, and miserly, the latter noting that he had not come out of his palace for eleven years, 'nor having once gone to the chase nor any other kind of amusement, to the great dissatisfaction of his people'.[1] Such a change in their patron's tastes must have been disastrous for his artists; and it is not surprising that the grand style, which called for costly materials, disappeared before the middle of the century. It could only flourish under the direct patronage of a wealthy sovereign, and with the waning of his interest painting altered its character rapidly.

Ismā'īl II (1576-8) re-established the library on his accession, and employed some well-known artists, Zayn al-'Ābidīn, Siyāwush, Sādiqī Beg, Khwāja Nasīr, Shaykh Muhammad of Shīrāz, 'Alī Asghar of Kāshān, 'Abd Allāh of Shīrāz, and perhaps Muhammadī of Herāt.[2] This Shāh, however, only lived for two years, after murdering his brother, the gifted and artistic Sultān Ibrāhīm. None of the subsequent Shāhs were bibliophiles of the standards of their great predecessors.

Manuscripts from about 1560, or even earlier, tend to be more stereotyped, less finely decorated, thinner pigments taking the place of the rich opaque body-colour of the last two centuries; gold is less lavishly used, drawing becomes more careless and mechanical, especially in the innumerable *Shāh-nāmas* of the period, usually large volumes very much of a type. But the change is not absolute, and many fine illustrated manuscripts of the middle and last half of the century still exist. Among those shown at Burlington House some striking examples came from Mr. Chester Beatty's collection, such as 180 (Pl. CVIII A) and 182, while the Bodleian Library's *Yūsuf u Zulaykhā*, dated 1569 (no. 207), is a favourable example of a rather later period.

Much of the best painting and drawing of Shāh Tahmāsp's reign was in the form of separate miniatures, not intended for the illustration of manuscripts. Several contemporary albums of such miniatures exist. The separate drawing was of course no new invention; it was at least as early as the previous century; but the practice became steadily commoner as the standard of the book arts, which formerly absorbed the best miniature work, declined. A number of the most celebrated sixteenth-century examples, portraits, none attempting close realism, single figures or more elaborate compositions were exhibited, mostly in the Architectural Room, such as the portrait of the Safawid Prince, belonging to M. Vever (no. 142), another very fine version of the same subject (Mr. Beghian, no. 144); some attractive 'royal picnic' groups, and several complex line-drawings of exquisite detail of hunting scenes and other subjects. Many new examples

---

[1] *Travels of Venetians in Persia* (Hakluyt Society, 1873).
[2] Iskandar Munshī (see Arnold, *Painting in Islam*, pp. 141-4. Sir Thomas Arnold is mistaken in understanding 'Ismā'īl Mīrzā' to apply to the founder of the dynasty). The first three of these, with 'Alī Asghar and Naqdī Beg, are credited with miniatures in a *Shāh-* *nāma* of about this period (Marteau and Vever, pls. CII-CIV). The names are apparently entered by a librarian. The miniatures are in an ambitious style, typical of the period. According to 'Ālī, Zayn al-'Ābidīn was a pupil of Mīr Musawwir, as to whom see Appendix I.

were sent by the Persian Government, in a great album[1] of Persian and Indian miniatures, and these were removed from the album for the purpose of being shown on the walls of Burlington House.

A rare painter of the first half of the century was exemplified in a work by Muhammad Mu'min, belonging to Mr. Beghian (no. 170). Muhammad Mu'min was a pupil of one Muhammad of Herāt,[2] presumably the artist of no. 130, which is dated 1522, and no. 144.

No attempt was made at a full representation of the company of Persian artists who were employed in Turkey, but a drawing by the greatest of these, Shāh Qulī, was shown, representing an angel bearing a cup (no. 153). This artist, originally of Tabrīz, was a pupil of the celebrated Mīrak. He painted at the court of Sulaymān the Magnificent (1520–66), who was enthusiastically interested in painting, and showered favours upon Shāh Qulī. He is extravagantly praised by the Turkish writers,[3] and the drawing, which cannot, unfortunately, be reproduced here, is a most accomplished one, executed with extreme virtuosity. No. 154 is almost certainly by the same artist; and so, very probably, is no. 156. A number of his works are at Istanbul.

A master of the line-drawing, generally lightly tinted, was Muhammadī, son and pupil of Sultān Muhammad.[4] He is rather better represented than most contemporary painters; fortunately, too, for he has an original and attractive style, with a lightness and lively humour which are his own. One of the best known of his drawings, depicting a scene in the country, with humped oxen working a plough, and women in tents spinning and conversing, is dated 986 A.H. (= 1578). It is at the Louvre.[5] A copy, by Riza-yi 'Abbāsī, of a portrait by Muhammadī of a young man reading a book, at the British Museum,[6] contains an inscription in which Muhammadī is referred to as 'of Herāt'; but nothing is known of his life. A very beautiful picture of two lovers, and a picnic scene, both now at Boston,[7] and a gay drawing of masqueraders, at Leningrad, reveal different aspects of Muhammadī's varied talents. A version of the last was shown at Burlington House (no. 190), and of one of the picnic scenes in no. 192.

Not all the drawings attributed to Muhammadī are above suspicion. Of those, not mentioned above, which were included in the Exhibition, no. 187, a drawing of a young dervish; no. 191, of a youth and a musician; and no. 188, a coloured portrait of a page, are perhaps genuine. 'Alī states that Muhammadī painted lacquered bindings, which had by this time begun their long vogue.

This artist has left a self-portrait, now at Boston.[8]

Two painters of Shāh Tahmāsp's reign are of particular importance, not only on account of their eminence in their art, but because of the leading part which they played in the formation of the Mughal school of painting in India. Their names were Mīr

---

[1] See Appendix III. [2] Sakisian, p. 88.
[3] Ibid., p. 121.
[4] Ibid., p. 123 (quoting 'Alī). He seems to preserve something of his father's manner.
[5] Ibid., fig. 161; Stchoukine, *Louvre Cat.*, xx. His

floruit was shortly after Tahmāsp's death, according to Iskandar, who also refers to him as 'of Herāt'.
[6] Sarre and Mittwoch, Abb. 4 B; Martin, pl. 110.
[7] *Ars Asiatica*, XIII, pls. XXII, XXIV.
[8] Ibid., pl. XXIII; Schulz, Taf. 159.

Sayyid 'Alī and 'Abd al-Samad. Sayyid 'Alī was one of the painters who collaborated, if the attribution is correct, in illustrating the great *Khamsa* of Nizāmī which was completed in 1543. His one illustration in that manuscript reveals him as a fine designer, with an uncommon feeling for scenes of rural life. Its subject is the visit of Majnūn to Laylā's tent; but the artist has gone out of his way to introduce a series of pictures of shepherds, children, and serving-women leading their everyday existence in the fields and in their richly carpeted tents.

About a year after the completion of this manuscript the Mughal Emperor Humāyūn, son and successor of Bābur, was compelled, after losing his Indian throne, to seek refuge and assistance in Persia; he visited Tabrīz, and at the court of the Shāh he became acquainted with the artist, whom he engaged to superintend the illustration of the Romance of Amīr Hamza, a task in which fifty painters are said to have been employed for many years.

Mīr Sayyid 'Alī was a native of Tabrīz, being the son of a certain Mīr Mansūr.[1] Humāyūn seems to have had a high opinion of his merits, and to have conferred on him the title of *Nādir al-Mulk* ('the Wonder of the Kingdom'). He was also a poet.[2] It was from the illustration of the Hamza romance that Mughal painting originates, for the task was an immensely ambitious one, entailing two thousand four hundred illustrations of unusually large size, and the artists included, besides Sayyid 'Alī and his brother, many Indians as well as foreigners.[3] The work was apparently completed in Akbar's reign, but meanwhile, in 1549, Mīr Sayyid 'Alī was superseded, temporarily at least, by 'Abd al-Samad, son of the Governor of Shīrāz, who came to Kabul, where Humāyūn had established himself since 1545, for the purpose of taking up his post.

Numerous illustrations of the Hamza romance, painted on cloth, have survived,[4] and they have formed the subject of a beautifully produced publication.[5] Two of them were shown at the Exhibition (Nos. 227, 228); these are not, however, probably the actual work of either of the two Persian artists.

Paintings by Mīr Sayyid 'Alī are of the greatest rarity. Apart from the *Nizāmī* picture, the following have been attributed to him; two examples belonging to M. Cartier,[6] one at Boston,[7] and two which were shown at the Exhibition.[8] None of these can be said with any confidence to be genuine. The Boston example, one of the *Hamza* illustrations, was tentatively attributed to Sayyid 'Alī by Dr. Coomaraswamy mainly on the grounds of similarity in the drawing of a flock of sheep with a similar motive

[1] See the *Ā'īn i Akbarī*, Blochmann's text, vol. 1, p. 254; translation, p. 590. It is probable that *Mansūr* is a mistake for *Musawwir*, 'the painter'. The two words are easily confused in Persian, a single dot making nearly all the difference. If *Musawwir* is correct, Mīr Musawwir would be the well-known Tabrīz artist, as to whom see pp. 115–16 above and Appendix I. His being a Sayyid makes the identification the more probable.
[2] He wrote under the pen-name Judā'ī. Specimens of his verses are given in the *Ā'īn* and the *Atish-kada* (Bombay ed., p. 341). He lived on in India under

Akbar, who, like his father, conferred a title on him.
[3] *Ma'āsir al-Umarā*, translated by Beveridge, p. 454.
[4] They are mostly in Vienna and Paris, at South Kensington, and in America.
[5] *Die indischen Miniaturen des Haemzae-Romanes*, hrsg. von H. Glück, Wien, 1925.
[6] Sakisian, figs. 152 and 190.
[7] Coomaraswamy, *Catalogue of the Indian Collections*, part VI (1930), plate I.
[8] Nos. 224 (pl. CIII A) and 225.

in the Nizāmī picture. Whether this painter is represented at all in the surviving *Hamza* pictures is not definitely known. But there is a stronger likelihood of Sayyid 'Alī, or alternatively 'Abd al-Samad, having painted the unique 'Emperors and Princes of the House of Tīmūr' at the British Museum,[1] which, like the *Hamza* pictures, is a large painting on cloth. This may well have been the first work commissioned by Humāyūn, and may date from a few years before the middle of the sixteenth century.[2] Mīr Sayyid 'Alī's successor, 'Abd al-Samad, called *Shīrīn-Qalam*, or 'Sweet-brush', had an interesting career in India. Akbar appointed him Master of the Mint at his capital, Fathpur Sīkrī, and he was subsequently made Dīwān of Multān, in 1586. He also had the distinction of teaching Akbar drawing. His son was an intimate friend of Jahāngīr, who mentions him several times in his Memoirs.

It is significant that both Mīr Sayyid 'Alī, a descendant of the Prophet, and 'Abd al-Samad, were men of high social position; but it would be incorrect to assume that these and similar instances point to a generally high status among painters, at this or at any period. Though the ruler's favour, if he happened to be interested in painting, conferred a certain prestige on the court artists, and though particular artists might command personal respect, there are several stories which prove that, both in Persia and in India, they were subject to considerable prejudice. In the case of 'Abd al-Samad prestige would have been enhanced from his wonderful skill as a calligrapher. So steady was his hand, and so marvellous his eyesight, that he is recorded to have written on a single poppy seed the short 112th chapter of the Qur'ān (which contains the phrase *allāhu al-samadu*, 'God is eternal').

Several of 'Abd al-Samad's paintings are known. In the Bodleian is a small sketch,[3] showing considerable realistic power, of an important incident in Akbar's early career, the arrest of Shāh Abu'l-Ma'ālī by Tuluq Khān Qūchī in 1556. The drawing may possibly be rather later than the incident depicted.

In Mr. Dyson Perrins' *Khamsa* of Nizāmī, written in 1593, is a full-page representation[4] of a hunting scene, of a type not uncommon in illustrations of the *Akbar-nāma*, crowded with figures of men and animals. It is close in style to Indian work of the period, and if the attribution to 'Abd al-Samad is genuine it shows very clearly the influence of environment in modifying the pure Persian conventions.

Both of these bear similar ascriptions—they can hardly be signatures, owing to the use of the honorific *Khwāja*—'the work of Khwāja 'Abd al-Samad'.

A not very distinguished group in the sixteenth-century Indian *Dārāb-nāma* at the British Museum[5] bears the inscription 'the work of Bihzād, corrected by Khwāja 'Abd al-Samad'. This Bihzād was an Indian painter.

---

[1] See Mr. L. Binyon's monograph on this subject, published 1930 by Order of the Trustees of the Museum.
[2] The Louvre collection contains a portrait which may be a self-portrait of Mīr Sayyid 'Alī (Stchoukine, *Miniatures indiennes . . . au Musée du Louvre* (1929), p. 12 and pl. II (a)).

[3] Reproduced in P. Brown, *Indian Painting under the Mughals*, pl. VIII, fig. 2.
[4] Reproduced in Martin, pl. 179; P. Brown, pl. 36.
[5] Or. 4615. Reproduced in Vincent Smith's *History of Fine Art in India and Ceylon*, p. 453 (2nd ed., pl. 150).

The five examples from Persia bearing this artist's name[1] throw valuable and favourable light on his style. He had a good deal, it seems, in common with Sayyid 'Alī, and, like him, excelled in the telling portrayal of detail, besides being an admirable animal-painter. Nos. 230 and 231 must be counted among the leading productions of the Indo-Persian style. Nos. 232 and 233 are, as the inscriptions testify, more rapidly executed work, intended, perhaps, as New-Year gifts for the Emperor.

Mughal painting, in its beginnings, learnt much from Persia, though long before the end of the sixteenth century it evolved a style which derived more and more from European and indigenous standards, while a little later, under the Emperors Jahāngīr and Shāh Jahān, when the art attained its highest achievements in portraiture and animal subjects, the Persian stream is often hardly discernible.

It was otherwise in Turkey, the only other country where Persian painting exercised any appreciable influence. Here, the Turks having no strong native tradition of painting, while Persian literature was for centuries widely read and imitated, Persian models were followed far more closely than in India. Many so-called Turkish paintings of the sixteenth century are undoubtedly the work of Persian artists, several of whom are known to have practised under the Ottoman Sultans. Only a few of these 'Turkish' miniatures were shown at Burlington House, two of which, by Shāh Qulī, have already been mentioned. A later painter of some renown was Walī Jān, of Tabrīz, pupil of Siyāwush Beg the Georgian. He has left several portraits and drawings of single figures. No. 237, a portrait of a dervish, bears his name, and M. Blochet, Sir Thomas Arnold, and M. Sakisian have reproduced several other specimens of this facile artist's work.[2] Walī Jān belongs, however, to the latter part of the century. His manner bears a close resemblance to that of Shāh Qulī. His master Siyāwush has also left one drawing, now at the Louvre, of a hunting scene,[3] a very elaborate composition. Some details about him are given by Iskandar Munshī.[4] He was formerly page to Shāh Tahmāsp, who encouraged his talent. Iskandar also gives[5] a long account of Sādiqī Beg, an Afshār Turk, famous for his skill as a portrait-painter and the marvellous fineness of his drawing. He was in turn a Dervish and a soldier, and wrote poetry. He, like Siyāwush, lived into the reign of Shāh 'Abbās, but fell out of favour owing to his overbearing disposition. He is perhaps the artist of no. 301, and of two drawings reproduced in Blochet, *Musulman Painting*, pls. 138 and 140. All of these bear the name Sādiq, but the names are not, apparently, signatures. One of these drawings, of a very modish lady of the court, or more probably of the *demi-monde*, is of superb elegance, and it is sad that so few of the 'thousands of marvellous portraits', of which Iskandar Munshī tells, by this attractive artist have come down to us.

But Sādiq belongs rather to the reign of Shāh 'Abbās, which will be considered in the following chapter.

[1] Nos. 229–33.
[2] Sakisian, figs. 164, 166; Blochet, *Musulman Painting*, pl. 147; Arnold and Grohmann, *The Islamic Book*, pl. 93.
[3] Sakisian, fig. 157; Marteau and Vever, no. 210.
[4] The passage is translated in Arnold, *Painting in Islām*, p. 143.
[5] Arnold, op. cit., p. 142.

CATALOGUE

A. BUKHĀRĀ MINIATURES

104 [501] MINIATURES from an album arranged by Mīr Maʿsūm Khwāja, the binder, in 1260/1844, by order of ʿAbd al-Khāliq Nizām al-Mulk Dastarkhānchī, and presented by the latter to the Mashhad shrine. Four paintings signed by Mahmūd (see p. 106 foll.).

Early XVI century. ¶ Lent by PERSIAN GOVERNMENT from the Mashhad shrine.

(*a*) Three damsels from China, inscribed 'Nāzanīnān i Chīn', 'Sweethearts of China'. Signed *Mahmūd Muzahhib.* One of the girls carries chop-sticks and a jar. 15·5×9 *cm.*

PLATE LXXVI A.

(*b*) Youth offering an apple to a lady. Signed, below the lady, '*amal i Mahmūd Muzahhib.* The inscription between them, 'The Qalmāq King', in another hand, is probably simply based on the costume of the man with his bell-shaped hat. The faces are partly erased and carelessly redrawn. (Another version is in the Museum of Fine Arts, Boston: *Goloubev Cat.*, pl. XXII, no. 42.) 20·5×11·5 *cm.* PLATE LXXVII B.

(*c*) Angel in blue, yellow and red. Signed *Mahmūd Muzahhib.* 17·5×9 *cm.*

(*d*) Portrait of Mīr ʿAlī Shīr Nawāʾī (1441–1501), inscribed 'Portrait of the great Amīr, Mīr ʿAlī Shīr'. Signed *Mahmūd Muzahhib.* Mīr ʿAlī Shīr wears a blue robe, over which is a brown cloak, and a white turban over a green *kulah.* 16×7 *cm.* PLATE LXXVI B.

The subject of this portrait was one of the leading figures in Persian literary history, and, with Jāmī, the most celebrated figure in the Islamic literary world during the second part of the fifteenth century. Born in 1441, he was the son of an Amīr of the court of Sultān Abu Saʿīd—grandfather of Bābur, and was an intimate friend and old schoolfellow of Sultān Husayn Bayqarā, who, on gaining the sovereignty of Herāt, sent for him from Samarqand, whither he had retired after quarrelling with Abu Saʿīd. He held various high official posts in Khurāsān, and acquired enormous wealth, which, however, he spent lavishly, endowing many charitable and religious institutions, and being a generous patron of literature and the arts. He was a distinguished writer in prose and poetry, both Eastern Turkī and Persian, though Bābur criticizes him for some of his compositions. He was, says Bābur, noted for his refined manners. 'He had neither son nor daughter, wife nor family; he let the world pass by, alone and unencumbered.... He took nothing from the Mīrzā; on the contrary, he each year offered considerable gifts.'[1] He was himself a musician and painter, and 'it was through his effort and supervision that Master Bihzād and Shāh Muzaffar became so distinguished in painting'.[2] He seems to have had a sense of humour. Bābur relates that one day at a chess-party he touched the hind parts of the poet Banāʾī and exclaimed, 'It is a sad nuisance in Herāt that a man cannot stretch out his leg without touching a poet's backside'. 'Nor draw it up again,' Banāʾī retorted.

There is another portrait of Mīr ʿAlī Shīr in the Serai Library at Istanbul, signed '*Alī.* Sakisian[3] thinks it may possibly be a self-portrait, but it seems more likely to be a copy of the one reproduced here, to which it is much inferior in quality.

105 [541 c] ʿĀRIFĪ'S *GŪY U CHAWGĀN*, 'The Ball and the Polo Stick', an allegorical poem[4] (written 1438–9). Copied by ʿAlī al-Husaynī at Herāt in 929/1523. Two miniatures and two illuminated 'dedication' pages. Formerly in the possession of the Great Mughal Jahāngīr (whose autograph it bears) and, later, of Fath ʿAlī Shāh.

22·5×15 *cm.* Marteau-Vever, no. 86. ¶ Lent by M. L. CARTIER, Paris.

(*a*) Frontispiece, decorated with angels. The right-hand page of the double-page opening containing the first lines of the poem, which is a mystical allegory, employing, throughout,

---

[1] Beveridge's translation of the Memoirs of Bābur, p. 272.
[2] Ibid.
[3] Op. cit., p. 63. It is in the album formerly numbered 37086, but now 1722.
[4] The text and a translation by Mr. R. S. Greenshields have recently been published. The translation contains three miniatures in colour of polo subjects.

elaborate images taken from the game of polo. These angels were quite commonly used as spandrel ornaments in the sixteenth century. No doubt originally, as perhaps here, they had a mystical significance, but later they came to be used purely decoratively. The elaborate background of double arabesques superimposed is a favourite one in the early sixteenth century and is even used as a dress-pattern. Though the manuscript was copied at Herāt the miniatures seem to be of the Bukhārā school and would therefore have been added later. PLATE LXXVIII B.

106 [716 D] 'ASSĀR'S *MIHR U MUSHTARĪ*, 'The Sun and Jupiter', copied by Ibrāhīm Khalīl at Bukhārā in 929/1523. Four full-page miniatures. Lacquer binding. A mystical romantic *masnawī* composed in 778/1377 by Muhammad 'Assār[1] of Tabrīz, relating the love and friendship of Mihr and Mushtarī, their separation, adventures, reunion, and simultaneous deaths.

26·5 × 17 *cm.* Schulz, Taf. 79, 80. ¶ Lent by KALEBDJIAN, Paris.

(*a*) The two friends Mihr, the son of the king, and Mushtarī, the son of the Wazīr, are entrusted to a learned teacher for their education. PLATE LXXX B.
(*b*) Mihr kills a ferocious lion which has attacked the company of merchants with whom he has become associated in the course of his wanderings. PLATE LXXIX B.
(*c*) Mihr, after his wanderings, is entertained by King Kaywān. He is here the king's guest at a moonlight drinking party. PLATE LXXIX A.
(*d*) The marriage of Mihr and the Princess Nawhīd, daughter of King Kaywān. PLATE LXXXA.

This fine manuscript, which is dated from Bukhārā, is an excellent guide to the state of painting in Transoxiana in the early part of the century when the school there was just coming into being. The miniatures are of a notably smooth facture and a pale colour-scheme.

107 [718 B] SA'DĪ'S *BŪSTĀN*, copied by 'Alī al-Husaynī in 931/1524 in *nasta'līq*. Headings in gold and colour. One *'unwān*, two miniatures. Bukhārā. Red leather binding, gold-stamped with medallion.

26 × 17·5 *cm.* ¶ Lent by M. H. VEVER, Paris.

(*a*) A saint riding a leopard and grasping a snake in his hand encounters the poet on foot. The figures in the background at their several tasks are decorative features unconnected with the main incident depicted. PLATE LXXXI A.
(*b*) Court scene.

108 [120 D] FOUR POEMS by Jāmī, copied respectively by Mīr Husayn al-Kātib al-Khāqānī al-Husaynī in 950/1543, Muhammad 'Alī b. Mahmūd al-Munajjim al-Khāqānī in Bukhārā in 954/1547, and Khwāja Jān in Bukhārā in 954/1547. The celebrated poet and scholar, 'Abd al-Rahmān b. Ahmad, known as Jāmī (d. 1493), wrote seven religious and romantic *masnawīs*, known as the *Haft Awrang*. Manuscripts of five, or a less number, of these are fairly numerous. Far the most famous is the *Yūsuf u Zulaykhā*, the subject of which is the story of Joseph and Potiphar's wife. The colophons contain the information that separate parts of the manuscript were transcribed under the care of Khwāja Sultān Mīrak Kitābdār (the Librarian). Nine miniatures. Black leather binding.

22 × 14 *cm.* ¶ Lent by A. CHESTER BEATTY, ESQ.

[1] Cf. Ouseley, *Biographical Notices of Persian Poets*, 1846.

109 [716 c] ALBUM. Anthology. Fifty-two folios of calligraphy ascribed to Mīr 'Alī, with double-page *sarlawh*, decorated margins, and six small figure miniatures of the Bukhārā school. Mid XVI century. Stamped leather binding. The album formerly belonged to Hamīda Bānū, wife of the Emperor Humāyūn, and mother of Akbar.

16·5 × 10 *cm.* ¶ Lent by Y. DAWUD, ESQ.

110 [541 F] JĀMĪ'S *TUHFAT AL-AHRĀR* or 'Gift of the Free', a religious *masnawī*, copied by Mīr 'Alī al-Husaynī, under the care of Sultān Mīrak Kitābdār. Bukhārā school. Dated 915/1509; but in view of the fact that one of the miniatures bears the date 955/1548, it is very probable that the date intended was 951/1544–5. A similar confusion is not uncommon in the dates of Bukhārā manuscripts. Mīr 'Alī *al-Husaynī* or *al-Harawī*, the calligrapher, was taken to Bukhārā in 1534 or 1535. Decorated text inside margins of different coloured gold-sprinkled paper. One *sarlawh*, two *'unwāns*, and three miniatures. Seals of Mughal emperors. An endorsement records the fact that the manuscript was in the library of the Emperor Akbar in 963/1556, the first year of his reign. It is therefore almost certain that it must have belonged to his father Humāyūn. Black leather binding with animal motives stamped in gold inside lattice-work.

28 × 18 *cm.* ¶ Lent by A. CHESTER BEATTY, ESQ. (Beatty Library, Dublin, Ms. 215).

(*a*) Taking augury from the flight of ducks.
(*b*) A Canaanite presenting Yūsuf with a mirror. At the top is an inscription, 'In the days of the Khāqān, just and generous, Abu'l-Ghāzī 'Abd al-'Azīz Bahādur Khān, in the year 955'. 'Abd al-'Azīz ruled at Bukhārā from 947 to 957 (1540–9). The date on this miniature corresponds to A.D. 1547/8.
(*c*) A youth declaring his love to a lady. He wears a purple cloak over a yellow under-garment, and a white turban with a green *kulah*. A blue sky is visible behind the golden hill (fol. 63).

PLATE LXXXI B.

These miniatures are typical of the work produced by the Herāt artists whom the Uzbeks forced or persuaded to take employment at their courts in Transoxiana after the fall of Herāt.

111 [541 A] JĀMĪ'S *TUHFAT AL-AHRĀR*, copied by Mīr Husayn, known as Mīr Kulangī. Headings in red, paper gold-sprinkled. Margins decorated in gold and colour with arabesque designs. The date reads 98, which must be intended for 980/1572. Bukhārā. Formerly owned by Muhammad Hasan. Two miniatures. Black leather cover; inside, figures of animals, birds and trees in inlaid coloured leather.

24·5 × 16 *cm.* ¶ Lent by A. CHESTER BEATTY, ESQ.

(*a*) Yūsuf on a throne, being presented with a mirror.
(*b*) Taking augury from duck's flight.
    Very inferior to the preceding manuscript of the poem owned by Mr. Chester Beatty (no. 110), which contains miniatures of the same subjects. It shows the decadence of the Bukhārā school after the middle of the century.

Huart (p. 211) mentions Mīr Husayn Kulangī of Bukhārā as a pupil of Mīr 'Alī. This mystical poem by Jāmī was obviously extremely popular in the sixteenth century and copies of it are frequently met with. It seems to have been an especial favourite at Bukhārā. In addition to these two manuscripts in the Chester Beatty collection mention may be made of four other Bukhārā copies:

(1) Arthur Sambon collection, Sale, Paris, May 1914, lot 190. Said to have been dated 1031, but evidently from the catalogue plate a Bukhārā manuscript.

(2) Claude Anet collection, Sale, Sotheby, 4 June 1920, lot 68. Copied by Mīr Husayn al-Husaynī in 962/1554. Three miniatures (one reproduced, which is close to no. 110 (a)).

(3) Marteau-Vever, no. 123 (Demotte collection). Copied by Mīr Husayn al-Husaynī, called Mīr Kulangī al-Hājī, in 1575. Two miniatures, of which one is reproduced.

(4) Octave Homberg Sale, lot 88 and plate xxxix. Frontispiece signed: *Mahmūd*. Colophon obliterated. These appear to be all quite distinct manuscripts.

112 [724 F] JĀMĪ'S *TUHFAT-AL-AHRĀR*, copied by Bābā Mīrak al-Tashkandī in 966/1558. Margins decorated in gold. Three miniatures in the Bukhārā style. Lacquer binding.

21 × 12·5 *cm*. Marteau-Vever, no. 89. ¶ Lent by M. H. VEVER, Paris.

(a) Musicians in a garden. The left half of a double-page frontispiece opening. The verses are from Hāfiz, and are not connected with the poem but solely with the miniature. They read:
'Delightful are the garden, the rose and the wine,
    Yet when the loved one is away they delight no longer.'
The combination in this miniature of cypress and fruit tree and of lute and harp is symbolical. The formal landscape and arrested figures are typical of the Bukhārā school, as is the brilliant, clear colouring, with pale blue sky. The date of the manuscript had been altered to 766, presumably by some dishonest owner.   PLATE LXXVIII A.

113 [716 E] A PREACHER AND HIS CONGREGATION. An illustration from Sa'dī's *Gulistān*, mounted in an album. The story illustrated tells how Sa'dī was preaching to an apathetic congregation in the mosque at Baalbek when a traveller from a distance cried out in applause; on which Sa'dī, encouraged, praised God for admitting strangers to divine knowledge. Bukhārā school: mid XVI century.

38·5 × 25 *cm*. From Johnson collection. ¶ Lent by INDIA OFFICE LIBRARY.   PLATE CII B.

114 [561] TWO LOVERS: a prince in vermilion cloak, and a lady in black embroidered cloak. Signed *'Abd Allāh*. Mid XVI century.

15·5 × 10 *cm*. C. Anet: *Burl. Mag.*, Nov. 1912, pl. 1 (E). Marteau-Vever, no. 142. ¶ Lent by M. H. VEVER, Paris.   PLATE LXXVII A.

The inscription 'painted by 'Abd Allāh' is in calligraphy in the panel in the middle of the left side. There is no reason to doubt it, as this miniature would appear to be Bukhārā work of 1550–70. A miniature signed by 'Abd Allāh and dated 972/1564 was included in a manuscript of earlier date sold at Sotheby's in 1921 (Anonymous sale: 25 October (Herramaneck collection), lot 180). Another signed miniature by his hand occurs in a copy of the *Dīwān* of Sultān Ibrāhīm Mīrzā b. Bahrām b. Shāh Ismā'īl Safawī (d. 978 /1570). The inscription is dated 99 for 990/1582. According to Iskandar Munshī, 'Abd Allāh had previously been in the service of Ibrāhīm Mīrzā.

115 [541 D] SHĀHĪ'S *DĪWĀN*, copied by Mīr 'Imād al-Husaynī.[1] Polychrome headings; gold marginal designs. Two miniatures of Garden Scenes (Bukhārā style). The copy bears the signatures of its former owners, Shāh 'Abbās, the Emperors Jahāngīr (1014/1605) and Shāh Jahān. Red morocco binding with inlaid gold details.

22 × 13·5 *cm*. Marteau-Vever, I, no. 100. ¶ Lent by A. CHESTER BEATTY, ESQ.

[1] Or *al-Hasanī*. Both spellings are found, but perhaps *al-Husaynī* is more likely to be correct, as Mīr 'Imād's master was Muhammad Husayn Tabrīzī. Mīr 'Imād of Qazwīn was a celebrated calligrapher in the reign of Shāh 'Abbās I. The miniatures are probably considerably earlier than the text.

115 A [120 H] *RUBĀʿIYYĀT* OF ʿUMAR KHAYYĀM, copied by Sultān ʿAlī al-Kātib in 911/1505. With five miniatures.

16·5×12·5 *cm. Ill. London News,* August 1930. ¶ Lent by PROFESSOR S. N. ASHRAF, Patna.

The quatrains of ʿUmar Khayyām (d. A.D. 1123), although celebrated in Europe, were scarcely ever illustrated in the East, and this illustrated copy, recently discovered in India, is therefore somewhat of a curiosity. It was exhibited at Burlington House beside the famous Bodleian Manuscript, dated A.D. 1461, which furnished Fitzgerald with the main basis for his English version.

The miniatures, which are in pleasing colours, consist of rather unpretentious figure subjects. They appear to have been executed in Bukhārā, and may be later than the date of the manuscript. The scribe is not necessarily the celebrated Sultān ʿAlī Mashhadī, who died in Herāt in A.D. 1513. Several other calligraphers of this name are mentioned by the chroniclers, for which see *Tazkira i Khushnavīsān,* by Ghulām Muhammad (Bibliotheca Indica edition), pp. 48–9. The most celebrated was Sultān ʿAlī of Qāyin, who taught Sultān Husayn's children, and died in 914/1508.

B. SAFAWĪ MINIATURES

116 [126 F] JĀMĪ'S *TUHFAT AL-AHRĀR,* writing ascribed, in a note in Persian, to Mīr ʿAlī. Double-opening page richly decorated. Two miniatures. Leather binding, coloured and inlaid, *c.* 1500.

26×17 *cm.* ¶ Lent by DR. HENRY F. SEMPLE.

117 [558] MINIATURE, from a manuscript of Nizāmī. The sandal-wood Pavilion. *c.* 1500.

27·5×17 *cm.* ¶ Lent by FITZWILLIAM MUSEUM, Cambridge.

118 [505] TWO LEAVES, from a manuscript of *Kalīla wa Dimna. c.* 1500.

15×7 *cm.* ¶ Lent by R. A. DARA.

(*a*) The hare entrapped.
(*b*) The monkey caught in a tree.

119 [715 C] MUHAMMAD ĀSAFĪ'S *DĀSTĀN I JAMĀL U JALĀL,* copied in *taʿlīq* in 908/1502 at Herāt by Sultān ʿAlī. Thirty-four miniatures. Profusely ornamented.

27×17 *cm.* Tornberg, *Cat.,* no. 171. Exh. Gothenburg 1928, Copenhagen 1929. Cat. no. 15. ¶ Lent by ROYAL UNIVERSITY LIBRARY, Upsala.

(*a*) The arrival of Jalāl and his guide at the turquoise dome. The dome has an amber ornament surmounting it, on which sits a golden bird which moves; from its beak, when it sings, comes quicksilver, which turns into pearls, with which the garden is filled. On each pearl Jamāl's name is written. On the dome the words 'al-Sultān al-ʿĀdil' are written, with the date 910 (A.D. 1504). PLATE LXXXII B.

(*b*) Jalāl among the fairies, of whom he inquires the way to Jamāl. PLATE LXXXII A.

This fine manuscript, written by the renowned Sultān ʿAlī Mashhadī[1] of Herāt, presents a problem by reason of the unusual character of the miniatures, which are totally unlike Herāt work of the period.

[1] It is not, however, certain that this is his work. The signature omits the words *al-Mashhadī,* and there was at least one other contemporary calligrapher of the same name. See under 115 A above.

The colours are rather coarse, with a good deal of crimson. The turbans, which have thick red batons, differ somewhat from the ordinary Safawī type, which is unknown at this date.

120 [502] A PRINCE ACCOSTED BY A SUPPLIANT. A miniature from a manuscript of Amīr Khusraw Dihlawī's *Khamsa*, copied in 909/1504, by ʿAlā al-Dīn Muhammad al-Harawī at Balkh.

21 × 12·5 *cm.* Marteau-Vever, no. 85. From the Sambon and Rosenberg collections. ¶ Lent by the METROPOLITAN MUSEUM, New York.

For other miniatures from this manuscript, which was formerly in the Mughal Imperial Library, see Marteau-Vever, nos. 84 and 88; Stchoukine, *Louvre Cat.*, nos. VI and VII; and for the colophon *Notices et Extraits*, t. XLI, pp. 161–3.

121 [715 B] ʿASSĀR'S *MIHR U MUSHTARĪ*, copied by Murshid al-Dīn Muhammadī in 912/1506. Ten miniatures. Brown leather gilt, with flap.

22 × 13 *cm.* ¶ Lent by R. S. GREENSHIELDS, ESQ.

122 [578] MINIATURE. A young lord, in a Safawī turban, kneeling, with a falcon on his glove. Early XVI century.

18 × 10·5 *cm.* Marteau-Vever, no. 162. ¶ Lent by M. A. HENRAUX, Paris.

123 [723 B] PORTRAIT OF A SEATED MAN IN SAFAWĪ HEAD-DRESS. Inscribed in calligraphy 'Portrait of Mawlānā ʿAbd Allāh Hātifī. Work of the master Bihzād.' Coloured drawing.

7·5 × 11 *cm.* Sakisian, fig. 129. ¶ Lent by ARMENAG BEY SAKISIAN, Paris.

ʿAbd Allāh Hātifī was the nephew and pupil of Jāmī, the leading scholar and poet of the fifteenth century, and was famous as the author of a *khamsa*, or set of five poems, of which the *Tīmūr-nāma* was one. He also began a poem on the achievements of Shāh Ismāʿīl, which was never completed owing to his death, in 1520 or 1521. He was a native of Kharjird, in the district of Jām, Herāt, where Shāh Ismāʿīl paid him the visit, in 1511, which led to the poet starting his unfinished poem. The calligraphic inscription may be contemporary, but is more probably later than the portrait, which shows Hātifī towards the end of his life.

124 [572] LINE-DRAWING. Bearded man seated and holding a cup. The name of Bihzād is written in the corner. Early XVI century. It is in any case one of the finest drawings of the period surviving.

20 × 13 *cm.* Martin, II, pl. 108 (as Sultān Muhammad). Marteau-Vever, no. 196. ¶ Lent by M. A. HENRAUX, Paris.

125 [560] LINE-DRAWING. Two men hunting on horseback. Attributed to Bihzād. Early XVI century.

9 × 14·5 *cm.* ¶ Lent by M. H. VEVER, Paris.

126 [619] MINIATURE. Young prince on horseback, with page. Unfinished. Early XVI century.

17·5 × 13 *cm.* ¶ Lent by M. CLAUDE ANET, Paris.

127 [546 c] *DĪWĀN* OF HĀFIZ, with an inscription in honour of Sām Mīrzā, b. Shāh Ismāʿīl, with miniatures by Shaykh-zāda and Sultān Muhammad. Fine contemporary lacquer binding with figures of angels, and a central panel with two youths in Safawī head-dress. Early XVI century.

29 × 18·5 *cm*. Marteau-Vever, nos. 94, 95; Sakisian, figs. 121 and 144–6. For binding Marteau-Vever, fig. 275. Exh. Musée des Arts Décoratifs, 1912. From the collection of M. Arthur Sambon. ¶ Lent by M. L. CARTIER, Paris.

The date of this manuscript, so important for its miniatures, is uncertain. According to Marteau-Vever the figures 16 are written after the signature of the artist, Sultān Muhammad, in the last miniature. This they naturally assume to be intended for the year 916/1510–11. But these figures are not clear, and in any case this date would be too early for the miniatures in view of the mention of Sām Mīrzā's name above the archway in the fourth miniature, signed by Sultān Muhammad. This prince, the youngest son of Shāh Ismāʿīl, was not born till 1517: he survived till 1576, when he was executed. As both Shaykh-zāda and Sultān Muhammad are known to have lived early in the sixteenth century, and as the latter instructed Sām's brother Tahmāsp in drawing, it is tempting to think that this miniature was being painted just at the time of Sām Mīrzā's birth, for his father or elder brother, and that Sultān Muhammad added this inscription in his honour, rather than that it was actually done for the prince himself at a date which would necessarily be some fifteen or twenty years later. 1517 would accord better with the style of painting, still under the influence of Herāt, than about 1540, which would make it contemporaneous with the great British Museum *Nizāmī*, which seems considerably more advanced.

(*a*) Polo. In the background two players receiving refreshments. The whole foreground is occupied by the six players and by spectators. The verses illustrated are as follows: 'May the ball of the sky be encircled by the curve of thy polo-stick | May the universe be thy polo-ground.' The figure-drawing is predominantly Herātī.　　　　PLATE LXXXIII B.

(*b*) A prince entertaining a lady in a garden. The prince is seated under a canopy on a carpet: a kneeling slave is handing him a cup. In front are two girls dancing with castanets. The scene illustrates the verse, 'Without the beloved's face the rose has no sweetness; without wine the spring has no sweetness'. The miniature is attributed by Martin to Mīrak and by Sakisian to Sultān Muhammad.　　　　PLATE LXXXIII A.

(*c*) A moving sermon. By Shaykh-zāda. A preacher delivering a sermon in a mosque, illustrating the opening lines of one of the *ghazals*, to the effect that pretentious preachers do not practise what they preach. The words *ʿamal i Shaykh-zāda*, 'the work of Shaykh-zāda', can just be detected, in very minute writing, at the extreme base of the picture, beneath the left hand of the two figures seated in the middle. Shaykh-zāda is mentioned by the Turkish writer ʿĀlī as a direct pupil of Bihzād, the only one for eastern Persia. Only two miniatures by him are known, the other being in an album (no. 37067) in the Serai Library at Istanbul. It is a large composition illustrating the preparation of a feast.[1] He has been falsely identified with Mahmūd, and a miniature reproduced by Martin (I, fig. 28) has an untrustworthy attribution.　　　　PLATE LXXXIV B.

(*d*) A prince, surrounded by his court. By Sultān Muhammad. The artist's name, written in calligraphy, is contained in the diamond-shaped ornamental detail directly under the prince. Above the archway on the right are the words *Al-Ghāzī Abu'l-Muzaffar Sām Mīrzā*, indicating that the manuscript was prepared for this prince. For Sultān Muhammad, who was a pupil of Āqā Mīrak and instructed Shāh Tahmāsp in painting, see above, pp. 114–15.　　　　PLATE LXXXIV A.

(*e*) A scene of drunkenness. By Sultān Muhammad. Hāfiz's songs of Love and Wine are interpreted by Sūfīs in their strictly allegorical sense, the Wine standing for Ecstasy, the Wine-house for the Monastery of the Sūfīs, and so on. Persian illustrators take the *ghazals* literally, but broad humour of the kind which this miniature exhibits is very rare. All the figures are drunk, even the angels. The lines illustrated are as follows: 'The Angel of Mercy took the Cup of Delight And dashed the dregs, like rosewater, on faces of Hūr and Parī.' The words

[1] *Vide* Sakisian, op. cit., pp. 80–1.

'The work of Sultān Muhammad 'Irāqī' are written in calligraphic white letters above the doorway through which the old man is issuing. The supposed date on this miniature is discussed above, p. 112.   PLATE LXXV.

128 [544 c] 'ASSĀR'S *MIHR U MUSHTARĪ*. Copied by Mīr 'Alī. Five miniatures, early Safawid.

24·5 × 14·5 *cm.* ¶ Lent by M. H. VEVER, Paris.

129 [544 B] JĀMĪ'S *KHAMSA*, copied in 928/1522 by 'Alī al-Husaynī al-Harawī by order of a royal personage whose name is illegible. Pages with headings in different colours. Text bordered by gold rulings. Margins with rich designs of birds, animals, and human beings, five *sarlawhs*. Three full pages at the beginning and four full pages at the end, with decorative work in gold. Five double-page miniatures, with ascriptions: no. 1 to Sultān Muhammad Shāhī; no. 2 to Haydar 'Alī, son of Master Bihzād's sister; no. 3 to Qāsim 'Alī Chihra-gushāy; no. 4 to Muzaffar 'Alī, son of Master Bihzād's brother; no. 5 to Maqsūd, pupil of Master Bihzād. Leather binding, stamped in gold; inside, red, green, blue, and gold lattice-work. One of the five poems, the *Tuhfat al-ahrār*, has another colophon with the date 886/1481. The miniatures have all been retouched and remounted, and the ascriptions are not contemporary. The miniatures are surrounded with elaborate illuminated framework.

34 × 23 *cm.* V. Minorsky, 'Two unknown Persian manuscripts', *Apollo*, Feb. 1931. ¶ Lent by GULISTAN MUSEUM, Tehran.

(*a*) A prince in a pavilion. Attributed to Sultān Muhammad Shāhī. This miniature would appear to be considerably later than 1522 and is not of a quality to justify an attribution to Shāh Tahmāsp's court painter.

(*b*) Dancing Dervishes. Attributed to Haydar 'Alī. Nothing is known of this Haydar 'Alī, here described as sister's son to Bihzād. A miniature of a horse with a groom wearing a Safawid turban bearing this artist's name is reproduced by Sakisian (fig. 156). There seems very little doubt that our miniature was done at Bukhārā, the colouring, drawing, and costume all agreeing with such an assumption. It is quite possible that Bihzād's nephew, like other members of the Herāt school, withdrew to Bukhārā and did not follow his famous uncle to Tabrīz. The ascription is written in a rather large hand among the trees of the right-hand page. PLATE LXXXV.

(*c*) Zulaykhā and the ladies of Egypt. Attributed to Qāsim 'Alī. Zulaykhā invites the ladies, who have been talking too freely of her love for Yūsuf, to her palace and sets fruit before them. On the appearance of Yūsuf they are so overcome by his beauty that they cut their fingers with the fruit-knives. In the right-hand page the entry of Yūsuf, carrying wine as Zulaykhā's slave, and in the foreground a lady who has fainted away from emotion being restored by massage of her feet and hands. In the left-hand page the late arrival of another lady. The ascription to Qāsim 'Alī is written in the upper left-hand corner over later regilding. It is certainly not to be credited, though the design may originally have been by him. Once more the colouring, especially the black background to the calligraphy introduced on the building, and the scanty foliage point to Bukhārā. Repr. *Burl. Mag.* LVIII, Feb. 1931 (frontispiece); *Apollo*, XIII, Feb. 1931, fig. IV.   PLATE LXXXVI.

(*d*) Attributed to Muzaffar 'Alī, son of Master Bihzād's brother. Presumably intended for the celebrated Safawid painter, pupil of Bihzād.

(*e*) Ladies dancing. Attributed to Maqsūd. An illustration to the *Sikandar-nāma*. Gold hills and blue sky. Maqsūd is mentioned by Mīrzā Haydar Dughlāt as a pupil of Bihzād. Repr. *Apollo*, XIII, Feb. 1931, fig. V.

130 [603] MINIATURE from Nizāmī's *Khamsa*. King Nūshīrwān and his Minister, attributed to Muhammad al-Harawī, dated 928/1522.

18 × 11·5 *cm.* ¶ Lent by AJIT GHOSE, Calcutta.

131 [542 B] MANUSCRIPT, containing specimens of minute calligraphy dated 930/1524 by (1) Mīr 'Alī of Herāt, (2) Muhammad Qāsim, (3) Sultān Muhammad Khandān, (4) Sultān Muhammad Nūr. With a miniature, signed by Bihzād, representing an old man and a youth in a meadow. Certified by the Mughal Emperors Akbar, Jahāngīr, and Shāh Jahān. 67 fols.

25 × 17 *cm.* ¶ Lent anonymously.

A preface in rhetorical style states that the collection contains examples of beautiful handwriting and a *shamsa* (i.e. 'sun'; it is a small circular miniature with a diameter of about 7 *cm.*) 'radiating light like the real sun'. It was compiled in the following way. A certain Wazīr Khwāja Malik Ahmad,[1] a patron of calligraphers, saw a page written by Mawlānā Shaykh Mahmūd, and was so greatly taken by its beauty and delicacy that he commissioned similar works from the most famous calligraphers of the day and formed the present collection.

After mentioning the names of the calligraphers, the preface states that the *shamsa* was executed by the 'paragon of the age, the sun of the zenith of skill, the marvel of the time, the master Kamāl al-Dīn Bihzād, in a way to cause jealousy to the *hūrīs*'. The miniature follows the preface and specimen of Shaykh Mahmūd's calligraphy and is on folio 3 recto. It represents an old man, bearing a rosary and leaning on a staff, conversing with a youth beside a stream in a flowery meadow, with a background of rocks and trees. It is signed in rather faded and extremely minute writing below the centre of the miniature just outside the border, 'painted by the slave (*al-'abd*) Bihzād'. To the left are the words, partly erased, 'The work of Master Bihzād', perhaps in the same hand as the verses above and below. The left hand and turban of the old man are slightly damaged by flaking, and the silver of the stream is blackened by oxidization. The landscape is painted in rather pale brown, greys, and greens, and the sky is golden. The old man wears a blue scarf over a dress in two shades of brown; the youth a green dress with blue-lined scarlet cloak. An elaborate rosette border surrounds the miniature.

Somewhat full details have been given as it is unfortunately impossible to publish a reproduction of this important miniature. It is rather strikingly similar to a miniature in Mr. Chester Beatty's *Hasht Bihisht*[2] of Amīr Khusraw (no. 78 (*b*)).

On the obverse of folio 1 are notes by the Mughal Emperors Jahāngīr and Shāh Jahān, to whose library the manuscript once belonged. There is also a note, apparently by Akbar, valuing it at 3,000 rupees: Shāh Jahān appraises it at 4,000 rupees, and both mention that it contained selections of writing, but neither mentions the miniature. In a note, however, by an official of the Imperial Library at the end of the volume is a mention of the '*shamsa* painted by the master Bihzād'. The date, 930/1524, is appended to the first and last specimens of calligraphy: it need not be accepted for the miniature as the volume is admittedly a collection. The page on which it is painted is larger than the written surface of the other pages in the volume, and it is unlikely that Bihzād would have been in Herāt when the collection was apparently made, in 1524. But judging from the style and quality of the miniature painting there is no reason to doubt the opinion of the collector who considered that he was prefixing a masterpiece by Bihzād to his volume of calligraphy.

132 [488] TWO CAMELS FIGHTING. By Bihzād. *c.* 1525. The camels are interlocked head on while their two keepers endeavour to separate them: the one by a rope round its foreleg, the other with a stick. In the background is a man spinning the camel hair. The two camels are in contrasting shades of light and dark brown, and have silk saddle-cloths. In a cartouche is an inscription which opens with words from

---

[1] Identified by M. Blochet (*Catalogue of the Exhibition of Muhammedan-Persian Art*, New York, 1914; no. 254) as Nizām al-Dawlat wa'l-Wazārat Ahmad Beg, minister of Herāt and Khurāsān in the reign of Shāh Ismā'īl, who was in Herāt in 928 A.H. and was sent to Tabrīz to report on his province. [Cf. *Habīb al-Siyar* (Bombay ed.), vol. III, pt. IV, pp. 103, 104.]

[2] Reproduced: F. R. Martin, *Les miniatures de Behzad dans un manuscrit persan daté 1485*, pl. 9. Martin, pl. 75.

the Qur'ān (88. 17), *'Will they not regard the camels how they were created?'* and goes on, 'The broken pen of the poor frustrated one, Bihzād, after attaining the age of 70 years and great experience, entered upon this matter; *and that which is asked from Allah is pardon in life'*. This would perhaps make the date about 1525. There is no reason to reject the attribution to Bihzād of a drawing which is fairly close to his earlier style but shows some concession to the new sixteenth-century fashions. The design afterwards becomes famous and is often found repeated in later Persian and Mughal work.

26 × 16·5 cm. ¶ Lent by GULISTAN MUSEUM, Tehran.　　　　PLATE LXXXVII A.

133 [489] TWO CAMELS FIGHTING. A copy of no. 132 by Nānhā, dated 1608/9. In the cartouche corresponding to that containing Bihzād's inscription is an endorsement in the autograph of the Emperor Jahāngīr which reads as follows: 'Allah is the greatest. This work of the master Bihzād was seen and copied by Nānhā the painter according to my orders. Written by Jahāngīr son of Akbar, Pādshāh, Ghāzī. 1017 A.H.' (A.D. 1608/9). Jahāngīr was very proud of the cleverness of his artists in copying pictures, and Sir Thomas Roe, the ambassador of James I to his court, has an amusing anecdote on the point, when Jahāngīr had copies made of a European miniature and defied Roe to detect the original among them. The copy is certainly extraordinarily close, the main difference being in the rather warmer tone of Nānhā's version. Nānhā is a well-known artist of the reigns of Akbar and Jahāngīr: he is represented by paintings in the *Bābur-nāma* and the *Anwār i Suhaylī* of 1610 in the British Museum (Add. 18579).

25·5 × 15·6 cm. ¶ Lent by GULISTAN MUSEUM, Tehran.　　　　PLATE LXXXVII B.

134 [543 A] NIZĀMĪ'S *KHAMSA*, dated 954/1547. 319 fols. Double-page *sarlawh* and five *'unwāns*. Twelve miniatures, nine of which bear the name of Bihzād in minute characters. A gold inscription written in India on the fly-leaf states that the manuscript was presented by the Shāh of Persia to the Emperor Shāh Jahān, and by him to Sa'd Allāh Khān Nawwāb, his wazīr (d. 1656). Inserted is a complimentary letter from Sultān Husayn Mīrzā to Shāh Ismā'īl (1502–24) which, according to an inscription on the reverse, sealed by the Minister of Shāh Jahān, accompanied the manuscript on this occasion.

33 × 21·5 cm. *Burl. Mag.*, XLVI, Feb. 1925, pp. 71, 72. ¶ Lent by MAJOR D. MACAULAY.

135 [718 E] NIZĀMĪ'S *KHAMSA*, copied partly in 915/1510 and partly in 934 /1527 in the shrine of Mawlānā Nizām al-Dīn Ibrāhīm. Two *'unwāns*, twenty-seven miniatures.

28 × 17 cm. ¶ Lent by M. H. VEVER, Paris.

136 [716 A] NIZĀMĪ'S *KHAMSA*, copied in 935/1528 by Murshid, surnamed

'Attār al-Shīrāzī. Seven '*unwāns*, blue and gold, and twenty-one miniatures. Stamped leather binding, lacquered; inside, lattice-work. ? Shīrāz.

29·5×18 *cm.* ¶ Lent by A. CHESTER BEATTY, ESQ. (Beatty Lib., Dublin, Ms. 195).

(*a*) The Caliph Ma'mūn having his hair shaved at the bath. Full use is made by the painter of this miniature of the bright blue bathing cloths as had been done by the artist, perhaps Bihzād, in the illustration of the same scene in the British Museum Nizāmī of 1494 (Or. 6810) [Martin and Arnold, pl. 7]. This illustration of a scene not often depicted is of considerable interest for the detailed study of a *hammām* interior. The inclined plane for the ox drawing the water over a pulley and the man being massaged in the lowest chamber are to be noted (fol. 33). PLATE LXXXVIII A.

137 [543 c] *ZAFĀR-NĀMA* by Sharaf al-Dīn 'Alī Yazdī. According to the colophon copied in 935/1529 by Sultān Muhammad Nūr, gilded by Mīr 'Azud, and illustrated by Bihzād. A fine Safawid manuscript presumably produced at Tabrīz. The many miniatures are rather complicated compositions in a cool tone, a clear slaty blue and yellow prevailing. They are quite unlike any known work of Bihzād, but may perhaps be attributed to Sultān Muhammad and his school.

35×21 *cm.* ¶ Lent by PERSIAN GOVERNMENT.

(*a*) Scene in a mosque. The incident illustrated is an instance, quoted with much approval by the historian, of Tīmūr's impartial justice. A famous doctor, Mawlānā Qutb al-Dīn of Shīrāz, was accused by Mawlānā Sā'id, also of that city, of having extorted a large sum of money from the people of Fārs under the pretext that it was required for a present to Tīmūr. Tīmūr ordered Qutb al-Dīn to be sent, bound, to Shīrāz to restore the money. The illustration shows Qutb al-Dīn exposed in fetters in the Shīrāz mosque, while Mawlānā Sā'id, having ascended the pulpit (on the left), reveals his iniquity to the applauding congregation. In the central structure is probably the governor or some high official. The mosques of Persia are open-air courts with buildings round them, a minaret and a high arch marking the prayer niche or *mihrāb*. PLATE LXXXIX B.

(*b*) The son of the Sultān of Rūm brought before Tīmūr. After his Georgian expedition the son of Murād I, the Ottoman Sultan, was brought before Tīmūr by some European envoys who had taken him prisoner and who sought alliance with the emperor. The chronicler says that the envoys were received with civility, the emperor presenting them with rich apparel and granting their requests. Just as the Persians in the manuscript are dressed in the Safawid turbans of the period so the European envoys wear the 'Holbein' costume of 1529, though the scene represented took place about 1390. The magnificent carpet is especially to be noted as it is evidently realistically drawn, and it is generally believed that some of the miniature painters were also carpet-designers. PLATE LXXXIX A.

138 [545 D] NIZĀMĪ'S *KHAMSA*, copied in 936/1529 by Murshid, surnamed 'Attār. Six '*unwāns*, thirty-three miniatures. Leather binding. ? Shīrāz (cf. nos. 136, 176).

29×16·5 *cm.* ¶ Lent by A. CHESTER BEATTY, ESQ.

139 [716 F] JĀMĪ'S *KHAMSA*, copied in 937/1531 by 'Abd Allāh al-Harawī in *nasta'līq* script. Headings in gold and different inks. One *sarlawh*, five '*unwāns*, eight miniatures (five double-page, three single). Contemporary lacquered pasteboard binding, with medallions and spandrels; inside, lacquer painting with scenes of hunting and other entertainments on gold ground; flap, with figures of angels. Presented to Trinity College by Dr. Thomas Gale in 1697.

24×17·5 cm. Palmer, *Cat.*, p. 17. ¶ Lent by TRINITY COLLEGE, Cambridge.

(*a*) Khizr and Elias bathing in the Waters of Life. Cf. no. 76. On the various versions of this story see article 'Al-Khaḍir' in the *Encyclopaedia of Islām*. PLATE XC A.

140 [718 c] MĪR 'ALĪ SHĪR NAWĀ'Ī'S *DĪWĀN*, in Chaghatay Turkish, copied by Hājjī Muhammad b. Malik Ahmad Tabrīzī in 938/1531. Three illuminations and eleven miniatures. Text with decorated headings.

28×18 cm. ¶ Lent by BIBLIOTHÈQUE ÉGYPTIENNE, Cairo.

(*a*) A polo scene. Musicians play during the game, as is the custom in parts of central Asia and the Himalayas to this day, the instruments being very similar. On the antiquity of polo in Iranian lands see Appendix VI to volume I of Sir William Ouseley's *Travels in Various Countries of the East*, 1819. There is an interesting article on the subject by Dr. Laufer in the April 1932 number of *Polo*. PLATE XC B.

141 [722 c] FIRDAWSĪ'S *SHĀH-NĀMA*, copied in *nasta'līq* by Muhammad in 938/1531. Forty-three miniatures, of which many are defaced with black ink. Leather binding; inside, lattice-work. XVI century.

38·5×24 cm. ¶ Lent by PERSIAN GOVERNMENT from the Ardabīl Shrine.

(*a*) Kay Kāūs in his flying contrivance. The foolish Shāh Kay Kāūs, beguiled by Iblīs, attempts to fly up to the sky. He fastens joints of meat on four spear-heads, which are fixed to the corners of his throne, beneath which four eagles are tied. The eagles fly upwards in an effort to reach the meat, and bear the throne aloft. Eventually they become exhausted and fall to the ground. An exquisite miniature in pale blue and gold. PLATE LXXXVIII B.

142 [565] MINIATURE. Portrait of a young Safawid prince, reclining on a cushion, and holding a book, inscribed with praises of his beauty. Attributed to Sultān Muhammad. Early XVI century. Identified, uncertainly, as Shāh Tahmāsp.

15·5×13 cm. Kühnel, *I.M.*, pl. 61; Martin, II, pl. 109. ¶ Lent by M. H. VEVER, Paris.

143 [620] MINIATURE. Portrait of a prince, seated on a stool, reading. Attributed to the school of Sultān Muhammad. XVI century.

26·5×14 cm. Exh. Gothenburg, 1928, cat. no. 33. ¶ Lent by NATIONAL MUSEUM, Stockholm.

144 [579] MINIATURE. A young prince (Shāh Tahmāsp?) in vermilion robe and mantle of gold brocade figured with scenes of capture, wearing a plumed Safawid turban. Signed *Muhammad Harawī*.

19·5×10·5 cm. ¶ Lent by E. BEGHIAN.

145 [568] LINE-DRAWING, TINTED. Youth seated, holding a book and a flower. Signed *Shaykh Muhammad*. Mid XVI century (?).

15·5×8·5 cm. Martin, pl. 109; Marteau-Vever, no. 184; *Meisterwerke*, pl. 29; Sakisian, fig. 122; Migeon, I, fig. 49; Kühnel, *I.M.*, fig. 77; Stchoukine, *Louvre Cat.*, no. XXII. Exh. Munich 1910, no. 746; Paris 1912; The Hague 1927, no. 29. ¶ Lent by M. RAYMOND KOECHLIN, Paris.

Several variations of this famous drawing exist, of which nos. 147 and 353 C were shown at the Exhibition. For Shaykh Muhammad see Sakisian, pp. 89–91, and p. 116 above.

146 [485] MINIATURE. Camel with highly ornamented saddle and saddle-cloth, with its keeper. Inscription: '*Painted and written by Shaykh Muhammad*, 964' (1556).

10·4×13·2 *cm.* Sakisian, fig. 85. ¶ Lent by ARMENAG BEY SAKISIAN, Paris.

For Shaykh Muhammad see under no. 145. It is doubtful whether or not there was more than one artist of this name, but if there was only one, his production would seem to have extended over eighty years. This drawing appears to be earlier than the date inscribed on it.

147 [719 L] DRAWING, slightly coloured. Portrait of a young prince kneeling and holding a green parrot. Similar to M. Koechlin's drawing (no. 145). It has been attributed to Shaykh Muhammad on the basis of a signature, which, however, is not clear. Third quarter XVI century.

14·5×8 *cm.* Sakisian, fig. 123. ¶ Lent by ARMENAG BEY SAKISIAN, Paris.

148 [274] MINIATURE. Seated page, bareheaded. First half XVI century.

14×7·5 *cm.* ¶ Lent by M. CLAUDE ANET, Paris.

149 [592] STENCIL. Combat between a dragon and a phoenix. Attributed to Mīrak.

22×16 *cm.* ¶ Lent by MAJOR D. MACAULAY.

150 [566] MINIATURE. Young man seated on the branch of a flowering tree, holding an open book. Attributed by Martin to the school of Bukhārā, by Marteau-Vever to that of Āqā Mīrak. West-Persia: mid-sixteenth century. The colouring is rather pale.

17·5×11 *cm.* Marteau-Vever, no. 154; Martin, pl. 101. ¶ Lent by M. H. VEVER, Paris.

151 [718 D] SHARAF AL-DĪN 'ALĪ YAZDĪ'S *ZAFAR-NĀMA*, copied by Murshid al-Kātib al-Shīrāzī in 939/1533. Thirty miniatures. Safawid: provincial style.

30×23 *cm.* ¶ Lent by INDIA OFFICE LIBRARY [Ethé, *Cat.*, 175].

(*a*) Tīmūr hunting near Multān. The *qamargha* or battue was an institution beloved of Tīmūr and his descendants. The game was surrounded by troops and driven towards the centre of a diminishing circle.　　　　　　　　　　　　　　　　　　　　　　　　　　PLATE XCI A.

(*b*) Tīmūr mourning for his grandson Shāh-zāda Muhammad. The death of this grandson, to whom Tīmūr was much attached, occurred in the spring of 805/1403 after the battle of Angora. There was a remarkable demonstration of grief, and the historian remarks that, instead of putting on their new spring garments, the courtiers dressed in mourning clothes of blue and black. The broken bow and arrows are symbolical. An account of Tīmūr's grief on this occasion and of the Mosque he ordered to be built as a memorial is given by Clavijo (Broadway Travellers ed., pp. 275–6).　　　　　　　　　　　　　　　　　　　　PLATE XCI B.

152 [545 B] JĀMI'S *YŪSUF U ZULAYKHĀ*, dated 940/1533. Two decorated pages and six miniatures. Lacquer binding.

> 24 × 15 cm. ¶ Lent by BIBLIOTHÈQUE ÉGYPTIENNE, Cairo.

> (*a*) The ascent of Muhammad to heaven by night. Though representations of the Prophet were entirely contrary to the teaching of the Traditions, they were not uncommon, though the artist frequently, as here, compromised with orthodoxy by veiling the face. The incident, often depicted, shows the Prophet riding upon the strange beast Burāq, represented, as usual, as a kind of sphinx with a mule-like body, with the angel Gabriel preceding him, and other angels in attendance, bearing vessels, one containing burning perfume. Both Muhammad and Burāq are surrounded with a great flame halo. Far the finest known example of this subject is contained in the famous *Khamsa* of Nizāmī in the British Museum (Or. 2265, fol. 195).   PLATE XCII A.

> (*b*) Zulaykhā, to win the love of Yūsuf and to declare her own to him, caused a house to be constructed containing pictures of them both, seated together and embracing, so that wherever he looked he should be reminded of her amorous designs.
>
> The illustration shows Zulaykhā, having introduced Yūsuf into the innermost chamber, beseeching him to look on her. Yūsuf, however, refuses to lift his eyes, but even on the carpet he sees the picture fashioned. Yūsuf, as a holy personage, wears a flame halo, which is repeated in the surrounding pictures.   PLATE XCII B.

> The illustrations present several unusual features, the rococo patterning, mainly in blue and mauve, in the second (pl. XCII B) being, however, not uncommon at this period.

153 [591] ANGEL, FLYING, WITH A CUP AND WINE FLASK. Line drawing with faint colour. Signed *Shāh Qulī*. Mid XVI century. Probably executed in Constantinople, where Shāh Qulī was painter in chief to Sulaymān the Magnificent (1520–66).

> 18 × 13·5 cm. ¶ Lent by E. BEGHIAN.

> Similar drawings are to be found in an album formerly at Yildiz (cf. Sakisian, fig. 101) and the Musée Jacquemart-André (cf. Blochet, *Musulman Painting*, pls. CXLVII, CXLVIII), one of which is signed by Walī Jān, who is also known to have worked at Constantinople and who would appear to have been a pupil of Shāh Qulī, though 'Alī records him as a pupil of Siyāwush, the Georgian.

154 [595] KNEELING FIGURE OF AN ANGEL AS A CUPBEARER. He has the sort of head-dress often found in Persian drawings of angels, which looks as if it were made of leaves. These may, however, possibly be intended for feathers. The dress is covered with an intricate design of arabesques, and two golden streamers hang from the breasts. Ink and light colours: elaborate double border. Unsigned, but probably by Shāh Qulī. Constantinople: mid XVI century.

> 19·5 × 12·5 cm. ¶ Lent by E. BEGHIAN.

155 [666] PEN DRAWING, slightly tinted. A flying genius, with a head-dress formed of leaves, holding a flask and a drinking-cup. Second half of the XVI century.

> 12 × 5·8 cm. *Katalog der Ausstellung im Städelschen Kunstinstitut*, 1932, pl. VII. ¶ Lent by FRAU MARIA SARRE-HUMANN, Berlin.

> This drawing also comes, like the two preceding numbers, from Constantinople, where such subjects enjoyed particular popularity.

156 [719 G] LIGHTLY-TINTED DRAWING. Balqīs, Queen of Sheba, reclining. Perched on a tree on the right is the hoopoe, the messenger of Solomon, holding his letter in its beak. Balqīs looks languorously at it. Her robe is decorated with arabesques centring round human and animal masks. In front a formal stream. Considered by Kühnel to be Turkish, mid-XVI century. Attributed by Martin to Shāh Qulī. False attribution to Bihzād.

> 18·5 × 4·5 *cm*. Martin, pl. 119; Marteau-Vever, no. 208; *Burl. Mag.*, Nov. 1912; Kühnel, *I.M.*, pl. 99. ¶ Lent by M. CLAUDE ANET, Paris.

157 [500] SOLOMON AND HIS FLYING THRONE, borne by angels. Ink drawing slightly enhanced with colour and gold.

> 28 × 17·5 *cm*. *Meisterwerke*, pl. 21; Martin, II, pl. 58. Exh. Munich 1910, no. 682. ¶ Lent by FRAU MARIA SARRE-HUMANN, Berlin.   PLATE XCIII A.

> Solomon is escorted by angels and *jinn*, bearing animals and offerings, playing on musical instruments or pouring flames from above. Among the various birds the *sīmurgh*, or phoenix, is prominent. The hoopoe (*hudhud*), Solomon's messenger to the Queen of Sheba, is seen at the top on the right. For Solomon's flying throne, see Sale (note to Chapter 27 of the Qur'ān): 'Eastern writers . . . say that he had a carpet of green silk on which his throne was placed . . . and that when all were in order, the wind, at his command, took up the carpet, and transported it, with all that were upon it, wherever he pleased; the army of birds at the same time flying over their heads.' The picture shows a rather different version. Judging from the landscape at the bottom, the caparisoning of the horse, and the decoration of the throne, this drawing must be of early Safawid date (as Schulz had suggested). Perhaps it might be given to Shāh Qulī, who drew angels of this type and was fond of the sort of *chinoiserie* which decorates Solomon's canopy or carpet.

158 [499] PEN DRAWING, lightly coloured. The garden of the fairies. Early XVI century.

> 28 × 17·5 *cm*. *Meisterwerke*, pl. 21; Kühnel, *I.M.*, pl. 47; Schulz, pl. 72; Sakisian, fig. 104; Martin, II, pl. 57. ¶ Lent by FRAU MARIA SARRE-HUMANN, Berlin.

> Representations of Paradise are rare. For other examples see Arnold, *P.I.*, pl. xxxv. In the present well-known drawing it is, however, doubtful whether the actual Paradise is intended. A winged *parī* is seated on a platform, set in the branches of a great *chenār* tree, with steps leading up to it. Other *parīs* attend on her, some playing on musical instruments, and a bearded *jinn* stands on guard at the foot of the tree. This was originally a companion picture to no. 157.

159 [577] LINE-DRAWING. Holy man riding a lion, with attendant angel. XVI century.

> 46 × 32 *cm*. Marteau-Vever, fig. 216; Martin, II, pl. 59. ¶ Lent by M. ADOLPHE STOCLET, Brussels.

> An illustration to the *Būstān* of Sa'dī (cf. no. 77 (a)). Though assigned by Martin to the middle of the fifteenth century, the drawing of the angel and the sage's face—not to speak of the cloud-forms or the landscape—would seem to indicate a much later date, perhaps mid-sixteenth century. A drawing in the Bibliothèque Nationale (Od. 41, fol. 26), showing a saint and a hunter, may be a companion piece by the same hand. It clearly belongs to the sixteenth century (cf. Blochet, *Musulman Painting*, pl. cxlv).

160 [556] LINE-DRAWING, on gold ground. A Turkman prince. This well-known drawing is discussed on pp. 89–90, above.

> 21 × 14·5 *cm*. Martin, pl. 83; Marteau-Vever, no. 192; *Meisterwerke*, pl. 25; Sakisian, fig. 97; Stchoukine, *Louvre Cat.*, no. XXIII. Exh. Munich 1910, no. 725; Paris 1912; The Hague 1927, no. 14. ¶ Lent by M. RAYMOND KOECHLIN, Paris.

161 [724 H] JĀMĪ'S *YŪSUF U ZULAYKHĀ*, copied by 'Ayshī in 944/1537. Margins decorated in gold, with gold headings. Two miniatures: the angel Parī-Shād, and Yūsuf with his brother. Stamped boards and leather binding.

26 × 15 *cm.* ¶ Lent by P. C. MANUK, ESQ., Patna.

162 [724 G] *SUWAR AL-KAWĀKIB*, 'Images of the Stars', translated by Nasīr al-Dīn Tūsī, copied in Yazd in 947/1540. Fifty-three astronomical drawings in black, gold, and a little colour. Leather cover.

24 × 16·5 *cm.* ¶ Lent by A. CHESTER BEATTY, ESQ.

The drawings appear to be copies of much older ones, as is not uncommon in astronomical works.

163 [601] A PRINCE, perhaps intended for the young Tahmāsp, picnicking in the mountains. A night scene with flambeaux and lanterns. In the foreground musicians and servants preparing food. All have Safawid turbans: the central figure has a double aigrette in his, while two of the older men have single plumes in their turbans. The grass is dark green and 'stippled' as in the Cartier manuscript (Pl. LXXXIII A). Perhaps workshop of Sultān Muhammad. *c.* 1530–40. From the Jahāngīr Album.

27·5 × 16·5 *cm.* Arthur Upham Pope, fig. 51. ¶ Lent by GULISTAN MUSEUM, Tehran.

164 [562] LINE-DRAWING. Young prince wearing a Safawid turban, holding a book. Inscribed Ghulām Hazrat Shāh Sayyid 'Alī ibn (?) Sayyid Muhammad.[1] *c.* 1540.

25 × 18 *cm.* Martin, II, pl. 107. ¶ Lent by M. H. VEVER, Paris.

165 [512] PRINCES IN A PAVILION. A full-page miniature, possibly from a manuscript. The quatrain at the top reads: 'Here is the assembly of joy and the delight of drinking,—Here is wine lawful, and repenting of wine unlawful.' Spacious Safawid style, *c.* 1540–50. In this case the full mount has been reproduced in order to show the way in which the Jahāngīr Album, of which this is a folio, was decorated. Jahāngīr's studio excelled in the portrayal of such delicately painted small birds.

32·5 × 19·5 *cm. Souvenir*, pl. 46. ¶ Lent by GULISTAN MUSEUM, Tehran.　　PLATE XCIV B.

166 [511] BATTLE SCENE. A miniature illustrating the *Khusraw u Shīrīn* of Nizāmī. Buzurg-ummīd, the old tutor and counsellor of Khusraw Parwīz, waits beside the prince's elephant with an astrolabe in his hand, so as to watch for the auspicious moment for attacking the rebel Bahrām Chūbīn. A big composition of the Tahmāsp period at Tabrīz; the oriflammed sun is very typical; cf. the British Museum Nizāmī of 1539–43. Illuminated border. Early Safawid, 1530–40.

40 × 26 *cm.* ¶ Lent by ROYAL SCOTTISH MUSEUM, Edinburgh.　　PLATE XCIV A.

[1] This can hardly be a signature of an artist 'Sayyid 'Alī, son of Muhammad', otherwise the word *Hazrat* would not be used.

167 [596] GOLD DECORATED PAGE, with animal scenes. Mid XVI century. Similar work to the border paintings in the famous British Museum Nizāmī of 1539–42 (Or. 2265), though not of such exquisite quality. From the Jahāngīr Album. No doubt originally an end-paper.

40 × 24 *cm.* ❡ Lent by GULISTAN MUSEUM, Tehran.

168 [553] HUNTING SCENE. Line-drawing with light colour and silver. The final scene of slaughter at a battue, with every sort of game represented. Representations of battues of this kind have a very ancient history, and to go no further back than the seventh century A.D., the Sasanian hunting reliefs at Tāq i Būstān, near Kermānshāh, display much the same motives as the miniatures of the Safawid period. One of the most striking of these, the presence of musicians, does not actually appear in this drawing. Note the early drawing of the musket in the hands of a man at the top on the right of the drawing. A drawing in the British Museum, Department of Prints and Drawings, 1920–9–17–254 [4], is very close in style and may be by the same hand. School of Sultān Muhammad (?): second quarter of the sixteenth century.

30·5 × 20·5 *cm.* ❡ Lent by E. BEGHIAN.   PLATE XCIII B.

169 [586] PORTRAIT OF A SAFAWID PRINCE wearing a red robe and a double-plumed turban, and holding a falcon on his gloved right hand. About 1520.

17·5 × 9 *cm. Souvenir,* plate facing p. 32. ❡ Lent by E. BEGHIAN.

170 [570] ARMED YOUTH IN BEIGE ROBE HOLDING A FLOWER. Full colour on duck's-egg ground. By Muhammad Mu'min, whose signature can be seen at the bottom in the corner on the left.

14·5 × 8·5 *cm.* ❡ Lent by E. BEGHIAN.   PLATE XCIX A.

Muhammad Mu'min worked in the early sixteenth century, but this drawing seems to be later work. M. Sakisian (p. 88) quotes 'Ālī to the effect that he was of Khurāsān and a pupil of Muhammad Harawī. He attributes a drawing of a similar subject in the Bibliothèque Nationale to his hand (Sakisian, fig. 119). The Muhammad Mu'min b. 'Abd Allāh i Marwārīd with whom Schulz confounds him was a calligrapher of Herāt who died in 1510.

171 [583] ELEGANT YOUNG MAN WITH A CUP, LEANING AGAINST A FLOWERING TREE. School of Sultān Muhammad. Full colours on a duck's-egg ground.

18 × 10 *cm.* ❡ Lent by PERSIAN GOVERNMENT from the Mashhad Shrine.

172 [627] TWO PAGES FROM A *SHĀH-NĀMA*; Gayūmars, the first Shāh, with attendants clothed in leopard skins. XVI century.

28·5 × 19·5 *cm.* Marteau-Vever, no. 103. ❡ Lent by M. H. VEVER, Paris.

173 [617] MINIATURE from Jāmī's *Yūsuf u Zulaykhā,* copied by 'Abd al-Hātif. Early Safawid. Ladies in a garden (faces repainted in the XVII century).

23 × 14·5 *cm.* ❡ Lent by A. CHESTER BEATTY, ESQ.

174, 175 [723 A and C] TWO ALBUMS.

49 × 35 *cm.* and 45 × 29 *cm.* ¶ Lent by Museum of Top-Kapu, Istanbul.

These two large albums contain a strange medley of miniatures of all sizes and calligraphic specimens, put together in a most haphazard manner. Based originally on sixteenth-century collections, they have both been re-bound, and the miniatures largely repainted, almost certainly
in Turkey, in comparatively modern times. Later work has also been added. Many of the
miniatures contain the names of the painters to whom they have been attributed, written in
calligraphy. Unfortunately the attributions, which are not apparently contemporary with the
paintings, cannot be trusted, famous names being added with little discrimination to mediocre
work. Chinese paintings occupy a number of pages, and many others are filled with single
figures painted in glaring colours. There are numerous paintings of Muhammad riding his
steed Burāq, some attributed to the artists Ahmad Mūsā and Muhammad Dūst.

The more interesting of the albums is no. 174, which was dedicated originally to Abu'l-Fath
Bahrām Mīrzā, brother of Shah Tahmāsp, in the year 951/1544. A large painting at the beginning is said to be by Shāh Tahmāsp himself.

Apart from some interesting specimens of calligraphy which must be genuine, the most
valuable pages are those containing the preface, which purports to be written by the scribe
Dūst Muhammad for Bahrām Mīrzā, brother of Shāh Tahmāsp, and which contains an account
of the Persian calligraphers and painters of the fifteenth and sixteenth centuries.[1]

(*a*) A line-drawing, stated to be by Shāh Muzaffar of Khurāsān. It represents Muhammad
riding on Burāq, and accompanied by the angel Gabriel, on his heavenly journey. It is ascribed,
in a calligraphic inscription, to *Nādir al-Asrī Ustād Shāh Muzaffar, Siyāh-qalum-naqqāsh* (i.e.
black-and-white artist) of Khurāsān. The particular interest of this inscription resides in the fact
that Bābur in his Memoirs writes of only two contemporary artists of Herāt, the famous Bihzād
and Shāh Muzaffar,[2] the latter of whom was distinguished for his portrait painting, and especially
for his dainty rendering of the hair. We know, too, from Bābur's cousin, Mīrzā Muhammad
Haydar Dughlāt, that Shāh Muzaffar was the son of a famous artist of the time of Abū Sa'īd,
named Mansūr, whom, however, he surpassed in some respects, his brush being so delicate and
refined that all were amazed at it. He died at the age of 24, having completed eight group
pictures (*majlis*). Some persons also, says the Mīrzā, possess black-and-white drawings (*qalam i
siyāhī-yi ū*) by him.[3]   PLATE XCV.

176 [547 B] QAZWĪNĪ'S *'AJĀ'IB AL-MAKHLŪQĀT*, 'Wonders of Creation', Persian translation, copied in 952/1545 by Murshid Shīrāzī, called 'Attār. 648
miniatures. Double-page frontispiece. 1 *'unwān*. Black and brown leather binding,
gold-stamped and inlaid with panels; inside, coloured lacquer. Formerly in Goloubev
Collection. ? Shīrāz.

31·5 × 18·5 *cm.* Arnold, *P.I.,* pl. 37 *a.* ¶ Lent by A. CHESTER BEATTY, ESQ. (Beatty Lib., Ms. 212).

(*a*) The island of Java, and the strange creatures that dwell there, including black-and-white
talking apes; white men with wings; multicoloured parrots, peacocks and other birds (fol. 108b).
                                                                                    PLATE XCVI A.
(*b*) The Mountain of Yalam, near Qazwīn, in which are many animals and human beings, all
turned to stone (fol. 127v).   PLATE XCVI B.
(*c*) Two monkeys. 'The King of Nubia sent two monkeys to the sister of the Caliph, one a
tailor, the other a carpenter' (fol. 459v).
(*d*) A bird which changes its colour, called Bū-qalamūn (the word usually means a chameleon).

---

[1] See Appendix I; and for notes on the album (174), [2] See Beveridge's translation, pp. 272 and 291.
Sakisian, pp. 53, 118–20. (The old number of this [3] See the article by Sir T. W. Arnold reprinted in
album was 3708 5. The new number is 1721.) Appendix II.

(e) The spring called Nātūl, in Egypt, whose water turns clay into mice (fol. 187).
(f) A bird which sings all night, so that the other birds gather round it (with d on fol. 465v).
(g) A hare which is a male one year and a female the next (fol. 442b).
(h) A duck (fol. 466).
  (c)–(h) of the same size as the original miniatures.   PLATE XCVII.

177 [563] LINE-DRAWING. A camel with his driver. Mid XVI century. From the collection of Charles Ricketts, R.A. Perhaps by Sultān Muhammad. One of the most admired drawings of the period.

20·2 × 27·2. Martin, II, pl. 118; Kühnel, *I.M.*, pl. 69. ❡ Lent by PHILIP HOFER, ESQ., New York.

178 [564] DRAWING, with light colour. Horse and groom. Signed *Rizā*. Late XVI century.

18 × 20 *cm.* Martin, II, pl. 161; Marteau-Vever, no. 176; *Burl. Mag.*, Nov. 1912. ❡ Lent by M. CLAUDE ANET, Paris.

On the horse's flank on the near side a flower is stamped. In this connexion the following passage from Sir John Chardin (Amsterdam, 1711, tome II, p. 27) is of interest: 'Tous les chevaux du roi sont marquez d'une grande tulipe ouverte à la cuisse du montoir, et il n'y a que les chevaux du Roi qu'on marque de ce côté-là, tous les autres qui sont marquez le sont de l'autre côté.' Chardin also remarks that henna, originally used against the cold, was afterwards applied at all seasons to horses as well as women as a decorative expedient.

179 [722 B] PAGES from a manuscript of Sa'dī's *Kulliyyāt* (complete works), *c.* 1550. Formerly in the library of Prince Zill al-Sultān. Four illuminated pages, and two with miniatures, brightly coloured.

29 × 16 *cm.* ❡ Lent by M. CLAUDE ANET, Paris.

180 [716 G] SA'DĪ'S *BŪSTĀN*, copied by Shāh Mahmūd al-Nīshāpūrī in Mashhad in 958/1551. Text and margins gold-sprinkled. One *sarlawh*, two *'unwāns*. Six miniatures, unfinished (line-drawings), attributed to Sultān Muhammad. Six spaces are left blank for miniatures. Leather binding, gold stamped.

25 × 16·5 *cm.* ❡ Lent by A. CHESTER BEATTY, ESQ. (Beatty Lib., Ms. 221, fol. 19b).

(a) King Khusraw detects his wazīr exchanging glances with a beautiful slave. PLATE CVIII A.

These unfinished miniatures are of considerable interest as showing the manner in which the miniature-artists worked. In this case there are signs of alteration and gilding has been applied to the wazīr's turban and saddle-cloth and to part of the sky. There is no solid evidence for the attribution to Sultān Muhammad.

181 [724 E] THE TIMURID SULTĀN HUSAYN'S *MAJĀLIS AL-'USH-SHĀQ*, 'Assemblies of Lovers', copied in 959/1552 by Farīd al-Kātib. Many miniatures.

29 × 18·5 *cm.* Ethé 1271; Arnold, *P.I.*, pls. XXXIII, XLV, XLVI, XLVIII (a). ❡ Lent by BODLEIAN LIBRARY, Oxford. [Ouseley Add. 24.]

182 [715 G] NIZĀMĪ'S *KHAMSA*, copied in 959/1552 by Muhammad Qāsim al-Hasanī. Twenty-eight miniatures in a fine provincial style.

32·5 × 21·5 *cm.* ❡ Lent by A. CHESTER BEATTY, ESQ.

The manuscript is a fine example of contemporary decoration, especially one double-page, with an unusual spiral pattern. The miniatures, which are drawn in an unusual and somewhat archaic style, Safawid turbans being entirely absent, are chiefly notable for the exquisite treatment of flowers, especially in a representation of Majnūn in the jungle, and the curiously large faces of the figures.

183 [615] MINIATURE. From the manuscript last mentioned. Alexander sailing to the West.

32·5 × 21·5 cm. ¶ Lent by A. CHESTER BEATTY, ESQ.

184 [720 A] QĀSIMĪ'S *SHĀH-NĀMA*, describing Shāh Tahmāsp's exploits. On the margin *Tīmūr-nāma* (a poem on the history of Tīmūr) by Hātifī (d. A.D. 1521). Marbled paper of different colours, richly decorated. Two *sarlawhs*, eleven miniatures of XVI century. Cover stamped outside and lattice-work inside. Given by Shāh 'Abbās to the Ardabīl shrine in 1017/1608. Form *nīm-waraqī*. Mid XVI century, west Persia.

33·5 × 23·5 cm. ¶ Lent by PERSIAN GOVERNMENT from the Ardabīl shrine.

(a) Tīmūr is attacked by demons in the mountains of Katwar. An illustration to the *Tīmūr-nāma*. The introduction of this fabulous story of man-rending demons from the Alexander legend into what the author expressly claims as a strictly veracious historical poem, is a good instance of the untrustworthiness of poetic history, considering that at the date that it was composed Tīmūr had been dead less than one hundred years. PLATE XCVIII B.

185 [144 M] JALĀL AL-DĪN RŪMĪ'S *MASNAWĪ*, Book V, copied by Sultān 'Alī b. Muhammad al-Mashhadī in 863/1458. One *'unwān*, two miniatures in early Safawid style added later. Gold-sprinkled margins. Leather binding with flap, gold-stamped; inside, fretwork (with pieces of glass affixed).

30 × 19·5 cm. ¶ Lent by M. H. VEVER, Paris.

Jalāl al-Dīn's great *Masnawī*, sometimes called the 'Persian Qur'ān', is only very exceptionally illustrated.

186 [545 C] SA'DĪ'S *KULLIYYĀT* (complete works), copied 964/1556 by 'Ināyat-allāh Shīrāzī. 497 fol., seventeen miniatures.

27 × 19 cm. *Catalogue of the Arabic and Persian Manuscripts in Edinburgh University Library*, no. 104. ¶ Lent by EDINBURGH UNIVERSITY LIBRARY.

187 [719 H] LINE-DRAWING. Young Dervish, holding a spear and a book. Signed *rāqimuhu* (drawn by) *Muhammadī*.

37·5 × 27·5 cm. Arnold, *P.I.*, pl. LXII (a). ¶ Lent by INDIA OFFICE LIBRARY. [Johnson Album XXVIII.] PLATE XCIX C.

188 [618] MINIATURE. Youth in dark-blue coat, leaning on a staff. Inscribed *Muhammadī*. (Above, a line in Chaghatay Turkish from 'Alī Shīr Nawā'ī.) Second half of XVI century.

17 × 7 cm. *Studio*, January 1931, colour plate. ¶ Lent by E. BEGHIAN.

189 [571] LINE-DRAWING WITH SOME COLOUR. Picnic in the mountains: a goatherd with his herd of goats. Another version of a drawing in the Bibliothèque Nationale, signed by Muhammadī (Martin, II, pl. 103; *Enluminures*, pl. LXXXIV). It may perhaps represent the work of a Bukhārā artist. *c.* 1550.

23·6×15 *cm.* Martin, II, pl. 104. ¶ Lent by PHILIP HOFER, ESQ., New York.   PLATE C.

190 [576] LINE-DRAWING. Gipsies dancing; two dressed in goat skins. Style of Muhammadī. *c.* 1575. This is a version of a well-known drawing at Leningrad— reproduced in Martin, pl. 102, and Kühnel, fig. 66.

15×10 *cm.* Arnold, *P.I.*, pl. XLVII. ¶ Lent by MISS E. J. BECK.

191 [716 H] LINE-DRAWING. Youth with pike and a musician, attributed to Muhammadī. Similar to a drawing reproduced in Martin, pl. 102 (right).

12×8 *cm.* Arnold, *P.I.*, pl. LXII (*b*). ¶ Lent by INDIA OFFICE LIBRARY. [Johnson Album XXVIII.]

192 [552] MINIATURE. Prince and lady seated with attendants in landscape; shepherd playing pipe. XVI century. Style of Muhammadī.

23×17 *cm.* ¶ Lent by M. H. VEVER, Paris.

193 [621] LINE-DRAWINGS, from an album. End of XVI century. In the style associated with Muhammadī.

(*a*) Youth offering a cup to another. 8×8·5 *cm.*
(*b*) Youths duelling. 9×11·5 *cm.*   PLATE CVII A.
(*c*) Doctors and pupil. 9×15 *cm.*
¶ Lent by INDIA OFFICE LIBRARY.

194 [584] THREE MUSICIANS AND A DANCER. Line-drawing with touches of black and gold. Mid XVI century. At the foot is a false signature of Bihzād: probably school of Sultān Muhammad. The mount is later than the miniature, and the verses have no connexion with it. They are couplets from the *Būstān* of Sa'dī and are not consecutive, indeed from separate chapters of the work (see Graf's edition, pp. 370 and 373). The first reads: 'Not every eye or eyebrow that you behold is fair—Eat the kernel of the pistachio, and throw away the husk.' And the second, below: 'The bosom of a dear mother is paradise, and her breasts a river of milk.'

10·5×9·5 *cm.* ¶ Lent by PHILIP HOFER, ESQ., New York.   PLATE C.

195 [574] RURAL SCENE, figures ploughing with zebus and carrying melons, from which it has been suggested that the scene is laid in Gīlān. In the style of Muhammadī. Light colours. A version of a favourite Persian composition.

20·5×12 *cm.* ¶ Lent by E. BEGHIAN.

196 [585] LIGHTLY TINTED DRAWING. Hunting scene. Style of Muhammadī.

17·5×12 *cm.* ¶ Lent by PERSIAN GOVERNMENT from the Mashhad Shrine.

197 [575] LINE-DRAWING. Young dervish with a skin on his shoulders and a club under his arm. End of XVI century.

10·5×2·5 *cm.* ¶ Lent by E. BEGHIAN.

198 [569] LINE-DRAWING. Dervishes, some dancing, others attended by young companions. XVI century. A spirited drawing, suggestive of the style of Muhammadī.

19×12 *cm.* ¶ Lent by PERSIAN GOVERNMENT from the Mashhad Shrine.

199 [509] MINIATURE. Lady in a blue dress, with a black and gold cloak, holding a carafe and a cup. Inscribed '*Abd Allāh Khān Uzbek,* which must be an attribution. Nothing is known of the artist. XVI century.

46×37 *cm.* ¶ Lent by PAUL J. SACHS, ESQ., through FOGG ART MUSEUM, Harvard University.

200 [608] LINE-DRAWING. Two youths romping. Mid XVI century. Perhaps by Muhammad Mu'min.

45×30 *cm.* Marteau-Vever, fig. 189. ¶ Lent by M. ADOLPHE STOCLET, Brussels.

201 [481] THREE DOUBLE LEAVES from a sketch-book, with drawings on both sides. The drawings, which cannot be dated precisely, must have been made by an artist of the Persian miniature-school at some time after the beginning of the sixteenth century. Included are geometrical and architectural designs, clouds, a tent, boots, head-gear, flames, and arabesques. An unusual subject is that of a naked woman issuing from a blazing brazier. In a very minute hand on the breasts of this presumably symbolical figure is the name of Bihzād.

10×5 *cm.* (each half-leaf). ¶ Lent by MAJOR D. MACAULAY.

202 [722 A] FIRDAWSĪ'S *SHĀH-NĀMA,* copied by Hasan b. Muhammad Ahsan at Shīrāz in 967/1560. Many miniatures.

40×28·5 *cm.* ¶ Lent by INDIA OFFICE LIBRARY.

203 [718 A] JĀMĪ'S *SILSILAT AL-ZAHAB,* 'Gold Chain', copied by Bābā-Shāh Isfahānī in 977/1569. Margin covered with floral and animal designs in gold. Fourteen miniatures. Bound in lacquered leather with figures of birds and flowers; inside, lattice-work.

24·5×16 *cm.* ¶ Lent by GULISTAN MUSEUM, Tehran.

204 [720 C] PERSIAN VERSION OF QAZWĪNĪ'S *WONDERS OF CREA-TION,* with miniatures and coloured diagrams. Copied in 974/1566.

35·5×23 *cm.* E. G. Browne, *Catalogue of the Persian MSS. in the University of Cambridge,* 1896, pp. 208-10. ¶ Lent by CAMBRIDGE UNIVERSITY LIBRARY.

205 [546 D] 'ĀRIFĪ'S *GŪY U CHAWGĀN*. Fifty-two folios, ten half-lines to a page. The first and last pages are gilt and illuminated with coloured arabesques. Two miniatures. Copied in 974/1566. Eighteenth-century lacquer binding.

20×12·5 *cm*. ¶ Lent by R. S. GREENSHIELDS, ESQ.

206 [724 C] MAWLĀNĀ NIZĀM'S *ĀSĀR AL-MUZAFFAR* (Early Muhammadan history), copied in 974/1567. Three miniatures. Red leather binding.

26×17·5 *cm*. ¶ Lent by A. CHESTER BEATTY, ESQ.

(*a*) Muhammad and 'Alī destroying idols at the Ka'ba.
(*b*) The Fortress of Hisn al-Qāmīs taken by 'Alī.
(*c*) Muhammad and 'Alī, veiled, appearing before an assembly of shaykhs.

207 [144 A] JĀMĪ'S *YŪSUF U ZULAYKHĀ*, dated 977/1569, written in *nasta'līq*. Richly illuminated and ornamented with marginal arabesques. Seven miniatures. Lacquer binding.

23×17·5 *cm*. Ethé, *Cat.*, no. 908. Exh. Oriental Congress, Oxford, 1928. Gray, pl. 11. ¶ Lent by BODLEIAN LIBRARY, Oxford [Greaves 1].

208 [582] PORTRAIT of a painter dressed in green, with spectacles, holding a writing tablet. XVI century. Inscribed: 'picture of Fānī the painter'.

16×8 *cm*. Martin, pl. 89; Marteau-Vever, no. 165. Exh. Paris 1912. ¶ Lent by M. CLAUDE ANET, Paris.

209 [604] LINE-DRAWING. Chinese lady playing a Chinese stringed instrument. XVI century. Apparently copied from a Chinese original.

46×32 *cm*. Marteau-Vever, no. 212. ¶ Lent by M. ADOLPHE STOCLET, Brussels.

210 [593] MINIATURE. Falconer dressed in green, with a falcon on his wrist. Warm ochre background. Second half of XVI century.

14·5×9·5 *cm*. Marteau-Vever, no. 16. ¶ Lent by M. CLAUDE ANET, Paris.

211 [547 C] NIZĀMĪ'S *KHAMSA*, in *lūlū-dār* script. Two decorated pages; nineteen miniatures in early Safawid style. Mid XVI century. Gold-stamped binding. Given by Shāh 'Abbās I to the Ardabīl Shrine in 1017/1608.

31×20 *cm*. ¶ Lent by PERSIAN GOVERNMENT from the Ardabīl Shrine.

(*a*) Khusraw and Shīrīn at the hunting ground. A scene full of movement which at first obscures the extent to which by this date the Safawid school had reduced their compositions to patterns. The arrangement in three planes, the almost complete balance, and the highly stylized vegetation and clouds are all signs of this and typical of the period.   PLATE CI A.
(*b*) Farhād, the sculptor, carries Shīrīn and her horse on his back to her castle. Her maidens look on in astonishment. The miniature exemplifies the not uncommon practice of Persian artists of suggesting weird shapes and faces in the drawing of rocks.   PLATE CI B.

212 [507] MINIATURE. Mary with the infant Jesus, at an oasis in the desert. XVI century.

19 × 12 *cm*. ¶ Lent by AJIT GHOSE, Calcutta.

213 SIX PAINTINGS from a manuscript, of very large format, of a Shī'ite book of auguries and pious precepts. Mid XVI century.

(*a*) [244 A] *Mi'rāj* (Muhammad's ascent to Heaven). 57 × 43·5 *cm*.
(*b*) [244 B] Solomon and the Queen of Sheba receiving offerings from attendant angels. The figure above is inscribed '*Satan the Accursed*'. 58 × 43·5 *cm*.
(*c*) [260 A] Adam and Eve, with haloes, riding on a dragon and a bird. 57 × 43 *cm*.
(*d*) [260 B] Devil descending from a tower upon a horseman. 57 × 43 *cm*.
¶ (*a*)–(*d*) Lent by M. H. VEVER, Paris.
(*e*) [262 A] 'Alī and Muhammad taking the fortress of Hisn al-Qamīs. In the seventh year of the Hijra (628) Muhammad led his armies to attack the Jewish oasis of Khaybar, 100 miles north of Madina. In the attack on the fortress of Hisn al-Qamīs 'Alī, having lost his shield, seized a door lintel which he used in its stead. 54·5 × 45 *cm*.
(*f*) [262 B] 'Alī and Muhammad in conversation with King Solomon, for whom demons are building a wall in the foreground. According to the Qur'ān, legions of demons were put in subjection to Solomon, who employed them especially in his building operations. 54·5 × 45 *cm*.
¶ (*e*) and (*f*) Lent by A. CHESTER BEATTY, ESQ.

214 [587] MINIATURE. Joseph landing in Egypt. XVI century.

20·5 × 11·5 *cm*. ¶ Lent by FITZWILLIAM MUSEUM, Cambridge.

Another version is in the Metropolitan Museum, New York, in a manuscript of Jāmī's *Yūsuf u Zulaykhā* dated 1523–4 (Dimand: fig. 16).

215 [599] NŪSHĪRWĀN AND HIS MINISTER. A miniature illustrating an episode in the *Makhzan al-Asrār* of Nizāmī. Nūshīrwān and his minister hear two owls conversing in a ruined village. In answer to the Shāh's inquiry the wazīr informs him that they are discussing the dowry of the daughter of one of them, who is to marry the other. He offers the ruin with one or two others, remarking that 'if the sovereign (i.e. Nūshīrwān) continues in disregarding the welfare of his people, I will give you a hundred thousand such ruins'. *c*. 1560.

12·5 × 11 *cm*. Exh. Detroit Institute of Arts, November 1930. ¶ Lent by PARISH-WATSON, New York.

216 [289] MINIATURE. Solomon and the Queen of Sheba with the wazīr Āsaf, surrounded by birds, beasts, angels, and jinn. On the throne is seated the hoopoe which acted as messenger between them. About 1560. Style of Āqā Rizā. Rather strong colouring. Attributed to Turkey by Kühnel.

25 × 18 *cm*. Marteau-Vever, no. 15; Sakisian, fig. 158; Kühnel, *I.M.*, pl. 95. ¶ Lent by M. H. VEVER, Paris.

217 [719 B] LINE-DRAWING, calligraphic. Dragon and Crescent. XVI century. A seal of a former owner bears the date 998/1590.

13·5 × 9 *cm*. ¶ Lent by J. V. S. WILKINSON, ESQ.

218 [613] DRAWING in ink and sanguine, tinted with gold. Mounted archer. XVI century.

26×27·5 *cm.* ¶ Lent by R. S. GREENSHIELDS, ESQ.

219 [551] MINIATURE. Solomon seated on a golden throne judging men, beasts, and genii (cf. Qur'ān, xxxviii). Decorations in gold and colours. Early XVI century.

10×20 *cm.* ¶ Lent by Y. DAWUD, ESQ.

220 [719 J] INK SKETCH. Young man mounted, and a suppliant. A satiric drawing. The suppliant has dismounted from an emaciated horse and is kissing the pastern of the other's horse. Both the suppliant and his horse are drawn on a minute scale. XVI century.

11·5×8·5 *cm.* Sakisian, fig. 149. ¶ Lent by ARMENAG BEY SAKISIAN, Paris.

221 [719 F] INK AND LIGHT COLOUR SKETCHES. Late XVI century.

17×9 *cm. each.* A. C. Edwards, *A Persian Caravan*, 1928, pl. facing p. 79. ¶ Lent by A. CECIL EDWARDS, ESQ.

(*a*) Rustam slaying a Dragon.
(*b*) Bahrām hunting.

222 [715 F] JĀMĪ'S *TUHFAT AL-AHRĀR*, copied by Khwānd (?) Sālik b. Mīrak in Samarqand in 990/1582. Twelve minute pen drawings on the margins inside octagonal medallions. Some signed *Bāqir*. An inscription at the end of the manuscript states that the book was left unfinished, and that the writer hesitates to complete his *qibla-gāhī's* (father or patron's) work.

19×13 *cm.* ¶ Lent by MAJOR D. MACAULAY.

223 [547 A] NIZĀMĪ'S *KHAMSA*, copied at Shīrāz by Qāsim the Scribe. Many miniatures. XVI century. The colophon has the date '92', which, in view of the style of the miniatures, is more likely to be intended for 992/1584 than for 920 or 922 (1514 or 1516).

37×27 *cm.* ¶ Lent by UNIVERSITY MUSEUM, University of Pennsylvania, Philadelphia.

(*a*) A garden scene. A typical Safawid composition showing youths and their instructors in literature and cooking. PLATE CII A.

224 [633] SCENE IN A MOSQUE SCHOOL. Attributed to Mīr Sayyid 'Alī. The painting depicts a variety of occupations both within and without the mosque school, in the niches outside which the pupils have left their shoes. Besides those that are reading and writing, one pupil is being bastinadoed and another is polishing paper for calligraphy. Cooking, washing, and bread-making are also going on, and above the muezzin is calling the Faithful to prayer. Such elaborate compositions seem to have been favoured by the early Persian masters who worked at the Mughal court in India. Third quarter of the XVI century.

27·5 × 15 cm. ¶ Lent by M. H. VEVER, Paris. PLATE CIII A.

225 [631] MINIATURE. Hawking scene with eight figures in a rocky landscape. Mughal school: third quarter of XVI century. Attributed to Mīr Sayyid ʿAlī.

21·5 × 13 cm. ¶ Lent by MRS. E. E. MEUGENS.

226 [606] PORTRAIT BUST, on linen. About 1550. This portrait, unusual both for the material on which it is painted and for its scale, has been identified by M. Sakisian as representing the Sultān Mehmet II, the conqueror of Constantinople, in spite of the fact that it does not show a marked resemblance to the Bellini portrait in the National Gallery nor to the medal by Costanzo, which are the only authentic portraits. The upper part from just above the turban is a later addition made in India probably in the reign of Jahāngīr, when the album in which the portrait is mounted was put together. From its presence in India then, as well as from the fact that the only other known paintings on stuff are of Mughal origin, it is possible that it represents some member of the Mughal house. It may therefore have been painted at Kābul, where Humāyūn was resident about 1550. It may even just possibly be a portrait of Humāyūn himself, though it has not his peculiar head-dress, and is not close to other portraits of him. On the other hand, some of the details of the costume appear to be Turkish.

30·5 × 18 cm. *Syria*, 1931, p. 168, fig. 2. ¶ Lent by GULISTAN MUSEUM, Tehran.

227 [636], 228 [626]. PAINTINGS, on linen, from the *Hamza-nāma.*[1] 1550–75.

(*a*) Hamza overturning Amīr i Maʿdī and his horse. [H. Glück, *Die Indischen Miniaturen des Haemzae-Romanes*, Vienna, 1925 (Abb. 2).] 68·5 × 49 cm. ¶ Lent by GERALD REITLINGER, ESQ.
(*b*) Scene of parting in front of a building. 66 × 49 cm. ¶ Lent by M. H. VEVER, Paris.

229 [632] HORSE LED BY A GROOM; behind is a hermit in a tower, placed in a rocky landscape. Inscribed *ʿAbd al-Samad, Shīrīn-qalam.* Probably later than the other works by this artist included in the Jahāngīr album; but the horse and the groom's costume are still of a Persian type.

13 × 20·5 cm. ¶ Lent by GULISTAN MUSEUM, Tehran.

230 [628] THE PRESENTATION OF A MINIATURE by Akbar to his father the Emperor Humāyūn. By ʿAbd al-Samad.

23 × 14 cm. ¶ Lent by GULISTAN MUSEUM, Tehran.

Humāyūn, who is seated on a platform built in a chenar tree, is receiving a painting which it is possible to recognize with a glass as this miniature. In the upper story of a pavilion on the left are musicians, and in the lower a prince, probably also the young Akbar, holding an open book. In front and just outside is a seated figure probably intended for the artist ʿAbd al-Samad; for by his side lies a book bearing the words *Allāh Akbar, al-ʿabd ʿAbd al-Samad,*

[1] See p. 119 *ante.*

Shīrīn-qalam, i.e. '*God is great* (the common play on the name of Akbar being intended), *the slave 'Abd al-Samad, Sweet-brush'*. On the back walls of the pavilion frescoes are clearly visible with repeating designs similar to those on Safawid textiles, of hunting scenes and lovers. In the foreground is the royal huntsman with grooms holding horses and the hunting cheetah.

Probably painted shortly before Humāyūn's death, which occurred in January 1556. Akbar was then in his fourteenth year, having been born in November 1542. The headgear is peculiar to Humāyūn's court. Above and below the miniature are some verses, added by the library staff when this album was made up about 1620 for Jahāngīr, which read as follows: 'The likeness of Shāh Humāyūn and Shāh Akbar—Was painted by the establishment of 'Abd al-Samad to display their skill—The picture shows the whole of this group—On the page that Shāh Akbar is showing to the Shah.' PLATE CIV B.

This miniature is of considerable interest, as a signed work of 'Abd al-Samad, as containing contemporary portraits of Humāyūn in maturity and of Akbar in youth, and as finely representative of the court scenes and elaborate compositions of the earliest Mughal period. A seventeenth-century Mughal copy is in the 'Miniature Room' at Schönbrunn (cf. W. Staude in *Belvedere*, 1931, Heft 5, fig. 90).

231 [630] DERVISH PRAISING GOD while his companions sleep. By 'Abd al-Samad. An illustration to a story in the *Gulistān* of Sa'dī. While the other travellers in a caravan are asleep after a journey, one of the company, uttering a loud cry, runs into the forest, being unable to keep silence when, as he explains, the birds are all praising God. The inscription in the label in the bottom left-hand corner of the miniature reads as follows: *The slave, Shikasta-raqam, 'Abd al-Samad Shīrīn-qalam* (Sweet-pen).' The section at the top filled with storks and other birds is a later addition made when the album was put together, and the verses at top and bottom were inserted at the same time.

23·5 × 14·5 *cm.* ¶ Lent by GULISTAN MUSEUM, Tehran. PLATE CV A.

232 [638] COMPOSITE PAGE. Above, two young men, one painting, one playing a stringed instrument, signed: *'Made by Mawlānā 'Abd al-Samad in half a day on New Year's Day* 958/1551.' Below, Majnūn in the desert, *c.* 1490.

27·5 × 15 *cm.* ¶ Lent by the GULISTAN MUSEUM, Tehran. PLATE CV B.

The upper part, which is in pale colouring and not very highly finished, may well be a picture of the young Akbar given to him by 'Abd al-Samad as a New Year's gift. It has been enlarged later to fit the page of the album. The lower part is a fine composition of the period of Bihzād. It has not been much cut down as is evident from an unacknowledged copy of 1028 A.H. signed by Rizā-yi 'Abbāsī (repr. Schulz, Bd. I, Taf. R). On the opposite page in the album was bound up a copy apparently made for Jahāngīr himself (see the following no.). So that it was evidently a famous composition of which this version may not be the original.

233 [640] COMPOSITE PAGE. Above, a groom leading a horse. Signed: *'Made by 'Abd al-Samad on New Year's Day*, 965/1557.' Below, Majnūn (copy of the lower part of 232). Inscribed *Pādshāh Salīm*, i.e. the Emperor Jahāngīr. The lower miniature must, of course, be a good deal later in date if it was actually executed for Jahāngīr, who was not born till 977/1569.

29 × 16 *cm.* ¶ Lent by GULISTAN MUSEUM, Tehran.

234 [642] MINIATURE. Safawid princes visiting a dervish. Painted, probably in India, about 1550.

27×12·5 cm. ¶ Lent by GULISTAN MUSEUM, Tehran.

235 [644] PICNIC SCENE. Safawid figures, but possibly executed in India.

32·5×19·5 cm. ¶ Lent by GULISTAN MUSEUM, Tehran.

236 [634] COURT SCENE. By Riżā'ī Jahāngīrī. A prince seated on a throne in a pavilion, surrounded by courtiers, musicians, and attendants. In the top left-hand corner is an inscription, probably by a library clerk, 'The work of Riżā'ī, murīd (disciple) of Pādshāh Salīm'. Jahāngīr, whose name before his accession was Salīm, refers in his Memoirs to a certain Āqā Riżā'ī of Herāt who joined his service when he was a prince [Rogers and Beveridge's translation, vol. II, p. 20]. No doubt he is the artist here intended. There is a difficulty in the word Pādshāh, which is a title that could only be given to the Emperor, but it is possible that this inscription was put on years after the drawing was made. If the prince depicted is intended to represent Jahāngīr it can hardly be later than 1585–90, for Jahāngīr was born in 1569. The colouring is strong and there is some European influence in the use of modelling in the drawing of the faces.

29×16·5 cm. ¶ Lent by GULISTAN MUSEUM, Tehran.   PLATE CIV A.

237 [581] LINE-DRAWING. Portrait of a dervish, wearing a bell-shaped hat and long-sleeved cloak. Signed *Walī Jān*. Late XVI century.

45×30 cm. Marteau-Vever, fig. 195; Martin, II, pl. 88 b; Sakisian, fig. 173. ¶ Lent by M. ADOLPHE STOCLET, Brussels.

Probably not the original of this well-known composition. Cf. the versions given by Martin, pl. 88.

238 [724 B] FIRDAWSĪ'S *SHĀH-NĀMA*, copied in 955/1548. Thirty-two miniatures of archaistic style, copying early Timurid work of the XV century. Lacquer binding : hunting scene and a hermit in a cave ; late XVI century.

25×16 cm. ¶ Lent by A. CHESTER BEATTY, ESQ.

239 [715 A] AHMAD AL-AFLĀKĪ'S *MANĀQIB AL-'ĀRIFĪN* (Lives of the Great Masters of the Mawlawī dervishes of Qonya), copied by Kamāl. Two '*unwāns*: nine miniatures. XVI century.

19×11·5 cm. Formerly owned by H. M. H. Fournier, French Ambassador at Stockholm. Zetterstéen, *Cat.*, no. 409. Exh. Gothenburg, 1928; Copenhagen 1929, cat. no. 26. ¶ Lent by ROYAL UNIVERSITY LIBRARY, Upsala. [Nov. 94.]

240 [597] MINIATURE. Angels and jinn warring against demons. XVI century.

19×12 cm. ¶ Lent by M. H. VEVER, Paris.

241 [645] LINE-DRAWING, from an album. End of XVI century. Agricultural scene. Signed *Mīrak*. Certainly not the work of the celebrated Āqā Mīrak of the period.

16·5×23 cm. ¶ Lent by INDIA OFFICE LIBRARY.

242 [611] MINIATURE. A battle scene. XVI century.

21 × 16 *cm.* ¶ Lent by GERALD REITLINGER, ESQ.

243 [721 E] JĀMĪ'S *HAFT AWRANG* (Seven Poems), copied by Muhammad Qiwām of Shīrāz. Eighteen miniatures. XVI century. The miniatures are very delicately executed. The Safawid turban is absent, and the date is probably in the third quarter of the century.

37·5 × 24·5 *cm.* Ethé, *Cat.,* no. 898; Arnold, *P.I.,* pl. XXXII. ¶ Lent by BODLEIAN LIBRARY, Oxford [Elliott, 149].

244 [497] MINIATURE IN TWO PANELS.

11 × 15·5 *cm.* ¶ Lent by NATIONAL MUSEUM, Stockholm.

(*a*) A camel. *c.* 1500.
(*b*) A chamberlain. *c.* 1600.

245 [286] TREE WITH BIRDS AND ANIMALS, including a monkey and two foxes. Line-drawing, slightly coloured, inscribed in Persian 'this is one of the marvels of Bihzād'. The drawing is on the reverse of a specimen of calligraphy, one of three pages executed by Zayn al-Dīn 'Alī and Muhammad Rizā in 993/1585 for Sultān Muhammad Qulī Qutb-Shāh of Golconda, Southern India. The drawing is of about the same period. Gold-decorated blue margins with monkeys.

14 × 23·5 *cm.* ¶ Lent by A. CHESTER BEATTY, ESQ.

246 [573] PAGE from an album, XVI century. Two miniatures. Probably later Turkish copies of sixteenth-century drawings. From the same album as no. 247.

25·5 × 15 *cm.* ¶ Lent by A. CHESTER BEATTY, ESQ.

(*a*) Lion attacking an antelope, signed *Āqā Mīr*.
(*b*) Camel with two attendants.

247 [637] DRAWING, slightly tinted. Dragon walking on rocks. XVI century. Probably Turkish. From the same album as no. 246.

12·5 × 20 *cm.* ¶ Lent by A. CHESTER BEATTY, ESQ.

PLATE LXXVI-A. 104 (*a*). Three damsels from China
By Mahmūd

PLATE LXXVI-B. 104 (*d*). Mīr ʿAlī Shīr Nawāʾī
By Mahmūd

PLATE LXXVII-A. 114. Lovers
By 'Abd Allāh. *Mid* XVI *century*
Bukhārā

PLATE LXXVII-B. 104 (*b*). Youth offering an apple to a Girl
By Mahmūd. *Early* XVI *century*
Bukhārā

PLATE LXXVIII-A. 112 (a). Musicians in a Garden. 1558
Bukhārā

PLATE LXXVIII-B. 105 (*a*). Frontispiece. 1522
Bukhārā

PLATE LXXIX-A. 106 (c). Mihr entertained by King Kaywān
Bukhārā, 1523

PLATE LXXIX-B. 106 (b). Mihr kills a ferocious lion
Bukhārā, 1523

PLATE LXXX-A. 106 (*d*). The Marriage of Mihr and the Princess Nawhīd
Bukhārā, 1523

PLATE LXXX-B. 106 (*a*). Mihr and Mushtarī at school
Bukhārā, 1523

PLATE LXXXI-A. 107 (a). A Saint riding on a leopard
Bukhārā, 1524

PLATE LXXXI-B. 110 (*c*). A youth declaring his love to a lady
Bukhārā, 1548

PLATE LXXXII-A. 119 (b). Jalāl among the fairies. 1504

PLATE LXXXII-B. 119 (*a*). Jalāl arrives at the turquoise dome. 1504

PLATE LXXXIII- A. 127 (*b*). A prince entertaining a lady

Between 1517 and 1540

PLATE LXXXIII-B. 127 (*a*). Polo

Between 1517 and 1540

PLATE LXXXIV-A. 127 (d). A Prince and his Court
By Sultān Muhammad
Between 1517 and 1540

PLATE LXXXIV-B. 127 (c). A moving sermon
By Shaykh-zāda
Between 1517 and 1540

PLATE LXXXV. 129 (b). Dancing Dervishes. Attributed to Haydar ʻAlī. 1522(?)

PLATE LXXXVI. 129 (*c*). Zulaykhā and the ladies of Egypt. Attributed to Qāsim ʿAlī. 1522(?)

PLATE LXXXVII-A. 132. Two camels fighting. By Bihzād, c. 1525

PLATE LXXXVII-B. 133. A copy of 132, made by Nānhā for Jahāngīr in 1608/9

PLATE LXXXVIII-A. 136 (*a*). The Caliph Ma'mūn being shaved after a bath. 1528

PLATE LXXXVIII-B. 141 (*a*). Kay Kāūs in his flying contrivance. 1531

PLATE LXXXIX- A. 137 (*b*). The son of the Sultān of Rūm brought before Tīmūr. 1529

PLATE LXXXIX-B. 137 (*a*). A scene in a mosque. 1529

PLATE XC-A. 139 (*a*). Khizr and Elias bathing in the
Water of Life. 1531

PLATE XC-B. 140 (*a*). A Polo Scene. 1531

PLATE XCI-A. 151 (*a*). Tīmūr hunting near Multan. 1533

PLATE XCI-B. 151 (*b*). Tīmūr mourning for his grandson. 1533

PLATE XCII-A. 152 (*a*). The ascent of Muhammad to heaven by night. 1533

PLATE XCII-B. 152 (b). Zulaykhā tempting Yūsuf. 1533

PLATE XCIII-A. 157. Solomon and his flying throne
First half of XVI *century*

PLATE XCIII-B. 168. The end of a *battue*
Second quarter of XVI *century*

PLATE XCIV- A. 166. Battle Scene. *c.* 1530–40

PLATE XCIV-B. 165. Princes in a Pavilion. *c.* 1540–50

PLATE XCV. 174. Muhammad mounted on Burāq. By Shāh Muzaffar(?)

PLATE XCVI-A. 176 (*a*). The island of Java

Shīrāz, 1545

PLATE XCVI B. 176 (*b*). The Mountains of Yalam, where all
life is turned to stone

Shīrāz, 1545

PLATE XCVII. (c) Two monkeys

PLATE XCVII.(d) The Bū-qalamūn, which changes colour

PLATE XCVII.(e) The spring Nātūl

All from no. 176. (?) Shīrāz, 1545

PLATE XCVII.(f) A bird which sings all night

PLATE XCVII.(g) A hare

PLATE XCVII.(h) A duck
All from no. 176. (?) Shīrāz, 1545

PLATE XCVIII- A. 101. Majnūn at the Ka'ba. 1501

PLATE XCVIII-B. 184 (a). Tīmūr is attacked by demons

Mid XVI *century*

PLATE XCIX-A. 170. Youth. By Muhammad Mu'min

PLATE XCIX-B. 286. Line-drawing
Early XVII *century*

Plate XCIX-C. 187. Young Dervish. By Muhammadī

PLATE C-A. 189. Picnic in the mountains. *c.* 1550

PLATE C-B. 194. Three musicians and a dancer. *Mid* XVI *cent*.

Plate CI-A.211 (a). Khusraw and Shīrīn at the hunting ground. c. 1550

PLATE CI-B. 211 (*b*). Farhād carrying Shīrīn and her horse. *c.* 1550

PLATE CII-A. 223 (*a*). A garden scene. Shīrāz, 1584(?)

PLATE CII-B. 113. A preacher and his congregation
(?)Bukhārā, *mid* XVI *century*

PLATE CIII-A. 224. Scene in a mosque school
Attributed to Mīr Sayyid ʻAlī

PLATE CIII-B. 95. Hunting scene (Hills repainted by Dawlat)
Late XV *century*

PLATE CIV- A. 236. A Court Scene. By Rizā Jahāngīrī

PLATE CIV-B. 230. Akbar presenting a miniature to his
father Humāyūn. By ʿAbd al–Samad

PLATE CV-A. 231. Dervish praising God while his companions sleep
By ʿAbd al-Samad

PLATE CV-B. 232. *Above*: Two young men in a garden
By 'Abd al-Samad, 1551
Below: Majnūn in the desert. *c*. 1490

VI

PAINTING UNDER SHĀH ʿABBĀS AND HIS SUCCESSORS

WHEN Sir John Malcolm visited Persia in 1800, he found that the names of almost all the Safawid Shāhs were forgotten, excepting that of ʿAbbās the Great, of which the British ʿElcheeʾ became quite tired, associated as it was with all great buildings, good sayings, liberal acts, and deeds of arms. It may, nevertheless, be useful to record the names and dates of the seventeenth-century Shāhs. They were Shāh ʿAbbās the Great (1587–1629); Safī (1629–42); ʿAbbās II (1642–66); Safī, who took the name Sulaymān (1666–94); and Husayn (1694), in whose reign the Afghan invasion of 1722 put an end to the dynasty.

Shāh ʿAbbās succeeded as a boy of sixteen to a throne greatly weakened and imperilled by ten years' unsettlement. Obliged at first to make terms with his enemies, he was able, by the early years of the seventeenth century, to secure his eastern frontier against the Uzbeks, to defeat the Turks decisively, to win back his lost provinces, and to put down the unruly elements among the Qizil-bāsh nobles. He was even greater as an administrator than as a soldier. By his farsightedness in conciliating the various elements of the population; by his wisdom in conceiving, and energy in carrying out, ambitious projects for the benefit of his people, he showed himself in advance of his age. In the words of Sir John Malcolm, 'Though possessed of great means, and distinguished as a military leader, he deemed the improvement of his own wide possessions a nobler object than conquest; he attended to the cultivation and commerce of Persia beyond all former monarchs . . . the bridges, caravansaries, and other useful public buildings that he erected were without number.'[1]

It is no wonder that such a ruler should have retained the affection of Persians up to modern times as the initiator of all benefits, in spite of a strain of odious cruelty in his nature, too well authenticated to be disregarded, and too horrible in its manifestations to be excused as the custom of the country or the age.

Shāh ʿAbbās moved the capital, in 1600, to Isfahān, which he filled with magnificent avenues and buildings, some of which are standing to-day, notably the *Masjid i Shāh*, of which a partial model was constructed for the Burlington House Exhibition, and the great bridge of ʿAlī-wirdī Khān.

Isfahān is still a beautiful city, and though its glory has faded it is possible, with the aid of the descriptions of contemporary European travellers, to form some kind of mental picture of its impressive and colourful splendour under the most sumptuous of the Safawids. 'Not inferior to the greatest and best-built city throughout the Orient,'

[1] Malcolm, *History of Persia*, vol. I, p. 378.

says Herbert[1] of the capital, though Herbert's best description of Persian magnificence, not to say gaudiness, is in his account of a provincial governor's court, on the occasion of the banquet given in 1628 in Shīrāz by 'the Duke' to Sir Dodmore Cotton, the British Ambassador, and Sir Robert Sherley. The feast was held in a 'stately banqueting-house, supported with twenty gilded pillars, the roof embossed with gold', and exquisitely painted. The ground was spread with 'extraordinary rich carpets of silk and gold; a state [i.e. canopy] at one end of crimson satin was erected, embroidered with pearl and gold, under which the Duke was to enthrone himself. Upon one side thereof was painted his Ormus trophies, no cost, no art being left out to do it to advantage.' During the entertainment 'young Ganymedes, arrayed in cloth of gold, with long crisped locks of hairs, went up and down bearing flagons of gold filled with choice wine, which they proffered to all the company one by one so long as the feast endured'. When the 'Duke' entered he was ushered in by thirty comely youths in crimson satin, wearing rich jewellery, swords in embroidered scabbards, with hawks upon their fists, each hood set with precious stones. The Duke himself was a dazzling figure wearing, over a silver embroidered blue satin coat, a long robe 'so thick-powdered with Oriental pearl and glittering gems as made the ground of it inperspicable'. After the return feast with the British Ambassador the Governor nearly fell off his horse—the result of a three hours' drinking bout, and had to be helped home by two of Cotton's suite.

Later in the century another acute observer, Chardin,[2] remarks (he has been referring to the *vivacité incomparable* of the colours in painting): 'Je n'ai vû nulle part de si belles couleurs qu'en *Perse*, pour l'éclat, pour la force, & pour l'épaisseur, tant des couleurs de l'*art*, que de celles de la *nature*. . . . On peut dire que ceux qui n'ont jamais été dans les Païs Orientaux, ne connoissent point l'éclat et le brillant de la Nature.'[3]

The age of Shāh 'Abbās saw the opening up of Persia to the West. Embassies from most of the European countries, merchants, private travellers, and technicians, visited the capital and the chief cities in increasing numbers, encouraged by the Shāh's enlightened policy towards non-Muslims and interest in foreign products, in this and the succeeding reigns; and many of them have left careful accounts of their impressions and experiences, covering every detail of the life and customs of the court and the population.

Several of these travellers speak, not always with approval, of the elaborate paintings with which the royal palaces and the houses of the rich were decorated. 'The painters were no Titians,' says Della Valle; he found the paintings badly executed, but the colours exquisite. The subjects, too, occasionally shocked him. Most of these were, it would seem, of battles, hunting scenes, and the like; but he objected to the 'display

[1] Sir Thomas Herbert (1606–82) visited Persia in 1628: he published his *Description of the Persian Monarchy* in 1634.
[2] Sir John Chardin (1643–1713), born in Paris: visited Persia as a merchant in jewels 1664–70 and 1671–7.
[3] *Voyages en Perse*, Amsterdam, 1711, Tome II, p. 78.

of the votaries of Venus and Bacchus', in some of them.[1] He notes, too, that some of the Bacchanalian figures were furnished with hats, so as to represent Europeans, with the intention, he thinks, of intimating that 'the Persians are not the only ones addicted to wine'.

The European accounts make it clear that in Shāh 'Abbās's reign there was a marked vogue for wall-painting, no doubt in part reflecting a personal taste of the monarch, who, like Shāh Jahān in India, seems to have been far more interested in building than in the arts of the book, which steadily decayed. Chardin found the bookbinders clumsy workmen, the paper not very good, and that of the country often replaced by European substitutes.[2]

But the miniature was still popular, as is clear from Chardin's remarks;[3] as at all periods, mural and miniature painting were practised simultaneously.

Examples of the mural art of the seventeenth century are still in existence, especially at two royal buildings at Isfahān.[4] The decoration, which is badly damaged, is mainly Persian in character; some of the figure-drawing is closely akin to the miniatures associated with the name of Rizā-yi 'Abbāsī; while there is a certain amount of European work, possibly by 'John the Dutchman', who was for many years in Shāh 'Abbās's service. Part of the Chihil Sutūn painting is distinctly in the Dutch style.[5] Olearius, in 1637, saw, in the audience hall at Isfahān, 'pieces of painting done in Europe and representing certain histories'.

The art, in general, of Shāh 'Abbās's reign has often been highly praised; the architecture, textiles, carpets, and pottery of the period all have their warm admirers; but an impartial critic cannot fail to detect in nearly all of it a falling-off in vitality and inventive power, manifesting itself in various ways; in the pottery, by a wholesale imitation of Chinese forms, and in textiles and carpets by a steadily increasing lifelessness of design and a deterioration in the colours.

In miniature painting the circumstances and the results were somewhat different, partly, no doubt, because the art was to some extent practised at this time independently of court patronage. It is much less aristocratic than before, and at the same time some examples display a new spirit of refreshing originality—alongside, it must be admitted, much uninspired work. Though the decadence was subsequently rapid, the standard of achievement was for a while, and within limits, remarkably high.

Iskandar Munshī, writing in 1616, remarks that, when Shāh Tahmāsp's interest in painting waned, some of the library officials (he is referring, apparently, to painters)

---

[1] Herbert, visiting the house of 'Hodge-Nazar' at Julfa, the Armenian quarter of Isfahān, a year before Shāh 'Abbās's death, notes that it was furnished with 'beastly pictures, such ugly postures as indeed are not fit to be remembered'. In Māzandarān, and on the 'Alī-wirdī Khān bridge, traces of such 'painted scenes of impurity' survived into modern times. On the subject of Muslim erotic painting generally see Arnold, *Painting in Islam*, pp. 84 seq.

[2] The best paper, however, came, as always, from Turkestan. It was prepared by soaping and was then polished with an egg-shaped crystal, or some other burnisher. 'Marbled' paper was often used.

[3] See below, p. 154, note 2.

[4] The Ali Qapi and the Chihil Sutūn. See J. Daridan et S. Stelling-Michaud, *La Peinture Séfévide d'Ispahan*, Paris, 1930. Some of the 'European' work is probably by a Persian artist imitating Western models.

[5] Pope, *Introduction to Persian Art*, p. 51.

were allowed to practise their art by themselves; and it is probable that this partly accounts for the scarcity of manuscripts *de luxe* after the middle of the sixteenth century. Commercial products, executed in haste to supply the demands of less wealthy and discriminating patrons, began even then to take their place; and single paintings and drawings, not intended for manuscripts, became commoner at about the same time. A change in the whole character of the art was inevitable, unless enthusiastic and liberal royal patronage was to be renewed.[1] There was in addition another influence which began to be felt towards the end of the century—that of Europe. Shaykh Muhammad, as has been said, is quoted as the first Persian artist to imitate European models and to set a new fashion, which must have received additional encouragement from the presents of European pictures which were made to the Shāhs by the European ambassadors and other visitors. Several instances of this are recorded. Shāh ʿAbbās the Great, like his later namesake, was especially fond of Europeans. Owing to the Sherleys' advice, and their British cannon-founder, he had been helped to victory against the Turks; and he employed European artificers and craftsmen in considerable numbers. The Dutch painter, 'John the Dutchman', was probably the first of the European artists employed at the court; there were others in subsequent years, of whom, however, little is known.

Nevertheless—and it is a curious fact in the circumstances, besides being a powerful testimony to the strength of the indigenous tradition—there is little trace of the close emulation of European technique till the seventeenth century was well advanced. In fact what distresses European observers like Chardin is precisely the failure of Persian painters to adopt the European conventions of perspective and chiaroscuro.[2]

Although, however, technique was only slowly westernized, European influence doubtless had something to do with the subjects which began to be depicted. A certain number of actual copies and adaptations of European paintings have survived;[3] and

[1] Patronage was not altogether lacking in the seventeenth century. There are, for instance, a number of drawings inscribed 'for the royal treasury' dating apparently from the reign of Shāh Safī, and ʿAbbās II was interested in painting, for a time at least. 'Le feu Roi savoit dessiner et peindre dès sa jeunesse' (Chardin). Tavernier says that he learnt his drawing from two Dutch artists.

[2] See Chardin, *Voyages en Perse* (Amsterdam, 1711), Tome II, pp. 204–5. The passage is worth quoting. After remarking that the Persians had lost their ancient knowledge owing to the religious ban on portraiture, he continues, 'A présent ils ne font rien du tout en bosse, & pour ce qui est de la *plate peinture*, il est vrai que les visages qu'ils représentent sont assez ressemblans, ils les *tirent* d'ordinaire de profil, parce que ce sont ceux qu'ils font le plus aisément: ils les font aussi de *trois quarts*, mais pour les *visages en plain* ou *de front*, ils y réussissent fort mal n'entendant pas à y donner les *ombres*: ils ne sauroient former une *attitude* & une *posture*. Les *figures* qu'ils font sont estropiées par tout, tant celles des oiseaux & des bêtes que les autres, & leurs *nuditez* sur tout: il n'y a rien de plus mal fait, de même qu'il n'y a rien de plus infame que leurs re-

présentations; mais en échange, ils excellent dans les *moresques*, & à la *fleur*, ayant sur nous l'avantage des *couleurs, belles, vives* & qui ne passent point. Ils ne font rien a l'*huile*, ou fort peu de chose, toute leur *peinture* est en miniature: ils travaillent sur du velin qui est admirable, c'est un carton mince plus qu'aucun autre que nous ayons, dur, ferme, sec et licé, où la peinture ne coule point. Leur *pinceau* est fin et délicat, et leur *peinture vive* et *éclatante*, il faut attribuer à l'air du Païs la beauté des couleurs: c'est un air sec qui resserre les corps, les durcit & les polit, au lieu que nôtre air humide étend & dissout les couleurs, & répand dessus une certaine crasse qui en empêche l'éclat. Ils ont aussi la plûpart des matieres pour la *peinture* plus fraiches & nouvelles, que nous ne les avons, comme le *lapis l'azul*. Ce *vernix* qu'ils ont si beau, et que nos Maîtres admirent tant, n'est fait que de *sandarac* & d'*huile de lin*, mêlez ensemble, & reduits en consistence de pâte ou d'onguent: lors qu'ils s'en veulent servir, ils le dissolvent avec l'*huile de nafte*, ou au défaut avec de l'*esprit de vin rectifié* plusieurs fois.'

[3] See Kühnel, figs. 82, 86; Sarre-Mittwoch, *Zeichnungen von Riza Abbasi*, Taf. 48 (b).

European clothes, hats, and pet dogs are found in pictures before 1630; the genre drawing was perhaps stimulated by examples of the schools of Northern Europe.

In the art of the manuscripts tradition tended to restrain innovations, but in the separate miniatures, not intended as book illustrations, the artists were less tied by custom. Fortunately a large number of these exist, most of the chief collections containing specimens. Apart from the fully coloured paintings, there are numerous sketches, in pencil or coloured chalk; others are, perhaps, drawn with a metal pen; some are partly tinted; some are in a sort of water-colour technique.

In the manuscript work we notice a loosening of the former closeness of co-operation between the various book arts. The illustrations force themselves, more obtrusively than before, into the margins.[1] Moreover, the illumination is often perfunctory, the quality of the pigments is sometimes very mediocre, and the types in the figure subjects are generally commonplace and lacking in dignity. The best miniature work is generally to be found outside the covers of the books, or in miscellaneous picture albums.

Independent paintings and drawings cannot always be accurately dated. The style of Muhammadī merges gradually into that of the seventeenth century, and older work was, as always, often imitated by later artists. A good general guide for dating figure-subjects is the head-gear, which becomes much more varied towards the end of the sixteenth century. The ordinary head-dress, from about this time, is a very voluminous turban, loosely and not very neatly tied, frequently, among the foppish young men so often depicted, with a long-stemmed flower setting off its elaborately negligent folds. Various other caps, furred and otherwise, were worn. The women, now and later, sometimes wore conical caps, perhaps embroidered with figures, but more often kerchiefs, plain or figured, sometimes stuck with plumes, and rows of pearls set over the forehead and fastened under the chin, 'so that their faces', as Olearius remarks, 'seemed to be set in pearls'. The effeminate-looking pages often wore kerchiefs, like the women. At the beginning of the third quarter of the seventeenth century the men still wore 'furred caps of sheepskin, the wool hanging down at the edges',[2] or large turbans or red caps; and the fan-shaped fur-edged head-dress of the later years of Shāh 'Abbās the Great and the reign of Shāh Safī (1629–42) appears in many miniatures.[3] Most of the subjects of the portraits of women were no doubt dancing-girls and courtesans—who were prominent figures in the cities. The standard of clothing generally was as luxurious as the wearers could make it, the women wearing finer stuffs—especially silks and brocades—than the men.[4] Their hair hung in tresses. Cloaks were often trimmed with fur. Jewellery—including nose-rings in parts of the country—was not only worn in profusion in the ordinary ways, but was used as a decoration for clothes and harness—the latter being an old Persian custom. Hands and feet were made red with henna, and girls had elaborate patterns painted on their limbs.

[1] e.g. in no. 273. This tendency, however, had begun to appear much earlier.
[2] Olearius.
[3] It began to be worn, apparently, early in the seventeenth century.
[4] Shāh 'Abbās himself, however, often affected quite simple clothes (*Herbert*, the Broadway Travellers series, 1928, p. 155).

The typical figure-painting and drawing of the period reflects the studied airs and affectations of a bizarre city life. Backgrounds may be painted in monochrome, with touches of gold in the impressionistically rendered foliage, and frequently Chinese *tai* clouds are introduced as purely decorative motives. Direct Far-Eastern influence has been detected in some of the monochrome drawings of the time of Shāh 'Abbās I,[1] and this is certainly possible in an age which copied Chinese ceramic models so deliberately. Some of the figure-drawing has a vaguely Japanese look.

Drawing and design had, however, a much wider range than that covered by the types just referred to. A valuable selection of varied examples is contained in a sketch-book belonging to Dr. Sarre, and published by him and Dr. Mittwoch, with facsimile illustrations and very full critical notes.[2]

These and other similar drawings are rather different from anything that had gone before; altogether more modern in spirit, for the most part. Keeping, in the main, to Asiatic conventions in the eschewing of shadows, and the absence of modelling and perspective, and preserving the Persian decorative intention, they show, here and there, the influence of Western contacts. Many of the figures and animal studies attempt a more or less complete realism and at times—though by no means always—the artist is concerned with the minute delineation of facial types. Features are often considerably worked up. Some of the drawings are valuable as indications of the artists' methods of work, successive corrections being plainly visible (nos. 338, 378).

As a whole, the drawings have a strong popular flavour, genre subjects and portrait studies of ordinary people, often set in naturalistic scenery, taking the place of the set themes of tradition. Shepherds and milkmaids, dervishes, doctors, and pilgrims, wayfarers meeting on a journey, a horse being watered, a falcon swooping on its prey—nothing is too ordinary to serve as a subject for these swift and vivid sketches, which often have scribbled across them minute details of occasion and date. Besides European pictures, Indian drawings were sometimes copied.[3]

The attribution of drawings of the period to individual artists is extraordinarily difficult, in spite of the dates and signatures.

The main problem centres round the elusive personality of Rizā-yi 'Abbāsī, a name only less famous than that of Bihzād. So much has been written about this artist, and so many difficulties attach to the whole subject, that it would be impossible, in a work of this nature, to attempt even a summary of all sides of the controversy.[4]

---

[1] Blochet, *Musulman Painting*, p. 83.
[2] *Zeichnungen von Riza Abbasi*, München, 1914. Several of these were shown at Burlington House. The sketches are not all by the same hand or of the same period.
[3] Sarre and Mittwoch, no. 28 a. On the possible relationship between the well-known Indian drawing by Bishan Dās of the interview between Shāh 'Abbās and the Mughal ambassador (1618/19) and the Persian version of the same subject by Rizā-yi 'Abbāsī, see Dr. Coomaraswamy's note in *Ars Asiatica*, XIII, pp. 78 and

79 and pl. LXXIII; Schulz, Taf. 179; Sakisian, fig. 181 and p. 143. See also Blochet, *Les Enluminares*, pp. 150-1 (pl. CVII c) on the version by Mu'īn.
[4] See especially Joseph von Karabacek, *Kaiserliche Akademie der Wissenschaften. Sitzungsberichte; Philosophisch-Historische Classe*, 167, Band 1 (Wien, 1911). Sarre and Mittwoch, in *Der Islam*, Band 11 (Strassburg, 1911), and *Zeichnungen von Riza Abbāsi* (München, 1914). All the standard works on Persian painting contain references to the subject, notably Kühnel, *I.M.*, pp. 35 et seq., and Sakisian, pp. 135–40.

In the first place, it should be noted that a very large proportion of drawings, covering most of the first half of the seventeenth century, contain signatures and inscriptions with the name *Riza* in various formulae.[1] There were doubtless many artists of this name in a Shī'a country, but the proportion is nevertheless large. Possibly, indeed certainly, many of the names were added by people other than the artists, who were not necessarily called *Riza* at all, to enhance their value, or because they resembled the work of a famous Riza.

If these drawings are examined, it will be noticed that the largest proportion are signed *Raqm i kamīna Rizā-yi 'Abbāsī*,[2] and that most of these have certain characteristics in common. They are decidedly mannered; a large number of them are single portraits of middle-aged men with curious long noses, and full-faced young pages and girls. The silhouette is often drawn in a very characteristic way, in bold and rather mechanical curves. The faces are expressive, but lack variety. This manner was no doubt easy to copy, and it had a considerable, and not a very healthy, effect on later practice. Several examples of this type were shown at Burlington House.

But Rizā-yi 'Abbāsī was capable of better work than the average of the typical drawings, with which he is generally credited, would suggest. Even if—on stylistic grounds —one excepts some of the examples which Dr. Sarre's closely reasoned study[3] ascribes to him, he is revealed as a born draughtsman of marked originality and a new realistic power, whose ingenious pencil delighted in seizing on the types of common people whom he met on his walks, and recording them in rapid economical strokes. His linear patterns sometimes have a seductive, undulating rhythm, as in the pairs of lovers with arms intertwined (nos. 314, 318). The inscriptions, it is worth noting, in Dr. Sarre's album and in some of the best of the other drawings seem to be in a different hand from the ordinary stereotyped signature[4] of this artist.

It has been observed[5] that the handwriting of the inscriptions on some of the 'Riza 'Abbāsī' drawings is identical (or almost so) with that of a certain Shafi' 'Abbāsī, who, according to a remark on a drawing[6] dated 1634, was a son of Riza-yi 'Abbāsī, and it is possible that he copied his father's work, passed it off as his own, and added detailed remarks to strengthen his pretensions.

1 Some idea of the differences in form of these inscriptions may be gathered from the following list, which does not claim to be exhaustive. We get *Rāqimuhu Rizā, Raqm i Rizā 'Abbāsī, Rizā-yi 'Abbāsī, Raqm i kamīna Rizā-yi 'Abbāsī, Raqm i kamīna Rizā Musawwir, Rizā Musawwir*. Then again, *Mashaqahu Āqā Rizā, Āqā Rizā, Rāqimuhu Āqā Rizā*. One drawing has what looks like a signature *Āqā Rizā-yi 'Abbāsī*, with two ascriptions, i.e. *Āqā Rizā* and *Rizā*, in different handwritings (Karabacek, fig. VII). Another (Martin, fig. 39) contains two notes. One states that it is a copy, after an original by Bihzād, made by *Rizā-yi Musawwir* in the year 1028 A.H. Above is a note by Shafi' 'Abbāsī that this 'composition by Āqā Rizā' was painted (i.e. perhaps completed by Shafi')

on a certain date in 1064 A.H.
2 Or the word '*Abbāsī* may be omitted.
3 *Zeichnungen von Riza Abbasi*. Many of the drawings in Dr. Sarre's album are unsigned.
4 The distinctive feature is the joining of the first two letters of the name *Riza*.
5 Kühnel, p. 37.
6 Formerly belonging to M. Demotte (see Sarre and Mittwoch, p. 13). Shafi' 'Abbāsī has left a number of paintings of birds and flowers, many of which are at Leningrad. He migrated to India, where he died in A.D. 1674. For a colour reproduction of one of his nature studies see Blochet, *Musulman Painting*, pl. 168. It was executed for Shāh 'Abbās II, as the inscription shows.

The name *ʿAbbāsī* was not the artist's own. It may either have been conferred on him by Shāh ʿAbbās to mark his appreciation of his protégé, or it may mark his descent from ʿAbbās, son of the Imām ʿAlī. Court poets sometimes took, or were given, the name of their patron, and the same is true of many calligraphers (Jaʿfar *Baysunghurī* for instance) —and there are parallels in the case of artists (e.g. *Yaʿqūbī* and *Jahāngīr-Shāhī*).

On the period of Riżā-yi ʿAbbāsī's floruit his sketches, if the dates of the inscriptions are correct, supply a good deal of information. A good number were produced early in the second quarter of the seventeenth century, but several bear earlier and later dates. The dates given in the drawings in Dr. Sarre's album range between 1598 and 1643; the latest signed and dated example being of 1638.

If Sarre's identification is accepted, the Mashhad pilgrim,[1] reproduced in Tafel I of his book, must be one of the earliest.

The date of Riżā-yi ʿAbbāsī's death is given in an inscription on a miniature[2] by Muʿīn, his friend, another version of which was shown at the Exhibition (no. 374, Pl. CXII A) as having taken place in 1044/1635. Some of Riżā-yi ʿAbbāsī's supposed drawings, however, are dated considerably later than this! Muʿīn's note says that the portrait was painted a month before Riżā's death, and completed forty years later in 1084 A.H. Possibly Muʿīn's memory failed him, or 'forty years' may have been used as the equivalent of 'many years', but he gives the exact months both of the execution of the original sketch and of its completion.

Some modern critics attribute a little group of miniatures to another Riżā, who is, it must be confessed, a decidedly enigmatical figure. He is distinguished from Riżā-yi ʿAbbāsī by the appellation *Āqā*. According to this theory, Āqā Riżā was a somewhat earlier painter than Riżā-yi ʿAbbāsī. The appellation *Āqā* or *Āghā* is an honorific; and it is unlikely that any painter would have the presumption to sign himself 'Āqā' anything. In cases of the term occurring in an inscription it is probable[3] therefore that this has been added by another hand, as in the case quoted above,[4] where the reference is certainly to Riżā-yi ʿAbbāsī. But there are a few miniatures, bearing the name Āqā Riżā, which certainly differ, stylistically, in some ways from those by Riżā-yi ʿAbbāsī. Whether they are all by one and the same hand, and how far the ascriptions or signatures are to be relied on, it is difficult to say. M. Sakisian has attempted a classification of the work of this artist,[5] including signed and unsigned examples.

Whoever is responsible for them, these miniatures include some of the most able figure-studies ever executed by the Isfahān artists. They are marked by great finesse and an admirable sense of design, while the line has marked peculiarities. It is a very sensitive line, tending to broaden out from extreme tenuity, but its main characteristic

---

[1] No. 258.

[2] Sakisian, fig. 179; Arnold and Grohmann, *The Islamic Book*, pl. 75. The portrait is apparently of a man of about 60 or 65 years of age, wearing spectacles, and painting a portrait of a youth in European dress, holding a wine-jar.

[3] Not, however, quite certain. *Āqā* may be an integral part of the name. In Schulz, Taf. 180, is a late drawing signed *Raqm i kamtarīn Āqā Bāqir*, 'the humble Āqā Bāqir'. See also note 2 on p. 159.

[4] *Ante*, p. 157 (footnote 1).

[5] *La Miniature Persane*, pp. 126–9.

is the calligraphic hooked hatching in the drawing of the ends of turbans and waist-bands, a kind of 'splutter' which is absent from the usually smooth contour drawing typical of Rizā-yi 'Abbāsī, though it does occur here and there in some of the sketches which seem, from other evidence, to be by this latter.

Drawings attributed to Āqā Rizā include the often-reproduced portrait of a young prince with his preceptor, belonging to M. Vever (no. 256); the seated boy of the Bibliothèque Nationale (reproduced in *Les Enluminures*, pl. LXXI; Sakisian, fig. 168); the girl[1] holding a necklace, in the Museum of Fine Arts, Boston (*Ars Asiatica*, XIII, pl. XLVI; Sakisian, fig. 167); and the coloured drawing of a girl with a fan (no. 257; Sakisian, fig. 171). No. 210 is somewhat in the same manner.

Several of the examples reproduced by Dr. Sarre closely resemble some of these, for instance figs. 10 and 32, while no. 1 exemplifies a kind of blend between the characteristic drawing of the two supposed artists.

There is, it must be admitted, a good deal of mystery about this painter;[2] and a careful study of the drawings attributed to him and to Rizā-yi 'Abbāsī reveals a certain amount of common ground between them,[3] while the confusion is increased by the fact that Rizā-yi 'Abbāsī seems to have been actually known as 'Āqā Rizā', as already noted.

Iskandar Munshī, writing in A.D. 1616, gives an account of a certain Āqā Rizā, which Sir Thomas Arnold has translated.[4] He was famous, according to this writer, for drawing single figures and portraits (*dar fann i yaka sūrat wa chihra-gushā'ī*), and for his delicate touch (*nazākat i qalam*); but in spite of enjoying royal favours he had, at the time when Iskandar wrote, neglected his art, taken to low company, and become poor and unpopular.

This description does not seem altogether to fit in with a painter like Rizā-yi 'Abbāsī, most of whose work is considerably later than 1616, and it may therefore apply rather more naturally to the earlier Āqā Rizā. But Iskandar notes that the painter was showing signs of amendment.

The whole problem has been further tangled by the unnecessary introduction of a certain 'Alī Rizā 'Abbāsī, a contemporary calligraphist of merit, about whom a certain amount is known. But ''Alī' is an essential part of this name, and the fact that it does not appear in any of the signatures in the miniatures is sufficient to prove that the

---

[1] Signed with the name *Rizā*, the first two letters of the name being joined, as in the typical signatures of Rizā-yi 'Abbāsī.

[2] Some fine miniatures which may be by this Āqā Rizā are contained in a *History of the Prophets* at the Bibliothèque Nationale (Supp. Pers. 1313). They are dated by M. Blochet, on dubious evidence, before the year 1556 (see Blochet, *Les Peintures*, pp. 298–9, pls. LIV–LV; *Les Enluminures*, pp. 116–17; pls. LXVII, LXVIII; *M.P.*, pls. CXXX–CXXXIII). One of these miniatures (rep. also in Arnold, *The Old and New Testaments in Muslim Religious Art*, pl. XI) contains the inscription—

apparently a signature—'the work of Āqā Rizā', and all are quite possibly by the same hand. Some of them show striking originality and dramatic power. Their real date can only be approximately guessed at; stylistically they would seem to belong to the later years of the sixteenth century.

[3] 'Es besteht trotz abweichender Signaturen und trotz grosser Qualitätsunterschiede ein enger Zusammenhang zwischen dem ganzen Rizâ-Material, der durch blosse Schultradition nicht zu erklären ist.' (Kühnel, p. 36.)

[4] *Painting in Islam*, p. 143.

calligraphist and the painter are entirely different persons. The identification rests partly on the rather bad writing of the word *ʿAbbāsī* in an inscription on a portrait of Riżā-yi ʿAbbāsī already referred to. This was read as *ʿAlī*, but the word is much more naturally read as *ʿAbbāsī*, and in any case *Riżā ʿAlī* is not the same as *ʿAlī Riżā*.

There is another Persian painter called Riżā who must be distinguished from Riżā-yi ʿAbbāsī, and who is a more definite figure than the Āqā Riżā already mentioned. He, too, is given the name Āqā Riżā in inscriptions. He painted several miniatures in a manuscript, produced at the Mughal court in India, and now at the British Museum (Add. 18579), of the *Anwār i Suhaylī*, early in the seventeenth century. These bear the names of Āqā Riżā, Āqā Muḥammad Riżā, and Muḥammad Riżā, with the additional appellation, in three instances, of *Murīd*, or *Murīd i Pādshāh* ('disciple', or 'disciple of the Emperor'). He can hardly be the artist of two much earlier portraits in the Museum of Fine Arts, Boston,[1] one of which contains the name Āqā Riżā, with the appellation *Murīd*. Jahāngīr, the Mughal Emperor, mentions a certain artist, Āqā Riżā'ī of Herāt, who was in his service before his accession (A.D. 1605). The emperor was not nearly so highly impressed with his work as by that of his son, Abu'l-Ḥasan, several of whose miniatures are in existence. Judging from these, Abu'l-Ḥasan was one of the finest of all the Mughal painters, and almost deserved the title of *Nādir al-Zamān* which Jahāngīr bestowed on him.

This Āqā Riżā's works are decidedly rare, but several which may be by him were bound up in the splendid album from Tehran.[2] The artist was clearly influenced greatly by his Indian surroundings, and his usual style is very different from that of typical Safawī painting. On the other hand, his illustrations in the *Anwār i Suhaylī* stand out distinctly from among the other miniatures on account of their more brilliant, and sometimes very pleasing, colouring, and one or two of them are stylistically close to Safawī work.[3]

Riżā-yi ʿAbbāsī had a number of imitators, among whom Ḥaydar *naqqāsh* was one of the best.[4] Others were Afżal, Muḥammad Yūsuf, Muḥammad Qāsim of Tabrīz, Muḥammad ʿAlī of Tabrīz, and Muʿīn, all of whom were represented at the Exhibition, with several more.

---

[1] Reproduced in Martin, I, figs. 29, 30; Coomaraswamy, *Ars Asiatica*, XIII (1929), nos. 110 and 111, pl. XLIII. See pp. 68–70 of the latter work.

[2] See pl. CIV A and Appendix III.

[3] M. Blochet considers that the painter of whom Jahāngīr speaks in his memoirs is a different artist from the Muḥammad Riżā of the *Anwār i Suhaylī*. See *Les Peintures Orientales de la Collection Pozzi*, pp. 40 et seq. The word *Riżā'ī* is an adjective, and *Āqā Riżā'ī* would presumably mean 'follower of Āqā Riżā', i.e. of the earlier of the two painters of Shāh ʿAbbās mentioned above. Nevertheless the facts that an Āqā Riżā and Abu'l-Ḥasan co-operated in painting the *Anwār i Suhaylī* illustrations, and that the latter here signs himself 'Dust of the threshold of Riżā' indicate that Āqā Riżā and Āqā Riżā'ī are the same. This con-clusion receives support from the inscriptions in two miniatures in the Gulistan Museum Album (see Appendix III). In one of these (no. 236) the name of the artist is given as Āqā Riżā'ī, with the same appellation 'disciple of Pādshāh Salīm' as is contained in one of the *Anwār i Suhaylī* miniatures, as well as in another miniature in the Gulistan Album, these words in the latter case being appended to the inscription *Raqm i Āqā Riżā*.

[4] This artist painted some effective miniatures in a *Nizāmī* at the Bibliothèque Nationale (Supp. Pers. 1029), dated 1620–24 (Blochet, *Les Peintures*, pls. LVI–LXV; *Les Enluminures*, pls. LXXXVIII–XC; *Musulman Painting*, pls. CLXIII–CLXVI). The early date, M. Sakisian thinks, indicates that he may have initiated the style of Riżā.

Afzal's[1] floruit was in the early part of the reign of Shāh 'Abbās II, while Muhammad Yūsuf—to be distinguished from an earlier Mīr Yusuf—painted in the fifties.[2] He was hardly a great master.

Muhammad Qāsim[3] (fl. 1660) followed the Rizā 'Abbāsī style fairly closely, but was not destitute of decorative skill. Neither, apparently, was Muhammad 'Alī,[4] his contemporary, whose drawing sometimes greatly resembles that of Qāsim. The figure-drawing of both tends to be stiff and wooden.

Several of the drawings attributed to Rizā-yi 'Abbāsī contain mentions of a certain Mu'īn, a friend of the artist. Presumably this is the same Mu'īn—though he must have been quite young at Rizā-yi 'Abbāsī's death, who has left a number of miniature paintings and drawings, often inscribed in the manner of his master—for he was Rizā's pupil —which he closely imitated. He appears to have lived from as early as 1617 to 1707, or rather later; but these dates are decidedly suspicious.[5]

Mu'īn *Musawwir* (the painter), as he signs himself, is not a happy colourist; his paintings are often dominated by a particularly ugly purple; his designs are incoherent, and his drawings, not without calligraphic facility, are unsatisfying and untidy, with few exceptions. There exists what may be a self-portrait (illustrated in Blochet, *Les Enlu-minures*, planche CVII) in which he is represented playing on the bagpipes.[6] It is not clear why M. Blochet states that Mu'īn passed his life in Constantinople, and in the absence of evidence a Persian domicile must be presumed. Mr. Dawud's miniatures[7] by Mu'īn are from the same *Shāh-nāma* manuscript as one in the British Museum (B.M. 1922–7–11–02), dated 1059/1649, depicting the death of Suhrāb.

Mu'īn has left a number of erotic pictures of a type unsuitable for public exhibition.

Apparently late in the reign of 'Abbās II (1642–66) a new fashion in clothes makes its appearance. The stiff brocaded coat has a pronounced waist, from which the skirts stick out at a sharp angle. The turbans, though still large and conspicuous, are much more closely wound and show an end at the top which gives a fluted outline to the silhouette. Portraits showing this style usually exhibit marked European traces in the modelling of the faces, as well as in other details. A good example is illustrated in Pl. CXII B.

The paintings of Muhammad Zamān, who signs himself as the son of Hājī Muhammad Yūsuf, represent a new departure. Shāh 'Abbās II, in his enthusiasm for Western things, sent him and some other Persians to Rome for purposes of study, early in his

---

1 No. 380. See Martin, p. 125 and pl. 149.

2 Nos. 364, 368. See Martin, pl. 166; *Ars Asiatica*, XIII; pls. L and LII; Schulz, Taf. 177.

3 Nos. 294 and 295. Blochet, *Musulman Painting*, pl. CLXVII; Kühnel, pl. 91; Martin, 165. The British Museum has a drawing of a kneeling man, inscribed *mashaqa Muhammad Qāsim* (B.M. 1920–9–17–0278 (2)), and there is another example of this artist's work in the Metropolitan Museum of New York (Schulz, Taf. 166).

4 No. 366. Schulz, Taf. 170, 171, 175, 178 (b); Kühnel, pl. 92; Stchoukine, *Louvre Cat.*, pl. XXIX. The first of these—a scene of a teacher with male and female pupils—has decided merits.

5 Nos. 371–7. Blochet, *Les Enluminures*, p. 150; Schulz, p. 203; Sakisian, p. 142; Coomaraswamy, p. 54. Reproductions of his work are to be found in most of the standard publications. Schulz, Taf. 169, reproduces a miniature from a manuscript dated as early as 1617. The style is, however, of the next generation.

6 For an account of the inscriptions in the Bibliothèque Nationale examples—among which this portrait is included—of Mu'īn's work see Blochet, *Les Peintures des Manuscrits Persanes de la Collection Marteau à la Bibliothèque Nationale*, p. 169.

7 No. 371.

reign. While in Italy or, according to another, less probable, account, in his childhood, he became a Christian. About 1646 he took refuge in India, as he found his Christianity embarrassing in Persia. In 1086/1675–6 he was again in Persia, where he was employed to fill three pages left blank in the great *Khamsa* of Nizāmī which had been prepared for Shāh Tahmāsp over a hundred years earlier (British Museum, Or. 2265). These three paintings are in an almost completely Italian technique,[1] like all his work; the costumes also being sometimes European.

Besides the British Museum *Nizāmī* he illustrated, in Isfahān, another copy of the same work in the same year (now in the Morgan Library, New York), while a *Visitation* and a *Flight into Egypt* reproduced by Martin (pl. 173) bear the dates 1089 and 1100 respectively.

At the Exhibition his work was shown in two illustrations to a *Shāh-nāma*, also dated 1086/1675, belonging to Mr. Chester Beatty.[2]

He seems to have been an accomplished man, who owned several Latin books, and wrote a History of China in Persian. He was friendly with the Jesuits in India, especially the noble and learned Father Busi.

Muhammad Zamān and his companions in all probability brought back from Rome examples of Italian paintings, which may have had something to do with the output of representations of the Holy Family, Christian saints and angels, which was so curious a phenomenon, for a Muhammadan country, in the eighteenth and nineteenth centuries.

Of this Europeanized painting little need be said, especially as it was largely practised in lacquer. Mention, however, may be made of the bird and flower painting of the period of Nādir Shāh (1736–47), and of Āghā Sādiq, who was especially celebrated in the period of Karīm Khān of Zand (1750–79). His pupil, Muhammad Hasan Khān, executed a number of life-sized portraits of Fath 'Alī Shāh and his sons, of a type well represented at Burlington House, while Muhammad Hasan Khān's pupil, Abu'l-Hasan Khān, also attained some eminence in Tehrān, the capital of the Qājār dynasty, as it is of Rizā Khān Pahlawī. These artists painted mainly in oils. What appears to have been the supreme example of the book-illumination of Bābā Mirzā, Fath 'Alī Shāh's chief Court painter, was lent to the Exhibition by His Majesty the King (No. 390).

The later lacquer-painting is too well known to need description, and the shops of European dealers can show thousands of examples of boxes, mirrors, and *qalam-dāns* decorated in this manner. Āghā Najaf, who died about the middle of the nineteenth century, was one of the most celebrated exponents of papier-mâché painting, very European in character, and not rising, in merit, above the chocolate-box standard. Nāsir al-Dīn Shāh (1848–96), who used himself to paint, tried to encourage the art, but his efforts were hampered by the strength of foreign influences and the lack of

---

[1] See the colour plate of one reproduced by Arnold, *P.I.*, pl. v.
[2] No. 384. For Paolo Zaman—for this was the name he assumed from the time of his visit to Rome—and his unusual career see N. N. Markovitch's article in the *Journal of the American Oriental Society*, xlv, 1925, pp. 106–9; Arnold, *Painting in Islām*, pp. 148–9; Sir E. D. Maclagan, *The Jesuits and the Great Mogul*, pp. 192, 200, 235–6, 244, and references on p. 261.

patronage of indigenous talent. Some of the nineteenth-century manuscript miniatures are quite pretty. With present-day painting, and the rival claims of the modernist and the archaizing movements, we are not concerned; nor with the activities of the professional 'fakers', who, whether operating from Persia or Europe, have executed some close imitations of old work, which have deceived many collectors, and who have displayed a technical dexterity comparable occasionally with that of the old miniaturists, and worthy of better employment.

Genuine book miniature painting has disappeared. Printing was first introduced into Persia about 1815, but neither printed nor lithographed books have been fortunate in their illustrators. Both types copy, very often, the forms of the old manuscripts, but the line-drawings with which they are sometimes provided are seldom of any great merit.

As to the future, it would be rash to speculate along what lines the eventual revival, which it is safe to predict in a nation of artists, is likely to develop.

CATALOGUE

248 [319 X (*a*)] A YOUNG MAN in a brocade coat, holding a falcon. *c.* 1570. Style of Muhammadī.　　　　　　　　　　　　　　　　　　　　　PLATE CVI.

18·2×9·7 *cm.* ¶ Lent by ESTATE OF V. EVERITT MACY, ESQ., New York.

249 [319 X (*b*)] A QUEEN conducting a prince to her private apartments. A page from a manuscript. Minute style. About 1575.

24×16 *cm.* ¶ Lent by ESTATE OF V. EVERITT MACY, ESQ., New York.

250 [598] LADY IN GREEN AND RED, standing and adjusting her aigrette. About 1580.

17×8 *cm.* Marteau-Vever, no. 156. ¶ Lent by M. H. VEVER, Paris.

251 [673] A KNEELING YOUTH in a figured robe, with a flower. Second half XVI century. Line-drawing.

15×8·5 *cm.* Sarre-Mittwoch, pl. 10. Exh. Berlin 1910, no. 151. ¶ Lent by FRAU MARIA SARRE-HUMANN, Berlin.

252 [557 B] LION STALKING AN ANTELOPE. Line-drawing. XVI century.

12·5×4·5 *cm.* ¶ Lent by MAJOR D. MACAULAY.　　　　　　　　　PLATE CVII B.

253 [557 A] A MAN SEATED ON A CARPET. Line-drawing. XVI century.

¶ Lent by MAJOR D. MACAULAY.

254 [120 E] JĀMĪ'S *TUHFAT AL-AHRĀR*, copied by Shāh Husayn Shihābī al-Harawī in 992/1584. Margins of polychrome paper, with gold designs. Two '*unwāns* in gold, blue and red, two miniatures, two pages gilded. Dark red leather binding stamped with gold medallions inside polychrome lattice-work.

29×18·5 *cm.* ¶ Lent by A. CHESTER BEATTY, ESQ.

(*a*) Joseph on a throne.
(*b*) Two lovers meeting.

This is probably not a Bukhārā manuscript. The turbans in the miniatures are rather large as they were under the Safawids at this date. The iconography is rather different from that in the illustrations of the same scenes in Mr. Chester Beatty's two Bukhārā manuscripts of this poem (nos. 110, 111).

255 [719 M] PEN DRAWING. Two men, one on horseback, the other on foot, hunting a lion in a rocky landscape. Attributed to Āqā Rizā. XVI century.

15·5×23 *cm.* Exh. Memorial Art Gallery, Rochester, 1930. Pennsylvania Univ. Museum, 1930. Detroit Inst. of Arts, 1930, cat. no. 42. ¶ Lent by DEMOTTE, New York.

256 [657] DRAWING IN GOLD with touches of colour on golden-brown ground. Youth conversing with a sage. With calligraphy by Mīr 'Alī, dated 937/1530. Inscribed: *mashaqahu Āqā Rizā*, 'The work of Āqā Rizā'.

9×16·5 *cm.* Marteau-Vever, no. 17; Sakisian, fig. 163. ¶ Lent by M. H. VEVER, Paris.

257 [721 G] MINIATURE. Girl with a fan. Signed: 'The work of Āqā Rizā.' Mid XVI century.

9·5×15·5 *cm.* Sakisian, fig. 171. ¶ Lent by ARMENAG BEY SAKISIAN, Paris.

A good deal of the style associated with Sultān Muhammad survives, with the bright colouring, but the drawing has become more calligraphic.

258 [672] LINE-DRAWING. A Mashhad Pilgrim. Inscribed: 'In sacred Mashhad; this was made at the end of Friday, the 10th of Muharram, in the princely house, for the friends, in the year 1007 (1598). Drawn by Rizā specially for Mīrzā Khwājagī Sāhib. May God preserve him.'

11·5×7 *cm.* Sarre-Mittwoch, pl. 1. Exh. Berlin 1910, no. 151. ¶ Lent by FRAU MARIA SARRE-HUMANN, Berlin.

259 [605] MINIATURE. Man in red and green with black head-dress, holding a bird. Late XVI century.

11·5×10 *cm.* ¶ Lent by M. H. VEVER, Paris.

260 [589] PRINCE DRESSED IN GREEN, embracing a lady, dressed in scarlet and purple. Late XVI century. The painting is inserted on a page from a *Shāh-nāma.*

22×11 *cm.* ¶ Lent by M. H. VEVER, Paris.

261 [724 A] JĀMĪ'S *YŪSUF U ZULAYKHĀ,* copied in 1004/1595 for Shīr-dil Khān Fakhr Isfahānī. Sixteen miniatures, in which the compositions are highly patternized.

30×20 *cm.* Ethé, *Cat.,* no. 910; Gray, pl. 13. ¶ Lent by BODLEIAN LIBRARY, Oxford. [Elliott, 418.]

262 [272] MINIATURE. Princess in green, with purple shawl. Late XVI century.

22×14·5 *cm.* ¶ Lent by M. CLAUDE ANET, Paris.

263 [629] TWO WARRIORS EMBRACING: behind, a party of dervishes dancing to a band. Latter part of XVI century.

26×16·5 *cm.* ¶ Lent by K. M. PANNIKKAR, ESQ., Delhi.

264 [727] *SHĀH-NĀMA OF FIRDAWSĪ.* Formerly the property of Warren Hastings. Profusely ornamented with many miniatures. Late XVI century.

44×27·5 *cm.* ¶ Lent by INDIA OFFICE LIBRARY. [Ethé, 2992.]

265 [625] DERVISH WEARING A LOIN-CLOTH. Line-drawing. XVI century.

10×5 *cm.* ¶ Lent by PERSIAN GOVERNMENT from the Mashhad Shrine.

266 [635] A PRINCE, in red, pouring out wine. Late XVI century.

12·5×21·5 *cm.* ¶ Lent by PERSIAN GOVERNMENT from the Mashhad Shrine.

267 [588] JOSEPH EXPOSED IN THE SLAVE-MARKET. Line-drawing, from an album. End of XVI century.

25×20 *cm.* ¶ Lent by INDIA OFFICE LIBRARY.

268 [268] TWO LINE-DRAWINGS from an album. End of XVI century.

(*a*) A Prince with attendants under a tree. 17×11 *cm.*
(*b*) A Dervish dancing under a tree. 17×10 *cm.*
¶ Lent by INDIA OFFICE LIBRARY.

269 [494] HOLY MAN with pupils by a stream. Late XVI century.

18×11·5 *cm.* ¶ Lent by PERSIAN GOVERNMENT from the Mashhad Shrine.

270 [285] HUNTING SCENE. Period of Shāh ʿAbbās I. A double-page opening, surrounded by an illuminated border. The scene is a *qamargah* or battue, in which every sort of game is being slaughtered. Two of the hunters are armed with guns. The miniatures are rather rubbed and have been mounted. On the reverse is an inscription, evidently written at the Mughal court, which states that in the course of a hunt, at which, besides the Shāh of Persia and the Mughal Emperor Humāyūn, the latter's wife, Hamīda Begam, and various other Mughal princes were present, Humāyūn received a good omen which decided him to attempt the reconquest of India (which he finally achieved in 1555). Humāyūn was entertained to several of these hunts by Shāh Tahmāsp in 1544, when he was in exile in Persia. The miniature is, however, certainly much later and the types are conventional, so that it is impossible to recognize either of the principal figures. No lady is shown.

20·5×13 *cm. (each half).* ¶ Lent by H. A. N. MEDD, ESQ., Delhi.

271 [510] THREE MINIATURES, from Hilālī's *Shāh u Gadā*, 'The King and the Dervish', copied in 946/1539 by Shāh Mahmūd Nīshāpūrī Shāhī. Miniatures of early XVII century.

(*a*) The dervish at the prince's drinking party. 22×17 *cm.*
(*b*) The prince gives the dervish his signet ring. 22·5×17 *cm.*
(*c*) The prince defeats his enemies in battle. 22·5×17 *cm.*
Martin, II, pl. 141–3; Schulz, p. 127, 131, 168; Arnold, *The Miniatures in Hilālī's mystical poem, The King and the Dervish*, Vienna, 1926; Munthe, G., *Persiska Miniatyr* (National Musei årsbok, Stockholm, 1923). Exh. Gothenburg 1928, Cat. nos. 20, 21, 22. ¶ Lent by NATIONAL MUSEUM, Stockholm.

272 [675] YOUNG MAN riding through a rocky landscape with a falcon on his wrist. An unfinished sketch, ink and carmine with grey-blue wash. The sketch in its present form would appear both from the landscape and the costume of the rider to date from the first half of the seventeenth century. There have, however, been a number of re-drawings by washing over with body colour and by overlaying the original page. It is quite possible that the original drawing, particularly of the horse, is of the sixteenth century. For a full description of the condition of the sketch see Sarre and Mittwoch, p. 26, where, however, a different conclusion is reached.

19 × 12 *cm.* Sarre-Mittwoch, pl. 8. Exh. Berlin 1910, no. 151. ¶ Lent by FRAU MARIA SARRE-HUMANN, Berlin.

273 [269, 271] TWO DECORATIVE DOUBLE-PAGES. The central part of each page is covered with illuminator's work except for a medallion in the middle. In these, and in the borders, figure-painting is introduced. On the first are scenes of picnicking and fighting; in the second of hunting. Period of Shāh 'Abbās the Great, of the style of which they are excellent examples.

40 × 26·4 *cm.* Martin, II, pls. 261–2; Marteau-Vever, nos. 115, 116. ¶ Lent by M. H. VEVER, Paris.

274 [677] YOUNG WOMAN IN A GREEN ROBE applying henna to her feet and finger-tips. *c.* 1600.

17 × 9·5 *cm.* ¶ Lent by E. BEGHIAN.

275 [600] LINE-DRAWINGS, *c.* 1600.
(*a*) Youth leaning on a slender staff. 15 × 9 *cm.*
(*b*) Youth with a conical, fur-brimmed cap; behind is a magpie sitting on a branch. Touches of gold and colour. 14·5 × 18·5 *cm.*
(*c*) Youth leaning on a long staff. Touches of colour. 12·5 × 6 *cm.*
¶ Lent by P. MANUK, ESQ., Patna.

276 [647] PAGE FROM A MANUSCRIPT OF NIZĀMĪ'S *KHAMSA*. Five figures standing on the bank of a stream, a sixth seated near them. Margin decorated with figures. *c.* 1600.

36·5 × 25 *cm.* ¶ Lent by M. DEMOTTE, Paris.

277 [650] PRINCESS, dressed in green, violet, and golden-brown. *c.* 1600.

16·5 × 10·5 *cm.* Marteau-Vever, no. 168. ¶ Lent by M. CLAUDE ANET, Paris.

278 [624] LADY IN GREEN DRESS, standing, with a cup in her hand. Formerly in the Ayrton collection. *c.* 1600 (cf. no. 277).

36·5 × 21·5 *cm.* Exh. Victoria and Albert Museum, 1875–85. ¶ Lent by Y. DAWUD, ESQ.

279 [697] SAGE TALKING TO A YOUTH. Drawing, slightly coloured. Gold-decorated mount. *c.* 1600.

20 × 14·5 *cm.* ¶ Lent by M. A. HENRAUX, Paris.

280 [719 K] A MAN ON HORSEBACK, with a monkey seated on his shoulder. Drawing, slightly coloured. *c.* 1600.

10 × 10 *cm.* Sakisian, fig. 107. ¶ Lent by ARMENAG BEY SAKISIAN, Paris.

281 [609] A YOUTH, in gold patterned robe, kneeling on one knee with a hawk perched on his gloved hand. Inscribed *Khusraw Sultān Awrang. c.* 1600.

15·5×8 *cm.* ¶ Lent by E. BEGHIAN.

282 [281] THREE DRAWINGS. *c.* 1600.

(*a*) Youth holding a bird in his right hand. Touches of gold and colour. 16×9·5 *cm.*
(*b*) Kneeling page holding a wine flask and cup. Touched with gold. On vellum. 16×10 *cm.*
(*c*) Standing youth with right hand extended. Touches of colour. 17·5×10 *cm.*
¶ Lent by P. C. MANUK, ESQ., Patna.

283 [610] YOUTH IN BLUE, kneeling, and handing a cup to a standing lady dressed in scarlet and purple. *c.* 1600.

20×11·5 *cm.* Marteau-Vever, no. 171. ¶ Lent by M. H. VEVER, Paris.

284 [721 F] A SAGE WITH PUPILS in a garden. Line-drawing, slightly coloured. *c.* 1600.

27·5×16 *cm.* ¶ Lent by HERR L. BÄCKSBACKA, Helsingfors.

285 [319 X (*c*)] A YOUTH HOLDING A GIRL IN HIS ARMS. *c.* 1600.

22×13·5 *cm.* ¶ Lent by ESTATE OF V. EVERITT MACY, ESQ., New York.

286 [654] LINE-DRAWING, slightly coloured. Bearded man under a tree in conversation with a youth. Two other men in the foreground. Stencilled green border. Early seventeenth century.

14×8·5 *cm.* ¶ Lent by A. CHESTER BEATTY, ESQ. (Beatty Lib., Ms. 260, fol. V). PLATE XCIX B.

287 [120 C] HILĀLĪ'S *SIFĀT AL-'ĀSHIQĪN,* copied *c.* 1600. Decorated margins. One double-page frontispiece miniature: a party of learned men on a terrace in a hilly landscape. Black leather binding, gold-stamped; inside, polychrome lattice-work.

24·5×15 *cm.* ¶ Lent by A. CHESTER BEATTY, ESQ.

Hilālī was educated at Herāt by Mīr 'Alī Shīr, and put to death as a Shī'a by 'Ubayd Allāh Khān, the Uzbek, in 1528-9. The *Sifāt al-'Āshiqīn* is one of the two *masnawī* poems composed by him.

288 [633 X] A BATTLE SCENE. A miniature from a manuscript. *c.* 1600.

23·5×15 *cm.* ¶ Lent by GERALD REITLINGER, ESQ.

289 [602 A] YOUTH DANCING WITH SCARF. Drawn in gold on bluish ground. Signed *Hāshim.* Line-drawing. *c.* 1600.

15×9 *cm.* ¶ Lent by P. MANUK, ESQ., Patna.

290 [602 B] MAN STANDING, wearing a turban and long cloak, holding a flask. Line-drawing, with touches of gold and colour. *c.* 1600.

13·5×4·5 *cm.* ¶ Lent by P. MANUK, ESQ., Patna.   PLATE CVIII C.

291 [728 A] FIRDAWSĪ'S *SHĀH-NĀMA*, copied in Qazwīn, in 1011/1602. Forty-six miniatures by Murād b. Alī. Binding with hunting scenes.

25×37 *cm.* Tornberg, *Codices orientales, Supplement*, Lund, 1853. Exh. Göteborg 1928. ¶ Lent by LUND UNIVERSITY LIBRARY, Sweden.

292 [726 G] FIRDAWSĪ'S *SHĀH-NĀMA*, copied in 1014/1605. One hundred and forty-six folios, two fully decorated pages, text with decorations. Sixty-seven miniatures. Leather binding, gold-stamped outside and inside.

33·5×20 *cm.* Munich Exhibition Catalogue, no. 718. ¶ Lent anonymously.

293 [720 B] KHWĀNDAMĪR'S *KHULĀSAT AL-AKHBĀR* (Universal History), copied in 900/1494. Fourteen full-page miniatures, of later date, mostly battle scenes. The last one unfinished.

23×35 *cm.* C. J. Tornberg, *Codices orientales, Supplement*, Lund, 1853. ¶ Lent by LUND UNIVERSITY LIBRARY, Sweden.

294 [660] PAGE HOLDING A WRITING. In blue and gold, by Muhammad Qāsim Musawwir. Early XVII century.

19×10·5 *cm.* ¶ Lent by E. BEGHIAN.

For signed work by Muhammad Qāsim see *Musulman Painting*, pl. CLXVII; Martin, II, pl. 165, 'Baghdad: Portrait of Wali, a page'; Schulz, pl. 166—a drawing in the Metropolitan Museum dated 114 (*sic*); and Kühnel, pl. 91 (in Czartoryski Museum, Cracow).

295 [663] THREE YOUNG MEN standing in front of a tree, one of them kissing the foot of another. Line-drawing, with touches of gold and colour. Ornamental borders. By Muhammad Qāsim. Early XVII century.

33·5×21·5 *cm.* ¶ Lent by MADAME GRETA STRÖMBOM, Stockholm.

296 [725 A] ANTHOLOGY. Text on marbled paper, with sumptuously decorated margins. One '*unwān*, fifteen miniatures of about 1610.

24×14·5 *cm.* ¶ Lent by M. H. VEVER, Paris.

297 [506] MINIATURES from Sa'dī's *Būstān*, copied by Muhammad Amīn, for Hasan Khān Shāmlū, whose seal has the date 1026/1617.

28·5×18 *cm.* ¶ Lent by A. CHESTER BEATTY, ESQ.
(*a*) Archer shooting an arrow at a cat.
(*b*) Young men inviting an old man to join their party.

298 [691] PORTRAIT OF A EUROPEAN. Ink and gold wash. Possibly intended for one of the two English adventurers Sir Anthony and Sir Robert Sherley, who first visited Persia in 1599. Little dogs of the sort shown in the miniature are represented in several others of the early seventeenth century. About 1600. This drawing is a variant of the finished miniature, signed by Riżā-yi 'Abbāsī and dated 1037/1628, reproduced by Sarre and Mittwoch (Abb. 5).

36×24 *cm.* ¶ Lent by MISS H. SCHLESINGER.   PLATE CIX A.

299 [683] PORTRAIT OF A YOUNG MAN in a puce jacket, green breeches, orange stockings, and a black hat. Perhaps intended for Sir R. Sherley. School of Rizā-yi ʿAbbāsī. Early XVII century.

20 × 11 *cm.* ¶ Lent by GERALD REITLINGER, ESQ.

300 [725 E] SAʿDĪ'S *BŪSTĀN*, copied, according to a note at the end, by Sultān ʿAlī Mashhadī. Richly illuminated headings, margins gold-sprinkled. Four miniatures. One, showing a group of persons discoursing in a kiosk by night, is a fine example of mid-sixteenth-century work. The others are considerably later, of the early seventeenth century. Modern Bukhārā leather binding.

29·5 × 19 *cm.* ¶ Lent by A. CHESTER BEATTY, ESQ.

301 [678] DRAWING, slightly coloured. Bearded man with red-striped turban and blue sash leading a child by the hand. Signed, in ornamental writing, *Sādiq* (or Sādiqī). First half of XVII century.

13 × 9·5 *cm.* ¶ Lent by A. CHESTER BEATTY, ESQ.

302 [319] LINE-DRAWING. A young woman sitting cross-legged. Signed *Sādiq*. On the border a Persian quatrain signed by the calligrapher, *Mīr Husayn al-Sahwī al-Tabrīzī*.

21·5 × 13·2 *cm.* ¶ Lent by ESTATE OF V. EVERITT MACY, ESQ., New York.

Mīr Husayn is mentioned by Huart among writers of *nastaʿlīq*: 'Mīr Husain of Tabrīz, who bore the name of al-Sahwī, left Persia (apparently at the same time as ʿAbd al-Samad) for India, where he died.'

303 [656] LADY IN RED twisting a thread. *c.* 1600. Possibly by Sādiq.

17·5 × 10 *cm. Souvenir*, colour plate. ¶ Lent by E. BEGHIAN.

304 [144 D] HILĀLĪ'S *SIFĀT AL-ʿĀSHIQĪN*, copied by Mīr ʿAlī in 929/1522 in the lifetime of the author. Gold-sprinkled margins. Two miniatures of early XVII century. Lacquer binding.

30 × 18·5 *cm.* ¶ Lent by BIBLIOTHÈQUE ÉGYPTIENNE, Cairo.

305 [658] YOUTH IN GREEN, seated and holding a wine-flask. Brown background decorated with foliage and clouds in gold. The Persian hemistich reads: 'A youth reclining overcome by intoxication.' Early XVII century.

10 × 16·5 *cm.* ¶ Lent by M. H. VEVER, Paris.   PLATE CIX B.

306 [594] MINIATURE, in *découpé* work. A lion springing on an antelope. The design in white has been cut out and attached to the gold ground. Early XVII century.

19 × 12·5 *cm.* ¶ Lent by EDWARD MARSH, ESQ.   PLATE CX B.

Probably executed at Constantinople, where this art was carried to a high level. At the end of the *Muraqqaʿ* 1720 in the Serai Library is bound up a fairly large number of specimens of such work.

307 [662] TWO YOUTHS, one reclining and the other holding a hawk. Early XVII century. The drawing of the trees in the background shows European influence. Drawing with touches of gold and colours. Border of gold designs.

11 × 17·5 cm. ¶ Lent by A. CHESTER BEATTY, ESQ.

308 [639] THREE MEN SHOEING A HORSE. Line-drawing, slightly coloured. Early XVII century.

22·5 × 13 cm. ¶ Lent by R. A. DARA.

309 [693] A PAIR OF LOVERS EMBRACING UNDER A TREE. Line-drawing slightly tinted. Early XVII century.

23 × 14 cm. ¶ Lent by E. BEGHIAN.

310 [614] TWO YOUTHS SEATED, one reading a book; the other, with eyes closed, resting against a tree. Early XVII century.

17·5 × 10·5 cm. Marteau-Vever, no. 169. ¶ Lent by M. H. VEVER, Paris.

311 [661] A PAIR OF LOVERS; border of birds and animals in a landscape. Early XVII century.

33 × 20 cm. ¶ Lent by M. H. VEVER, Paris.

312 [664] YOUTH IN LONG RED ROBE holding a golden flask and a cup. Early XVII century.

18 × 10 cm. ¶ Lent by E. BEGHIAN.

313 [728 B] FIRDAWSĪ'S *SHĀH-NĀMA*, early XVII century. Two *sarlawhs*, two frontispieces, of which the one representing King Solomon was added in the XIX century. Numerous miniatures.

39 × 25 cm. ¶ Lent by SENEHI, Paris.

314 [695] TWO LOVERS EMBRACING. Signed *Rizā 'Abbāsī*. Full colours. A youth, clad in a green dress, is clasping in his arms his beloved, who is dressed in purple. Dark-brown background with gold foliage. Dated 1029/1620, but may be rather later.

18 × 11·8 cm. Kühnel, *I.M.*, pl. 80. Exh. Munich 1910, no. 747. Migeon, fig. 54. ¶ Lent by FRAU MARIA SARRE-HUMANN, Berlin.

315 [687] GOAT AND GOATHERD. Line-drawing, lightly touched with blue and red. Signed *Rizā-yi 'Abbāsī*, 1031/1622.

18 × 8 cm. Exh. Detroit Institute of Arts, November 1930. ¶ Lent by PARISH-WATSON, New York.

316 [719 N] FOLDING ALBUM of quatrains. Copied by 'Abd al-Rashīd in 1032/1623. Animal and floral designs on the margins. On the last page, signed

Rizā-yi 'Abbāsī, is a portrait of Āqā 'Abd al-Rashīd, presumably the writer of the book. 'Abd al-Rashīd, calligrapher, of Isfahān, died about 1647. Modern morocco binding.

23 × 12·5 *cm.* ¶ Lent by P. C. MANUK, ESQ., Patna.

317 [694] SHEPHERD with a fat-tailed sheep and a goat in a landscape. Drawing with light colour. Inscribed: 'Drawn by the humble Rizā-yi 'Abbāsī. Completed on Monday the 7th day of the month of Ramazān the blessed 1041 [28 March 1632 A.D.] for an album [*jarīda*].'

21·5 × 11·5 *cm.* ¶ Lent by MISS H. SUTHERLAND.   PLATE CXI B.

A contemporary version of the miniature is in an album at Leningrad (reproduced by Martin, II, pl. 159, Kühnel, pl. 83). This miniature, which has a mutilated inscription in the upper left-hand corner, in which part of the signature of Rizā 'Abbāsī is still visible, is much stronger in drawing.

318 [690] LOVERS, SEATED ON THE GROUND. The miniature is somewhat close to no. 314, and may be the original. The youth is here clasping the head of his beloved. Inscribed: 'Completed on Saturday 24th of the month of Shawwāl (propitiously) 1041 [A.D. 1632] by the humble Rizā-yi 'Abbāsī.'

35·5 × 23·5 *cm.* Kühnel, *I.M.,* pl. 79. Marteau-Vever, no. 173. ¶ Lent by M. J. J. MARQUET DE VASSELOT, Paris.

319 [665] A MAN KNEELING ON THE GROUND near a tree and grasping snakes. Pen drawing, slightly coloured. Inscribed: 'Completed on Friday, 10th Shawwāl, 1041 [1632]. Drawn by the humble Rizā-yi 'Abbāsī.'

16 × 26 *cm.* (oblong). Kühnel, *I.M.,* fig. 85; Martin, pl. 158. Exh. Memorial Art Gallery, Rochester, 1930; Pennsylvania Univ. Museum, 1930; Detroit Inst. of Arts, cat. no. 45. ¶ Lent by DEMOTTE, New York.

320 [667] POLO-PLAYER. Line-drawing, slightly coloured, in black and carmine. Attributed to Rizā 'Abbāsī. Inscribed: 'Done in the middle of Sha'bān the revered, 1052 A.H. (= Nov. 1642). May it prosper!'

15·5 × 10 *cm.* Sarre-Mittwoch, pl. 33. Exh. Berlin, 1910, no. 151. *Souvenir,* pl. 48. ¶ Lent by FRAU MARIA SARRE-HUMANN, Berlin.

321 [655] THE MASTER AND HIS PUPIL. On an elaborate mount, covered with arabesques in gold and colour. With a doubtful signature or ascription to Rizā-yi 'Abbāsī. *c.* 1620.

33 × 25·5 *cm.* Sakisian, fig. 184; Migeon, I, fig. 46. Exh. Munich 1910, no. 799. ¶ Lent by MUSÉE DES ARTS DÉCORATIFS, Paris.

322 [688] MAN RIDING A HORSE IN THE RAIN. Drawing, slightly coloured. Signed: *Raqm i kamīna Rizā-yi 'Abbāsī.* The horse's nostrils are slit, in accordance with a custom apparently prevalent in the East at this time. For a note on a drawing by Pisanello showing this practice, see G. F. Hill, *Drawings by Pisanello,* Bruxelles; Paris, 1929: pp. 34, 35, pl. XVII.

13 × 17·5 *cm.* Martin, II, pl. 163. ¶ Lent by M. CLAUDE ANET, Paris.

323 [705] PORTRAIT OF A YOUTH sitting under a tree with a flask. Signed *Rizā-yi ʿAbbāsī*.

19 × 9·5 *cm.* Rabino, *Les Provinces Caspiennes*, pl. 30. ¶ Lent by H. RABINO, ESQ., Cairo.

324 [622] MINIATURE touched with colour. Portrait of a seated man, signed, 'The work of the poor Rizā' (Rizā ʿAbbāsī?). XVII century.

27 × 18 *cm.* Exh. Gothenburg, 1928, Cat. no. 37. ¶ Lent by NATIONAL MUSEUM, Stockholm.

325 [284] LINE-DRAWING. Bust of a woman. Inscribed: 'Drawn by Rizā-yi ʿAbbāsī for the son of Khadīja.'

12 × 6·5 *cm.* Rabino, *Les Provinces Caspiennes*, pl. 88. ¶ Lent by H. RABINO, ESQ., Cairo.

326 [649] PORTRAIT OF A YOUTH. Inscribed *Kāmrān Shāh Hindī*. Signed *Rizā-yi ʿAbbāsī*. Line-drawing with touches of purple and blue.

15·5 × 16 *cm.* ¶ Lent by E. BEGHIAN.

327 [725 D] LINE-DRAWING, partly coloured. Seated dervish. Signed *Raqm i kamīna Rizā-yi ʿAbbāsī*.

12·5 × 7·5 *cm.* Arnold, *P.I.* LXIV, A. ¶ Lent by INDIA OFFICE LIBRARY [Johnson Album XXII].

328 [692] YOUTH IN BLUE with plum-coloured coat, green sash, and gold collar, holding a cup. Signed *Raqm i kamīna Rizā-yi ʿAbbāsī*. XVII century.

19·5 × 10 *cm.* ¶ Lent by A. CHESTER BEATTY, ESQ.

329 [696] PAGE STANDING, in orange waistcoat, purple coat, blue sash, figured gold brocade trousers. Signed *Raqm i kamīna Rizā-yi ʿAbbāsī*. XVII century.

19 × 9 *cm.* ¶ Lent by A. CHESTER BEATTY, ESQ.

330 [612] LIONESS AND CUBS. Inscribed: 'Drawn by the humble Rizā ʿAbbāsī.' Ink and light colour. Formerly in the Ayrton collection.

32·5 × 21·5 *cm.* Exh. Victoria and Albert Museum, 1875–85. ¶ Lent by Y. DAWUD, ESQ.
PLATE CVII C.

331 [674] THE CLOTH MERCHANT. A bearded man kneeling on a carpet, busied with lengths of cloth. Ink drawing on white paper. Attributed to Rizā-yi ʿAbbāsī, but in the calligraphic style more generally associated with the name of Āqā Rizā. But see Sarre and Mittwoch, p. 36.

17 × 11 *cm.* Sarre-Mittwoch, pl. 32. Exh. Berlin 1910, no. 151. ¶ Lent by FRAU MARIA SARRE-HUMANN, Berlin.

332 [684] PICNIC. Attributed to Rizā-yi ʿAbbāsī. A drawing, slightly coloured. Formerly in Ayrton collection.

23 × 13 *cm.* Exh. South Kensington Museum, 1875–85. ¶ Lent by Y. DAWUD, ESQ.

333 [652] PORTRAIT OF A PERSIAN YOUTH, seated and reading a sheet of writing, by a yellow tree. Attributed to Rizā-yi 'Abbāsī.

15×8 cm. ¶ Lent by SIR CECIL HARCOURT SMITH.

334 [646] THREE-QUARTER-LENGTH PORTRAIT of a Persian youth smelling a flowering branch which he holds in his right hand. Attributed to Rizā-yi 'Abbāsī. Early XVII century.

10·5×16·4 cm. ¶ Lent by SIR CECIL HARCOURT SMITH.

335 [725 F] JĀMĪ'S *LAYLĀ WA MAJNŪN*, copied in 1033/1623. One miniature in Rizā-yi 'Abbāsī style: Laylā speaking to the messenger from Majnūn, under a date-palm.

25·5×17 cm. ¶ Lent by A. CHESTER BEATTY, ESQ.

336 [659] PAGE FROM AN ALBUM. Youth in striped cloak of blue, green, and brown, standing and holding a flask. Rizā-yi 'Abbāsī style, with large and elaborate turban. An inner border contains panels of calligraphy by 'Abd al-Rahīm,[1] *'anbarīn-qalam* (amber-pen), with five minute paintings of birds. The outer border is decorated with birds among foliated arabesques, typical of the court style of the Emperor Jahāngīr.

24·5×13 cm. ¶ Lent by GULISTAN MUSEUM, Tehran.

337 [682] MINIATURE. Bahrām and a princess in a red and yellow pavilion. XVII century.

21×11 cm. ¶ Lent by GERALD REITLINGER, ESQ.

338 [668] A GIRL SEATED, stooping over a book. Grey-blue, transparent wash. Unfinished, showing traces of corrections in the drawing of the hands and drapery. XVII century.

10×9·5 cm. Sarre-Mittwoch, pl. 7; Kühnel, *I.M.*, pl. 84. Exh. Berlin, 1910, cat. no. 151. ¶ Lent by FRAU MARIA SARRE-HUMANN, Berlin.

339 [651 (*a*)] MINIATURE. Seated figure of a man leaning forward, before a rocky background. XVII century.

14·5×8·5 cm. ¶ Lent by P. MANUK, ESQ., Patna.

340 [651 (*b*)] PEN DRAWING FOR A MINIATURE. A victorious warrior, carrying the head and leading the horse of his enemy, whose stripped corpse lies on the ground. XVII century.

17×13 cm. ¶ Lent by P. MANUK, ESQ., Patna.

[1] This calligrapher migrated to India from his native town of Herāt, became one of Akbar's court calligraphers, and was given his title by Jahāngīr. The well-known *Khamsa* of Nizāmī, belonging to Mr. Dyson Perrins, was copied by him.

341 [681] GIRL IN LIGHT GREEN ROBE with a high head-dress and veil, seated, holding a flask and cup. XVII century.

13×9 *cm.* ¶ Lent by E. BEGHIAN.

342 [725 H] *TRADITIONS*, with a Persian paraphrase, in verse, by Jāmī, copied, at Mashhad, in 964/1557 by Mahmūd of Nīshāpūr. With a fanciful portrait of Jāmī (in the style of the early XVII century) inserted.

15·5×11 *cm.* ¶ Lent by A. CHESTER BEATTY, ESQ.

343 [414 C] A RECLINING FIGURE. School of Riżā-yi 'Abbāsī. XVII century.

25×17 *cm.* ¶ Lent by HON. HAROLD NICOLSON.

344 [713] KINGFISHER UNDER A TREE. Painting, on linen.

15×9·5 cm. ¶ Lent by SIR CECIL HARCOURT SMITH.

345 [616] STUDY OF FLOWERS AND INSECTS, in gold and colour. XVII century.

14·5×9·5 *cm.* ¶ Lent by E. BEGHIAN.

346 [653] DRAWING. An oak tree, with a dragon entwined. Inscribed: *Āqā 'Ināyat Allāh Iṣfahānī.*

18×11·5 *cm.* ¶ Lent by SIR CECIL HARCOURT SMITH.

347 [699] A WOOD-CUTTER. Drawing, with touches of colour. XVII century.

16·5×10 *cm.* ¶ Lent by DEMOTTE, Paris.

348 [680] RECLINING WOMAN, semi-nude, suckling a child. XVII century.

15×18 *cm.* ¶ Lent by E. BEGHIAN.

349 [676] SEMI-NUDE LADY wearing a white peignoir and holding a scarf. XVII century.

17·5×9·5 *cm.* ¶ Lent by E. BEGHIAN.

350 [702] MINIATURE. Young dandy wearing a fez and a cloak. XVII century.

40×26 *cm.* ¶ Lent by MALLON, Paris.

351 [283] HEAD AND SHOULDERS OF A WOMAN. Line-drawing. XVII century.

12×7·5 *cm.* ¶ Lent by H. RABINO, ESQ., Cairo.

352 [282] PAIR OF MINIATURES from a History of the Prophets. XVII century.

24×15 *cm.* (*each*). ¶ Lent by Y. DAWUD, ESQ.
(*a*) Jonah and the Whale.
(*b*) Joseph sold into captivity.

[175]

353 [273] LINE-DRAWINGS, XVII century.

(*a*) Lady standing, holding out her right hand. 17·5 × 10 *cm.*
(*b*) Youth kneeling on one knee, holding a cup. Touched with gold. 15·5 × 9·5 *cm.*
(*c*) Line-drawing of a seated youth, holding a book in his right hand. A version of no. 145.
12·5 × 7 *cm.*
¶ Lent by P. C. MANUK, ESQ., Patna.

354 [648] A FESTAL PARTY IN A GARDEN. Five figures. Gold and light colours. School of Rizā-yi ʿAbbāsī.

18 × 10 *cm.* ¶ Lent by E. BEGHIAN.

355 [719 D] YOUTH WITH HAWK AND ITS PREY. Line-drawing, slightly coloured, from an album. XVII century.

7·5 × 7 *cm.* ¶ Lent by INDIA OFFICE LIBRARY.

356 [554] ZODIACAL FIGURE OF THE ARCHER (*Sagittarius*). Upper part (full face) human, in blue, red, and gold; body animal, in arabesque pattern. Decorated border in blue and gold. XVII century; probably drawn in India.

14 × 18·5 *cm.* ¶ Lent by A. CHESTER BEATTY, ESQ.

357 [725 B] JĀMĪ'S *SUBHAT AL-ABRĀR*, copied by Nūr al-Dīn b. Muhammad al-Qāshānī (?) in 946/1539. Gold-sprinkled and gold-decorated margins, text with headings in different inks, one ʿunwān, three miniatures of the first half of XVII century, added later. Lacquer binding with floral designs. Formerly in the Imperial Library, Delhi.

26·5 × 16 *cm.* ¶ Lent by A. CHESTER BEATTY, ESQ.

358 [719 A] PERSIAN LADY STANDING, carrying a pear in her left hand. By Bahrām ʿAbbāsī. XVII century.

13 × 7·5 *cm.* ¶ Lent by HERR L. BÄCKSBACKA, Helsingfors.

359 [641] LADY IN RED, GOLD, AND BLUE, dancing with a purple scarf. False signature of *Mahmūd Muzahhib*. Rizā-yi ʿAbbāsī style. The composition may perhaps be a copy after a design by Mahmūd such as those exhibited under no. 104.

17 × 9 *cm.* ¶ Lent by the PERSIAN GOVERNMENT from the Mashhad Shrine.   PLATE CXI A.

360 [701] PICNIC IN A GARDEN. School of Rizā-yi ʿAbbāsī. XVII century.

28·5 × 19 *cm.* ¶ Lent by SIR CECIL HARCOURT SMITH.

361 [607] TWO CAMELS FIGHTING. XVII century.

23 × 15 *cm.* ¶ Lent by DEMOTTE, Paris.

362 [709, 711] TWO MINIATURES from a Cosmography. XVII century. (*a*) Adam naming fishes and beasts. (*b*) Adam and Eve.

12 × 10 *cm.* (*each*). ¶ Lent by COMMANDER W. ROSS.

363 [679] LADY SLEEPING, with two youths, dressed in seventeenth-century costumes, contemplating her. One of the kneeling figures occurs in a miniature in the Claude Anet collection (no. 364).

23 × 12 cm. (*oblong*). ¶ Lent by E. BEGHIAN.

364 [670] KNEELING PAGE holding a cup and a flask; dressed in blue, green, gold, and red. Signed *Mīr Yūsuf*.[1] First half XVII century.

16 × 10·5 cm. Martin, II, pl. 156. ¶ Lent by M. CLAUDE ANET, Paris.

365 [725 C] *DĪWĀN* OF HĀFIZ. Text inside gold rulings, lines disposed in different ways. Four hundred and fifty folios with four hundred and twenty-four miniatures. Some signed *Muhammad Salīm Tabrīzī*, 1049/1639. Red leather, gilt-stamped binding. XVII century.

20 × 19 cm. ¶ Lent by MRS. A. P. H. HOTZ.

366 [590] MONKEY RIDING ON A BEAR, waving a club; a fox and a hare in the background. Signed *Muhammad ʿAlī*. This may be by the Muhammad ʿAlī of Tabrīz, who was highly reputed in the mid-XVII century (Schulz, p. 193). But the name would be a very common one.

33 × 28 cm. From the Léonce Rosenberg collection. ¶ Lent by R. S. GREENSHIELDS, ESQ.

PLATE CX A.

367 [623] A NUDE FIGURE OF A WOMAN STANDING. Drawn in sanguine, with some gold and colour. Mid-XVII century. Nude subjects are rare in Persian miniatures.

16 × 9·5 cm. ¶ Lent by P. MANUK, ESQ., Patna.

PLATE CVIII B.

368 [643] PERSIAN LADY standing under tree with a cup in her hand. Pen-and-ink sketch, signed '*the work of Muhammad Yūsuf*' (op. 1640–75). A drawing by Muhammad Yūsuf in the Gonse collection was reproduced in the *Gazette des Beaux-Arts*, 1893, 3ᵉ période; tome X, p. 493.

18 × 10·5 cm. ¶ Lent by Y. DAWUD, ESQ.

PLATE CIX C.

369 [689] A YOUNG PRINCE in a short black coat, green knee-breeches, orange stockings, and crimson slippers, carrying a brown mantle and a conical hat with a feather. Inscribed *Shāhzāda Bahrām Khūqandī* (?). XVII century.

18 × 8·5 cm. ¶ Lent by E. BEGHIAN.

370 [414 B] TEN PAGES from Saʿdī's *Būstān*, copied in 1059/1649 by Nāsir Kitābdār for the Jānid Abuʾl-Mansūr ʿAbd al-ʿAzīz Bahādur Khān of Transoxiana. Elaborately decorated margins with different designs chiefly in gold.

18·5 × 11 cm. ¶ Lent by A. CHESTER BEATTY, ESQ.

1 See p. 161.

371 [698, 700] TWO MINIATURES by Mu'īn Musawwir from a *Shāh-nāma*. Another miniature, signed by Mu'īn, from the same manuscript is in the British Museum collection (1922–7–11–02) and is dated 1059/1649.

34×15 *cm.* (*each*). ¶ Lent by Y. DAWUD, ESQ.

(*a*) Bīzhan rescued from the well.
(*b*) Rustam before the Shāh.

372 [686] DRAWING, with touches of colour. A man carrying a cock. Inscribed: 'Done on Thursday, 11th of the month of Zi'l-Hajja, 1066/1656, for another relative of Āqā —— [illegible]. May it be blessed, Mu'īn Musawwir.'

8·5×12 *cm.* Rabino, *Les Provinces Caspiennes*, pl. 65. ¶ Lent by H. RABINO, ESQ., Cairo.

373 [267] TWO LINE-DRAWINGS. Both apparently drawn and inscribed by Mu'īn Musawwir.

(*a*) Portrait of a woman, wearing a nose-ring, inscribed: 'Portrait of the refuge of chastity Minnat Jān (?). Done in Rabī' al-Ākhar, 1067 [1657].' 16·5×7 *cm. Les Provinces Caspiennes*, pl. 3.
(*b*) Portrait of a seated dervish, eating fruit. Inscribed: 'In Rabī' al-Awwal 1074 [1663] for my relative Hātim Beg. May it be blessed.' 15·5×6 *cm. Les Provinces Caspiennes*, pl. 48.

¶ Lent by H. RABINO, ESQ., Cairo.

374 [708] A PORTRAIT OF RIZĀ-YI 'ABBĀSĪ, the painter, making a drawing. By Mu'īn Musawwir. The inscription on the left reads: 'The portrait of my deceased master, now in Paradise—God's mercy and forgiveness on him!—Rizā-yi 'Abbāsī the painter, executed in the year 104 (? = 1040/1630), and finished on the 5th of the month of Safar 1087 [19th April 1676] as a memorial for an album. Good fortune to it! Executed by Mu'īn Musawwir. God pardon his sins!' A very similar portrait is in the collection of B. Quaritch.[1] In that case the inscription states that the portrait was painted in 1044/1635, that Rizā-yi 'Abbāsī died in the same year, and that the portrait was finished on the 14th of Ramazān in the year 1084 [24th December 1673] by Mu'īn Musawwir in accordance with the wishes of his (Mu'īn's) son. There is nothing improbable in the artist having made two copies of an old drawing of his master. The main differences between the two versions consist in the treatment of the face, especially the eyes, the turban, and the subject of the drawing on which Rizā is at work. In the other version a page in European costume, holding a wine-flask, is depicted. The line seems somewhat more incisive than in the later version.

20×12·5 *cm.* From the Engel-Gros collection. Exh. Philadelphia Sexcentennial Exhibition, 1928; Pennsylvania Museum, Philadelphia, 1926; Detroit Institute of Arts, November 1930. ¶ Lent by PARISH-WATSON, New York. PLATE CXII A.

375 [704] A CAMEL AND A TURBANED MAN. Drawing with touches of colour. Inscribed: 'On the night of Wednesday the 28th of Shawwāl 1089 A.H. [1678]

---

[1] Martin, I, fig. 32; Sakisian, pl. c; Arnold and Grohmann, pl. 75; *Journal of Indian Art*, XVII, no. 135, July 1916.

these two [sic] camels designed by the late Ustād Bihzād Sultānī (mercy on him !) were drawn by Mu'īn Musawwir.' The signature is written in the flamboyant manner characteristic of Mu'īn.

13 × 18·5 cm. Rabino, Les Provinces Caspiennes, pl. 16. ¶ Lent by H. RABINO, ESQ., Cairo.

376 [414 A] SIX MINIATURES, signed raqam zad Mu'īn Musawwir; from a Shāh-nāma, copied in the second half of the XVII century.

35·5 × 22 cm. (the page). ¶ Lent by A. CHESTER BEATTY, ESQ.

377 [707] KNEELING DERVISH. Miniature attributed to Mu'īn Musawwīr. Second half of the XVII century.

11 × 6 cm. ¶ Lent by M. CLAUDE ANET, Paris.

378 [669] A DERVISH BLOWING A HORN. Lightly coloured, with chalky grey-blue wash. Line-drawing. Unfinished, with the feet sketched in two positions. The face and some other parts of the drawing show European influence in the use of modelling. Mid-XVII century.

13 × 7·5 cm. Sarre-Mittwoch, pl. 6. Exh. Berlin 1910, no. 151. ¶ Lent by FRAU MARIE SARRE-HUMANN, Berlin.

379 [719 C] PEN DRAWING, slightly coloured. A Persian lady seated in a landscape, in company of an old woman leaning on a staff. Possibly by Muhammad 'Alī. Mid-XVII century.

10 × 8 cm. Exh. Memorial Art Gallery, Rochester, 1930. Pennsylvania Univ. Museum, 1930. Detroit Inst. of Arts, 1930, cat. no. 53. Blochet, Demotte Catalogue, no. 132, pl. 45. ¶ Lent by DEMOTTE, New York.

380 [725 G] MINIATURE, slightly coloured. Dervish by a fire. Signed Afzal. c. 1650.[1]

21 × 13 cm. Martin, II, pl. 149. ¶ Lent by M. CLAUDE ANET, Paris.

381 [270] LADY STANDING, dressed in striped robe. Mid-XVII century.

12·5 × 20 cm. ¶ Lent by C. G. N. MORGAN, ESQ.

382 [703] A PERSIAN PRINCE ON HORSEBACK with three attendants, one in European and one in Indian dress. Inscribed: Yā Sāhib al-zamān, 'O Lord of the Time.' The prince wears the exaggeratedly waisted dress and peculiar turban characteristic of the latter part of the seventeenth century. He is perhaps Shāh Sulaymān (1667–94) in the early part of his reign, which began when he was 20 years of age. The European dress of one of the servants is characteristic of an age of increasing European contacts, of which Persian art has begun to show considerable traces, especially in modelling and in landscape effects. The painting has been attributed to

---

[1] Martin mentions a miniature by Afzal dated 1054/1644 and a Shāh-nāma at St. Petersburg dated 1642–50, containing miniatures signed by him.

Muhammad Zamān, as to whom see above, pp. 161–2. He was sent by the Shāh to study art in Rome, and several existing examples of his work show a strange blend of the traditions of East and West.

> 14·5 × 22 cm. ¶ Lent by M. CLAUDE ANET, Paris.　　　　　　PLATE CXII B.

383 [706] PORTRAIT, inscribed *Shāh Sulaymān*, i.e. the Safawid Shāh Sulaymān (1667–94). He is kneeling, in a green, waisted coat and the large turban of the period, and holds a spray of roses. In the sky is a flight of birds as in Mughal portraits. Red decorated border. 1670–80.

> 12 × 9 cm., with the border 45·5 × 30 cm. ¶ Lent by A. CHESTER BEATTY, ESQ.

384 [671] EIGHT MINIATURES from a *Shāh-nāma. c.* 1675. The manuscript is of unusual size and finely executed, obviously for a royal library. There are fifteen miniatures in all, most of which are in the style of Rizā-yi 'Abbāsī's followers. A few, however, show marked European influence, and (*a*) and (*f*) below are by Muhammad Zamān, who actually studied in Italy (*vide* pp. 161–2).

> 39·5 × 26 cm. ¶ Lent by A. CHESTER BEATTY, ESQ.
> (*a*) The Sīmurgh coming to help Rūdāba at the birth of Rustam. Signed in 1086/1675 by Muhammad Zamān.
> (*b*) The Sīmurgh carrying Zāl to his nest.
> (*c*) Rustam killing the white elephant.
> (*d*) Farīdūn crossing Āb i daryā.
> (*e*) Minūchihr pursuing his father's murderer.
> (*f*) The head of the murdered Īraj is brought before his father Farīdūn. Evidently by Muhammad Zamān.
> (*g*) Tahmūras warring against the Dīws.
> (*h*) Rakhsh, Rustam's charger, killing a lion.

385 [685] LINE-DRAWING. Portrait of a dervish with a pointed beard, seated. Dated Thursday, 15th Rabī' II, 1103/1691.

> 7 × 11 cm. Rabino, *Les Provinces Caspiennes*, pl. 79. ¶ Lent by H. RABINO, ESQ., Cairo.

386 [287] DOUBLE-PAGE MINIATURE, mounted for an album. The scene is evidently an illustration to the *Shāh-nāma*, and represents (on the right) Rustam pleading before the Shāh. In the background on the left is an army encamped. Strong and crude colouring, showing European influence. Late XVII century.

> 32·8 × 38·8 cm. ¶ Lent by GULISTAN MUSEUM, Tehran.

387 [710] PORTRAIT OF A YOUTH holding a quince. End of XVII century.

> 14·5 × 8 cm. ¶ Lent by COMMANDER W. ROSS, R.N.

388 [288] TWO MINIATURES. XVII century.

> (*a*) Four men in a boat. 15 × 13·7 cm.
> (*b*) Two men in a boat, snaring birds. 12·5 × 13·6 cm.
> ¶ Lent by COMMANDER W. ROSS, R.N.

389 [714] PORTRAIT of a young man, seated, half-length. The face is modelled in the European style. The tall black head-dress persisted into the nineteenth century and is found in book-illustrations after 1850. Late XVIII century.

57·5×40 cm. A. C. Edwards, *A Persian Caravan*, 1928. ¶ Lent by A. CECIL EDWARDS, ESQ.
PLATE CXIII B.

390 [726 A] POEMS of Fath 'Alī Shāh (poetical name Khāqān), dated *Shawwāl*, 1216/1802. Profusely illuminated throughout, in gold and colours, red being prominent. The outer borders contain well-executed figures of birds, animals, and foliage in gold on a dark-blue ground. Lacquer binding with bird and flower subjects, signed by Mirzā Bābā, *Naqqāsh-bāshī* (i.e. Chief Court Painter), and dated 1216 A.H. Several fine *sarlawhs*, that on fol. 1 containing representations of the Lion and Sun of Persia.

On fols. 12 *v.* and 13 are portraits of the first two rulers of the Qājār dynasty, Āqā Muhammad Khān, the eunuch Shāh (crowned 1796), and Fath 'Alī Shāh, his nephew and successor (1797–1834). The portraits are signed *Raqm i kamtarīn ghulām Mirzā Bābā Naqqāsh-Bāshī*. That of Fath 'Alī Shāh is dated 1216 A.H. Both the Shāhs are depicted kneeling on carpets, richly worked in pearls and jewels, against garden backgrounds. The manuscript is an outstanding example of the Court art of the period.

43×28·5 cm. ¶ Lent by HIS MAJESTY THE KING.

This manuscript is mentioned by Sir W. Ouseley in his *Travels in . . . the East* (vol. iii, pp. 372–3; 1823). It was included among the gifts dispatched to the Prince Regent of England in 1812. Ouseley says that ˙Mirzā Bābā took seventeen years over the miniatures and illumination of the book. This seems to be the longest time on record.
Portraits of Fath 'Alī Shāh are numerous. He was proud of his jewels and of his long black beard and thin waist, and he is often portrayed surrounded by his sons, fifty-seven of whom—not to speak of forty-six daughters—survived him. A portrait of him, in oils, by this same Mirzā Bābā, is in the India Office, London. It is dated 1213 A.H.

391 [712] PORTRAIT of Āqā Yūsuf, a Hamadān grandee, *c.* 1860, by Abu'l-Hasan Ghaffārī Kāshānī, Sanī' al-Mulk.

47×23 cm. A. C. Edwards, *A Persian Caravan*, 1928. ¶ Lent by A. CECIL EDWARDS, ESQ.

392 [726 E] PERSIAN TRANSLATION IN MANUSCRIPT of Queen Victoria's *Leaves from the Journal of our Life in the Highlands*. Translated by command of the Shāh. Bound at Tehran, 1885. Binding executed and signed by Rizā Tālaqānī, 1302/1885.

22·5×17·5 cm. ¶ Lent by HIS MAJESTY THE KING.

393 [726 B] HOLY MEN BOILING AN EGG DURING THE FAST. Demons are emerging from the flame. A satiric drawing. XIX century. Above and below are two panels of birds and flowers, of rather earlier date.

23×15 cm. ¶ Lent by HERR L. BÄCKSBACKA, Helsingfors. PLATE CXIII A.

394 [726 F] THE PRINCE AND THE PHILOSOPHER. Modern Tehran school. Signed *Mīrzā Nūr Allāh*.

30×18 cm. A. C. Edwards, *A Persian Caravan*, 1928. ¶ Lent by A. CECIL EDWARDS, ESQ.

PLATE CVI. 248. A young man with a falcon. *Style of Muhammadī*

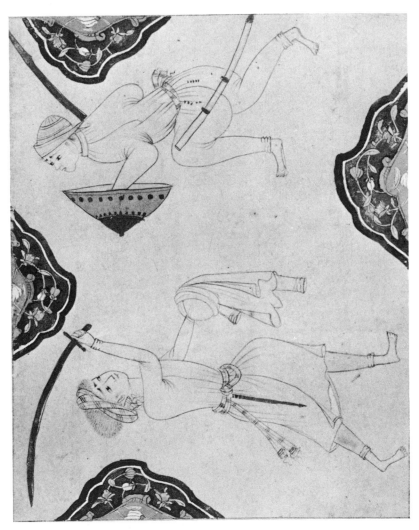

PLATE CVII- A. 193 (*b*). Youths duelling. *Late* XVI *century*

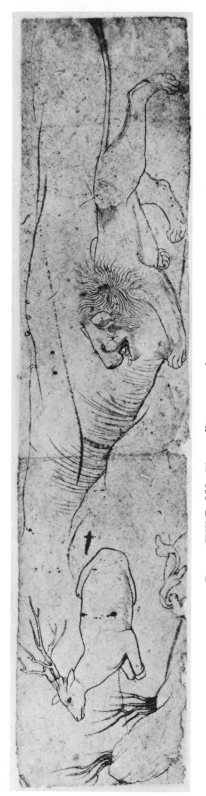

PLATE CVII-B. 252. Lion stalking an antelope. XVI *century*

PLATE CVII-C. 330. Lioness and Cubs. *Signed*: Riżā ʿAbbāsī

PLATE CVIII-A. 180 (*a*). The Wazīr and the
Page (*unfinished*). 1551

PLATE CVIII- B. 367. Nude figure. *Mid* XVII *century*

PLATE CVIII-C. 290. Line drawing. *c.* 1600

PLATE CIX-A. 298. A European
Early XVII *century*

PLATE CIX-B. 305. A drunken youth
Early XVII *century*

PLATE CIX-C. 368. Ink sketch. By Muhammad Yūsuf
Mid XVII *century*

PLATE CX-A. 366. Monkey riding a bear
By Muhammad 'Alī. *c.* 1650

PLATE CX-B. 306. Design in *découpé* work

Early XVII *century*

PLATE CXI- A. 359. Dancing girl. *Mid* XVII *century*

PLATE CXI-B. 317. Shepherd. By Rizā-yi 'Abbāsī, 1632

PLATE CXII-A. 374. Portrait of Rizā–yi ʿAbbāsī
By Muʿīn Musawwir. 1676

PLATE CXII-B. 382. Persian prince and attendants. c. 1670

PLATE CXIII- A. 393. Holy men boiling an egg during the fast. A satire.
Late xix *century*

PLATE CXIII-B. 389. Portrait. *Late* XVIII *century*

DŪST MUHAMMAD'S ACCOUNT OF PAST AND PRESENT PAINTERS

THE nineteen pages containing this document are bound up in the album in the Topkapu Serai Library known as Bahrām Mīrzā's Album. The account was, it is believed, first noticed by the Turkish scholar Dr. Mehmet Aga-Oglu, who intends to publish it. What follows is merely an abstract of the more important passages.

The writer, Dūst Muhammad, is mentioned by the Turkish historian 'Ālī. He was a native of Herāt and the son of one Sulaymān. Besides being a calligrapher he also painted miniatures, several of which are known, and two which purport to be by him are included in the Album.

The text is written in a clear nasta'līq, the first two pages being richly ornamented. The date is given in a chronogram at the end as 951/1544.

The writer, after a long preamble, in very flowery language, says that Prince Abu'l-Fath Bahrām Mīrzā[2] became much interested in calligraphy, and ordered Dūst Muhammad to collect the scattered leaves of past and living masters and to form the present album, to which this is added as a fitting preface. After giving an account of the calligraphers of former times he introduces his remarks on 'the painters and illuminators of the past' by praising the arts of painting and illumination for their beauty and their function of adorning fine writing. The first to reveal their glory, says he, was 'Alī b. Abi Tālib [the Caliph], whose pen opened the gates of these two arts to mankind, and who produced several leaves 'known to painters as Islāmī'.

As a further encouragement to the humble painters Dūst Muhammad says that the books of the great reveal that painting derives from the Prophet Daniel. After Muhammad's death certain of the Companions undertook a journey to Rūm to propagate the faith, and conversed with the Emperor Heraclius. After some conversation the Emperor sent for a box, out of which he took a glorious painting, which he told them was a portrait of Adam. He also showed them portraits of the other Prophets, including one of Muhammad, on seeing which they were overcome with emotion. On their asking Heraclius the origin of the paintings he told them as follows. Adam was desirous of seeing the prophets of his offspring. Accordingly God sent him a box with thousands of compartments, each containing a piece of silk, on every one of which one of the prophets was depicted. It was called the 'Box of Testimony'. Adam kept it in his treasury, situated far in the West. From there it was transferred by Zu'l-Qarnayn to

---

[1] See p. 139 (no. 174).
[2] Brother of Shāh Tahmāsp. He died, according to the account given by another brother, Sām Mīrzā, in the Tuhfa i Sāmī, in 956 A.H. He was then only 33 years old. Sām Mīrzā, who wrote a year later, speaks of him as luxury-loving and profuse, of a keen intelligence, and skilled in calligraphy, especially nasta'līq, drawing (tarrāhī), poetry, and music.

Daniel, who copied the portraits with his marvellous brush. It was from that time that the tradition of painting had its origin on earth; and the paintings which Heraclius displayed were Daniel's handiwork.[1]

In the time of Jesus, son of Maryam, Mānī claimed to be the Prophet, and used paintings to enforce his teachings. When men asked him to show them a miracle he took a piece of silk and retired to a cave, the entrance of which was closed up, for a year. At the end of that time he emerged with the silk covered with wonderful figures, men, beasts, trees, and birds; and that silk was the famous Arzhang of Mānī, to which Sa'dī refers in his *Gulistān*.

It was, it appears, owing to Mānī that painting was introduced into 'Irāq and subsequently Cathay (Khatā).

Dūst Muhammad then refers to the story of Shāpūr the artist, who painted portraits of Khusraw which he placed in Shīrīn's pleasure-garden. Moreover, he continues, the art of painting flourished both in Cathay and in the territory of the Franks till the Sultanate of Abu Sa'īd Khudā-Banda.[2]

It was then that Ustād Ahmad Mūsā, who learned his art from his father, withdrew the covering from the face of painting, and invented the kind of painting which is current at the present time. An *Abu Sa'īd-nāma*, a *Kalīla wa Dimna*, and a *Mi'rāj-nāma*, copied by Mawlānā 'Abd Allāh, were illustrated by this painter; also a History of Chingīz,[3] which was afterwards in the library of Sultān Husayn Mīrzā.

Besides him was Amīr Dawlat Yār, who had been one of Sultān Abu Sa'īd's slaves. He was a pupil of Ahmad Mūsā. He excelled in black-and-white drawing (*qalam siyāhī*), so that even the matchless Walī Allāh acknowledged the marvel of his skill.

Again, there was, among his [Ahmad Mūsā's] pupils, Ustād Shams al-Dīn, who learned his art in the reign of Sultān Uways.[4] He illustrated a *Shāh-nāma* copied by Khwāja Amīr 'Alī. When Sultān Uways died Shams al-Dīn worked for no other master.

Shams al-Dīn's pupil Khwāja 'Abd al-Hayy was in distressed circumstances, but Shams al-Dīn rescued him from manual toil and gave him instruction. Accordingly in the reign of Sultān Ahmad of Baghdād, a great patron of the arts,[5] he excelled all others. He instructed the Sultān in painting, and the Sultān contributed a black-and-white illustration to an *Abu Sa'īd-nāma*.

[1] The story has obvious reference to the traditions that God showed Adam all the generations of men with their prophets, and that he concealed the secrets of his wisdom in a treasure cave, from which Daniel recovered them.

[2] The Il-khānī ruler (1317–35). It is just possible that Dūst Muhammad is confusing him with his predecessor Uljaytū, *Khudā-Banda* (1305–16), in whose reign the *Jāmi' al-Tawārīkh* of 1310–11 A.H. was written. But see the next note.

[3] The *Chingīz-nāma* of Ahmad of Tabrīz, which was dedicated to Abu Sa'īd, is presumably intended.

[4] 1356–74. Dawlatshāh (Browne's edition, p. 262) mentions this ruler's skill in drawing figures with the 'pen of Wāsit', and says that Khwāja 'Abd al-Hayy who was supreme in the art, derived instruction from him.

[5] Sultān Ahmad Jalā'ir reigned from 1382 to 1410. Dawlatshāh (*Tazkirat al-shu'arā*, p. 306) says of him that he composed good poetry in Arabic and Persian, and was a master of all kinds of accomplishments, including painting and illumination, bow- and arrow-making, and the engraving of seals. He was a calligrapher, writing six different hands, and a great lover of music, composing several musical works.

When the conquering army of Tīmūr overthrew Baghdād[1] he took 'Abd al-Hayy back with him to his capital of Samarqand. There the Khwāja died. After his death all the masters emulated his work.

A pupil of Shams al-Dīn was Ustād Junayd[2] of Baghdād.

Another was Pīr Ahmad, *Bāgh-shimālī*, the zenith of his time. No one could rival him. He reached the age of 50.

And Baysunghur Mīrzā brought from Tabrīz Ustād Sayyid Ahmad, *naqqāsh*, and Khwāja 'Alī, *musawwir*, and Ustād Qiwām al-Dīn the binder, of Tabrīz, and ordered them to produce a book in their best style, in shape and pages and illustrations exactly like the 'war' of Sultān Ahmad of Baghdād.[3]

The writing of this book was entrusted to Hazrat Mawlānā Farīd al-Dīn Ja'far.[4] The binding was done by Qiwām al-Dīn, who was the inventor of cut-pattern work[5] on bindings; the illumination and illustrations were by Amīr Khalīl.

Here Dūst Muhammad, after remarking that Amīr Khalīl was absolutely unrivalled and unique in his own method (*dar tarīq i khud*), tells a long anecdote to illustrate the familiar terms on which he stood with Baysunghur—Khalīl kicked the Prince by mistake on the forehead during a frolic, and the Prince magnanimously protected him from the results.

He then continues his 'history'. Before Baysunghur's 'war' [i.e. the great book] was completed the Prince died, and was succeeded by his eldest son 'Alā al-Dawla Mīrzā, who was anxious to finish it. And he assembled this company of artists in his own library, and supported them generously. At this time, also, he sent to Tabrīz for Khwāja Ghiyās al-Dīn, son of Ahmad the gold-beater. The Khwāja obeyed him, and came and worked in the Herāt library, painting some of the war-pictures with strife-exciting colours, and washing them with blood and tears, and completing the work. When Amīr Khalīl saw those paintings he decided to give up painting.

And after that Prince Ulugh Beg[6] marched from Samarqand on Khurāsān, and vanquished 'Alā al-Dawla Mīrzā. Mawlānā Shahāb al-Dīn 'Abd Allāh and Mawlānā Zahīr al-Dīn Azhar and all the library staff were carried off by him to Samarqand, where

---

[1] In 1393.

[2] It is provoking that Dūst Muhammad gives no details of this painter, who is, without a doubt, the artist of the important British Museum manuscript (Add. 18113) containing the poems of Khwājū Kirmānī, which bears the date 798/1396 and was copied at Baghdād by the celebrated calligrapher Mīr 'Alī of Tabrīz.

[3] The meaning is not quite clear. It is an historical fact that Baysunghur, then 20 years of age, was sent by his father, the Emperor Shāh Rukh, to restore order at Tabrīz in November 1420. Anarchy had broken out on the death of Qara Yūsuf, who had made Tabrīz his capital on defeating Sultān Ahmad ten years earlier; Tabrīz, as well as Baghdād, being included in Sultān Ahmad's kingdom. Baysunghur restored order, and it was presumably on this occasion that he took the

painters back to Herāt—an important event in Persian art history. Whether the book illustrated by these artists was actually the *Shāh-nāma*, now in the Gulistan Library, which was exhibited at Burlington House, is not absolutely certain, but the calligrapher was in each case Mawlānā Ja'far, and it is likely that the artists were the same.

[4] Also, it should be noted, of Tabrīz.

[5] *Munabbat-kārī*. As noted by Sir Thomas Arnold, in *The Islamic Book*, p. 98, the first appearance of this work, executed by cutting strips of leather into patterns and superimposing them over a coloured ground, appears in a binding executed in Baghdād in 1407.

[6] Son of Shāh Rukh, and Governor of Turkestan. On Shāh Rukh's death in 1447 'Alā al-Dawla seized Herāt and contested the supremacy with his uncle.

he treated them with all possible kindness and consideration. He ordered them to make a history of himself.[1]

Also there was Amīr Rūh Allāh,[2] called Mīrak Naqqāsh, a Herātī, one of the Sayyids who were makers of bows. He was at first a calligrapher, but after his father's death he took to scribe's work, besides bow-making. Later he entered the service of Mawlānā Walī Allāh, and took to illumination, going on from that to painting, in which he became unequalled. And in the time of the late Sultān Husayn Mīrzā[3] he received great favours and was made head of the library.

His pupil and successor (shāgird i khalaf) was Kamāl al-Dīn Bihzād, the best of the modern painters and chief of illuminators and writers, zenith of the age. His gifts are apparent in the work of his brush in the present album. He was honoured by employment in the library of His Majesty Shāh Tahmāsp, who showed him manifold favours. And in his service he died, and was laid to rest beside the tomb of Shaykh Kamāl.[4] The date of his death is contained in a verse by Amīr Dūst Hāshimī: *Nazar Afgan Ba Khāk i Qabr i Bihzād*.[5]

The writer then enumerates the court calligraphers of Shāh Tahmāsp, beginning with Shāh Mahmūd Nīshāpūrī, and including Kamāl al-Dīn Rustam 'Alī, celebrated for his writing in colours (rang-nawīsī), and himself. He then passes to the contemporary painters.

First comes Ustād Nizām al-Dīn Sultān Muhammad, the zenith of the age. Among the paintings by him in a *Shāh-nāma* of the Shāh is an illustration of people clothed in leopard skins, such that the hearts of the boldest of painters were grieved and they hung their heads in shame before it.

Then there is the Sayyid Āqā Jalāl al-Dīn Mīrak al-Hasanī, unique in the time, confidant of the Shāh, unequalled as a painter and portraitist. Also the illustrious and skilful portrait-painter Sayyid Mīr Musawwir.[6] These two Sayyids painted in the royal library, illustrating especially a royal *Shāh-nāma* and a *Khamsa* of Nizāmī so beautifully that the pen is inadequate to describe their merits. Moreover, they adorned an arched *jām-khāna* [mirror-house] for Prince Bahrām in the most exquisite and masterly manner, making it as beautiful as paradise peopled with fair youths and hūrīs.

Another portrait-painter, who is also a skilled poet, is Mawlānā Muhammad, known as Qadīmī.

Another is that unrivalled artist in line (tarrāh) Ustād Kamāl al-Dīn Husayn, while

---

[1] Ulugh Beg was murdered by his son 'Abd al-Latīf in 1449.
[2] In a manuscript in the British Museum (Add. 7669) dated 965/1558 is an anecdote about Mīrak, by Khwāndamīr, who gives his name as 'Sayyid Rūh Allāh, called Khwāja Mīrak Naqqāsh'. He was entrusted with the calligraphy of the Jāmi' mosque at Herāt when it was being repaired in 904/1499, but was so remiss that he held up the work of the faience

workers.
[3] Ruler of Khurāsān 1468–1506.
[4] Kamāl of Khujand, a well-known poet, praised for his saintly character. He died at Tabrīz about A.D. 1400.
[5] 'Regard the dust of the grave of Bihzād.' The numerical value of the letters of 'dust of the grave of Bihzād' is 942 (i.e. A.D. 1535–6).
[6] Mīr Naqqāsh was, according to 'Alī, the director of Shāh Tahmāsp's library (see Sakisian, p. 111).

Ustād Kamāl al-Dīn 'Abd al-Ghaffār and Ustād Hasan 'Alī are likewise notable painters.

Dūst Muhammad has a paragraph on the illuminators and others of the staff of the royal library. Among these he mentions *Mīrak al-muzahhib*, praised by all keen-sighted ones for his glorious work in margins and *sarlawḥs*; also his son, Qiwām al-Dīn Mas'ūd, whose work resembled his father's; the binders Kamāl al-Dīn 'Abd al-Wahhāb, known as Khwāja Kākā, and Mawlānā Muhsin.

The account closes with some verses in honour of Bahrām Mīrzā, containing the date[1] of the completion of the album, i.e. 951/1544.

This preface must rank as one of the two or three primary sources for the history of Persian miniature art. It was written at a time when the great school of Persian painting was still in a flourishing state and when, no doubt, the libraries of the Safawid princes were rich in material. The view of a regular development of painting in Persia, from the Il-khānī period to the writer's own day, is amply borne out by all the evidence. On the other hand, the connected descent from master to pupil, as implied by the author, shows every sign of being a literary device for enlivening the monotony of a list. But it will be noted that there are breaks in the succession after the Jalā'ir painters, and also after the defeat of Baysunqur's son 'Alā al-Dawla by Ulugh Beg. In each case the artists are said to have been carried off to Samarqand. The nineteenth-century idea, expressed, for instance, by M. Blochet in *Inventaire et description des miniatures des manuscrits orientaux conservés à la Bibliothèque Nationale* (1897–1900), of the Timurid school as Transoxanian has since been abandoned by this[2] and other writers. It would be unfortunate if it should be revived in any way as a result of the publication of this new reference, particularly as it does not probably represent an independent tradition.

The material in the preface falls into five parts: the account of the origins of painting, its history in the fourteenth century under the Mongols and Jalā'irs, the section on Baysunqur and his son, and those on the later Timurid and early Safawid periods. These five divisions correspond, more or less, with the first five chapters of this book. In his treatment of the origins the author presents a number of old legends without departing far from their known details. The next section is of far greater interest, and gives a number of new names for the fourteenth century. Of the names that Dūst Muhammad mentions for this period, two, 'Abd al-Hayy[3] and Pīr Ahmad,[4] are otherwise known from literary sources, while a third, Junayd, is represented in the British Museum collection. There is no reason to doubt the accuracy of the other names, but they must remain rather barren for lack of any work attributable to them. But there are two extremely important implications in the account, first, that miniature-painting rose

---

[1] The words which give the date are: *Abū'l-Fath Bahrām i 'Ādil Nihādī.*

[2] Cf. *Les Peintures*, p. 160, note.

[3] Dawlatshāh, p. 262.

[4] 'Alī, quoted by Sakisian, p. 64, gives Sayyid Ahmad of Tabrīz as Bihzād's master (!).

to be a fine art in Persia in the reign of Abu Saʿīd, and second, that the Jalāʾir sultāns were the principal, if not the only, heirs of the Mongol school. The first is a manifest piece of dramatic exaggeration, even if it is recalled that the reign, which extended from 1317 to 1335, probably saw the production of the Demotte *Shāh-nāma* (no. 29), which may be called the first typically Persian masterpiece: no such sudden 'with-drawing of the covering from the face of painting' is probable, or acceptable as a hypothesis in the face of the evidence of the manuscripts.

The exclusive claim of Tabrīz and the Jalāʾir house after the death of Sultān Uways is difficult to reconcile with their political weakness and the disturbed state of the city in the later part of the fourteenth century, though their patronage was of undoubted value. Both Husayn b. Uways (d. 1382) and his brother Ahmad (d. 1410) suffered exile in Egypt: in 1385 Tabrīz was captured by the Golden Horde: it was recovered by Ahmad in 1386, but held to ransom by Tīmūr in 1387. In 1392 it was in fief to Mīrān-shāh: in 1406 Ahmad was able to return, but almost immediately it fell to Qara Yūsuf; and in 1410 came Ahmad's final defeat and death. It is true that many other parts of Persia suffered almost as much, but Shīrāz seems to have remained a less troubled and therefore a wealthier place. It would be strange if Baysunqur should have been able to recruit his library staff entirely from Tabrīz in 1420, after all these con-querors had passed the same way before him. In fact there is a difficulty in the text of Dūst Muhammad; for, while he says that Baysunqur brought two artists, Ustād Sayyid Ahmad and Khwāja ʿAlī, from Tabrīz to make him an epic volume, he goes on to say that the illustrations to this book were by Khalīl, who is thus introduced without a place of origin being mentioned. Of him we only know that he worked at the court of Shāh Rukh and was esteemed the greatest painter of the day. The evidence of the surviving manuscripts all goes to prove that, at the very beginning of the Timurid period, Shīrāz was the principal centre of miniature-painting. Is it not probable that Khalīl was trained in this school?

A little farther on, Dūst Muhammad states that ʿAlā al-Dawla b. Baysunqur sent to Tabrīz for Khwāja Ghiyās al-Dīn to work at the still unfinished epic of his father. Here, on one of the few points at which we can check his account, it seems that he must be mistaken. For Ghiyās al-Dīn had been attached by Baysunqur to Shāh Rukh's embassy to China in 1419/20, and his account of it survives. Yet Dūst Muhammad evidently implies that it was not till after 1433 that Ghiyās al-Dīn first visited Herāt. This mistake does not inspire great confidence in the accuracy of his account in details.

No doubt, as he approaches his own age, he is more to be relied on; and there is no reason to doubt the particulars that he gives of Bihzād, Sultān Muhammad, and Jalāl al-Dīn Mīrak. It is possible that the royal manuscripts of the *Shāh-nāma* and Nizāmī, which he mentions as made for Tahmāsp, are those now belonging to Baron Edmond de Rothschild and the British Museum (Or. 2265).

APPENDIX II

MĪRZĀ MUHAMMAD HAYDAR DUGHLĀT ON THE HERĀT SCHOOL OF PAINTERS

By T. W. ARNOLD

[The following article, by the late Sir Thomas Arnold, is reprinted from Vol. v, Part IV (1930) of the *Bulletin of the School of Oriental Studies*, London Institution, by kind permission of the Editor, Sir E. Denison Ross. Its interest and importance are obvious, and it has often been referred to in the preceding text of this book. Additional notes are in square brackets.]

MUSLIM historians have put on record such scanty and insufficient materials for the biographies of painters that any fresh information deserves attention, especially if it is provided by a contemporary of the painters in question. The following extracts from the *Ta'rīkh-i-Rashīdī* have hitherto escaped notice; the Persian text of this interesting work has not yet been printed, and these passages were not included in the abbreviated translation which Sir E. Denison Ross published in 1895. But he recently drew my attention to them, and kindly placed at my disposal two manuscripts of the text in his private possession, and, further, revised and amended my translation; to his erudition are due whatever merits it may possess.

In addition to the two manuscripts above mentioned, I consulted one in the India Office Library (No. 39 (Ethé 2448), foll. 153–4*b*) and two in the British Museum (Or. 157, foll. 152*b*–4; and Add. 24090, foll. 133–4*b*). There are variants in the text provided by these five manuscripts, but they are of little importance, as they appear generally to arise from carelessness on the part of one or other of the scribes.

The author, Mīrzā Muhammad Haydar, is too well known a personage to require any notice here; suffice it to say that he lived between A.D. 1500 and 1551, and was thus contemporary with most of the artists to whom he refers. His interest in them was probably due to the fact (mentioned by his cousin Bābur) that Mīrzā Haydar himself added the cultivation of the art of painting to his other accomplishments, having been (as he himself tells us) a pupil of Mawlānā Darvīsh Muhammad.[1]

'*Painters.*—Shāh Muzaffar is the son of Master Mansūr. In the reign of Sultān Abū Saʿīd he (Mansūr) was unsurpassed, he is a master in his art,[2] he has a delicate, fine brush, and no other painter's brush has ever attained the same delicacy, with the exception of that of Shāh Muzaffar; but he was somewhat more refreshing[3] (as an artist) in that his strokes were firmer. But Shāh Muzaffar surpassed him in many respects, for he had an exceedingly delicate brush, so clean and refined and matured[4] that the eyes of all beholders were amazed. He died at the age of twenty-four. During

[1 Muhammad Haydar Dughlāt Mīrzā visited Herāt in childhood. He based his account of Herāt on the memoirs of others (see Sir E. Denison Ross's translation, p. 193), and presumably, in the case of the painters, also on the statements of his painting-master and others.]

[2 'a master in his art': *ustād*.]

[3 *khunuktar*.]

[4 *nāzukī*, *sāfī*, *malāhat*, and *pukhtagī* are the words used.]

his lifetime he completed eight group pictures[1] (i.e. large compositions), and some persons possess examples of his pen and ink drawings.[2] The masters of this art hold him in very high esteem.

'Bihzād. As a painter he is a master,[3] though he does not come up to Shāh Muẓaffar in delicacy of touch, but his brush is firmer and he surpasses him in his preliminary sketches and his grouping of his figures.[4]

'To an earlier period belongs Khwājah 'Abd al-Ḥayy who lived under the Khāqāns of the house of Hūlāgū, who were rulers of 'Irāq. It is the belief of these artists that he was a saint,[5] and in the end he repented, and wherever he could lay his hands upon any of his own works he washed them off or burnt them; consequently exceedingly few of his works can now be found. He is unrivalled in purity and delicacy and firmness of brush, indeed in all the characteristics of the art of painting. After Khwājah 'Abd al-Ḥayy come Shāh Muẓaffar and Bihzād, and after these up to our own times there has been none like them. Both of the two latter enjoyed the patronage of Mīr 'Alī Shīr.[6]

'Qāsim 'Alī, portrait-painter.[7] He is a pupil of Bihzād and his works come near to those of Bihzād,[8] but in this style[9] (of painting) any expert connoisseur can recognize that the works of Qāsim 'Alī are rougher than those of Bihzād and that his original designs are more unsymmetrical.[10]

'Maqṣūd is a second Qāsim 'Alī, (also) a pupil of Bihzād; his brush is in no way inferior to that of Qāsim 'Alī. But his original designs and finish[11] are crude[12] compared with those of Qāsim 'Alī.

'Mawlānā Mīrak Naqqāsh. He is one of the marvels of the age, and he is the master of Bihzād. His original designs are more mature[13] than those of Bihzād, though his finish is not equal to that of Bihzād. But he had to do all his work when he was not actually in attendance on the Mīrzā,[14] either on journeys or at the court, either in the house or in the open air; consequently he was never able to settle down to work in his studio and stick to his easel (lit. paper). It is somewhat extraordinary that in spite of his occupations he used to engage in various kinds of athletics that are the very reverse of painting and drawing, and used to practise many violent exercises, such as wrestling and boxing, whereby he gained a reputation. It is strange indeed that he should have combined the painting of pictures with activities of this kind.

'Another master is Bābā Ḥājī. He had an expert brush in painting, but his original designs were unsymmetrical.[15] Throughout the whole of Khurāsān he is inimitable in

[1 'group pictures': *majlis*.]
[2 *qalam i siyāhī*.]
[3 *ustādīst*.]
[4 *Qalam i wai mahkamtar ast tarh u ustukhwān i ān az wai bihtar ast. Tarh* means 'drawing'. The meaning of *ustukhwān* is rather obscure; literally 'bones', so, perhaps, of 'main design'.]
[5 *walī*.]
6 The talented friend and minister of Sulṭān Ḥusayn Mīrzā (*ob.* 1501).
[7 *chihra-gushāy*.]

[8 *kārhā i wai qarīb i Bihzād ast*.]
[9 *uslūb*.]
[10 *asl tarh i ū bī andāmtar ast*. See note 4. Perhaps 'unsymmetrical' is too definite. The word for 'rougher' is *durushttar*.]
[11 *pardākht*.]
[12 *khām*.]
[13 *pukhtatar*.]
14 i.e. Sulṭān Ḥusayn Mīrzā, who ruled in Harāt from 1470 to 1506.
[15 *bī andām*.]

sketching designs and drawing in charcoal.[1] There is a story that in a certain gathering, in order to show off (his skill) he drew fifty circles and a half, which were exactly like those made by a pair of compasses, and there was not a hair's difference, big or small, between them.

'Master Shaykh Aḥmad, brother of Bābā Ḥājī, and Mawlānā Junayd and Master Ḥusām al-Dīn the poignard-maker, and Mawlānā Walī—all these are skilled masters and no one of them is superior to the other.

'Mullā Yūsuf is a pupil of Bihzād; he can work so rapidly that in ten days he can finish what it would take those masters one month to do; but he has not such an agreeable brush as those masters; his gilding is superior to his painting.

'Mawlānā Darvīsh Muḥammad, who is my master, is a pupil of Shāh Muẓaffar; he has no equal in fineness of brush, nay he has even surpassed Shāh Muẓaffar. But he is not so symmetrical or expert or refined, and he is apt to make very crude strokes. He once drew a picture of a man on horseback, lifting up a lion on the point of a javelin; the whole of it only covers the surface of a single grain of rice.

'There are a great many (other) painters, and so many of them are masters and proficient in their art that it is impossible to give an account of them all.

'*The Workers in Gold.*—Yārī is a master in gilding, but his writing is better than his gilding. He is a pupil of Mullā Walī, but he has outstripped his master. Mawlānā Maḥmūd was a better gilder[2] than Yārī, and he had planned an exceedingly delicate preface (of a manuscript) for Mīrzā Sulṭān Ḥusayn, but it remained incomplete, though he had worked upon it for seven years.

'In that period there were many workers in gold, but the only masters among them were the two that have already been mentioned.'

[1 *zughāl giriftan.*]   [2 *muzahhib.* Rather 'illuminator'.]

APPENDIX III

THE ALBUM FROM THE GULISTAN MUSEUM

AMONG the objects sent over to the Exhibition by the Persian Government was an album containing specimens of calligraphy and miniatures by Persian and Mughal artists. It contained ninety-two folios, so arranged that a double-opening of calligraphy alternated with two pages of miniatures, and measured 40×24·5 centimetres. It was bound in a nineteenth-century Persian binding, but the mounting, and therefore the compilation, was evidently the work of the Imperial Mughal library. The border decorations, many of which are of great beauty, are in exactly the same style as those in the famous Jahāngīr album at Berlin.[1] In fact it appears to be of the same size and may actually have been a companion volume.

The work by Persian artists in the Gulistan Museum album was of such importance that permission was obtained by the Committee to unbind the volume temporarily, and in this way it was possible to show twenty-one of its paintings on the walls of Burlington House. These will be found described in their places in our Catalogue.[2] The earliest of them dates from the end of the fifteenth century, and the latest—apart from the last, which is almost certainly a later addition to the album—is the copy of Bihzād's camel-fight made by Nānhā for the Emperor Jahāngīr in 1608/9 (no. 133). Probably about the same date is the re-working by Dawlat on no. 95. Among the Mughal miniatures, which were not exhibited, there was signed work by Manohar, Basāwan, Bishan Dās, and Mansūr, in addition to Dawlat and Āqā Rizā. These are all leading artists who flourished under Jahāngīr. Apart from no. 133, which bears Jahāngīr's autograph note, several of the pages seem to show a close personal connexion with him, while the copy which forms the lower part of no. 233 is possibly from his own hand. Everything, in fact, goes to prove that this album was one compiled for the Emperor's personal use. How it came to Persia is unknown, but it may be conjectured that it formed part of Nādir Shāh's loot from the capture of Delhi in 1739.

[1] For this album see the fully illustrated monograph by Drs. Kühnel and Goetz, *Indische Buchmalereien aus dem Jahangiralbum der Staatsbibliothek zu Berlin*, Berlin, 1924.

[2] The numbers are: 81, 87, 91, 95, 96, 132, 133, 163, 165, 167, 226, 229, 230, 231, 232, 233, 234, 235, 236, 336, and 386. Two of these are double-page compositions.

BIBLIOGRAPHY[1]

ANET, CLAUDE. Exhibition of Persian Miniatures at the Musée des Arts Décoratifs, Paris. *Burlington Magazine*, vol. XXII, 1912, pp. 9–17, 105–17.
The 'Manafi i-Heiwan' [of J. P. Morgan]. *Burlington Magazine*, vol. XXIII, 1913, pp. 224–31, 261.

ARNOLD, SIR THOMAS W. *Painting in Islam*. Oxford, 1928. Quoted as Arnold, *P.I.*
The Miniatures in Hilālī's Mystical Poem, the King and the Dervish. Vienna, 1926.
Bihzād and his Paintings in the Zafar-nāmah MS. London, 1930. [The Robert S. Garrett MS.]
Survivals of Sasanian and Manichaean Art in Persian Painting: the Charlton Lecture. Newcastle-on-Tyne, 1924. Quoted as Arnold, *Survivals*.
The Old and New Testaments in Muslim Religious Art. The Schweich Lectures of the British Academy, 1928. London, 1932.
Mīrzā Muḥammad Ḥaydar Dughlāt on the Herāt School of Painters (1550–1). *Bulletin of the School of Oriental Studies*, vol. v, pt. iv.

ARNOLD, SIR T. W., and GROHMANN, A. *The Islamic Book. A contribution to its art and history from the seventh to the eighteenth century*. Florence, 1929.

BINYON, LAURENCE. *The Poems of Nizami* [The British Museum MS. of 1539–43, Or. 2265]. Described by L. B. London, 1928.
A Persian Painting of the Mid-fifteenth Century. *Burlington Magazine*, vol. LVII, 1930, pp. 256–7.
The Persian Exhibition: II. Paintings. *Burlington Magazine*, vol. LVIII, 1931, pp. 9–15.

BLOCHET, EDGARD. *Catalogue des manuscrits persans de la Bibliothèque Nationale*, 3 tom. Paris, 1905–28 (in progress). Quoted as Blochet, *Catalogue*.
Les Peintures des manuscrits orientaux de la Bibliothèque Nationale. Paris, 1914–20. [Société française de reproductions de manuscrits à peintures.] Quoted as Blochet, *Peintures*.
Les Enluminures des manuscrits orientaux de la Bibliothèque Nationale. Paris, 1926. Quoted as Blochet, *Enluminures*.
Les Peintures des manuscrits persans de la collection Marteau à la Bibliothèque Nationale. *Fondation Eugène Piot. Monuments et Mémoires*. Tom. xxiii, 1918–19, pp. 129–214.
Notices sur les Manuscrits arabes et persans de la collection Marteau. Paris, 1923. This is contained in *Notices et extraits publiés par l'Académie des Inscriptions et Belles Lettres*, tom. 41. Quoted as *Notices et extraits*, tom. 41.
Les Peintures de la collection Pozzi. Paris, 1928. [Société française de reproductions de manuscrits à peintures.] This volume contains an index to the last four items.
Musulman Painting, twelfth to seventeenth century. Translated from the French by Cicely M. Binyon. London, 1929. Quoted as Blochet, *Musulman Painting*.
Catalogue of an Exhibition of Persian Paintings . . . held at the Galleries of Demotte, Inc. New York [1929]. Quoted as Demotte, *Cat.*
On a Book of Kings of about 1200 A.D. *Rupam*, no. 41, January 1930.

COOMARASWAMY, ANANDA K. *Les Miniatures orientales de la collection Goloubew au Museum of Fine Arts de Boston*. Paris et Bruxelles, 1929. [*Ars Asiatica*, tom. XIII.] Quoted as *Goloubew Catalogue*.

DIMAND, M. S. *A Handbook of Mohammedan Decorative Arts*. New York, 1930.

ETHÉ, H. *Catalogue of Persian . . . Manuscripts in the Bodleian Library*. 2 vols., 1889, 1930. Quoted as *Ethé*.

GLÜCK, HEINRICH. *Die indischen Miniaturen des Haemzae-Romanes*. Wien, 1925.

GLÜCK, HEINRICH, and DIEZ, ERNST. *Die Kunst des Islam*. Berlin, 1925. Quoted as Glück and Diez.

[1] Only the principal works consulted are included.

BIBLIOGRAPHY

GRAY, BASIL. *Persian Painting*. London, 1930. Quoted as Gray.

GROUSSET, RENÉ. *The Civilizations of the East: the Near and Middle East*. London, 1931.

HUART, C. *Les Calligraphes et les miniaturistes de l'Orient musulman*. Paris, 1908. Quoted as Huart.

JACKSON, A. V. WILLIAMS, and YOHANNAN, ABRAHAM. *A Catalogue of the collection of Persian Manu-scripts . . . presented to the Metropolitan Museum of Art, New York, by Alexander Smith Cochran*. New York, 1914.

KARABACEK, JOSEF VON. Riza-i Abbasi, ein persischer Miniaturenmaler [*Sitzungsberichte der philo-sophisch-historischen Klasse der k. Akademie der Wissenschaften*, Bd. CLXVII]. Wien, 1911.

KÜHNEL, ERNST. *Miniaturmalerei im islamischen Orient*. Berlin, 1922. Quoted as Kühnel, *I.M.*
Die Baysonghur-Handschrift der Islamischen Kunstabteilung [*Jahrbuch der preussischen Kunst-sammlungen*, Bd. 52, Heft III]. Berlin, 1931.

KÜHNEL, ERNST, and GOETZ, HERMANN. *Indische Buchmalereien aus dem Jahangiralbum der Staats-bibliothek zu Berlin*. Berlin, 1924. [English edition: London, 1925.]

MARTEAU, GEORGES, and VEVER, HENRI. *Miniatures persanes exposées au Musée des Arts Décoratifs*, 2 tom. Paris, 1913. Quoted as Marteau-Vever.

MARTIN, F. R. *The Miniature Painting and Painters of Persia, India, and Turkey from the eighth to the eighteenth century*. 2 vols. London, 1912. Quoted as Martin.
Les Miniatures de Behzad dans un manuscrit persan daté de 1485. Munich, 1912.
Miniatures from the period of Timur. Vienna, 1926.
The Nizāmī MS. from the Library of the Shāh of Persia, now in the Metropolitan Museum at New York. Vienna, 1927.
A Portrait by Gentile Bellini found in Constantinople. *Burlington Magazine*, vol. IX, 1906, pp. 148–9.
Two Portraits by Behzad, the Greatest Painter of Persia. *Burlington Magazine*, vol. XV, 1909, pp. 4–8.

MARTIN, F. R., and ARNOLD, SIR T. W. *The Nizami MS. illuminated by Bihzad, Mirak and Qasim Ali . . . British Museum (Or. 6810)*. Vienna, 1926.

MIGEON, GASTON. *Manuel d'art musulman*, tom. II, *Les Arts plastiques et industriels*. Paris, 1907; 2nd edition, 2 tom., Paris, 1927.

MINORSKY, VLADIMIR. Two unknown Persian Manuscripts. *Apollo*, February, 1931.

MITTWOCH, EUGEN. Zu Josef von Karabaceks 'Riza-i Abbasi', eine Entgegnung. *Der Islam*, Bd. II, 1911, pp. 204–19.

MUNICH. *Die Ausstellung von Meisterwerken muhammedanischer Kunst in München, 1910*. Heraus-gegeben von F. Sarre und F. R. Martin. 3 Bd. München, 1912. [Bd. I contains the minia-tures.] Quoted as *Meisterwerke*.

MUNTHE, G. Persiska Miniatyr [The Hilālī Ms. of 1539]. *National Musei årsbok*. Stockholm, 1923.

PERSIAN ART. *An Illustrated Souvenir of the Exhibition of Persian Art at Burlington House, London, 1931*. Quoted as *Souvenir*.

POPE, ARTHUR UPHAM. *Introduction to Persian Art since the Seventh Century A.D.* London, 1930.

RIEFSTAHL, R. MEYER. Miniatures from a manuscript of al-Jazari. *Art Bulletin*, vol. XI, pp. 206–14. New York, 1929.
Primitive Rugs of the 'Konya' Type in the Mosque at Beyshehir. *Art Bulletin*, vol. XIII, pp. 177–220 [especially pp. 204–8]. New York, 1931.

SAKISIAN, ARMENAG, BEY. *La Miniature persane du XIIᵉ au XVIIᵉ siècle*. Paris et Bruxelles, 1929. Quoted as *Sakisian*.
La Miniature à l'Exposition d'Art persan du Burlington house. *Syria*, tom. XII, 1931, pp. 163–72.
L'École de miniature pré-mongole de la Perse orientale. *Revue des Arts asiatiques*, tom. VII, no. 3, 1932.

BIBLIOGRAPHY

SARRE, FRIEDRICH. Eine Miniatur Gentile Bellinis, gemalt 1479–1480 in Konstantinopel. *Jahrbuch der k. Preuszischen Kunstammlungen*, Bd. XXVII, 1906, pp. 302–6. *Nachtrag*, Bd. XXVIII, 1907, pp. 51, 52.
Zu Josef von Karabaceks 'Riza-i Abbasi'. Eine Entgegnung. *Der Islam*, Bd. II, 1911, pp. 196–203.

SARRE, F., and MITTWOCH, EUGEN. *Zeichnungen von Riza Abbasi*. München, 1914.

SCHULZ, PHILIPP WALTER. *Die persisch-islamische Miniaturmalerei. Ein Beitrag zur Kunstgeschichte Irans.* 2 Bd. Leipzig, 1914. Quoted as Schulz.

STCHOUKINE, IVAN. *Musée Nationale du Louvre. Les miniatures persanes.* Paris, 1932. Quoted as *Louvre Cat.*

UPTON, JOSEPH M. Notes on Persian Costumes of the sixteenth and seventeenth centuries. *Metropolitan Museum Studies*, vol. II, pp. 206–20. New York, 1930.

WILKINSON, J. V. S. *The Shāh-nāmah of Firdausī; with 24 illustrations from a fifteenth-century manuscript formerly in the Imperial Library, Delhi, and now in the possession of the Royal Asiatic Society* . . . With an introduction . . . by Laurence Binyon. London, 1931.
Fresh Light on the Herāt Painters. *Burlington Magazine*, vol. LVIII, 1931, pp. 61–7.

CONCORDANCE

BETWEEN THE NUMBERS IN THE EXHIBITION AND THE PRESENT BOOK

Exh. nos.	Cat. nos.	Exh. nos.	Cat. nos.	Exh. nos.	Cat. nos.	Exh. nos.	Cat. nos.
25	14 (a)	288	388	441	29 (n)	476 (a–c)	71 (a–c)
41	18 (c)	289	216	442	29 (m)	477	73
44	24 (b)	319	302	443	29 (x)	478 (a–n)	78 (a–n)
50	16 (d)	319 X (a)	248	444	29 (l)	480 (a–l)	77 (a–l)
67	29 (t)	(b)	249	445	29 (a)	481	201
71	29 (e)	(c)	285	446 (a)	29 (b)	482	82
120 B	78	414 A	376	(b)	29 (c)	483	81
C	287	B	370	447 (a)	28 (m)	484	88
D	108	C	343	(b)	28 (n)	485	146
E	254	D	72	448 (a)	28 (f)	486	94
H	115 A	415	14 (b)	(b)	28 (g)	487	93
126 F	116	416	14 (c)	449	28 (o)	488	132
127 T	48	417	14 (d)	450	34 (a)	489	133
144 A	207	418	21	451	34 (b)	490	91
B	20	419 (a)	18 (a)	452	10 (d)	491	87
D	304	(b)	18 (b)	453	10 (c)	492	89
M	185	420	16 (a)	454	15	493	85
177 ⎤		421	12	455 (a)	55 (a)	494	269
181 ⎟ 15		422	19	(b)	55 (b)	495	95
190 ⎟		423	24 (c)	(c)	55 (c)	496	96
191 ⎦		424	24 (d)	456	36	497	244
218 (a–d)	29 (p–s)	425	24 (e)	457	31	498	74
219 (a–e)	28 (a–e)	426	16 (c)	458	50	499	158
244 (a, b)	213 (a, b)	427	16 (b)	459	66	500	157
260 (a, b)	213 (c, d)	428 (a)	16 (f)	460	38	501	104
262 (a, b)	213 (e, f)	(b)	16 (g)	461	56	502	120
267	373	429	24 (f)	462	39	503	76
268	268	430	16 (e)	463	63	504	86
269	273	431 (a)	28 (h)	464	41	505	118
270	381	(b)	28 (i)	465 (a)	10 (a)	506	297
271	273	(c)	28 (k)	(b)	10 (b)	507	212
272	262	(d)	28 (l)	466	53	508	92
273	353	432	29 (o)	467	45	509	199
274	148	433	29 (f)	468	35	510	271
281	282	434	29 (h)	469 (a–h)	48 (a–h)	511	166
282	352	435	29 (k)	470	54	512	165
283	351	436	29 (g)	471	47	531 A, B	17
284	325	437	29 (u)	472	55 (d)	C	1
285	270	438	29 (i)	473	40	D	2
286	245	439	29 (w)	474	37	532 A	22
287	386	440	29 (d)	475 (a–i)	67 (a–i)	B	8

Exh. nos.	Cat. nos.	Exh. nos.	Cat. nos.	Exh. nos.	Cat. nos.	Exh. nos.	Cat. nos.
532 C	23	546 A	103	591	153	637	247
533 A	24 (a)	B	84	592	149	638	232
B	3	C	127	593	210	639	308
534 A	13	D	205	594	306	640	233
B	5	547 A	223	595	154	641	359
C	4	B	176	596	167	642	234
535 A	6	C	211	597	240	643	368
B	9	551	219	598	250	644	235
C	7	552	192	599	215	645	241
536 A	11	553	168	600	275	646	334
B	32	554	356	601	163	647	276
537 A	25	555	98	602 (a)	289	648	354
B	26	556	160	(b)	290	649	326
C	27	557 (a)	253	603	130	650	277
538 A	46	(b)	252	604	209	651 (a)	339
B	49	558	117	605	259	(b)	340
C	65	559	75	606	226	652	333
539 A	42	560	125	607	361	653	346
B	57	561	114	608	200	654	286
C	33	562	164	609	281	655	321
D	52	563	177	610	283	656	303
E	58	564	178	611	242	657	256
F	30	565	142	612	330	658	305
G	59	566	150	613	218	659	336
H	60	567	90	614	310	660	294
540 B	70	568	145	615	183	661	311
C	69	569	198	616	345	662	307
D	68	570	170	617	173	663	295
541 A	111	571	189	618	188	664	312
B	44	572	124	619	126	665	319
C	105	573	246	620	143	666	155
D	115	574	195	621	193	667	320
E	74	575	197	622	324	668	338
F	110	576	190	623	367	669	378
542 A	80	577	159	624	278	670	364
B	131	578	122	625	265	671	384
C	97	579	144	626	228	672	258
D	79	580	61	627	172	673	251
543 A	134	581	237	628	230	674	331
B	83	582	208	629	263	675	272
C	137	583	171	630	231	676	349
544 A	101	584	194	631	225	677	274
B	129	585	196	632	229	678	301
C	128	586	169	633	224	679	363
545 A	102	587	214	633 X	288	680	348
B	152	588	267	634	236	681	341
C	186	589	260	635	266	682	337
D	138	590	366	636	227	683	299

CONCORDANCE

Exh. nos.	Cat. nos.	Exh. nos.	Cat. nos.	Exh. nos.	Cat. nos.	Exh. nos.	Cat. nos.
684	332	710	387	719 C	379	723 B	123
685	385	711	362	D	355	C	175
686	372	712	391	E	99	724 A	261
687	315	713	344	F	221	B	238
688	322	714	389	G	156	C	206
689	369	715 A	239	H	187	E	181
690	318	B	121	J	220	F	112
691	298	C	119	K	280	G	162
692	328	E	51	L	147	H	161
693	309	F	222	M	255	725 A	296
694	317	G	182	N	316	B	357
695	314	716 A	136	720 A	184	C	365
696	329	C	109	B	293	D	327
697	279	D	106	C	204	E	300
698	371	E	113	721 A	100	F	335
699	347	F	139	C	62	G	380
700	371	G	180	D	43	H	342
701	360	H	191	E	243	726 A	390
702	350	718 A	203	F	284	B	393
703	382	B	107	G	257	E	392
704	375	C	140	H	64	F	394
705	323	D	151	722 A	202	G	292
706	383	E	135	B	179	727	264
707	377	719 A	358	C	141	728 A	291
708	374	B	217	723 A	174	B	313
709	362						

INDEX OF LENDERS

[The numbers refer to the catalogue entries in this book.]

INDEX OF LENDERS

GENERAL INDEX

GENERAL INDEX

GENERAL INDEX

Dover Books on Art

FOOT-HIGH LETTERS: A GUIDE TO LETTERING, M. Price. 28 15½ x 22½" plates, give classic Roman alphabet, one foot high per letter, plus 9 other 2" high letter forms for each letter. 16 page syllabus. Ideal for lettering classes, home study. 28 plates in box.   20239-9 $600

A HANDBOOK OF WEAVES, G. H. Oelsner. Most complete book of weaves, fully explained, differentiated, illustrated. Plain weaves, irregular, double-stitched, filling satins; derivative, basket, rib weaves; steep, broken, herringbone, twills, lace, tricot, many others. Translated, revised by S. S. Dale; supplement on analysis of weaves. Bible for all handweavers. 1875 illustrations. 410pp. 6⅛ x 9¼.   20209-7 Clothbound $7.50

JAPANESE HOMES AND THEIR SURROUNDINGS, E. S. Morse. Classic describes, analyses, illustrates all aspects of traditional Japanese home, from plan and structure to appointments, furniture, etc. Published in 1886, before Japanese architecture was contaminated by Western, this is strikingly modern in beautiful, functional approach to living. Indispensable to every architect, interior decorator, designer. 307 illustrations. Glossary. 410pp. 5⅝ x 8⅜.   20746-3 Paperbound $2.50

THE DRAWINGS OF HEINRICH KLEY. Uncut publication of long-sought-after sketchbooks of satiric, ironic iconoclast. Remarkable fantasy, weird symbolism, brilliant technique make Kley a shocking experience to layman, endless source of ideas, techniques for artist. 200 drawings, original size, captions translated. Introduction. 136pp. 6 x 9.   20024-8 Paperbound $2.00

COSTUMES OF THE ANCIENTS, Thomas Hope. Beautiful, clear, sharp line drawings of Greek and Roman figures in full costume, by noted artist and antiquary of early 19th century. Dress, armor, divinities, masks, etc. Invaluable sourcebook for costumers, designers, first-rate picture file for illustrators, commercial artists. Introductory text by Hope. 300 plates. 6 x 9.
20021-3 Paperbound $2.00

VITRUVIUS: TEN BOOKS ON ARCHITECTURE. The most influential book in the history of architecture. 1st century A.D. Roman classic has influenced such men as Bramante, Palladio, Michelangelo, up to present. Classic principles of design, harmony, etc. Fascinating reading. Definitive English translation by Professor H. Morgan, Harvard. 344pp. 5⅜ x 8.
20645-9 Paperbound $2.50

Dover Books on Art

ARCHITECTURAL AND PERSPECTIVE DESIGNS, Giuseppe Galli Bibiena. 50 imaginative scenic drawings of Giuseppe Galli Bibiena, principal theatrical engineer and architect to the Viennese court of Charles VI. Aside from its interest to art historians, students, and art lovers, there is a whole Baroque world of material in this book for the commercial artist. Portrait of Charles VI by Martin de Meytens. 1 allegorical plate. 50 additional plates. New introduction. vi + 103pp. 10⅛ x 13¼.

21263-7 Paperbound $2.50

PRINTED EPHEMERA, edited and collected by John Lewis. This book contains centuries of design, typographical and pictorial motives in proven, effective commercial layouts. Hundreds of the most striking examples of labels, tickets, posters, wrappers, programs, menus, and other items have been collected in this handsome and useful volume, along with information on the dimensions and colors of the original, printing processes used, stylistic notes on typography and design, etc. Study this book and see how the best commercial artists of the past and present have solved their particular problems. Most of the material is copyright free. 713 illustrations, many in color. Illustrated index of type faces included. Glossary of technical terms. Indexes. 288pp. 9¼ x 12.

21037-5 Clothbound $15.00

DESIGN FOR ARTISTS AND CRAFTSMEN, Louis Wolchonok. Recommended for either individual or classroom use, this book helps you to create original designs from things about you, from geometric patterns, from plants, animals, birds, humans, landscapes, manmade objects. "A great contribution," N. Y. Society of Craftsmen. 113 exercises with hints and diagrams. More than 1280 illustrations. xv + 207pp. 7⅞ x 10¾.

20274-7 Paperbound $2.75

ART AND THE SOCIAL ORDER, D. W. Gotshalk. Is art only an extension of society? Is it completely isolated? In this delightfully written book, Professor Gotshalk supplies some workable answers. He discusses various theories of art from Plato to Marx and Freud and uses all areas of visual arts, music and literature to elaborate his views. "Seems to me the soundest and most penetrating work on the philosophy of art to appear in recent years," C. J. Ducasse, Brown Univ. Addenda: "Postscript to Chapter X: 1962." Bibliography in notes. Index. xviii + 255pp. 5⅜ x 8½.

20294-1 Paperbound $1.75

HANDBOOK OF DESIGNS AND DEVICES, C. P. Hornung. A remarkable working collection of 1836 basic designs and variations, all copyright-free. Variations of circle, line, cross, diamond, swastika, star, scroll, shield, many more. Notes on symbolism. "A necessity to every designer who would be original without having to labor heavily," ARTIST AND ADVERTISER. 204 plates. 240pp. 5⅜ x 8.   20125-2 Paperbound $2.00

THE UNIVERSAL PENMAN, George Bickham. Exact reproduction of beautiful 18th-century book of handwriting. 22 complete alphabets in finest English roundhand, other scripts, over 2000 elaborate flourishes, 122 calligraphic illustrations, etc. Material is copyright-free. "An essential part of any art library, and a book of permanent value," AMERICAN ARTIST. 212 plates. 224pp. 9 x 13¾.   20020-5 Clothbound $12.50

AN ATLAS OF ANATOMY FOR ARTISTS, F. Schider. This standard work contains 189 full-page plates, more than 647 illustrations of all aspects of the human skeleton, musculature, cutaway portions of the body, each part of the anatomy, hand forms, eyelids, breasts; location of muscles under the flesh, etc. 59 plates illustrate how Michelangelo, da Vinci, Goya, 15 others, drew human anatomy. New 3rd edition enlarged by 52 new illustrations by Cloquet, Barcsay. "The standard reference tool," AMERICAN LIBRARY ASSOCIATION. "Excellent," AMERICAN ARTIST. 189 plates, 647 illustrations. xxvi + 192pp. 7⅞ x 10⅝.   20241-0 Clothbound $6.50

AN ATLAS OF ANIMAL ANATOMY FOR ARTISTS, W. Ellenberger, H. Baum, H. Dittrich. The largest, richest animal anatomy for artists in English. Form, musculature, tendons, bone structure, expression, detailed cross sections of head, other features, of the horse, lion, dog, cat, deer, seal, kangaroo, cow, bull, goat, monkey, hare, many other animals. "Highly recommended," DESIGN. Second, revised, enlarged edition with new plates from Cuvier, Stubbs, etc. 288 illustrations. 153pp. 11⅜ x 9.

20082-5 Paperbound $2.50

VASARI ON TECHNIQUE, G. Vasari. Pupil of Michelangelo, outstanding biographer of Renaissance artists reveals technical methods of his day. Marble, bronze, fresco painting, mosaics, engraving, stained glass, rustic ware, etc. Only English translation, extensively annotated by G. Baldwin Brown. 18 plates. 342pp. 5⅜ x 8.   20717-X Paperbound $2.75

Dover Books on Art

THE COMPLETE BOOK OF SILK SCREEN PRINTING PRO-DUCTION, J. I. Biegeleisen. Here is a clear and complete picture of every aspect of silk screen technique and press operation—from individually operated manual presses to modern automatic ones. Unsurpassed as a guidebook for setting up shop, making shop operation more efficient, finding out about latest methods and equipment; or as a textbook for use in teaching, studying, or learning all aspects of the profession. 124 figures. Index. Bibliography. List of Supply Sources. xi + 253pp. 5⅜ x 8½.

21100-2 Paperbound $2.75

A HISTORY OF COSTUME, Carl Köhler. The most reliable and authentic account of the development of dress from ancient times through the 19th century. Based on actual pieces of clothing that have survived, using paintings, statues and other reproductions only where originals no longer exist. Hundreds of illustrations, including detailed patterns for many articles. Highly useful for theatre and movie directors, fashion designers, illustrators, teachers. Edited and augmented by Emma von Sichart. Translated by Alexander K. Dallas. 594 illustrations. 464pp. 5⅛ x 7⅛.

21030-8 Paperbound $3.50

CHINESE HOUSEHOLD FURNITURE, G. N. Kates. A summary of virtually everything that is known about authentic Chinese furniture before it was contaminated by the influence of the West. The text covers history of styles, materials used, principles of design and craftsmanship, and furniture arrangement—all fully illustrated. xiii + 190pp. 5⅝ x 8½.

20958-X Paperbound $2.00

THE COMPLETE WOODCUTS OF ALBRECHT DURER, edited by Dr. Willi Kurth. Albrecht Dürer was a master in various media, but it was in woodcut design that his creative genius reached its highest expression. Here are all of his extant woodcuts, a collection of over 300 great works, many of which are not available elsewhere. An indispensable work for the art historian and critic and all art lovers. 346 plates. Index. 285pp. 8½ x 12¼.

21097-9 Paperbound $4.00

Dover publishes books on commercial art, art history, crafts, design, art classics; also books on music, literature, science, mathematics, puzzles and entertainments, chess, engineering, biology, philosophy, psychology, languages, history, and other fields. For free circulars write to Dept. DA, Dover Publications, Inc., 180 Varick St., New York, N.Y. 10014.